QUANTITATIVE ANALYSIS FOR MANAGERIAL DECISIONS

QUANTITATIVE ANALYSIS FOR MANAGERIAL DECISIONS

CHAIHO KIM

GRADUATE SCHOOL OF BUSINESS
UNIVERSITY OF SANTA CLARA

ADDISON-WESLEY PUBLISHING COMPANY
READING, MASSACHUSETTS · MENLO PARK, CALIFORNIA
LONDON · AMSTERDAM · DON MILLS, ONTARIO · SYDNEY

ISBN 0-201-03739-4
ABCDEFGHIJ-MA-798765

PREFACE

This text is intended for a one- or two-semester course in which quantitative analytical methods are taught to students who plan to pursue managerial careers in business and industrial organizations. We believe that the text will also be helpful to students who plan to pursue administrative careers in other types of organizations, such as governmental agencies, educational institutions, and health care centers.

The text assumes only a minimal mathematical background on the part of the students. For example, the knowledge of calculus, matrix algebra, or probability is not assumed. Thus, the discussions in the text specifically avoid the use of calculus or matrix algebra. In the case of probability, a somewhat concise but nevertheless self-contained chapter on probability is provided.

A pedagogical issue which is rather difficult to resolve in a text such as this is that of determining a proper balance between the emphasis on techniques and that of applications. We have assumed that, for a potential manager or administrator, studying the applications should be given priority over studying the techniques. Therefore, we have put much more emphasis on applications than on techniques.

In the same vein, we have placed more emphasis on model building than on computational algorithms. Thus, we have avoided discussions of the esoteric niceties of the different algorithms. In addition, we have placed model building discussions in the first portion of a chapter, whenever an entire topic is covered in a single chapter; or in the first of a series of chapters, whenever a topic is covered in more than one chapter. We believe that such an arrangement of the discussions will enable an instructor to deemphasize the computational algorithms almost completely, if he chooses to do so.

We hope that we have included most of the important major topics which should be covered in a text such as this. However, due to space limitations and pedagogical considerations, we have left out some of the topics which we wished to include. We have, for example, left out nonlinear programming because it would have required the use of calculus. In this respect, we wish to state that our selection of the topics, as well as their arrangement in the text, were considerably influenced by the advice of those who have reviewed the text.

We believe that the text contains enough material for a two-semester course. It should, therefore, provide considerable flexibility in topical selections for a one-semester course. The topical arrangement in the text is certainly influenced by our desire to offer the maximum flexibility in selecting the topics for one semester, or a one-quarter course. The chart at the end of this preface shows the various sequences of chapters which may be studied without loss of continuity.

I would like to express my special thanks to Dean Charles Dirksen of the Graduate School of Business for providing me with secretarial and other assistance. Without his generous help completion of this text would not have been possible.

Several persons have read the manuscript in various stages of its development and offered me suggestions for improving the manuscript. Many of their suggestions have been incorporated into the text, although I am entirely responsible for any errors and shortcomings that may remain. Among those who have read the manuscript, I would like to express my thanks to Professors Frank S. Budnick, University of Rhode Island; John Coffman and George Worm, Georgia State University; Ira Horowitz, University of Florida; Jay T. Knippen, University of South Florida; Jack B. ReVelle, University of Nebraska at Omaha; Barry Shore, Northeastern University, Chris A. Theodore, Boston University; and Fredrik P. Williams, North Texas University. My thanks are also due to my colleagues Shail Parikh, Zeb Vancura, and Jin Yen. I would also like to thank Mike Sisois for reading the manuscript and developing the computer program which produced the tables in Appendix 3.

I would like to thank Mrs. Caroline Luplow and Mrs. Toni Goodale for typing as well as editing several drafts of the manuscript.

I would like to thank the staff at Addison-Wesley for the assistance provided me during the manuscript development stage and during the copy editing and production stage of this text.

To my wife, Taeock, I express my appreciation for being a constant source of encouragement during the years the manuscript has been in preparation.

Santa Clara, California   C.K.
October 1975

ORGANIZATION CHART

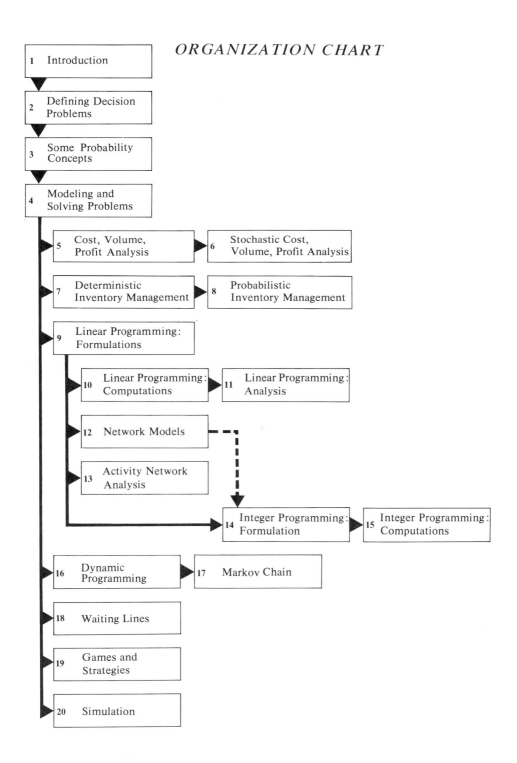

1 Introduction

2 Defining Decision Problems

3 Some Probability Concepts

4 Modeling and Solving Problems

5 Cost, Volume, Profit Analysis

6 Stochastic Cost, Volume, Profit Analysis

7 Deterministic Inventory Management

8 Probabilistic Inventory Management

9 Linear Programming: Formulations

10 Linear Programming: Computations

11 Linear Programming: Analysis

12 Network Models

13 Activity Network Analysis

14 Integer Programming: Formulation

15 Integer Programming: Computations

16 Dynamic Programming

17 Markov Chain

18 Waiting Lines

19 Games and Strategies

20 Simulation

CONTENTS

CHAPTER

1

INTRODUCTION

Business managers frequently make decisions whose consequences will be evaluated in terms of some quantitative measurements. For example, a company president makes decisions to influence company profit. A production manager makes decisions to control his production cost. A sales manager makes decisions affecting the sales in his sphere of influence. Profit, cost, and sales are all measurable quantitatively.

Before making a decision a manager should analyze all the factors that might have some bearing on the consequences of his decision. Specifically he should examine the relations between those factors which will affect his decision and others which will be affected by that decision.

Some of these factors may easily lend themselves to quantification; others may not. It seems, however, that quantification of at least some of these relations is essential in the analysis preceding any decision whose consequences will be evaluated in quantitative terms. An analysis which goes into a managerial decision is called a *quantitative analysis* when the relations studied are quantified.

1.1 PROGRESS IN QUANTITATIVE ANALYSIS

If we trace the history of business, we will find that quantitative analysis for business decisions is a practice as old as business itself. However, until World War II the techniques of quantitative analysis for managerial decisions were quite simple and unsophisticated.

During World War II the countries engaged in the war were confronted with enormous problems of planning and coordinating various military and economic activities. Teams of able minds from the government and from the military, business, and university communities were assembled in a number of these countries, for example, England and the United States, to plan and coordinate the war effort. Since many of the activities were interdependent, the analysis of them must take into account the nature of this interdependence. But since hundreds, perhaps thousands, of activities had to be taken into account, the requisite analysis became very complex, indeed, unmanageable.

It became apparent that new techniques must be developed to make sound analysis possible. Many new analytical techniques were indeed developed in that period. One common characteristic was to establish, as the first step, quantitative relations among the activities to be taken into account.

After the war the development of such analytic techniques has continued at an even more rapid pace. In fact, during the last twenty-five years there has been virtually an explosion in the development of analytical techniques for purposes of military, government, business, and other kinds of planning. In the process a number of scientific disciplines devoted to the development and applications of these techniques have emerged: for example, operations research, management science, and the decision sciences.

1.2 APPLICATION IN BUSINESS

During the early 1950s a number of large corporations in the United States began to apply some of these new techniques. The pioneers were perhaps the petroleum companies, which have since very successfully applied linear programming and other techniques to the problem of scheduling their refineries. A 1962 survey by Hausberg, Lundgren, and Roberts* of 86 refineries revealed the various ways in which a number of techniques had already been applied. Table 1.1 is a numerical breakdown of the 241 quantitative models employed by 86 of 127 refineries that answered the questionnaire.

Table 1.1 Types of Computer Models

Applications	Linear program	Simulation	Critical path	Miscellaneous	Total
Process scheduling					
integrated multiple refinery	21	4	—	—	25
complete refinery	46	36	—	3	85
fuel products	15	7	—	—	22
lubrication products	7	2	—	—	9
gasoline blending	43	9	—	4	53
others	6	3	—	—	9
Work scheduling	—	5	16	—	21
Storehouse control	2	5	—	7	14
Total	140	71	16	14	241

* E. W. Hausberg, W. E. Lundgren, and J. H. Roberts, "Survey of computer use in refinery scheduling," a paper presented to the Division of Refining, American Institute of Petroleum, May, 1962.

So successful were the applications of these techniques to refinery scheduling that the companies soon extended the use of these and other techniques to the problems of exploration, production, distribution, and routing of tankers.

Like the petroleum companies, the chemical and pharmaceutical companies also had rather early starts in applying these techniques. In as early as 1954 some of the major chemical and pharmaceutical companies were already applying these techniques to solving the problems of production scheduling, process optimization, inventory control, and distribution. Table 1.2 summarizes the findings of two surveys of leading chemical and pharmaceutical companies, one by Ackoff in 1955* and the other by Hess in 1962.†

Table 1.2   Percentage of Companies Utilizing Operations
Research Techniques

Application area	Survey year	
	1955	1962
Production	80%	91%
Finance	0	54
Accounting	20	54
Purchasing	10	27
Top management	10	45
Sales and marketing	20	91
Advertising	0	36
Transportation, shipping	30	91
Inventory	80	91
Personnel	not available	27
Research	not available	64
Long-range planning	not available	54
Number of companies	10	11

The 1962 survey, for example, indicates that 91 percent of the companies replied that they used these techniques in the areas of production, sales and marketing, transportation and shipping, and inventory management.

We will not trace the history of the applications of operations research and management science techniques in each industry. We should point out, however, that by the late 1950s almost all the major industries, including iron and steel, communications, transportation, paper, textile, food processing, and aerospace, were making use of these techniques.

As quantitative analysis began to play an increasingly more important role in decision-making and the planning of modern business enterprises, many large corporations began to establish special departments at their headquarters to

* Russell L. Ackoff, "A survey of operations research," a paper presented at the Operations Symposium, University of Pennsylvania, December 14, 1955.

† S. W. Hess, "Operations research in chemical and pharmaceutical industries," in David B. Hertz and Robert T. Eddison (Ed.), *Progress in Operations Research*, Vol. II, Wiley, 1964.

carry out such analysis. In 1969 Turban* conducted a survey that gives a glimpse of operations research activities at the largest American corporate headquarters (nonmilitary). Four hundred seventy-five American corporations were selected from *Fortune's* list of top 500, and questionnaires were sent to their directors of operations research or management science; 107 valid responses were returned.

Some of the significant findings of the survey are the following. Of the 107 corporations responding, forty-seven had departments that conducted operations research or management science types of activities. An additional thirteen corporations reported that they planned to establish such departments in the near future. Thus about 56 percent of the reporting corporations either had or were planning to have such departments at the time of the survey.

The survey also disclosed that 4.4 percent of these departments were established prior to 1950, 15.2 percent between 1951 and 1959, 50 percent between 1960 and 1965, and 30.4 percent after 1966. Thus there was an impressive rate of growth in the establishment of special departments to conduct operations research and management science types of activities. Turban concluded that by the middle of the 1970s about two-thirds of the large American corporations would have such departments.

---

* Efraim Turban, "A sample survey of operations research activities at the corporate level," *Operations Research*, Vol. 20, May–June, 1972.

DEFINING DECISION PROBLEMS

Before proceeding to the description of how a specific managerial decision can be analyzed quantitatively, perhaps we should describe in general the process by which any decision is reached.

We define a *decision process* as a sequence of activities which must be performed in reaching a decision. The manner in which these activities are performed may differ from one individual to another; even for the same individual it may differ from one decision situation to another. We can, however, identify these activities by their common characteristics.

First, we can divide the activities into classes: those which are needed to define a decision problem, and those which are needed to solve the problem once it has been defined. The sequence of activities needed to define a decision problem will be called the *definition process*, and the sequence of activities needed to solve the problem will be called the *solution process*.

In this chapter we shall discuss the definition process. The solution process will be considered in Chapter 4, after we have discussed some elementary probability concepts in Chapter 3.

2.1 DEFINITION PROCESS

If one is to make a managerial decision intelligently, he should obviously examine all the factors which might have some bearing on the consequences of his decision. The definition process of a decision problem may be defined as the set of activities required to enumerate these factors in some systematic fashion.

The factors which bear on the consequences of a managerial decision may be grouped into two categories. There are some factors which the manager can control and others which are beyond his control.

The manager can control the controllable factors in various ways, called *decision alternatives*. The first activity in the definition process, then, is to list all the decision alternatives that are available to the manager.

Those factors which are beyond the control of the manager can also take on various forms. Every form in which these factors may present themselves will be called an *environmental setting*. The second activity in the definition process, therefore, is to list all the possible environmental settings that might confront the manager.

On the basis of the preceding discussion it should be evident that the consequences of a decision are really a function of the decision alternatives and environmental settings. That is, a specific combination of a decision alternative chosen and a particular environmental setting that presents itself will uniquely determine the consequences of the decision. Therefore, in order to evaluate the wisdom of choosing any specific decision alternative in a given environmental setting, the manager must be able to describe the consequences that will result from his choice of that decision alternative in the given environmental setting. The third element in the definition process, therefore, is to describe the consequences of each combination of decision alternative and environmental setting.

The elements in the definition process of a decision problem may now be summarized as follows:

1. listing all the available decision alternatives;
2. listing all the possible environmental settings;
3. evaluating the consequences of each decision alternative against each environmental setting.

We shall now illustrate these activities for some specific decision problems.

Example 1. Oil Drilling Problem   The Richwell Oil Company is considering whether to drill an offshore parcel of leased land for oil. The drilling will be very expensive. Of course, if oil is discovered, the company will receive in return many times the cost of the initial drilling.

Richwell Oil can in fact reach a variety of decisions regarding the drilling question. However, ultimately it is a question of drilling or not drilling. Therefore, the decision alternatives are the following:

1. to drill the leased land
2. not to drill the leased land

Many factors are beyond the control of Richwell Oil in connection with this problem. The most important of these is the existence or nonexistence of oil in the area. Therefore, we may list the environmental settings as follows:

1. The leased land contains oil.
2. The leased land does not contain oil.

Having specified the decision alternatives and environmental settings, we can now proceed to evaluate the consequences of choosing a given alternative

Table 2.1

| Decision | Environmental settings | |
alternatives	Oil	No oil
Drill	large profit	forfeit drilling cost
Don't drill	forfeit large profit	avoid drilling expense

against a specific environmental setting. For example, suppose that the company decides to drill the leased land and it turns out that there is no oil. Then the company will have lost money to the amount of the drilling cost. The set of consequences of all available alternatives against all possible environmental settings is given by Table 2.1. The table is also a summary definition of the decision problem for Richwell Oil.

Example 2. Fashion Shop Problem   The Latest-in-Design Fashion Shop buys a fur coat of a particular design for $4000 per coat and sells it for $7000 during the season. However, when the season is over, the selling price of the coat will have to be marked down to $2000.

The decision to be made by the fashion shop is how many coats it should order. We may describe the decision alternatives as:

1. not to order any
2. order 1 coat
3. order 2 coats, etc.

The environmental condition beyond the control of the shop that will be crucial to the outcome of the decision by the fashion shop is the actual number of coats which will be in demand during the season. Thus the possible environmental settings are:

1. zero demand
2. a demand for 1 coat
3. a demand for 2 coats, etc.

Let us now evaluate the consequences of choosing a given decision alternative against a specific environmental setting. We observe that the fashion shop will make $3000 profit on every coat sold during the season but lose $2000 on every coat ordered but not sold during the season. The total amount of profit (or loss) as a function of the number of coats ordered and the number of coats demanded during the season is given in Table 2.2.

The table shows, for example, that if the shop orders 2 coats when only 1 coat will be demanded during the season, it will make a profit of $1000. This is easy to verify. The fashion shop will have to pay $8000 for the 2 coats it orders, but it will receive $7000 for the coat sold during the season and $2000 for the remaining coat sold after the season. The profit is $1000.

Table 2.2

Alternatives (quantity ordered)	Environment (number of coats in demand)		
	0	1	2
0	0	0	0
1	−2000	3000	3000
2	−4000	1000	6000

The remaining parts of the table may be verified in a similar manner. Table 2.2 summarizes the decision problem for the fashion shop.

2.2 UNDERSTANDING THE ENVIRONMENTAL SETTING

What often makes it difficult for a manager to reach a decision is the recognition that the outcome of his decision will be affected by events that are not predictable at the time of his decision. That is, a manager must often make decisions in environments which are not completely known to him.

In a given decision situation, however, a manager may have a great deal of knowledge concerning his environment or no knowledge at all. Three grades may be used to characterize the quality of his knowledge of the relevant environment.

Case of Certainty   This is a case in which the manager knows exactly what his decision environment is. For example, in the oil drilling problem the company management may know that the leased land contains oil. Or in the fashion shop problem the shop manager may know that exactly 2 coats will be demanded during the season.

Case of Risk   In this situation the manager is not entirely sure what the environmental setting is, but does know, for example, that he is more likely to be in one environmental setting than in another. Alternatively, we may define a risk situation as one in which the likelihood for the different environmental settings are known.

Thus in the oil drilling problem the oil company may have arrived at the following likelihoods:

Condition of leased land	Likelihood
Oil	0.2
No oil	0.8
	1.0

Or, in the case of the fashion shop the manager may have arrived at the following likelihoods:

Number of coats in demand	Likelihood
0	0.3
1	0.5
2	0.2
	1.0

Both are cases of risk.

Case of Uncertainty   In this case the manager is completely ignorant of the relevant environment.

Thus in the oil drilling problem the oil company management may have absolutely no idea as to whether or not the leased land contains oil so that it cannot even say what the likelihood is of there being oil. Similarly, the fashion shop manager may have no idea as to how many coats will be demanded during the season. Then he does not know the likelihood of any number of coats being demanded during the season.

EXERCISES

1.   Perma-Cell Battery Company is asked by a government agency whether it wants to do contract research to develop a new type of power cell for the government space program. The contract calls for a $200,000 expenditure, of which the government will underwrite fifty percent, regardless of whether the company develops the power cell or not. If the company does develop the power cell, it will then manufacture the power cell for the government space program. Since the total number of such power cells required for the space agency is fairly well established, Perma-Cell is in a position to determine with a reasonable amount of accuracy the profit which will accrue to the company in the event that it does develop the power cell. The estimated profit is $1,000,000.

Based on the information provided above:

a. List the decision alternatives for Perma-Cell Battery Company.
b. List the environmental settings for the decision.
c. Evaluate the consequences of each decision alternative against each environmental setting.

2.   In Exercise 1 suppose that the management of Perma-Cell is *reasonably* sure that it will develop the new type of power cell. How would you characterize the decision environment?

3.   Modern Television Store is a retailer of television sets manufactured by Zemax Television Company. The store is in the process of placing the last order for this year's models. New models will come out in two months.

Among current models the store is presently out of stock on Model Super Delux 10. The cost of this model, including transportation, is $800 per set. All models of television sets manufactured by Zemax are fair traded. The selling price of Super Delux 10 will be $1050 until next year's models come out. Then the manufacturer will reduce the selling price of this model to $750.

Since the store will be ordering some other models as well at this time, and since it does not want to overextend its debt, it will not order more than three sets, if any, of this model at this time. Based on the information provided above:

    a. list the decision alternatives;
    b. list the environmental settings;
    c. evaluate the consequences of these decision alternatives against the environmental settings.

4. Based on your experience with stores such as Modern Television, how would you describe the decision environment of Modern Television?

CHAPTER

3

SOME PROBABILITY CONCEPTS

Usually a manager has at least some understanding of the environment in which he has to make a decision; that is, usually the decision environment is neither completely known nor completely unknown to him. Therefore he must make a decision in a risk environment.

If a manager is to make a wise decision in a risk environment, he must be able to inteligently assess the various likelihoods associated with this environment and manipulate them in some logically consistent manner. We shall now turn our attention to this problem.

3.1 LIKELIHOOD AND PROBABILITY

Suppose the manager of Latest-in-Fashion of the last chapter tells us that the likelihood of exactly one coat being sold is very high, and that of exactly two coats being sold is quite high. We may assume him to mean that the likelihood of exactly one coat being sold is greater than that of exactly two coats being sold, but we do not know how much greater. This kind of ambiguity can be avoided by converting likelihood assessments into numbers. A *probability* is a number that expresses a likelihood assessment.

Another advantage of converting likelihood assessments into probabilities is that there are well-established rules of logic for manipulating probabilities. We shall discuss some of these rules later; but first, we shall discuss the meaning of the word "probability" in detail.

We say that a phenomenon is a *random phenomenon* if on any occasion its outcome is one among many possible outcomes whose individual likelihoods are either known or can be assessed. For example, a coin toss will result in our getting either heads or tails. If the coin is fair, the likelihoods of getting heads or tails are equal and therefore known to us. Thus a coin toss is a random phenomenon.

As another example, consider our familiar fashion shop. The manager of the shop may be able to assess the likelihood of a certain number of coats being demanded during the current season, based on his experience of demands for similar coats during past seasons. The demand for the coat may therefore be considered a random phenomenon.

Given a random phenomenon, our interests are usually in some of its possible outcomes. Suppose we can give a description of a certain outcome. Such a description, in probability theory, is called an *event*. In other words, an event is a description of an outcome of a random phenomenon.

In the case of a coin toss, an event of interest may be "getting heads." Where the demand for coats is concerned, an event of interest may be "at least one coat being sold during the season."

Once we have identified an event of interest to us, we can then calculate the likelihood that it will occur. A *probability* is a number that expresses the likelihood that a certain event will actually occur.

Any number may be used to indicate probabilities. However, it has been found convenient to restrict the range of such numbers so that they lie between 0 and 1. Thus a zero probability means that the event is impossible, and a probability of 1 means that the event is certain to occur. If an event is neither impossible nor certain to occur, then its probability must be greater than 0 but less than 1.

3.2   PROBABILITY AXIOMS

Two events are said to be *mutually exclusive* if both of them cannot occur at the same time. For example, "getting heads" and "getting tails" in a coin toss are mutually exclusive, since we cannot get heads and tails at the same time.

Suppose we decompose all the possible outcomes of a random phenomenon into a set of mutually exclusive events and call the set a *sample space*. Then we may want to assign probabilities to all the events in the sample space. There are three axioms, called the *probability axioms*, which govern the assignment of probabilities to the events in a sample space.

Probability Axioms

1. The probability of any event must be at least 0 and at most 1.

2. The probability of either one or the other of two mutually exclusive events is equal to the sum of the two individual probabilities.

3. The probabilities of all the events in a sample space must add up to 1.

Let us now consider the probability assessment for Richwell Oil of the last chapter. Let $p(o)$ be the probability that the leased land contains oil, and $p(n)$ be the probability that there is no oil. The first axiom says that $p(o)$ and $p(n)$ must each be at least 0 and at most 1. The second axiom says that the probability of the leased land either containing or not containing oil is equal to the sum of $p(o)$ and $p(n)$. The third axiom says that the sum of $p(o)$ and $p(n)$ must be 1. Thus if we let $p(o) = 0.2$ and $p(n) = 0.8$, then all three axioms will be satisfied.

3.3   ASSESSING PROBABILITIES

The probability axioms, however, do not tell us how we should actually assess the probabilities of the events in a sample space. There are three principal approaches to the assessment of probabilities.

Equally Likely Approach

Assume that there are m different events in a sample space, and suppose we have no reason to believe that any one event is more likely to occur than any other. Then we may assume that all m events are equally likely, and we can let the probability of each event be $1/m$. This is the *equally likely approach* to assessing probabilities.

   In tossing a fair coin we may assume that both heads and tails are equally likely to occur. Therefore, we can let $p(h) = 0.5$ and $p(t) = 0.5$, where $p(h)$ is the probability of getting heads.

   The equally likely approach is a very convenient way of assessing probabilities when there is symmetry among the events in question, such as the results in tossing a coin or a die. However, it is not suitable for situations where there is no symmetry among the events.

Relative-Frequency Approach

Suppose now that a random phenomenon can be repeated. We can observe the percentage of the times that a certain event occurs as the phenomenon is repeated many times. The observed percentage may be considered the probability of that event. For example, assume that we are to toss a coin which is known to be biased. Suppose that we have tossed the coin 1000 times and obtained heads 300 times and tails 700 times. Then we may let $p(h) = 0.3$ and $p(t) = 0.7$. This way of assessing probabilities is called the *relative-frequency approach*.

   The relative-frequency approach is very widely used in assessing probabilities in situations where sampling or replication of experiments is possible. It is often called the *objective approach*, because the probabilities determined through sampling or replication of experiments are likely to be free of the subjective biases of the persons determining these probabilities.

Personalistic Approach

There are, however, situations where neither the equally likely approach nor the relative-frequency approach is appropriate in assessing the probabilities.

   Consider the problem of determining the probability of a leased parcel of land containing oil. The equally likely approach is not appropriate, because the existence and nonexistence of oil are not symmetrical events. The relative-frequency approach is not appropriate, because the geological makeup of the leased land is likely to be unique in some respects and therefore cannot be considered as a duplication of other places.

   We may, however, nevertheless be able to come up with a reasonably good assessment of the probability that there is oil by evaluating seismographic recordings and conducting other geological studies. This is called the *per-sonalistic approach* or *subjective approach*.

3.4 PROBABILITY CALCULATIONS

Let us assume that we have a lot of 1000 items manufactured by a supplier. An item may be defective in finish or in mechanism. Assume that the conditions of the whole lot lend themselves to the following breakdown:

	Defective mechanism	Good mechanism	Total
Defective finishes	40	160	200
Good finishes	60	740	800
Total	100	900	1000

Marginal and Joint Probabilities

Suppose that we are to draw an item from the lot. The probability of an item being defective in finish is 0.2 and that of its being good in finish is 0.8. These are called a set of *marginal probabilities*. The information pertaining to these probabilities may be found on the right-hand margin of the above table. If we denote the probabilities of the item being defective in finish and good in finish, respectively, by $p(f)$ and $p(\bar{f})$, then one set of marginal probabilities is $p(f) = 0.2$ and $p(\bar{f}) = 0.8$.

Let $p(m)$ and $p(\bar{m})$, respectively, stand for the probabilities of the item having defective mechanism and good mechanism. Then $p(m) = 0.1$ and $p(\bar{m}) = 0.9$ constitute the other set of marginal probabilities for the lot.

Suppose we now ask, "What is the probability that an item drawn from the lot is defective both in finish and in mechanism?" This probability must be 0.04, since there are 40 such items in the lot of 1000. We will denote this probability by $p(f$ and $m) = 0.04$ and call it a *joint probability*. Then $p(\bar{f}$ and $m) = 0.06$ is another joint probability which indicates that the probability of an item having good finish and defective mechanism is 0.06.

The set of all joint probabilities, as well as both sets of the marginal probabilities, are given below for easy reference in subsequent discussions:

$p(f$ and $m) = 0.04$	$p(f$ and $\bar{m}) = 0.16$	$p(f) = 0.2$
$p(\bar{f}$ and $m) = 0.06$	$p(\bar{f}$ and $\bar{m}) = 0.74$	$p(\bar{f}) = 0.8$
$p(m) = 0.10$	$p(\bar{m}) = 0.90$	

Probability Addition

Suppose that an item in the lot is not usable if it is defective either in finish or in mechanism. In the lot of 1000 items we note that there are 200 items which have defective finishes and another 60 items which have good finishes but have defective mechanisms. Thus a total of 260 items are not usable. Therefore, the probability of an item not being usable is 0.26. Alternatively, we might say that the probability of an item being defective either in finish or in mechanism is 0.26. In notation we write $p(f \text{ or } m) = 0.26$.

Given the marginal and joint probabilities, we can calculate $p(f \text{ or } m)$ as follows:

$$p(f \text{ or } m) = p(f) + p(m) - p(f \text{ and } m) \quad \text{Add.}$$
$$= 0.2 + 0.1 - 0.04 = 0.26. \quad \times$$

This equation is a special case of the probability rule

$$p(a \text{ or } b) = p(a) + p(b) - p(a \text{ and } b).$$

If a and b are mutually exclusive, however, the last term of the above equation will drop out, since $p(a \text{ and } b) = 0$ when a and b are mutually exclusive.

Example 1. Advertising Problem Sharp Razor Blades Company advertises its razor blades on television and in magazines. Market research has revealed that 30 percent of the potential buyers will see the television advertisements, 20 percent will see the magazine advertisement, and 10 percent will see both advertisements. What percentage of the potential buyers will see at least one of the two types of advertisements? $p(t \text{ or } m) = p(t) + p(m) - p(t \text{ and } m)$

A different way of asking is "What is the probability that a randomly selected person from the group of potential buyers will see either the television or magazine advertisement?" In notation, this probability may be represented by $p(t \text{ or } m)$, where t is the television advertisement, and m the magazine advertisement. According to the probability addition rule, therefore,

$$p(t \text{ or } m) = p(t) + p(m) - p(t \text{ and } m)$$
$$= 0.3 + 0.2 - 0.1 = 0.4.$$

Thus 40 percent of the potential buyers will see at least one of the two types of advertisements.

Conditional Probabilities

Let us now return to our lot of manufactured items. Support that we are to draw an item from the lot containing defective finishes. What is the probability that an item so selected has a defective mechanism as well? Note that there are 200 items with defective finishes, of which 40 also have defective mechanisms. The probability in question is 0.2. We denote this probability by $p(m \mid f) = 0.2$. This notation may be read, "Given that an item has defective finish, the probability of its having a defective mechanism is 0.2." This probability is called a _conditional probability_, since in asking for the probability of an item having a defective mechanism, the condition of its finish is already assumed to be given.

Reviewing the process by which we obtained $p(m \mid f) = 0.2$, we realize that

$$p(m \mid f) = \frac{p(f \text{ and } m)}{p(f)} = \frac{0.04}{0.20} = 0.2.$$

This is a special case of the following probability rule:

$$p(b \mid a) = \frac{p(a \overset{\cap}{\text{ and }} b)}{p(a)}.$$

Applying the above rule, we can obtain, for example,

$$p(m \mid \tilde{f}) = \frac{p(\tilde{f} \text{ and } m)}{p(\tilde{f})} = \frac{0.06}{0.80} = 0.075,$$

which may be read, "Given that an item has good finish, the probability of its having a defective mechanism is 0.075." This is, of course, another example of conditional probability.

Probability Multiplications

It was proposed that $p(b \mid a) = p(a \text{ and } b)/p(a)$. If we multiply both sides of the above equation by $p(a)$, we obtain

$$p(a \text{ and } b) = p(a)p(b \mid a),$$

which indicates that a joint probability is the product of a marginal probability and a conditional probability.

Example 2. New Product Evaluation   Innovative Ideas International is considering whether or not to provide financial support for an inventor who approached the company with a very innovative idea.

The factors to be considered by the company in making the decision are: (1) the likelihood that the inventor will succeed in converting his idea into a product, and (2) the likelihood that the product, once developed, can be sold to a manufacturing company that will actually produce and market it. Innovative Ideas International assesses that the probability of the inventor's developing the product is 0.4, that is $p(d) = 0.4$. The company also has the assessment that, once the product has been developed, the probability of the company's being able to sell the product to a manufacturer is 0.8; that is, $p(s \mid d) = 0.8$.

What the company wants is the probability, once it has provided financial support for the inventor, that the investment will eventually return a profit; and it will do so only if the inventor succeeds in turning his idea into a product and the company succeeds in selling the product, if developed, to a producer. This probability may be expressed in notation as $p(d \text{ and } s)$. According to the probability multiplication rule, therefore, we have

$$p(d \text{ and } s) = p(d)p(s \mid d) = (0.4)(0.8) = 0.32.$$

Thus the probability of the venture succeeding is 0.32.

3.5   DERIVING PROBABILITIES

Frequently the information we have available cannot be readily used to assess the probabilities of some events that interest us. We may, however, nevertheless be able to calculate the probabilities by applying the probability rules which we have already described.

Let us again return to our lot of manufactured items. In our preceding discussion we assumed that all the joint probabilities and both sets of marginal probabilities were given. Let us now assume, instead, that only one set of marginal probabilities are given,

$$p(f) = 0.2, \qquad p(\tilde{f}) = 0.8,$$

along with the corresponding conditional probabilities

$$p(m \mid f) = 0.2, \qquad p(m \mid \tilde{f}) = 0.075,$$
$$p(\tilde{m} \mid f) = 0.8, \qquad p(\tilde{m} \mid \tilde{f}) = 0.925.$$

Suppose that we now want to find out the percentage of items in the lot which have defective mechanisms. We note that this probability is not explicitly given. However, it can be calculated by means of the probability rules.

Deriving Joint Probabilities

It was stated that $p(a \text{ and } b) = p(a)p(b \mid a)$. Applying this rule to the set of marginal and conditional probabilities explicitly given to us, we have

$$p(f \text{ and } m) = p(f)p(m \mid f) = (0.2)(0.2) \quad = 0.04,$$
$$p(f \text{ and } \tilde{m}) = p(f)p(\tilde{m} \mid f) = (0.2)(0.8) \quad = 0.16,$$
$$p(\tilde{f} \text{ and } m) = p(\tilde{f})p(m \mid \tilde{f}) = (0.8)(0.075) = 0.06,$$
$$p(\tilde{f} \text{ and } \tilde{m}) = p(\tilde{f})p(\tilde{m} \mid \tilde{f}) = (0.8)(0.925) = 0.74.$$

These are the joint probabilities pertaining to our lot.

Deriving Marginal Probabilities

An item that has a defective mechanism has either a defective finish or a good finish. If $p(m)$ denotes the probability of an item having a defective mechanism, then

$$p(m) = p(f \text{ and } m) + p(\tilde{f} \text{ and } m) = 0.04 + 0.06 = 0.10.$$

Alternatively,

$$p(\tilde{m}) = p(f \text{ and } \tilde{m}) + p(\tilde{f} \text{ and } \tilde{m}) = 0.16 + 0.74 = 0.90.$$

These calculations show that 10 percent of the items in the lot have defective mechanisms.

There is a more convenient way of deriving these marginal probabilities. Let us present the derived joint probabilities in a table:

	m	$\tilde{m}$	Given marginal probabilities
f	0.04	0.16	0.20
$\tilde{f}$	0.06	0.74	0.80
Derived marginal probabilities	0.10	0.90	1.00

Then a *given* marginal probability may be obtained by adding a row of joint probabilities, and a *derived* probability may be obtained by adding a column of joint probabilities.

Example 3. Market Share Determination   The Easy Learning Textbook Company is about to come out with a revised edition of a text for introductory accounting. As soon as the textbook is published, the company will send examination copies to instructors of introductory accounting. Its mailing list, however, is incomplete and covers only 80 percent of those who will be teaching the course.

On the basis of its experience with the first edition of the book, the company has arrived at the following probability assessments: (1) 30 percent of the instructors who receive the examination copies will adopt the text, (2) 10 percent of those who do not receive examination copies will nevertheless adopt the text. The company wants to know the percentage of the instructors for introductory accounting who will adopt the text.

Let r denote that an instructor will receive an examination copy and $\tilde{r}$ that he will not, a that he will adopt the text and $\tilde{a}$ that he will not. Then $p(r) = 0.8$ and $p(\tilde{r}) = 0.2$; $p(a \mid r) = 0.3$, $p(\tilde{a} \mid r) = 0.7$, $p(a \mid \tilde{r}) = 0.1$, and $p(\tilde{a} \mid \tilde{r}) = 0.9$. Thus we can initially obtain the following joint probabilities

$$p(a \text{ and } r) = p(r)p(a \mid r) = (0.8)(0.3) = 0.24,$$

$$p(\tilde{a} \text{ and } r) = p(r)p(\tilde{a} \mid r) = (0.8)(0.7) = 0.56,$$

$$p(a \text{ and } \tilde{r}) = p(\tilde{r})p(a \mid \tilde{r}) = (0.2)(0.1) = 0.02,$$

$$p(\tilde{a} \text{ and } \tilde{r}) = p(\tilde{r})p(\tilde{a} \mid \tilde{r}) = (0.2)(0.9) = 0.18,$$

which can also be presented in tabular form:

	a	$\tilde{a}$	Given marginal probabilities
r	0.24	0.56	0.80
$\tilde{r}$	0.02	0.18	0.20
Derived marginal probabilities	0.26	0.74	1.00

Adding the first column of the joint probabilities, we find that the probability of an instructor's adopting the text is 0.26. This amounts to saying that 26 percent of those who will be teaching introductory accounting will adopt the text.

3.6   REVISING PROBABILITIES

It is not uncommon that we will revise our thinking on a subject after learning something new about it. Thus we may want to revise our probability assessments pertaining to a random phenomenon after some observation.

Let us again return to our lot of manufactured items. The joint and marginal probabilities pertaining to the lot are again presented below:

	m	$\tilde{m}$	Marginal probabilities
f	0.04	0.16	0.20
$\tilde{f}$	0.06	0.74	0.80
Marginal probabilities	0.10	0.90	1.00

Assume that an item is drawn from the lot but that we have not examined it yet. What is the probability that it has a defective finish? We have to say that the probability is 0.20, since 20 percent of the items in the lot have defective finishes. This probability is sometimes called a *prior probability*, since the assessment is made before we have learned anything about the item drawn. Suppose now we examine the item and discover that it has a defective mechanism. What should now be our assessment of the probability that the item has a defective finish as well? This is equivalent to the question, "Given that an item has a defective mechanism, what is the probability of its also having a defective finish?" In notation, this probability is $p(f \mid m)$. Note that this is a conditional probability. Its value is

$$p(f \mid m) = \frac{p(f \text{ and } m)}{p(m)} = \frac{0.04}{0.10} = 0.4.$$

This probability is sometimes called a *posterior probability*, since the probability assessment is made after we have learned something about the item drawn.

Bayes' Theorem

This posterior probability may, however, be ascertained in one step without reference to the table of joint probabilities. Assume again that we are given the prior probabilities $p(f) = 0.2$ and $p(\tilde{f}) = 0.8$ and the conditional probabilities $p(m \mid f) = 0.2$, $p(\tilde{m} \mid f) = 0.8$, $p(m \mid \tilde{f}) = 0.075$, and $p(\tilde{m} \mid \tilde{f}) = 0.925$. Re-examining the equation

$$p(f \mid m) = \frac{p(f \text{ and } m)}{p(m)}$$

we note that

$$p(m) = p(f \text{ and } m) + p(\tilde{f} \text{ and } m).$$

But $p(f \text{ and } m) = p(f)p(m \mid f)$ and $p(\tilde{f} \text{ and } m) = p(\tilde{f})p(m \mid \tilde{f})$. Thus

$$p(f \mid m) = \frac{p(f)p(m \mid f)}{p(f)p(m \mid f) + p(\tilde{f})p(m \mid \tilde{f})}.$$

This probability rule is called *Bayes' theorem*. Applying this theorem, we have

$$p(f \mid m) = \frac{(0.2)(0.2)}{(0.2)(0.2) + (0.8)(0.075)} = \frac{0.04}{0.04 + 0.06} = 0.4,$$

which is the posterior probability we are looking for.

Example 4. Evaluating Advertising Effectiveness   From the warranty cards filed by the buyers of its 1973 models Zemax Television Company has learned that 90 percent of those who bought its 1973 models had been exposed to the company's advertisements. Separate market research has revealed that 40 percent of those who bought the competitor's models had also been exposed to the Zemax advertisements. During 1973, 20 percent of all television sets sold were manufactured by Zemax Television. To evaluate the effectiveness of its 1973 advertising programs, the company management has asked the following question: "Among the buyers of 1973 models, what percentage of those who had been exposed to the Zemax advertisements actually bought its models?"

Let b denote that a person bought a Zemax model and $\bar{b}$ that he did not, e that the person had been exposed to the Zemax advertisements and $\bar{e}$ that he had not been so exposed. The proposed question now becomes, what is $p(b \mid e)$?

The prior probabilities are: $p(b) = 0.2$ and $p(\bar{b}) = 0.8$. We also have $p(e \mid b) = 0.9$ and $p(e \mid \bar{b}) = 0.4$. Applying the Bayes theorem, we find that

$$p(b \mid e) = \frac{p(b)p(e \mid b)}{p(b)p(e \mid b) + p(b)p(e \mid \bar{b})}$$

$$= \frac{(0.2)(0.9)}{(0.2)(0.9) + (0.8)(0.4)} = \frac{0.18}{0.50} = 0.36.$$

Thus 36 percent of those who had been exposed to the Zemax advertisements actually bought its models.

3.7   STATISTICAL INDEPENDENCE

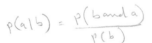

$$p(a \mid b) = \frac{p(b \text{ and } a)}{p(b)}$$

Let a and b be the two events of interest. Event a is said to be *statistically independent* of event b if $p(a \mid b) = p(a)$, and event b is statistically independent of event a if $p(b \mid a) = p(b)$. Then a is statistically dependent on b if $p(a \mid b) \neq p(a)$.

Loosely speaking, one event is statistically independent of another event if the occurrence of one is not affected by that of the other. Let d and a, for example, respectively stand for drawing a diamond and drawing an ace from a deck of cards. What is the probability that a card drawn from a complete deck is a diamond? It is $\frac{1}{4}$. In symbols, $p(d) = \frac{1}{4}$. Suppose that the card drawn is an ace. What is the probability that the card is a diamond? It is still $\frac{1}{4}$, since there are four aces in the deck. In symbols, $p(d \mid a) = \frac{1}{4}$. Therefore, $p(d \mid a) = p(d) = \frac{1}{4}$, and d is statistically independent of a. A little reflection will show that a is also statistically independent of d.

Let us now return to the probability multiplication rule $p(a \text{ and } b) = p(a)p(b \mid a)$. Assuming that a and b are statistically independent so that $p(b \mid a) = p(b)$, we can modify our rule to say

$$p(a \text{ and } b) = p(a)p(b)$$

if a and b are statistically independent events.

Example 5. Reliability Problem   A certain mechanical system contains components *a* and *b*. The system will work only if both *a* and *b* work. The
probability of *a* working is 0.9, and that of *b* working is 0.7. Also *a* and *b*
work independently of each other. What is the probability that the system will
work?

Since *a* and *b* work independently of each other, we can assume that the
workings of *a* and *b* are statistically independent. Therefore,

$$p(a \text{ and } b) = p(a)p(b) = (0.9)(0.7) = 0.63,$$

which is the probability that the system will work.

3.8 RANDOM VARIABLES

We defined a random phenomenon to be one the likelihoods of whose
outcomes are either known to us or can be assessed. In our discussion so far
the outcomes of a random phenomenon were either described in words or
symbolized by numbers. There are, however, situations where we want to
symbolize the outcomes of a random phenomenon by a set of numbers. A
random phenomenon is called a *random variable* if the outcomes of that
phenomenon are symbolized by a set of numbers.

Suppose that a coin is to be tossed and that the outcomes are described as
heads and tails. Then the coin toss is not a random variable because the
outcomes are described in words. However, assume that "heads we will win a
dollar, and tails we will lose a dollar." Then the possible outcomes of the coin
toss may be symbolized by a set of numbers: 1 and −1. We may, then consider
the coin toss as a random variable.

Probability Distribution

Given a random variable, we may want to devise a convenient way of
associating its numerical outcomes with their probabilities. A *probability distribution* is a description of how we may associate the numerical outcomes of a
random variable with their corresponding probabilities.

Suppose, for example, the coin to be tossed for the dollar is fair. Then the
probability of our winning a dollar is 0.5, as is the probability of our losing a
dollar. Our assessment of this coin toss may therefore be summarized as
follows:

Amount of win	Probability
1	0.5
−1	0.5
	1.0

This table shows the probability distribution of the random variable in question.

Example 6. Sales Distribution Per Suader is a salesman of large computers. He figures that in any given month the probability of his not selling any computer is 0.4, that of selling one is 0.3, and those of selling two and three are respectively 0.2 and 0.1. This assessment of his sales potential, then, may be summarized as follows:

Number of computers sold	Probability
0	0.4
1	0.3
2	0.2
3	0.1
	1.0

This table shows the probability distribution of Per Suader's monthly computer sales.

Having this probability distribution can be useful to Per Suader in many ways. Suppose that he is entitled to a bonus for any month during which he sells two or more computers. Then using the information contained in the probability distribution, he can see that the probability of his receiving a bonus for any given month is 0.3. $\frac{2}{10} + \frac{1}{10} = \frac{3}{10}$

3.9 MEAN, VARIANCE, AND STANDARD DEVIATION

The *mean* of a random variable is the weighted sum of the numerical outcomes of that random variable, where the weights used are the probabilities corresponding to the outcomes. Let us consider the probability distribution given by the following table:

Numerical outcome	Probability
x_1	$f(x_1)$
x_2	$f(x_2)$
x_3	$f(x_3)$

The mean, denoted by a Greek letter μ, may be defined as

$$\mu = x_1 f(x_1) + x_2 f(x_2) + x_3 f(x_3).$$

The mean of a random variable is sometimes called the *expected value* of that random variable.

The *variance* of a random variable is the weighted sum of the square deviations of the numerical outcomes of the random variable, where the weights used are again the probabilities corresponding to the outcomes. Let us denote the variance by a Greek letter σ^2. Then

$$\sigma^2 = (x_1 - \mu)^2 f(x_1) + (x_2 - \mu)^2 f(x_2) + (x_3 - \mu)^2 f(x_3).$$

$\sigma^2 = \sum_i (x_i^2) f(x_i) - \mu_x^2$ $\left(\text{see Ham. p223} \right) \longrightarrow$

The square root of a variance is called the *standard deviation* of the random variable. The standard deviation is denoted by the Greek letter σ.

Example 7. Personnel Management Problem The personnel manager of the Process Data Company has sampled the works of two key-punch operators. On the basis of the samples he has arrived at the following probability distributions for the hourly punching errors of the two operators:

Number of errors	Probability Operator A	Operator B
1	0	0.1
2	0.3	0.2
3	0.4	0.4
4	0.3	0.2
5	0	0.1
	1.0	1.0

The mean error of operator A may be calculated as follows:

Number of errors	Probability	$\left(\begin{array}{c}\text{Number of}\\ \text{errors}\end{array}\right)$(Probability)	
2	0.3	(2)(0.3)	= 0.6
3	0.4	(3)(0.4)	= 1.2
4	0.3	(4)(0.3)	= 1.2
	1.0	Weighted sum	= 3.0 $= \mu$

Our calculations show that the mean error is 3 for operator A; that is, operator A will make 3 errors per hour on the average.

A similar calculation for operator B will show that the mean error for him is also 3. Is there then no difference between the performances of the two operators? The answer is yes, for the following reasons. While the mean errors are the same for the two operators, the variations in the number of errors is smaller for A than for B. Thus the performance of operator A may be considered to be more consistent than that of operator B.

The variations in the number of errors for the two operators may be measured by the variances or standard deviations. The variance for operator A is 0.6:

Number of errors	Probability	$\left(\begin{array}{cc}\text{Number of} & \text{Mean}\\ \text{errors} & \text{error}\end{array}\right)^2$(Probability)	
2	0.3	$(2-3)^2(0.3)$	= 0.3
3	0.4	$(3-3)^2(0.4)$	= 0
4	0.3	$(4-3)^2(0.3)$	= 0.3
	1.0	Weighted sum	= 0.6

$\sigma^2 = [4(.3) + 9(.4) + 16(.3)] - (3)^2 = 9.6 - 9 = .6 \qquad \sigma = \sqrt{.6} = .7746$

The standard deviation in the number of errors for operator A is $\sqrt{0.6} = 0.775$.

A similar calculation for B will show that the variance and standard deviation in the number of errors for him are 1.2 and 1.095, respectively. These numbers are larger than those for A. But, then, we already noted that the variation in the number of errors for operator B was larger than that for operator A.

3.10 NORMAL PROBABILITY DISTRIBUTION

If we are to apply probability concepts to the analysis of managerial decision problems, one of the first steps we must take is to decide on the specific probability distribution to be used for the underlying random variable. Two approaches may be used for this purpose. We may use the actual probability distribution for the random variable or a theoretical probability distribution which approximates the actual probability distribution. An advantage of using a theoretical probability distribution is that it will usually simplify much of the calculations.

Normal Probability Distribution

The *normal probability distribution* is one such theoretical probability distribution, perhaps the most important one. It is illustrated by Figure 3.1, where the area under the curve represents the probability. We note that this probability distribution is bell shaped and symmetric with respect to μ, where μ is the mean of the distribution.

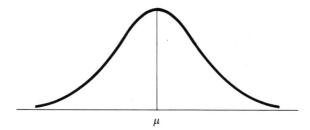

μ

Figure 3.1

A normally distributed random variable is said to be a *standard normal variable* if $\mu = 0$ and $\sigma = 1$. Appendix 1 at the end of this book is a table of probabilities for the standard normal variable. This table shows, for example, that

$$p(0 \le z \le 1.0) = 0.3413,$$
$$p(0 \le z \le 1.5) = 0.4332,$$
$$p(0 \le z \le 2.0) = 0.4772,$$

where z is a dummy notation for the standard normal variable.

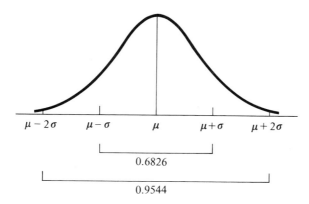

Figure 3.2

An important character of normally distributed random variables is that, given a positive number k, the probabilities of the random variables assuming a value between μ and $\mu + k\sigma$ are the same regardless of the values of μ and σ. This means that if x is a random variable with $\mu = 100$ and $\sigma = 20$, then $p(100 \le x \le 120) = 0.3413$; and if y is a random variable with $\mu = 400$ and $\sigma = 100$, then $p(400 \le y \le 500) = 0.3413$.

Since a normal probability distribution is symmetric with respect to μ, if the probability of the random variable assuming a value between μ and $\mu + \sigma$ is 0.3413, then the probability of the variable assuming a value between $\mu - \sigma$ and μ is also 0.3413. Then the probability of the random variable assuming a value between $\mu - \sigma$ and $\mu + \sigma$ is 0.6826 (see Figure 3.2). Using Appendix 1, we can easily show that the probability of the random variable assuming a value between $\mu - 2\sigma$ and $\mu + 2\sigma$ is approximately 0.95 (0.9544, to be precise), as illustrated in the figure.

Example 8. Airline Reservation Table 3.1 is a record of how long it took to service the incoming calls at a Trans Global Airline reservations center. We observe that 5 percent of the incoming calls required service times of 0.5 to 1.5 minute; that is, the probability is 0.05 that an incoming call will require a

Table 3.1

Service time (minutes)	Number of calls	Probability
0.5–1.5	100	0.05
1.5–2.5	500	0.25
2.5–3.5	900	0.45
3.5–4.5	300	0.15
4.5–5.5	200	0.10
	2000	1.00

service time of 0.5 to 1.5 minute. The probabilities for different required service times are established in a similar way and are shown in the right-hand column of the table. This column, therefore, gives the actual probability distribution of the random variable representing the service time. Such a probability distribution will be called an *empirical probability distribution*, since it is obtained from empirical data.

We shall next illustrate how we can approximate the above empirical probability distribution with a normal probability distribution. We must first calculate the mean and standard deviation for the empirical probability distribution. Let us assume that the average service time of all those calls requiring 0.5 to 1.5 minute is exactly 1 minute, and the average service time of those requiring 1.5 to 2.5 minutes is exactly 2.0 minutes, and so on. Then the mean and variance of the service times may be calculated as follows:

t	$f(t)$	$tf(t)$	$(t - \mu)^2 f(t)$
1	0.05	0.05	$(4)(0.05) = 0.20$
2	0.25	0.50	$(1)(0.25) = 0.25$
3	0.45	1.35	$(0)(0.45) =\ \ \ 0$
4	0.15	0.60	$(1)(0.15) = 0.15$
5	0.10	0.50	$(4)(0.10) = 0.40$
	1.00	Sum = 3.00	Sum = 1.00

where t is the required service time and $f(t)$ is the corresponding probability. The calculations reveal that the mean and variance are 3 and 1, respectively. Thus the standard deviation must also be 1.

The empirical probability distribution and a normal probability distribution having a mean of 3 and standard deviation of 1 are shown in Figure 3.3. This

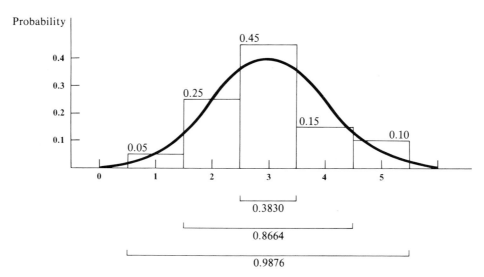

Figure 3.3

figure yields the following comparison of probabilities:

Service time (minutes)	Actual probability based on empirical distribution	Approximate probability based on normal distribution
2.5–3.5	0.45	0.3830
1.5–4.5	0.85	0.8664
0.5–5.5	1.00	0.9976

Based on this comparison we may conclude that the normal probability distribution is a reasonably good approximation of the empirical probability distribution.

EXERCISES

1. An electrical system contains two components A and B. The probability of A working is 0.8, that of B working is 0.7, and that of A and B both working is 0.6. The system will work so long as either A or B works. What, then, is the probability of the system working?

2. The Cosmox Company has received a government contract to develop a space vehicle and it has subcontracted the job of developing a certain key component of the vehicle to two different subcontractors, say A and B. The company believes that the probability of A developing the component is 0.7, that of B developing the component is 0.8, and that of both A and B developing the component is 0.6. What is the probability that the component in question will be developed at all?

3. Tokyo Electronics International is concerned over the prospect of passage of a certain trade bill in the United States Congress. Its assessment is that the chances of the bill being passed by the House of Representatives is 0.7, that of it being passed by the Senate is 0.5, and that of it being passed by both the House and the Senate is 0.4. Suppose now that the bill is actually passed by the House of Representatives. What, according to the given assessment, is the probability that the bill will also pass the Senate?

4. Sound Investment Company is trying to evaluate the growth potential of its portfolio holdings during the next year. At the moment the economy is in a recession. The company believes that the probability of the economy recovering from the recession during the next year is 0.6. It also believes that the chance is 80 percent that the portfolio holdings will grow once the recession is over. If the recession continues, the chance of the portfolio holdings growing during the next year is believed to be 30 percent. What is the company assessment of the probability that the portfolio holdings will grow during the next year?

5. A.B.C. Manufacturing is planning to bring out a new product. The management of the company believes that there is a 70-percent chance that the new product will generate an additional profit if competing companies do not bring out a similar product. It also believes that the chance is only 40 percent that the new product will generate additional profit for the company if the competitors bring out a similar product. Suppose the company management believes that the chances of competing companies' bringing out a similar product is 60 percent. What, then, is the chance that the new product will generate an additional profit for A.B.C.?

6. The Frontier Technology Company is planning to submit a proposal to a government department for a research grant. The company is aware that the department may receive several similar proposals, but it feels that among its competitors only the Advanced Science Associates has the technical know-how to carry out the research. The probability of Advanced Science Associates' submitting a proposal is assessed to be 0.8. The company also feels that the probability of its getting the grant is 0.6 if Advanced Science Associates submits a proposal, and 0.9 if the latter does not submit a proposal. What, according to this assessment, is the probability that Frontier Technology will get the research grant?

7. At a production facility 30 percent of the workers are classified as efficient and the remaining 70 percent are classified as not efficient. Among the efficient workers 40 percent had some college education and 60 percent did not. Among the inefficient workers 20 percent had some college education and 80 percent did not. Suppose that the personnel manager decides to use the above information in evaluating new applicants. What will be his assessment of the probability that an applicant will turn out to be an efficient worker, given that the latter had some college education?

8. Frank Yen is a mortgage lending officer at the Friendly California Bank. Examining his loan files, he classifies 80 percent of the mortgage loans made by him as good and the remaining 20 percent as bad. Among the good loans 70 percent involved 20-percent down payments and the remaining 30 percent involved 10-percent down payments. Among the bad loans 20 percent involved 20-percent down payments and the remaining 80 percent involved 10-percent down payments. Suppose that a loan applicant agrees to a down payment of 20 percent. What is the probability that the loan will turn out to be a good one?

9. The Wildcat Oil Company is trying to decide whether to drill a well in a parcel of land or sell the rights to it. Before making a decision the company wants to assess the probability of there being oil in the land. It plans to examine the seismographic readings. If the leased land contains oil, the probability of getting a positive seismographic reading is 0.8; but if there is no oil, the probability of getting a positive reading is 0.3. Before taking the seismographic readings, however, the company makes the assessment, based on other geological studies, that the probability of the leased land containing oil is 0.2. Suppose now, that a positive seismographic reading is obtained. What is the assessed probability that the leased land contains oil?

10. Suspicious Thomas feels that the probability of Honest Brown's lying to him is 0.8 and tells the latter about this feeling. Honest Brown then suggests a lie detector test. The test indicates that Honest Brown is not lying. If Suspicious Thomas knows that this particular lie detector test is only 70 percent reliable, what should be his assessment of the probability that Honest Brown has lied to him?

11. Richwell Oil Company has completed a promotional campaign to acquire new credit card customers, having mailed out 200,000 promotional letters to potential customers. In 100,000 of these letters the company promised to send a kitchen knife for each application for a credit card. In the remaining 100,000 letters it promised instead to send a recipe book. The company receives 40,000 applications for its credit card, of which there are 25,000 requests for the recipe book. Is the rate of response to promotional letters dependent on what the company promised to send to the applicants?

12. An electrical system contains two parallel components. The probability of each component working is 0.9. The components work independently of each other. The system works only if either one of its two components works. What is the probability that the system will work?

13. An electronic system contains three serial components. The probability of each component working is 0.9. The components work independently of each other. The system will work only if all three components work. What is the probability that the system will work?

14. Clean Soap Company plans to introduce two new brands of soap this year. In the past only 40 percent of the new brands introduced by the company were favorably received by the consumers. Assuming that the success or failure of either new brand introduced by the company is not influenced by that of the other, what is the probability that both new brands will be favorably received by the consumers? What is the probability that at least one of the two will be favorably received?

15. Going through his personnel records, an office manager has arrived at the following probability distribution of the number of employees absent from the office on a given day:

Number of workers absent	Probability
0	0.10
1	0.20
2	0.35
3	0.30
4	0.05
	1.00

What is the probability that 3 or more workers will be absent on a given day?

16. Calculate the mean, variance, and standard deviation for the probability distribution given in exercise 15.

17. A production manager at a factory has arrived at the following probability distribution of the number of daily machine breakdowns:

Number of machine breakdowns	Probability
0	0.4
1	0.3
2	0.2
3	0.1

What is the probability of at least one machine breaking down on a given day?

18. Calculate the mean, variance, and standard deviation for the probability distribution given in exercise 17.

19. Joe's Service Station has been selling on the average 2000 gallons of gasoline per day, with a standard deviation of 500 gallons. The daily sales of gasoline are normally distributed. What are the probabilities that the station will sell on a given day (a) between 1500 and 2500 gallons, (b) between 2500 and 3000 gallons, and (c) more than 3000 gallons?

20. Crackless Cement Company has won a subcontract to do the concrete work in a major construction project. The construction specifications state that the minimum 28-days strength of the concrete be 3000 p.s.i. (pounds per square inch). The company has experimented with two different mixes, say *A* and *B*. Mix *A* yields a mean 28-days strength of 3300 p.s.i., with a standard deviation of 100 p.s.i. Mix *B* yields a mean 28-days strength of 3,500 p.s.i., with a standard deviation of 250 p.s.i. Suppose that the company wants to maximize the probability of meeting the specification requirements. Which of the two mixes should it use, assuming that the 28-days strengths of both mixes *A* and *B* are normally distributed? Explain your answer.

CHAPTER

4

MODELING AND SOLVING PROBLEMS

In Chapter 2 we found that, to define a decision problem, it was necessary to specify the relations among environmental settings, decision alternatives, and a set of consequences. We had to devise a rule which assigned a unique consequence to each possible combination of environmental setting and decision alternative. Such a rule is sometimes called a *model* depicting a decision problem. Alternatively, we may define a *decision model* as a function which specifies a unique consequence for each combination of environmental setting and decision alternative.

The role of the model in a decision process is illustrated in the diagram below:

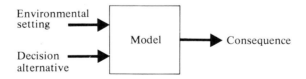

A decision model is then, in a sense, a black box which will indicate a consequence when a particular environmental setting and a particular decision alternative are fed into it.

Let us consider some specific examples.

Example 1. Oil Drilling Problem   Returning to the Richwell Oil situation of Chapter 2, we recall that in defining the problem we assumed that if there was oil and if the company decided to drill, then the latter would reap a large profit.   **31**

This assumption may be shown diagrammatically as follows:

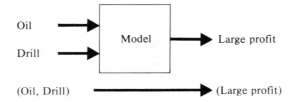

Figure 4.1 shows what the consequence is for every possible combination of decision alternative and environmental setting. It may be considered as a model for the oil drilling problem.

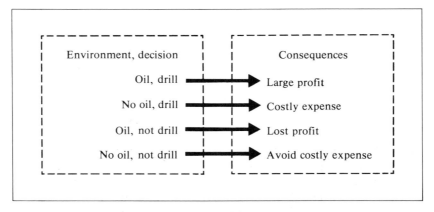

Figure 4.1

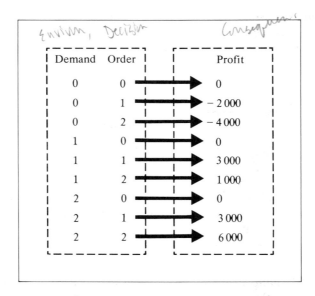

Figure 4.2

Example 2. Fashion Shop Problem The model for the Latest-in-Design Fashion shop problem of Chapter 2 may be constructed in a similar way. When we first encountered the problem, we pointed out that the fashion shop would make a profit of $3000 if it ordered one coat and there was a demand for two coats during the season. We can symbolize this as follows:

Demand   Order   Profit

(2   ,   1)   ($3000)

The full model defining the decision situation for the fashion shop is given in Figure 4.2.

4.2 QUANTIFICATION OF MODELS

Let E be an environmental setting, D be a decision alternative, and C be the corresponding consequence. Then a decision model may be expressed as

$$C = f(E, D),$$

where f indicates that C is a function of E and D.

To familiarize ourselves with the above notation, let us return to the Richwell Oil situation. The fact that the company will reap a large profit if it decides to drill and if the leased land contains oil may be written:

$$\text{Large profit} = f(\text{oil, drill}).$$

And in the case of the fashion shop problem, the fact that the fashion shop will make a profit of $3000 if there is a demand for two coats and only one coat is ordered may be written:

$$3000 = f(2, 1).$$

In the equation $C = f(E, D)$, C, E, and D are called the *variables* of the function f. They are so called because each represents something that is variable.

In our subsequent discussion we will call D, representing a decision, a *decision variable*, and E, representing an environmental setting, an *environmental variable*.

We observe that in defining our fashion shop problem all the variables were allowed to assume only numerical values. When a variable is allowed to assume numerical quantities, we say it is a *quantitative variable*. A model which defines a decision problem in terms of quantitative variables is called a *quantitative model*. Thus the fashion shop model is a quantitative model; but our oil drilling model is not a quantitative model.

If the need arises, we can always transform a nonquantitative model into a quantitative model. How this is done is illustrated below.

Consider the oil drilling problem. In the original definition we allowed E to be a nonquantitative variable. But we can also define E to be:

$$E = \begin{cases} 1 & \text{if the leased land contains oil,} \\ 0 & \text{if the leased land does not contain oil.} \end{cases}$$

Then it becomes a quantitative variable. D was not a quantitative variable in our original definition of the problem, but can be made into a quantitative variable by the definition

$$D = \begin{cases} 1 & \text{if the decision is to drill,} \\ 0 & \text{if the decision is not to drill.} \end{cases}$$

So far we have transformed E and D into quantitative variables in a somewhat arbitrary manner. These transformations may not be very important in our subsequent analysis of the problem.

The case is different with transforming C into a quantitative variable. We recall that C may stand for a large profit, costly drilling expense, etc. Therefore, if we are to make C a quantitative variable, we must determine the exact amount of profit that will arise from a successful drilling and also the exact amount of loss in the event that the drilling yields a dry hole. In practice these quantities are extremely difficult to determine. Yet, it is hard to conceive that Richwell Oil can reach a drilling decision without determining these quantities.

Let us now assume that a successful drilling will yield $100 million in profit and an unsuccessful drilling will mean a $10 million loss. We can then construct a matrix of consequences indexed against the decision alternatives and environmental settings, as shown below:

Decision alternatives	Environmental settings	
	oil	no oil
drill	100	−10
not drill	0	0

This act of information can in turn be converted into a model, as shown in Figure 4.3. Now the model is quantitative.

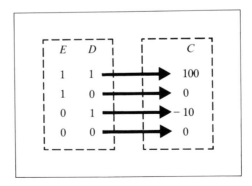

Figure 4.3

4.3   USE OF MATHEMATICAL EXPRESSIONS

Even though we can utilize in our analysis the diagrammatic models given in the preceding sections, the analysis can be made easier if the models are given in terms of standard mathematical expressions. We shall, therefore, illustrate how one of our example problems can be mathematically defined.

Consider the fashion shop problem. We let

d = number of coats demanded during the season,
q = number of coats ordered,
p = amount of profit.

We recall that each coat costs \$4000 and will be sold for \$7000 during the season. Therefore, if the demand for the coat during the season is equal to or exceeds the number of coats ordered, then the fashion shop will make \$3000 per coat ordered. The profit in this situation may be defined as:

$$p = 3000q \quad \text{if} \quad d \geq q.$$

On the other hand, suppose that the demand for the coat is less than the number of coats ordered. Then the fashion shop will still make \$3000 for each coat sold during the season, but it will lose \$2000 for each left-over coat. We write $q - d$ for the number of coats left over. Then the profit situation may be defined as follows:

$$p = 3000d - 2000(q - d) \quad \text{if} \quad d < q.$$

Summarizing our conclusions, we have the following model for the fashion shop:

$$p = 3000q \qquad\qquad\qquad\quad \text{if} \quad d \geq q,$$
$$p = 3000d - 2000(q - d) \quad \text{if} \quad d < q.$$

4.4   SOLUTION PROCESS

It was pointed out in Chapter 2 that a decision process may be decomposed into a definition process and a solution process. Our discussions in Chapter 2 and so far in this chapter, however, were mostly confined to the definition process. We shall now consider the solution process. A solution process was defined as a sequence of activities needed to solve a decision problem. But we have yet to explain what we mean by "*solving a decision problem.*"

In our discussion of the definition process we pointed out that environmental settings are the factors which bear upon a problem and which are yet beyond the control of the decision-maker. The only influence that the latter can exercise over the problem is by means of a selection of decision alternative. Thus solving a decision problem is the same as selecting a suitable decision alternative.

Now if the solution process is equivalent to the selection of a suitable decision alternative, then there must be a way of distinguishing a more suitable decision alternative from a less suitable one. However, one decision may be very suitable for one purpose and not so suitable for another purpose. This means that before a manager begins searching for a suitable decision alternative, he must decide on the criteria of suitability. Such criteria will be called the *decision criteria*. Therefore, formulating the decision criteria belongs in the sequences of activities constituting the solution process.

Even though the manager cannot select his own environmental setting, his selection of the decision alternatives must take into account the likelihoods of the different environmental settings. The second part of the solution process is therefore to evaluate his knowledge of these likelihoods.

Ultimately, however, the solution process must yield a decision alternative. Thus the third and final part of the solution process is the selection of a decision alternative. This selection, however, must be based on the first two parts of this entire sequence of activities.

Let us now elaborate on these activities.

4.5 DECISION CRITERIA

We shall describe some of the criteria that can be used in evaluating the suitability of different decision alternatives.

In any managerial decision-making situation there is a set of goals to be achieved. The decision criteria are the yardsticks by which the degree of attainment of these goals can be measured.

Suppose that the primary goal is to maximize profit. Then the proper criterion for judging the relative suitability of different decision alternatives is the amount of profit that will be generated by each alternative as compared to the yield of other alternatives.

Suppose, however, that the primary goal is not really to maximize the profit, but to attain a certain satisfactory level of profit. Then the preferred decision alternative is that one which will almost guarantee the desired level of profit. The criterion for judging the suitability of a decision alternative, therefore, can be the probability that the given decision alternative will yield at least that level of profit.

The amount of profit and the probability of attaining a specified level of profit are, however, only two among a variety of criteria that may be used to judge the suitability of decision alternatives. We shall introduce a number of other decision criteria as our discussion progresses.

4.6 ENVIRONMENTAL SETTING

The second step in the solution process is to evaluate the manager's knowledge of his decision environment. This, however, was discussed in Chapter 2.

4.7 SELECTING A DECISION ALTERNATIVE

Now as to the actual selection of a decision alternative, let us consider an illustration of how a chosen decision criterion, together with a particular conception of the environmental setting, will determine a particular decision alternative.

Example 3. Fashion Shop Problem   Returning to our familiar fashion shop, let us explore how a decision on the number of coats to be ordered can be made depending on the assumptions.

Case of Certainty.   Assume that the manager has certain knowledge that there will be a demand for exactly one coat during the season. Assume also that he wants to maximize profit. When the demand is for one coat, the amount of profit as a function of the order quantity is given by:

Order quantity	Profit
0	0
1	3000
2	1000

The decision which will maximize profit is to order exactly one coat.

Case of Risk.   Let us assume that the manager has no certain knowledge of exactly how many coats will be wanted during the season, but believes that the probability distribution of the demand is as shown below:

Number of coats	Probability
0	0.3
1	0.5
2	0.2
	1.0

Then the number of coats to be ordered by the fashion shop may nevertheless be influenced by the choice of decision criterion.

Maximize Expected Gain

Assume that the manager wants to maximize his profit. The expected amounts of profit for the different order quantities can be calculated as follows:

Order quantity			
0	0.3(0) + 0.5(0) + 0.2(0)	=	0
1	0.3(−2000) + 0.5(3000) + 0.2(3000)	=	1500
2	0.3(−4000) + 0.5(1000) + 0.2(6000)	=	500

The right decision, therefore, is to order one coat.

Maximize a Probability

On the other hand, the shop manager may very well try to maximize the probability of attaining a specified profit level. For example, he may want to maximize the probability of profit exceeding $5000. Then the decision alternative will have to be reached in the following manner. If he does not order any coat, then the profit will be zero regardless of the demand so that the probability of profit exceeding $5000 is zero. Similarly, the probability is zero if he orders only one coat, because in that case the maximum possible profit is $3000. On the other hand, the shop will make $6000 profit if the manager orders two coats and both are sold. Since the probability of having a demand for two coats is 0.2, the probability of profit exceeding $5000 is also 0.2. Therefore, ordering two coats will maximize the probability of profit exceeding $5000.

Minimize a Probability

The manager might, however, wish to minimize the probability of loss. Now, the probabilities of loss associated with the different order quantities are as follows:

Order quantity	Probability of loss
0	0
1	0.3
2	0.3

We see that the probability is minimized when the order quantity is zero.

Case of Uncertainty

Let us assume now that the manager is completely ignorant about the demand for fur coats. Then again the preferred decision alternative will depend on the decision criterion.

Maximax Profit

One possible decision criterion is to maximize the maximum possible profit. Given this criterion, the manager would first want to determine the maximum possible profit associated with each decision alternative. Then he would choose the alternative which yields the largest maximum possible profit.

The maximum possible profit for each decision alternative is given in the right-hand column of the following profit and loss table.

| | Demand | | | Maximum |
Order quantity	0	1	2	possible profit
0	0	0	0	0
1	−2000	3000	3000	3000
2	−4000	1000	6000	6000

Obviously ordering two coats will maximize the maximum possible profit.

Minimax Loss

Another possible criterion is to minimize the maximum possible loss. If this criterion is adopted, it will be necessary first to determine the maximum possible loss associated with each decision alternative. Then the preferred alternative is the one which will have the smallest maximum possible loss.

The maximum possible loss for each decision alternative is given in the right-hand column of the following profit and loss table.

Order quantity	Demand			Maximum possible loss
	0	1	2	
0	0	0	0	0
1	−2000	3000	3000	−2000
2	−4000	1000	6000	−4000

This table shows that not ordering any coat will minimize the maximum possible loss.

EXERCISES

1. Return to the problem of Richwell Oil described in Example 1. Assume again that a successful drilling will yield $100 million in profit and an unsuccessful drilling will entail a $10 million loss.

a. Suppose the company is absolutely sure that the leased land contains oil. What, then, will be the company's decision if its objective is to maximize profit?
b. Suppose the company believes that the probability of the leased land containing oil is 0.2. What will be the company decision if its decision criterion is to (1) maximize the expected profit, (2) maximize the profit exceeding $50 million, or (3) minimize the probability of loss exceeding $5 million?
c. Suppose the company is completely uncertain as to whether the leased land contains oil. What should be its decision if its objective is to (1) maximize the maximum possible profit or (2) minimize the maximum possible loss?

2. Return to the problem of Perma-Cell Battery of Exercise 1, Chapter 2. The company is asked by a government agency whether it wants to do contract research to develop a new type of power cell. The contract calls for a total expenditure of $200,000, of which the government will underwrite 50 percent, regardless of whether or not the company develops the power cell. If the company in fact develops the power cell, it will manufacture the power cell for the government space program, in which case the estimated profit from the manufacturing operation is $1,000,000.

a. Formulate nonquantitative and quantitative models for the decision problem confronting Perma-Cell Battery.
b. Suppose Perma-Cell is absolutely sure that it will develop the power cell. Which decision alternative is the company likely to choose? Explain.
c. Suppose Perma-Cell believes that the probability of the company's developing the power cell is 0.3. Which decision alternative will the company choose, given each of the following decision criteria: (1) maximize the expected profit, (2) maximize the probability of profit, and (3) minimize the probability of loss?

d. Suppose Perma-Cell is altogether uncertain whether it will develop the power cell. Which decision alternative will the company choose, given each of the following decision criteria: (1) maximize the maximum possible profit and (2) minimize the maximum possible loss?

3. Return to the problem of Modern Television (Exercise 2, Chapter 2). Among this year's models the store is currently out of stock with respect to Model Super Delux 10. The cost of this model, including transportation, is $800.00 per unit. The selling price for the model will remain at $1050.00 until the next year's models come out in two months, at which time it will drop to $750.00. The store manager does not want to order more than 3 sets of this model.

a. Formulate a decision model without using mathematical expressions for Modern Television.
b. Describe this model in mathematical expressions.
c. Suppose Modern Television is absolutely sure that exactly 2 sets of this model will be sold before the new models come out. Assuming that the store wants to maximize profit, what is the right decision for the store?
d. Suppose Modern Television believes that the demand probability distribution for this model before the new models come out, is as follows:

Number of sets demanded	Probability
0	0.4
1	0.3
2	0.2
3	0.1

How many sets of the model should the store order, given the following criteria: (1) maximize the expected profit, (2) maximize the probability of the profit exceeding $700, and (3) minimize the probability of loss?
e. Suppose Modern Television is completely uncertain as to the demand for this model before the new models come out. How many sets should it order, given each of the following decision criteria: (1) maximize the maximum possible profit and (2) minimize the maximum possible loss?

CHAPTER

5

COST, VOLUME, PROFIT ANALYSIS

One very simple quantitative analysis that is useful in managerial decisions is the break-even analysis. A key assumption underlying this analysis is that there are two types of costs: one which is fixed regardless of the volume, where volume refers to the quantity of sales or production; and another which varies with the volume. The *break-even point* is then defined to be the volume necessary to recover both types of costs, the fixed as well as the variable.

The simplicity of the analysis, however, should not be taken as a measure of its usefulness. In July 1971 there was a hearing in the United States Senate on whether the federal government should guarantee a $200 million loan by a banking consortium to the Lockheed Aircraft Corporation, which was on the verge of bankruptcy. One major controversy which emerged during the hearing was the exact break-even point for the company's Tri-star jet aircraft program. The company claimed that the break-even point was between 195 to 205 planes, whereas a defense department study showed that the company would have to sell more than 350 aircraft to break even on the project.*

Finding a break-even point, however, is not the only use for the break-even analysis. It can also be used to evaluate a whole group of questions pertaining to the relations among the volume, cost, and profit. For this reason the analysis is sometimes also called the *cost, volume, profit analysis.*

There are, however, two types of cost, volume, profit analysis: the *profit prediction analysis* and the *break-even analysis.* We shall now consider how each of the two types of analysis can help resolve some managerial decision problems.

---

* *The Wall Street Journal,* July 12, 1971, p. 5.

5.1   PROFIT-PREDICTION ANALYSIS

First, let us describe a situation which calls for a managerial decision.

The Spacecraft Printing Company specializes in printing works for scholarly journals and monographs. A university research bureau wants the company to print a monograph. The research bureau will decide in advance the number of copies to be printed, as well as the amount per copy that it will pay Spacecraft Printing.

The decision alternatives available to Spacecraft Printing are quite clear:

1. accept the work,
2. reject the work.

To choose the correct decision alternative, however, the company must determine the amount of profit or loss associated with each decision alternative. If it rejects the work, there will not be any profit or loss for Spacecraft Printing. However, if it accepts the work, its profit or loss will be a function of the revenue per copy of the monograph, the total number of copies printed, and various costs associated with the work.

We observe that the per copy revenue, the total number of copies to be printed, and the various costs associated with the printing work are, on the whole, not controllable by Spacecraft Printing; they are the environmental variables associated with the decision problem.

Cost Segregations

Let us now list some of the costs which the Spacecraft Printing will have to bear in the event that it decides to print the monograph.

First, it will have to do the composition work, otherwise known as the typesetting. Thus there will be the cost of composition. Then the monograph will have to be printed and bound. Therefore, there will be printing and binding costs.

The cost of printing and binding, however, will vary with the number of copies to be produced. For example, the total printing cost may very well double if the number of copies is doubled. It is therefore a *variable cost*. On the other hand, the composition cost is a *fixed cost* because it does not vary with the number of copies printed.

Revenue, Volume, Cost, and Profit Relations

We mentioned earlier that, in the event that Spacecraft Printing undertakes this work, its profit or loss will be a function of the revenue per copy, the number of copies printed (also referred to as the volume of printing), and the costs associated with the printing. Let us now examine the relations between these variables.

First, we let

$$q = \text{volume of printing,}$$
$$R = \text{unit revenue (or revenue per copy),}$$

V = unit variable cost (or variable cost per copy),

F = total fixed cost,

P = amount of profit or loss (where a minus sign will indicate loss).

Further, we let TR be the total revenue for volume q. Then TR must be equal to q times the unit revenue R:

$$TR = Rq.$$

If TC is the total printing cost for q, then TC must be the sum of the total fixed cost F and the total variable cost Vq, where Vq is the total variable cost. Thus

$$TC = F + Vq.$$

Since profit is equal to total revenue minus total cost $(P = TR - TC)$, we have

$$P = Rq - (F + Vq) = -F + (R - V)q.$$

If we let $M = R - V$, then

$$P = -F + Mq,$$

$$P = -F + (R-V)q$$

where M is called the *unit contribution margin.*

Formulation of Model

We can now formulate the decision model for Spacecraft Printing. The environmental variables are: the unit revenue R, the volume of printing q, the total fixed cost F, and the unit variable cost V. The decision variable x can now be defined as follows:

$$x = \begin{cases} 1 & \text{if Spacecraft Printing does undertake the job,} \\ 0 & \text{if Spacecraft Printing does not undertake the job.} \end{cases}$$

The model that we formulate must be able to indicate the amount of profit or loss for any given combination of decision and environment. We note that the profit is zero if the decision is not to undertake the job, whereas it is given by

$$P = -F + (R - V)q$$

if the job is accepted.

Now suppose we let

$$P = x[-F + (R - V)q].$$

Then P is a function of the decision variable x as well as the environmental variables F, q, R, and V. We note that $P = 0$ if $x = 0$, and $P = [-F + (R - V)q]$ if $x = 1$. Therefore, P is the amount of profit or loss for any given combination of decision and environment. Thus the function given above may be considered a model for the decision problem of Spacecraft Printing. Figure 5.1 is a schematic diagram for this model.

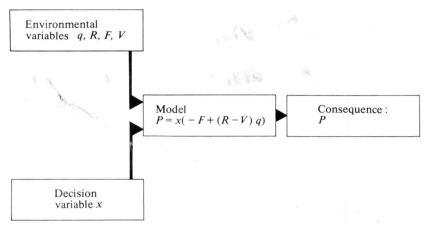

Figure 5.1

Obtaining a Solution

To obtain a solution for the model, we must first decide on a decision criterion and then consider the quality of information available on the environmental variables q, R, F, and V.

Selecting a decision criterion can be very easy. Spacecraft Printing may simply want to maximize its profit.

Determining the quality of available information on q, R, F, and V, however, is not likely to be so simple. For example, it is highly unlikely that Spacecraft Printing knows the exact values of F and V. Consider the unit variable cost V. This cost will be determined by the amount of paper used in each copy of the printed monograph, the number of machine and man hours required to print and bind each copy, the type of binding used, and so on. The company may be able to make a very good estimate of these costs, based on its past experience. But it cannot determine the exact unit variable cost with absolute accuracy. Thus the information that Spacecraft Printing has on the environmental variables falls under the category of risk. Spacecraft Printing knows only the probability distribution of the environmental variables.

The solution to the decision problem becomes involved if the environmental variables in the model are assumed to be random variables. We shall illustrate such a solution in the next chapter.

In the rest of this chapter, however, we shall assume that Spacecraft in fact knows the exact values of the environmental variables q, R, F, and V; that is, it is completely certain of its information. This assumption will simplify the solution. Moreover, it is very frequently made in practice.

Illustration

Let us now assume that the contract is for Spacecraft Printing to print 2000 copies of the monograph and receive $2.50 per copy from the university research bureau. We further assume that the total fixed cost is $1000 and the unit variable cost is $1.50. Thus we have

$$q = 2000, \quad R = 2.50, \quad V = 1.50, \quad F = 1000.$$

Substituting these values into the equations for P, we have

$$P = x(-F + Mq) = x(-1000 + (1)(2000)) = 1000x,$$

where $x = 1$ if the company signs the contract and $x = 0$ if it does not. Then $P = 1000$ if $x = 1$ and $P = 0$ if $x = 0$. Therefore, $x = 1$, or signing the contract, will maximize the profit.

Applications

The kind of decision problem faced by Spacecraft Printing frequently arises in other business enterprises. We shall, therefore, illustrate how the analysis that was carried out for Spacecraft may also be applied to other similar decision situations.

Example 1. Aircraft Development   McBee Aircraft Company has been quite successful with the sale of its huge jumbo jets. The company is in the process of deciding whether to develop an airplane which is slightly smaller but faster than the present jumbo jet.

Much of the existing technology for the jumbo jet can be applied to the development of this new airplane. Nevertheless, the company expects that it will cost $500 million to develop the new plane. Once the development program has been completed, the production cost will be $15 million per plane. Upon inquiry with various airlines, the company has received an initial commitment to buy 60 of these new airplanes, if the plane is ever developed, at a quoted price of $25 million per plane.

Since the development cost will not be influenced by the number of airplanes produced later, it is part of the fixed cost. Thus, if R is the revenue per plane, q the number of planes sold, F the total fixed cost, and V the variable cost per plane, then

$$q = 60, \quad R = 25,000,000,$$
$$V = 15,000,000, \quad F = 500,000,000.$$

Let x be the decision variable where $x = 1$ if the company develops the new airplane and $x = 0$ if it does not develop the plane. Then

$$P = x[-F + (R - V)q]$$
$$= x[-50,000,000 + (25,000,000 - 15,000,000) \times 60]$$
$$= 100,000,000x.$$

We note that $P = 100,000,000$ if $x = 1$ and $P = 0$ if $x = 0$. Therefore, it is better to develop the new airplane.

Example 2. Leasing Options   The administrative offices of the Graduate School of Business at the University of Saratoga is currently paying 5¢ per copy for the use of its office duplicator. The manufacturer proposed an alternate leasing option to the school in which the school pays a lump sum of $5000 per year for the use of the equipment regardless of the number of copies made. The school may keep the old lease option if it desires.

It is not very difficult to see that the school should switch to the new payment plan if it expects to duplicate more than 100,000 copies a year, but keep the old option if it expects to duplicate fewer than 100,000 copies a year. Thus, if there is advance knowledge of how much the machine will be used, there will not be any need to explicitly formulate a model to resolve the decision problem for the school.

We shall, however, nevertheless formulate a model that will give answers consistent with the preceding analysis.

To make a decision on the two leasing options, the school does not need to know the absolute values of the two costs, only their relative values. Let x be the decision variable where $x = 1$ if the school switches to the new lease option and $x = 0$ if it keeps the old lease option. We can consider the lump sum payment of $5000 as the total fixed cost for the new leasing option, and the 5¢ per copy paid under the old lease option as the saving or revenue per copy for the new lease option. Thus $F = 5000$ and $R = 0.05$ for the new lease option. Let q be the number of copies to be duplicated in a year. If we define

$$P = x[-F + (R - V)q] = x(-5000 + 0.05q),$$

then P may be regarded as the relative profit of the two lease options in the following sense: if $P = 1000$ *when* $x = 1$, for example, the model tells us that the new lease option will entail a saving of $1000 over the retention of the old lease; and conversely, there will be a relative loss if $P = -1000$ when $x = 1$.

For example, let $q = 120,000$. Then the old lease option will cost the school $6000, or $1000 more than the new lease. This is verified by

$$P = x[-5000 + 0.05(120,000)] = 1000x = 1000$$

when $x = 1$.

5.2 SENSITIVITY OF PROFIT PREDICTION

In the preceding section we dealt with the prediction of profit assuming that the volume, unit revenue, total fixed cost, and unit variable cost are constant. But in some situations, the manager can in fact vary one or more of these variables, for example, raise the unit revenue by raising the selling price. In other situations, changes may be imposed by external factors. Such changes will affect the total profit, so that it will be necessary to evaluate how the profit will vary with changing variables.

Let us now return to the problem of the Spacecraft Printing Company. Earlier we assumed that

$$q = 2000, \quad R = 2.50, \quad V = 1.50, \quad F = 1000.$$

We shall now examine how the profit will vary as we vary the value of one of these variables.

$2.50q - (100 + 1.5q)$

Varying the Volume

Let us first assume that volume q is a variable. Then the total revenue TR and the total cost TC are

$$TR = 2.50q, \qquad TC = 1000 + 1.5q,$$

so that

$$P = -1000 + (2.5 - 1.5)q = -1000 + q.$$

The variations in total revenue and total cost as functions of the volume are illustrated in Figure 5.2. The variation in profit as a function of the volume is illustrated in Figure 5.3. Thus Figure 5.3 shows that if the volume is increased by 1000 copies, then the total profit will increase by $1000.

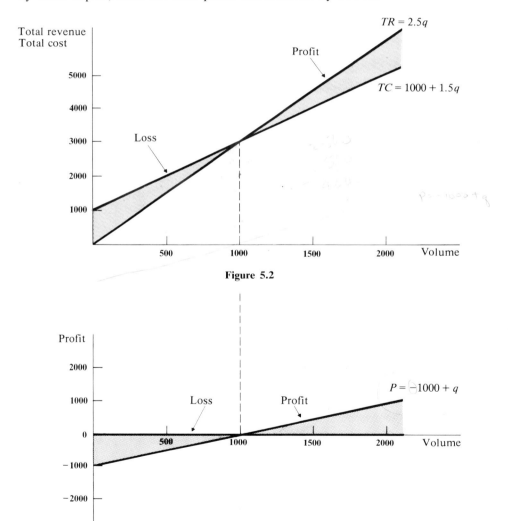

Figure 5.2

Figure 5.3

Varying the Contribution Margin

Let us now fix $q = 2000$ and $F = 1000$ and vary either R or V or both, so that the contribution margin M will vary. Then

$$P = -1000 + 2000M.$$

The variation in profit as a function of the contribution margin M is illustrated in Figure 5.4, where it is shown that if the contribution margin is increased by 0.5, total profit will increase by $1000. This is not very surprising since it was assumed that the volume is 2000 copies.

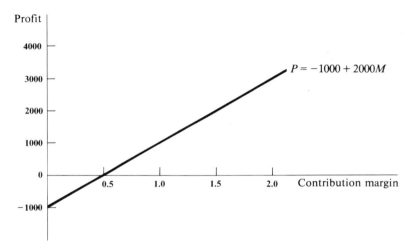

Figure 5.4

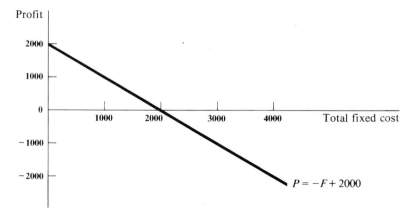

Figure 5.5

Varying the Total Fixed Cost

Let us now fix $q = 2000$, $R = 2.50$, $V = 1.50$, and vary the total fixed cost F. Then

$$P = -F + (2.50 - 1.50)2000 = -F + 2000.$$

The variation in profit as a function of the total fixed cost F is illustrated in Figure 5.5. We can see that if the total fixed cost is increased by \$1000, then total profit will decline by exactly the same amount.

5.3   BREAK-EVEN ANALYSIS

We shall again begin our discussion by describing a decision problem which might call for a break-even analysis.

Example 3   The Easia Travel Company sponsors group travels between San Francisco and a city in the Far East. It charters an airplane for a specified fixed sum. Each group, however, stops overnight in Tokyo before arriving at the final destination. Easia must pay for the hotel rooms, meals, bus fares, and so on, for the group. The total amount of such expenses will, of course, vary with the number of people in the group. Easia will charge a fixed amount to each person in the group.

The company has already decided on the amount per person it will charge. It also knows the cost of chartering an airplane. Furthermore, it has a very good idea as to the per person hotel, meal, and other expenses in Tokyo.

The uncertain element in its decision to sponsor a particular group in question is the number of persons who will join the group. As a first analysis, Easia wants to determine the number of persons needed for the company to break even.

Let us define the *break-even volume* as the number of persons needed in the group to break even and let

R = per person charge for the trip,
F = fixed lump sum cost of chartering an airplane,
V = cost per person in Tokyo,
$\bar{q}$ = break-even volume.

We know that at the break-even volume, total revenue is exactly equal to total cost. Thus

$$R\bar{q} = F + V\bar{q}$$

Transferring the variables and solving for $\bar{q}$, we have

$$\bar{q} = \frac{F}{R - V} = \frac{F}{M}.$$

Thus the break-even volume is simply equal to the total fixed cost divided by the unit contribution margin.

Illustration

For the Easia Travel Company let us assume that it will cost $22,500 to charter an airplane, $30 per person in Tokyo, and each person will be charged $180 for the trip:

$$R = 180, \qquad V = 30, \qquad F = 22,500.$$

Then $M = 180 - 30 = 150$, and the break-even volume is

$$\bar{q} = \frac{F}{M} = \frac{22,500}{150} = 150.$$

That is, it will take 150 persons to break even.

Once the break-even volume has been determined, Easia Travel can decide to sponsor or not to sponsor the trip depending on whether it believes that the actual number of persons who will join the group is greater or less than the break-even volume.

We observe that the above break-even model does not involve all the elements in a decision problem. For example, it does not involve the decision variable. Also it does not specify the consequence for a given combination of decision and environment.

We can, however, modify the model in such a way that it not only incorporates the decision variable but also predicts the consequence for any combination of decision and environment.

Let q be the actual volume, in contrast to the break even volume $\bar{q}$. Then if Easia Travel sponsors the trip, its total profit will be given by

$$P = (q - \bar{q})M,$$

where M is the contribution margin.

Let x be the decision variable where $x = 1$ if the Easia Travel Company sponsors the trip and $x = 0$ otherwise. Then the company profit as a function of the decision and environmental variables may be defined as

$$P = x[(q - \bar{q})M].$$

Assume now that 200 people for example, will join the group. Then

$$P = x[(200 - 150)150] = 7500x,$$

or

$$P = 7500$$

if Easia Travel sponsors the trip.

5.4   SENSITIVITIES OF THE BREAK-EVEN VOLUME

In Section 5.3 we examined the variations in profit with changes in environmental variables such as unit revenue, the fixed and unit variable costs. Let us now examine the variations in break-even volume as we change some of the same variables.

Varying the Total Fixed Cost

Returning to our Easia Travel illustration, we let

$$R = 180, \qquad V = 30,$$

but assume that the total fixed cost F is a variable. Then the break-even volume $\bar{q}$ is

$$\bar{q} = \frac{F}{180 - 30} = \frac{F}{150}.$$

The break-even volume as a function of the total fixed cost is illustrated in Figure 5.6. We note that it is a linear function. Furthermore, the break-even volume will increase by one whenever the total fixed cost is increased by $150.

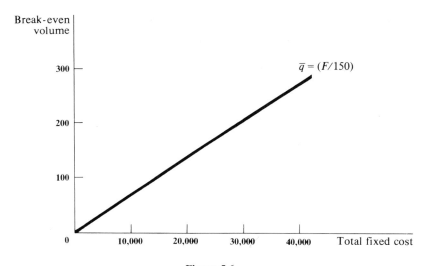

Figure 5.6

Varying the Contribution Margin

Again consider Easia Travel Company, but let us now hold the total fixed cost at $22,500 and vary either the unit revenue or unit variable cost so as to vary the unit contribution margin M. Then the break-even volume $\bar{q}$ is

$$\bar{q} = 22{,}500/M.$$

The break-even volume as a function of the unit contribution margin is illustrated in Figure 5.7. We note that it is a nonlinear function. For example, the break-even volume declines by 225 units when the contribution margin is increased from $50 to $100, but it declines by 15 units when the contribution margin is increased from $250 to $300.

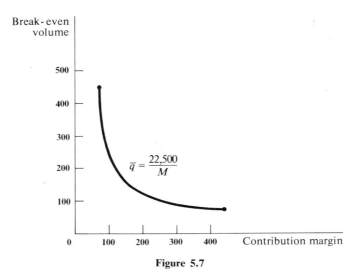

Figure 5.7

5.5   COMPARISON ANALYSIS

So far we have confined the application of our analyses to the evaluation of single projects. We will now extend the application to cases where two different projects are under consideration.

Profit Comparison

Let us now return to the McBee Aircraft problem. Our earlier assumptions were that the development cost for the new airplane could be $500 million, the unit production cost would be $15 million, and the selling price would be $25 million.

Suppose now the company can spend another $300 million for development in order to bring down the unit production cost by $5 million to $10 million. Is such an additional development expenditure justified? The answer depends on the number of airplanes which can be sold at the new reduced cost.

Let F_1 and V_1, respectively, be the original development cost and unit production cost; and let F_2 and V_2, respectively, be the corresponding new costs:

$$F_1 = 500,000,000, \qquad V_1 = 15,000,000,$$
$$F_2 = 800,000,000, \qquad V_2 = 10,000,000.$$

Let x be the decision variable where $x = 1$ if the decision is to adopt the first alternative and $x = 0$ if the decision is to adopt the second alternative. Then the model for the profit as a function of the decision and environment is given by

$$P = x(-F_1 + M_1 q) + (1 - x)(-F_2 + M_2 q),$$

where M_1 is the contribution margin under the first alternative and M_2 is the

$R = 25M$

contribution margin under the second alternative. We observe that $P = -F_1 + M_1q$ if $x = 1$, and $P = -F_2 + M_2q$ if $x = 0$.

Assume, for example, that 80 airplanes will eventually be sold. Then $q = 80$, $M_1 = 10,000,000$, and $M_2 = 15,000,000$, so that $P = 25,000,000$

$$P = x(-500,000,000 + 10,000,000(80))$$
$$+ (1 - x)(-800,000,000 + 15,000,000(80))$$
$$= -500,000,000 + 10,000,000(80) = 300,000,000$$

if $x = 1$ and

$$P = -800,000,000 + 15,000,000(80) = 400,000,000$$

if $x = 0$. Thus the second alternative will maximize the profit for McBee Aircraft.

If we wish, we can also ascertain the volume at which the two alternatives become equally profitable. Let us call this volume the *break-even volume* between the two alternatives. Then we can determine the break-even volume as follows. Let

$$P_1 = -500,000,000 + 10,000,000q$$

and

$$P_2 = -800,000,000 + 15,000,000q,$$

where P_1 and P_2 are respectively the amounts of profit associated with the two alternatives for a given volume of airplanes sold.

Figure 5.8 shows P_1 and P_2 as functions of the volume. The break-even

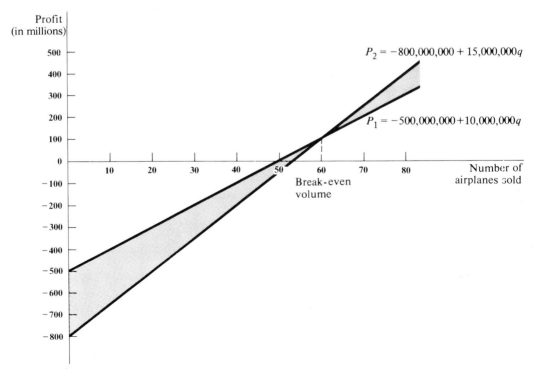

Figure 5.8

volume is evidently 60 airplanes. That is, if more than 60 airplanes can be sold, then spending $800 million for development will be more profitable. But if fewer than 60 airplanes can be sold, then spending $500 million for development will be more profitable or less unprofitable.

We can also determine the break-even volume algebraically by setting the equation

$$-500,000,000 + 10,000,000q = -800,000,000 + 15,000,000q$$

and solving for q:

$$q = \bar{q} = \frac{800,000,000 - 500,000,000}{15,000,000 - 10,000,000} = 60,$$

where $\bar{q}$ is the break-even volume.

Cost Comparison

Example 4   California Mutual is an insurance company in California. It is in the process of negotiating a yearly service contract for the typewriters used in the company. Approximately 1000 typewriters will be covered by the service contract.

The manufacturer of the typewriters has offered the following two options:

1. $30,000 plus $5000 times the average number of service hours required per typewriter during the year.
2. $10,000 plus $10,000 times the average number of service hours required per typewriter during the year.

Let C_1 = 30,000 + 5000q and C_2 = 10,000 + 10,000q, where q is the average number of service hours required per typewriter during the year. Then C_1 and C_2 represent the total annual costs of the two options.

Let x be the decision variable where $x = 1$ if the first option is chosen and $x = 0$ if the second option is chosen. Then the annual cost as a function of the decision and environment is given by

$$C = x(30,000 + 5000q) + (1 - x)(10,000 + 10,000q),$$

where C is the annual cost. We note that $C = C_1 = 30,000 + 5000q$ if $x = 1$, and $C = C_2 = 10,000 + 10,000q$ if $x = 0$.

Assume, for example, that an average of 6 hours will be required for each machine: $q = 6$. Then

$$C = x(30,000 + 5000q) + (1 - x)(10,000 + 10,000q)$$
$$= 30,000 + 5000q = 60,000$$

if $x = 1$ and

$$C = x(30,000 + 5000q) + (1 - x)(10,000 + 10,000q)$$
$$= 10,000 + 10,000q = 70,000$$

if $x = 0$. Thus the first option will minimize the annual cost of servicing the typewriters.

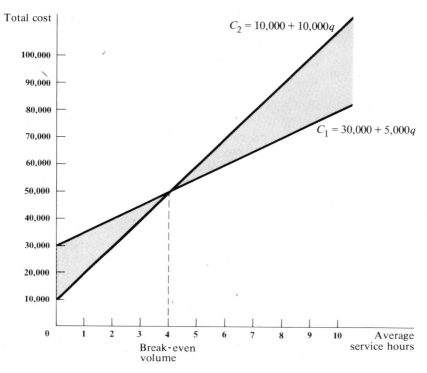

Figure 5.9

Let the break-even volume be defined as the average number of service hours per machine that will make the costs of the two options equal. Then it can be ascertained graphically as shown in Figure 5.9: the break-even volume is 4 hours. Thus if the average service time per machine exceeds 4 hours, then the first option will cost less, whereas if the average service time is less than 4 hours, then the second option will cost less.

We can also determine the break-even volume algebraically. Setting

$$30,000 + 5000q = 10,000 + 10,000q$$

and solving the equation for q, we have

$$\bar{q} = \frac{30,000 - 10,000}{10,000 - 5000} = 4.$$

5.6 INAPPROPRIATE APPLICATIONS

Even the most judicious applications of the cost, volume, and profit analysis sometimes produce errors. Inappropriate applications of the analysis can certainly lead to very serious errors.

We will discuss two types of inappropriate applications of the analysis: first, application to decision situations where our simplifying assumptions regarding unit revenue, total fixed cost, and unit variable cost do not hold; second, application in which the analysis is carried out with unit revenue and cost figures which do not reflect their definitions. Let us consider some of these errors.

Unit Revenue

We have assumed in our discussion that the unit revenue is constant regardless of the volume. This assumption implies, for example, that a company can sell any quantity (small or large) of product or service at a fixed price. This may be true if the quantity of the product supplied by the company is only a tiny fraction of the total quantity of the product supplied by all the suppliers. Otherwise, the company can often influence the volume of its own sales of this product by changing the unit selling price. It can, for example, increase the volume of the product sold by lowering the unit selling price.

If, however, an additional volume of sales can be brought about only by lowering the unit selling price the total revenue is no longer a linear function of the volume, as was assumed in our earlier discussion. Then we have to modify our analysis to take into account a nonlinear relation between total revenue and volume.

Total Fixed Cost

We have defined total fixed cost as the cost that does not vary with volume. A careful examination of our analysis will further show that total fixed cost is taken to be a lump sum cost which is incurred if and only if the project under consideration is actually undertaken. This means that in determining the total fixed cost, we should include those lump sum costs which will be incurred if the project in question is actually undertaken and explicitly exclude those costs which will be incurred regardless of whether the project is undertaken. This rule, however, is quite frequently violated in the actual applications of the cost, volume, and profit analysis.

For purpose of periodic income statements accountants classify certain types of cost as fixed for the period. They include, for example, general administrative expenses, depreciations, taxes, insurance premiums, etc. These expenses, however, are unavoidable period expenses for a company as a whole and are likely to be incurred regardless of whether a certain new project is undertaken. Then they should not be included in the total fixed cost for the project under consideration. Nevertheless, it is standard practice in many cost, volume, and profit analyses to allocate a certain percentage of such period expenses as part of the total fixed cost for the project in question. Such a practice obviously tends to make new projects appear less attractive than they might otherwise appear and thus leads to wrong decisions.

There is another issue concerning total fixed cost. Our definition is that the total fixed cost does not vary with volume. Frequently, however, such a definition is valid only for a certain range of the volume. For example, in the case of Easia Travel Company, if the company believes that between 100 and 200 persons will join the trip, it is likely to charter a regular jet. However, if it believes that between 300 and 350 persons will be on the trip, then it is likely

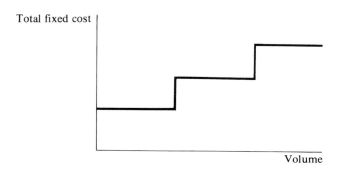

Figure 5.10

to charter a jumbo jet. The costs of chartering the two types of airplane will certainly be different. The total fixed cost for Easia Travel Company is really a step function of the volume, as illustrated in Figure 5.10. We expect that in many instances the total fixed cost is a step function of the volume. But if so, our analysis must explicitly take into account this character of the total fixed cost.

Unit Variable Cost

As with unit revenue, we have assumed that unit variable cost is constant, regardless of the volume, so that total variable cost is a linear function of volume.

There are, however, factors which will tend to make the unit variable cost vary with the volume. Quite often the unit material cost will decline with increasing volume on account of quantity discounts. On the other hand, sometimes large-volume production is possible only by means of very extensive utilization of the existing facilities and personnel, for example multiple shifts and overtime labor, which tends to increase the unit variable cost.

Economists generally believe that the unit variable cost initially tends to decrease as volume increases, but after the volume reaches a certain level, further increase in volume will cause the unit variable cost to increase. They believe that typically the unit variable cost as a function of volume is something like the graph in Figure 5.11.

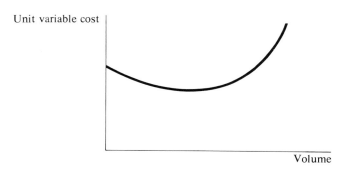

Figure 5.11

A number of important statistical studies, however, indicate that the unit variable cost tends to be fairly stable over a wide range of the volume. Nevertheless, the assumption that the unit variable cost is constant needs a careful scrutiny before it is incorporated into an analysis.

EXERCISES

1. Brown Camera Company is very successful in selling its cameras. The company does not, however, manufacture any camera which will produce printed pictures "instantly."

The research department of the company has been working on the development of such a camera. Recently a process has indeed been developed that can be used to produce the camera. However, it will require another $10 million to perfect the process; $15 million has already been spent.

Once the process has been perfected, another $20-million investment will be needed to build a manufacturing plant.

Material, labor, and other direct costs for the production and selling of the camera are estimated to be $40 per camera. The retail price of the camera will be $150.00. The company will sell it to the distributors for $90.00.

   a. Suppose that the company expects to sell 1,000,000 units. Should it proceed with the camera project? Explain your answer.

   b. Suppose that, instead of $10 million, it will require another $25 million to perfect the process. Will the total profit change assuming the same sales figure of 1,000,000 units?

   c. Suppose that there is a rise of $25 to $65 per unit in materials, labor, and other direct costs for the production and marketing. How will the total profit be affected, assuming that sales remain at 1,000,000 units?

   d. Suppose that the company can raise its selling price to the distributors by $10 to $100, while maintaining the sales figure of 1,000,000 units. How will the total company profit be altered?

2. Assume that it will cost Brown Camera Company $10 million to perfect the process, $20 million to build the manufacturing plant, that the material, labor, and other direct costs for the production and marketing of the camera are $40 per unit, and the selling price to the distributors will be $90 per unit.

   a. Determine the break-even volume.

   b. Suppose that instead of $10 million, $25 million will be needed to perfect the process. How will the change affect the break-even volume?

   c. Suppose that the material, labor, and other direct costs for producing and marketing the camera will rise by $25 to $65 per unit. How will the break-even volume be affected?

   d. Suppose that the company can raise its selling price by $10 to $100 per unit. What will happen to the break-even volume?

3. Pacific Airline maintains a daily schedule between San Francisco and Honolulu, Hawaii. The airplanes used for this route each have a seating capacity of 180. The fixed cost of making a one-way flight between the two cities is $8000. It includes the cost of gasoline, wages paid to the flight crew, landing fees, and other lump sum expenses specifically connected with the flight, but it does not include the general overhead expenses of the airline. Ticket price depends on whether it is one way or round trip, whether it is first class or tourist. The average ticket price for a one-way trip, however, is calculated to be $120. The unit variable cost per passenger is $20, which includes the cost of a meal, drinks, refreshments, etc.

a. Suppose that a given flight is 50 percent full. How much will the airline profit from the flight (profit being defined as the total revenue from the flight, less the total cost specifically attributable to the flight)?
b. If the fixed cost is increased by $2000 how will the profitability of the flight carrying 50 percent of the capacity be affected?
c. If the airline raises the average ticket price by $10, how will the profitability of such a flight be affected?

4. Assume that the total fixed cost for a Pacific Airline flight is $8000, the average ticket price is $120, and the unit variable cost is $20.

a. What is the break-even volume for a flight?
b. If the total fixed cost is increased by $2000, what will happen to the break-even volume?
c. Suppose the airline raises the average ticket price by $10. What will happen to the break-even volume?

5. Safevox is a large European automobile manufacturer. It is seriously considering whether to build a 2 million square feet assembly plant on the east coast of the United States. The projected cost for the plant is $100 million. The assembly plant will have the capacity to produce 100,000 automobiles a year.

Other factors besides the cost consideration will also influence the company's ultimate decision. One is the "buy American" sentiment which appears to be growing in the United States. Nevertheless, the cost will be a crucial consideration in the decision.

Safevox estimates that it will cost only $20 million to expand its European assembly plant capacity by 100,000 cars a year. The American workers will be paid higher wages than their European counterparts, although this added cost will be compensated by savings in the shipping costs and tariffs. There are also intangible costs to consider, such as the slower delivery from the European plant to the American market.

The total variable cost per car is estimated to be $3600 if the assembly is done in Europe. This includes the shipping costs, the United States tariffs, and other intangible costs of assembling in Europe for the American market. The total variable cost per car, with assembly in United States, is estimated to be $3500.

The company sells its cars to the American distributors for $4000 per car on the average. At present the company sales are approximately 50,000 cars a year in the United States.

Let us assume that Safevox will decide whether to build the American plant or expand the European plant, on the basis of a 10-year projection.

a. Suppose Safevox will sell 50,000 cars a year on the average for the 10-year period. Which alternative is preferable? Explain your answer.
b. Suppose Safevox will sell 100,000 cars a year on the average for the 10-year period. Which alternative is preferable? Explain your answer. *sensitivity Analysis*

6. For Exercise 5 determine the total number of cars sold during the 10-year period which will make the two alternatives equally desirable. Illustrate such a break-even volume graphically.

6

STOCHASTIC COST, VOLUME, PROFIT ANALYSIS

In our discussion of the cost, volume, and profit analysis in Chapter 5 we assumed that the unit revenue, total fixed cost, and unit variable cost are known with certainty. However, as pointed out elsewhere, the unit revenue and cost figures that we use in such an analysis may be quite different from their actual values. So in Chapter 5 we proposed various types of sensitivity analysis to evaluate the effect of the discrepancies between the assumed unit revenue and cost figures and their actual values.

In this chapter we shall use another approach to evaluate these discrepancies. Whenever we use certain numerical figures as costs and unit revenue in an analysis, we must have a good reason to believe that these figures are likely to be good approximations of their actual values. Even if we may not know precisely the actual values, we should have some idea as to the ranges within which these values are likely to fall.

We can therefore assume that unit revenue and costs are random variables whose probability distributions can be ascertained subjectively. This is the approach taken in this chapter. But first we shall illustrate how such probability distributions may be subjectively ascertained.

Example 1. Publication Decision   Consider again the problem of Spacecraft Printing Company. We recall that the company is confronted with a decision whether to undertake the printing of a monograph.

In the discussion in Chapter 5 we assumed that Spacecraft Printing would print 2000 copies of the monograph and the university research bureau would pay the company $2.50 per copy. We also pointed out that the cost of composition comprised most of the fixed cost, estimated at $1000. The major elements of the variable costs, estimated at $1.50 per copy, were those of printing and binding. Under the circumstances the estimated profit margin per copy was $1.00, so that the estimated total profit was

$$\begin{array}{l}\text{Estimated} \\ \text{total profit}\end{array} = \left(\begin{array}{l}\text{Estimated} \\ \text{profit margin}\end{array}\right)(\text{Volume}) - \left(\begin{array}{l}\text{Estimated} \\ \text{fixed cost}\end{array}\right)$$

$$= (\$1.00)(2000) - (\$1000) = \$1000.$$

Spacecraft Printing, however, is not absolutely sure about its estimates of the fixed and unit variable costs. Consequently, it cannot rule out the possibility that it might actually incur a loss instead of making a profit. If it should lose money in the venture, it would be due to either the fixed cost or the unit variable cost or both exceeding the estimated values.

The company now decides to examine these costs again. After carefully studying the figures for similar projects in the past, it comes to the following conclusions. Even though it is not absolutely sure that the fixed cost will in fact be $1000, it is at least 95 percent sure that the fixed cost will be between $400 and $1600. Similarly, it is 95 percent sure that the unit variable cost will be between $1.00 and $2.00. Suppose the company further assumes that the two costs are normally distributed random variables, in which case about 95 percent of the probability distribution will lie within two standard deviations from the mean. Thus the company can assume the mean and standard deviation of the fixed cost to be $1000 and $300, respectively (Figure 6.1). Similarly, it can take the mean and standard deviation of the unit variable cost to be $1.50 and $0.25, respectively (Figure 6.2).

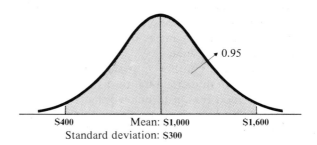

Figure 6.1

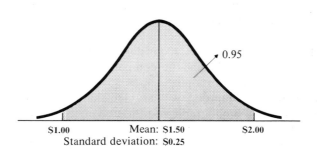

Figure 6.2

6.1 STATISTICAL PROPOSITIONS

Before proceeding further with probabilistic analysis of cost, volume, and profit, let us describe some concepts which will be utilized in the following sections.

Proposition 1   Let X and Y be two statistically independent random variables whose means are μ_x and μ_y and whose standard deviations are σ_x and σ_y. Then if $T = X + Y$, the mean and standard deviation of T are, respectively,

$$\mu_T = \mu_x + \mu_y \qquad \sigma_T = \sqrt{\sigma_x^2 + \sigma_y^2}.$$

But if we define $T = X - Y$, then

$$\mu_T = \mu_x - \mu_y, \qquad \sigma_T = \sqrt{\sigma_x^2 + \sigma_y^2}.$$

We observe that the mean of T is either the sum of or the difference between the means of X and Y, depending on whether $T = X + Y$ or $T = X - Y$, whereas the standard deviation of T is always the square root of the sum of variances of X and Y.

We shall next consider one simple application of the preceding proposition.

Example 2   Let us return to the Spacecraft Printing example. We have an expected unit variable cost of $1.50 with a standard deviation of $0.25.

Instead of just estimating these costs directly, the company may decide to do more detailed calculations. Company records reveal that the mean values of printing and binding costs are $1.00 and $0.50, whereas their standard deviations are 16¢ and 12¢ respectively. If we let

$$V = \text{unit variable cost,}$$
$$A = \text{unit printing cost,}$$
$$B = \text{unit binding cost,}$$

then

$$V = A + B,$$

so that

$$\mu_V = \mu_A + \mu_B = 1.00 + 0.50 = 1.50,$$

$$\sigma_V = \sqrt{\sigma_A^2 + \sigma_B^2} = \sqrt{(0.16)^2 + (0.12)^2} = 0.20.$$

Thus the mean and the standard deviation of the unit variable cost are $1.50 and $0.20, respectively.

We recall that the university research bureau has agreed to pay $2.50 per copy. If we let

$$R = \text{unit revenue,}$$

then the mean of R is $2.50 and the standard deviation of R is zero. Now we can let

$$M = \text{unit contribution margin,}$$

where $M = R - V$. Then

$$\mu_M = \mu_R - \mu_V = 2.50 - 1.50 = 1.00,$$
$$\sigma_M = \sqrt{\sigma_R^2 + \sigma_V^2} = \sqrt{(0)^2 + (0.2)^2} = 0.20.$$

The mean and the standard deviation of the unit contribution margin will be $1.00 and $0.20, respectively.

Proposition 2   Let X be a random variable and k be a constant. If $T = kX$, then

$$\mu_T = k\mu_x, \qquad \sigma_T = k\sigma_x.$$

We shall again consider an application of the proposition.

Example 3   Let us assume for Spacecraft Printing that the mean unit variable cost is $1.50, with a standard deviation of $0.20. Suppose we now wish to determine the expected total variable cost and its standard deviation for printing 2000 copies of the monograph. Then if S is the total variable cost,

$$\mu_S = 2000\mu_V = (2000)(1.50) = 3000,$$
$$\sigma_S = 2000\sigma_V = (2000)(0.2) = 400.$$

The mean and the standard deviation of the total variable cost are $3000 and $400, respectively.

6.2 PROFIT-PREDICTION ANALYSIS

Let us now reevaluate the decision problem confronting Spacecraft Printing Company in light of the assumption that the unit revenue, total fixed cost, and unit variable cost are all random variables.

First, we let

q = volume of printing,

R = unit revenue as a random variable,

V = unit variable cost as a random variable,

F = total fixed cost as a random variable,

M = unit contribution margin as a random variable,

where q, R, F, and V are environmental variables. Let x be the decision variable:

$$x = \begin{cases} 1 & \text{if Spacecraft Printing takes the job,} \\ 0 & \text{if it does not take the job.} \end{cases}$$

If P is the profit for Spacecraft, then we can again express P as a function of the decision and the environment:

$$P = x[-F + (R - V)q].$$

If Spacecraft Printing decides against taking the job, then

$$P = x[-F + (R - V)q] = 0[-F + (R - V)q] = 0.$$

If it decides to take it, then

$$P = x[-F + (R - V)q] = -F + (R - V)q,$$

since in this case $x = 1$. A schematic diagram for the model is provided in Figure 6.3, where the upper-case letters now represent random variables and the lower-case letters represent the nonrandom (or deterministic) variables.

We observe that the profit P is itself a random variable. For our subsequent analysis it would be helpful to know (1) the mean value of P, (2) the standard deviation of P, and (3) the shape of the probability distribution of P.

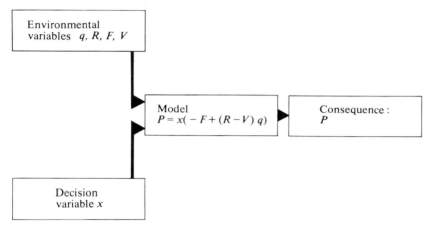

Figure 6.3

Let μ_P and σ_P respectively denote the mean value and standard deviation of P. By Propositions 1 and 2, we have

$$\mu_P = -\mu_F + (\mu_R - \mu_V)q, \qquad \sigma_P = \sqrt{\sigma_F^2 + (\sigma_R^2 + \sigma_V^2)q^2}.$$

Or,

$$\mu_P = \mu_F + \mu_M q, \qquad \sigma_P = \sqrt{\sigma_F^2 + \sigma_M^2 q^2},$$

where μ_M and σ_M respectively denote the mean value and standard deviation of the unit contribution margin.

Illustration

If we assume for the printing company that

$$\mu_F = \$1000, \qquad \sigma_F = \$300,$$
$$\mu_M = \$1, \qquad \sigma_M = \$0.20,$$

then

$$\mu_P = -\mu_F + \mu_M q = -1000 + (1)(2000) = 1000,$$
$$\sigma_P = \sqrt{\sigma_F^2 + \sigma_M^2 q^2} = \sqrt{(300)^2 + (0.2)^2(2000)^2} = 500.$$

The mean value and standard deviation of the profit are $1000 and $500, respectively.

We can further show that the profit P is normally distributed if the total fixed cost F and the unit variable cost V are normally distributed.

Decision Criteria   Given this situation of Spacecraft Printing Company, it is no longer apparent that one of the decision alternatives is clearly preferable to the other. Therefore, different decision criteria may lead the company to different decision alternatives.

Maximize Expected Profit.   Suppose that Spacecraft Printing wants to maximize its expected profit. The expected profit is zero if Spacecraft decides not to take the job, but $1000 if it takes the job. Thus the latter alternative will maximize the expected profit.

Minimize Probability of Loss.   Suppose, on the other hand, Spacecraft Printing wants to minimize the probability of loss. Quite obviously this probability will be zero if Spacecraft decides against the project.

Let us calculate the probability of loss in the event that Spacecraft does undertake the project. We have already shown that P is a random variable with a mean value of $1000 and a standard deviation of $500. As illustrated in Figure 6.4, zero profit is 2 standard deviations from the mean profit. Therefore, using the table of normal probability distributions, we can ascertain that the probability of loss is 0.0228.

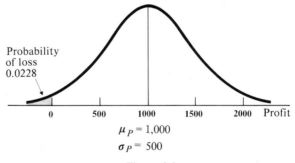

Figure 6.4

Therefore, to minimize the probability of loss, the company would not take the job. Of course, this conclusion is very obvious in the given decision situation. However, we shall later describe a situation where the issues are not so obvious.

Example 4. Aircraft Development   Consider now McBee Aircraft Company, which is in the process of deciding whether to develop an airplane that is slightly smaller but faster than its jumbo jet. The expected development cost is $500 million, and the company is 95 percent sure that the actual development cost will be between $300 million and $700 million. Once the plane is developed, the expected cost of producing an airplane is $15 million and the company is 95 percent sure that the actual production cost will be between $9 million and $21 million. The average selling price of the airplane will be $25 million, but the actual price will depend on the number of planes purchased by each airline and other factors surrounding each purchase. The company believes, however, that 95 percent of the airplanes will be sold at prices between $23 million and $27 million per plane. Assuming that the probability distribution of the development cost, unit production cost, and selling price is normal, then we can use the notation:

$$\mu_F = 500, \qquad \sigma_F = 100,$$
$$\mu_R = 25, \qquad \sigma_R = 1,$$
$$\mu_V = 15, \qquad \sigma_V = 3,$$

where the numbers are in millions of dollars. Then

$$\mu_P = -\mu_F + (\mu_R - \mu_V)q = -500 + (25 - 15)q,$$
$$\sigma_P = \sqrt{\sigma_F^2 + (\sigma_R^2 + \sigma_V^2)q^2} = \sqrt{(100)^2 + [(1)^2 + (3)^2]q^2},$$

where q is the number of airplanes to be sold.

Suppose, for example, that 80 airplanes are expected to be sold: $q = 80$. Then

$$\mu_P = -500 + (25 - 15)80 = 300,$$
$$\sigma_P = \sqrt{(100)^2 + [(1)^2 + (3)^2](80)^2} = \sqrt{100,000 + 640,000} \cong 272.$$

The expected profit is $300 million, and the standard deviation of profit is approximately $272 million.

While the prospect of earning $300 million may be intriguingly attractive, the company cannot overlook the fact that an actual profit of $300 would be contingent on the research and development cost being exactly $500 million, the unit production cost being exactly $15 million, and the unit selling price being exactly $25 million. However, cost overruns are not uncommon with the airplane manufacturers such as McBee. A serious cost overrun either in research and development or in production could bankrupt the company.

What, then, is the probability that the company will actually lose money if it proceeds with the development project? Since the mean profit is $300 million with a standard deviation of $272 million, zero profit is 1.1 standard deviations from the mean, as shown in Figure 6.5. Using the table of normal probability distribution, we find that the probability is 0.1357 that the company will lose money.

What should McBee Aircraft do in light of the preceding analysis? That depends on the decision criteria. If the company wants to maximize the expected profit, then it will proceed with the new aircraft development project. On the other hand, if it wants to minimize the probability of loss, then it will not proceed with the project. A more realistic aim may be to maximize the expected profit so long as the probability of loss is not greater than some

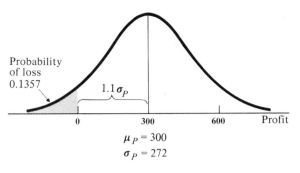

Figure 6.5

reasonable level. For example, if the probability of loss is not to exceed 0.2, then the company will decide to proceed with the project, the probability of loss being only 0.1357.

6.3 PROBABILISTIC BREAK-EVEN ANALYSIS

In Chapter 3 we defined the break-even volume $\bar{q}$ as

$$\bar{q} = F/M,$$

where F is the total fixed cost and M the unit contribution margin. If we let both F and M be random variables, then $\bar{q}$ also becomes a random variable. In this case $\bar{q}$ is a ratio of two random variables, and the probabilistic analysis of it becomes very difficult. Therefore, we shall not discuss probabilistic break-even analysis here. Readers who are interested in this topic may, however, consult the references at the end of the book.

6.4 COMPARISON ANALYSIS

So far in our discussion of probabilistic analyses we have been primarily concerned with evaluating single projects. Let us now turn to the problem of evaluating two mutually exclusive projects.

Consider the problem of the Safevox Automobile Company, which is in the process of deciding whether to expand its existing European assembly plant or build a new assembly plant in the United States. The feasibility studies done on the two alternatives have yielded the following information.

The expected cost of expanding the European assembly plant is $20 million with a standard deviation of $2 million. The expected cost of building a new assembly plant in the United States is $100 million with a standard deviation of $20 million.

The expected unit variable cost of assembling a car in Europe and delivering it to an American distributor is $3700 with a standard deviation of $200. The corresponding figures for a car assembled in the United States are $3600 and $300.

The expected unit selling price is $4000 with a standard deviation of $100, assuming that the price will not be affected by the decision in question.

Let F_1 and V_1 be the total fixed cost and the unit variable cost associated with the European assembly plant, and F_2 and V_2 be the corresponding costs associated with the American plant. Then in notation we have

$$\mu_{F_1} = 20,000,000, \qquad \mu_{F_2} = 100,000,000,$$
$$\sigma_{F_1} = 2,000,000, \qquad \sigma_{F_2} = 20,000,000,$$
$$\mu_{V_1} = 3700, \qquad \mu_{V_2} = 3600,$$
$$\sigma_{V_1} = 200, \qquad \sigma_{V_2} = 300,$$

and

$$\mu_R = 4000, \qquad \sigma_R = 100.$$

Let x be the decision variable where $x = 1$ if the decision is to expand the European plant and $x = 0$ if the decision is to build an American plant. If P is the profit, then

$$P = x[-F_1 + (R - V_1)q] + (1 - x)[-F_2 + (R - V_2)q],$$

where q is the number of cars to be sold. We assume that Safevox will make its decision on the basis of its projected value of q for the first 10-year period.

We observe again that $P = -F_1 + (R - V_1)q$ if $x = 1$ and $P = -F_2 + (R - V_2)q$ if $x = 0$. Thus

$$\mu_P = -\mu_{F_1} + (\mu_R - \mu_{V_1})q = -20,000,000 + (4000 - 3700)q$$
$$\sigma_P = \sqrt{\sigma_{F_1}^2 + (\sigma_R^2 + \sigma_{V_1}^2)q^2} = \sqrt{(2,000,000)^2 + ((100)^2 + (200)^2)q^2}$$

if $x = 1$ and

$$\mu_P = \mu_{F_2} + (\mu_R - \mu_{V_2})q = -100,000,000 + (4000 - 3600)q$$
$$\sigma_P = \sqrt{\sigma_{F_2}^2 + (\sigma_R^2 + \sigma_{V_2}^2)q^2} = \sqrt{(20,000,000)^2 + [(100)^2 + (300)^2]q^2}$$

if $x = 0$.

Assuming, for example, that 1,000,000 cars will be sold during the first 10 years, that is $q = 1,000,000$, then

$$\mu_P = -20,000,000 + (4000 - 3700)\, 1,000,000 = 280,000,000,$$
$$\sigma_P = \sqrt{(2,000,000)^2 + ((100)^2 + (200)^2)(1,000,000)^2} \cong 223,600,000$$

if $x = 1$ and

$$\mu_P = -100,000,000 + (4000 - 3600)1,000,000 = 300,000,000,$$
$$\sigma_P = \sqrt{(20,000,000)^2 + [(100)^2 + (300)^2](1,000,000)^2} \cong 316,300,000$$

if $x = 0$. Thus if Safevox expands its European plant, the expected profit is $280 million with a standard deviation of $223.6 million; and if Safevox builds an American plant, the expected profit is $300 million with a standard deviation of $316.3 million.

What should Safevox do in light of the preceding observations? Again that depends on the decision criteria.

Maximize Expected Profit. Suppose that Safevox wants to maximize the expected profit. Then it will decide to build a plant in the United States, since the expected profit associated with this decision is $20 million more than that of expanding the European plant.

Minimize Probability of Loss. Suppose, on the other hand, that Safevox wants to minimize the probability of loss. Then there are the following considerations. Since expanding the European plant will yield an expected profit of $280 million with a standard deviation of $223.6 million, zero profit is 1.25 standard deviation from the expected profit. And assuming that profit is normally distributed, the probability of incurring a loss is 0.1056. Building a plant in the United States, however, will yield an expected profit of $300 million with a standard deviation of $316.3 million. In this case zero profit is 0.95 standard deviation from the expected profit, so that the probability of incurring a loss is 0.1711.

Thus expanding the European plant will minimize the probability of loss.

EXERCISES

1. Cipolla Precision Instrument Company is considering the feasibility of developing a memory system utilizing the laser beam. The company is 95 percent sure that the research and development cost for project will be between $5 and $13 million. It also believes that once the memory system has been developed, it can manufacture each system for about $400,000, with a 95-percent certainty that the actual unit manufacturing cost will be between $200,000 and $600,000. Assume that the probability distributions of the research and development cost and the unit manufacturing cost are normal.

    a. What are the expected value and standard deviation of the research and development cost?
    b. What are the expected value and standard deviation of the unit manufacturing cost?

2. If the Cipolla Precision Instrument Company of Exercise 1 plans to market the memory system for $700,000 per unit and expects to sell 40 units of this system:

    a. What is the expected profit if the company proceeds with the development of the memory system?
    b. What is the probability that the company will lose money by undertaking the project?

3. Hays Aircraft Company is in the process of deciding whether to proceed with the research and development of a supersonic transport airplane, known as the SST. The company is 95 percent sure that the research and development cost will be between $1 billion and $3 billion. It is also 95 percent sure that once the new airplane has been developed, the unit cost of producing this airplane will be between $6 and $14 million. The planned selling price is $20 million per airplane.

Suppose that the probability distributions of research and development cost and unit production cost are normal.

    a. What are the expected value and standard deviation of the research and development cost?
    b. What are the expected value and standard deviation of the unit production cost?

4. Hays Aircraft (Exercise 3) expects to sell 300 of this airplane.

a. What is the expected profit of undertaking the development project?
b. What is the probability that the company will lose money by undertaking the project?

5. Nicholson Homes is a builder of tract houses and condominiums in northern California. It is in the process of starting the construction of a 200-unit condominium project. The decision confronting Nicholson Homes is whether to prefabricate some parts of each condominium unit. The company estimates that, without prefabrication, the average building cost per unit, including the land, will be $35,000, with a 95-percent certainty that the actual unit construction cost will lie between $31,000 and $39,000. If prefabrication is done, the average unit construction cost may drop to $30,000, with a 95-percent chance that it will be between $26,000 and $34,000.

In order to prefabricate some parts of each condominium unit, however, the company will have to build a new manufacturing facility, and there is a 95-percent chance that the cost of building the facility will be between $600,000 and $1,000,000.

The average selling price of a condominium unit will be $42,000. The company expects that 95 percent of the units will be sold at prices between $40,000 and $44,000.

Assume that all costs and unit prices are normally distributed.

a. What are the expected value and standard deviation of the cost of building the prefabrication facility?
b. What are the expected value and standard deviation of the unit construction cost without prefabrication?
c. What are the expected value and standard deviation of the unit construction cost with prefabrication?
d. What are the expected value and standard deviation of the unit selling price?

6. Given the answers to Exercise 5:

a. Suppose Nicholson Homes wants to maximize the expected profit. Which alternative should it choose?
b. Suppose the company wants to maximize the probability of earning at least $1,000,000 from the project. Which alternative should it choose?

7. A university library is considering whether to computerize its acquisition and cataloging process. If the process is computerized, machines will perform much of the information search activities which go into the ordering and cataloging of a book. A preliminary study has revealed the following:

The estimated cost of computerizing the process is $500,000. The actual cost, however, is likely to vary from the estimated cost, with a 95-percent chance of falling between $400,000 and $600,000.

At present the average cost of ordering and cataloging a book is $5, and 95 percent of the books cost between $3 and $7 to order and catalog. The computerized process is expected to bring down the average order and cataloging cost to $4 per book, with a 95 percent chance of the cost falling between $3 and $5.

Assume that the cost of computerizing the process and the costs of ordering and cataloging the books are normally distributed.

a. What are the expected value and standard deviation of the cost of computerizing the acquisition and cataloging process?

b. What are the expected value and standard deviation of the cost to order and catalogue a book at present?

c. What are the expected value and standard deviation of the unit cost of computerized ordering and cataloging?

8. Let us assume that the university library of Exercise 7 will make its decision on the basis of a 10-year projection of library operations. At present the library orders about 30,000 books a year. Thus it expects to order 300,000 books during the 10-year period.

a. Suppose the library wants to minimize the expected total acquisition and cataloging cost for the 10-year period. Which alternative should it choose?

b. Suppose the university has budgeted only $2,000,000 for library acquisition and cataloging during the 10-year period. The library wants to minimize the probability of the total cost exceeding $2,000,000 during the 10-year period. Which alternative should it choose?

CHAPTER

DETERMINISTIC INVENTORY MANAGEMENT

The items that are stored or reserved for meeting future demands are called *inventories*. Such items may be materials, machines, money, or even human beings. The need for inventories arises in almost every facet of business operations, so that business managers must make a variety of decisions regarding inventories. The problems of deciding on the optimal levels of inventories are called *inventory management problems*.

7.1 STRUCTURE OF INVENTORY PROBLEMS

Figure 7.1 depicts a hypothetical water supply system of a household. The system is obviously little used these days. But an examination of it can help us in understanding the nature of inventory management problems.

To devise an inventory control scheme, we have to know what the nature of the demand is. For example, what can we say about the water consumption of a household during any given period of time? It is highly unlikely that we will know in advance the exact quantity needed for the household. On the other hand, we are also unlikely to be completely ignorant of the quantity of consumption. On the basis of our past experience we should have some idea as to how much will be consumed and the likelihood of the actual consumption varying from the expected consumption by a specified amount. All this is merely to say that we know only the probability distribution of a family's demand for water.

There are three possibilities in respect to our knowledge of the demand: that the demand per unit of time is known in advance; even though the demand itself is not known, its probability distribution is known; it is completely unknown.

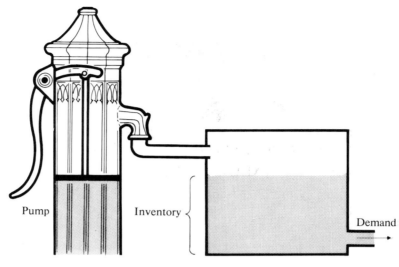

Figure 7.1

As in the case of household demand for water, it is quite unlikely that the manager of a business operation will know with certainty the exact quantitative need for an item in his operation. On the other hand, it is equally unlikely for him to be completely ignorant of the need. Thus the realistic assumption is that he knows the probability distribution of that need.

Next let us consider the problem of controlling the water supply for the household. Two questions arise:

   1. How often should water be pumped?
   2. How much water should be pumped every time?

The analogous questions for inventory management are:

   1. How often should an item be ordered (or produced)?
   2. How much should be ordered (or produced) every time?

We may say that an inventory problem has been solved when both of the above questions have been answered.

In the case of water supply we have assumed, in a sense, that the demand for water is not controllable by us but that we can control the pumping operation. There is, however, one aspect of the pumping operation that is not usually controllable. Those who are familiar with the kind of water pump shown in Figure 7.1 know that water does not flow at the instant we start pumping. In fact, the amount of priming required before water begins to flow out of the pump is usually a variable quantity.

Similarly in inventory management, it usually takes some time for an order to arrive. The time period between the placement of the order and the arrival of the order is called the *lead time*. In most situations the lead time is a variable quantity. Consequently, the most realistic assumption we can make regarding the lead time is that we know only its probability distribution. However, the mathematical models incorporating such assumptions are often quite difficult to solve analytically. Therefore, it is common practice in formulating inventory models to assume that the lead time is either zero or a known constant.

7.2 CONTROL SYSTEMS

Consider again the household water supply system. Two types of control system may be devised for it: the *time-clock system* and the *alarm-ring system*.

Time-Clock System

We may decide to pump water at regular, fixed intervals, say 24 hours. Thus we may decide to pump water into the tank at 6 o'clock every morning. This system is equivalent to having a time clock set for the pumping operations.

A similar system may be utilized in inventory management. For example, we may place a new order every 60 days. Such an ordering policy is frequently called a *fixed-period* policy.

Alarm-Ring System

In a water supply system we may also install an electronic device that will activate an alarm system whenever the water level in the tank falls to a specified level. Then whenever the alarm rings, we will start pumping water.

We can devise a similar system for inventory management, where the inventory level is continuously monitored and whenever it reaches a specified level, a new order is placed. Such a control system is known as a *continuous-review system, two-bin system, s and S system, or fixed-quantity system*.

7.3 INVENTORY COSTS

The difficulty of deciding on an optimal inventory level lies in the fact that there are disadvantages to having either a large inventory or a small inventory. A large inventory will cost more to maintain than a small one, but a small inventory is apt to result in shortages.

An experienced manager may be able to weigh the relative disadvantages somewhat intuitively and come up with reasonably good inventory-level decisions. However, as business operations become more complex so that it becomes more difficult for an individual to keep up with the operational details, intuitive approaches may not work too well. Furthermore, today more and more inventory control systems are being computerized, and the intuitions of a manager cannot very well be programmed for a computer. There is a need for a more exacting analysis.

The first step in such an analysis is to quantify the disadvantages associated with the different inventory levels, for example by weighing the disadvantages on a cost scale. The costs associated with inventory levels may be classified into two categories: (1) those attributable to having an inventory, called *inventory holding cost*, and (2) those attributable to not having an inventory, called *inventory stock-out cost*.

There are several components in the inventory holding cost: (1) capital cost, (2) storage cost, (3) insurance cost, and (4) deterioration cost, etc. In general, the inventory holding cost tends to vary with the inventory level.

Capital cost is the amount of money tied up in the inventory. It is usually the most important component of the inventory holding cost, varying more or less proportionally with the value of the inventory holding. If the cost of money is constant, then the capital cost will vary in direct proportion to the value of the inventory holding.

Storage cost is the cost of storing the inventory holding. It may be negligible when, for example, the inventory is stored in a warehouse with an empty space. In that case the cost is not likely to vary with the inventory level. On the other hand, it may be quite substantial, for example, if the inventory is placed on display counters, where counter spaces are assumed to have opportunity costs. Then the cost is likely to vary proportionately with the inventory level.

Insurance cost is the premium and other costs of insuring the inventory holding against fire and other causes of damage. Unless the business operations in question are very hazardous, this is not likely to be a sizable component of the inventory holding cost. Nevertheless, it will vary with the inventory level.

Deterioration cost is the cost of having to discard some of the inventory holdings because of deterioration. This cost is likely to be incurred if, for example, the inventory holdings consist of perishable goods.

The *inventory stock-out cost* is harder to identify. It depends on the type of demand to be satisfied by the inventory holding. If what is in the inventory is intended for sale, then the stock out cost may consist in: (1) the amount of lost profit due to lost sales and (2) the actual cost of having to back order. Moreover, whether the sales are lost for good or satisfied by back order, there may be some loss of goodwill, which has a dollar value hard to calculate. On the other hand, if the inventory is intended to satisfy material requirements for a production process, then the stock-out cost may consist of the cost of having to stop the production process.

If there are no other costs associated with inventory control besides these, then we may be able to minimize the costs by simply replenishing the inventory holdings frequently and in small quantities. Unfortunately things are not quite so simple. For example, there is also what is called *replenishment cost*, which tends to increase with the frequency of replenishment, and it may be either (1) an order cost or, (2) a set-up cost.

The *order cost* is the cost of placing an order when the inventory has to be replenished externally. It may include: (1) the cost of the manager's time needed to initiate an order, (2) the clerical costs of processing the purchase order forms, (3) the fixed component, if any, of the shipping cost, (4) the costs of receiving and placing the order into inventory, (5) the clerical costs of processing the bill and making the payment, and (6) the cost of any computer processing required to expedite the order and update inventory records, etc.

On the other hand, if an order is replenished internally, a new production run must be set up and this has its cost, called the *set-up cost*. It may include: (1) the cost of the manager's time needed to initiate and schedule a new production run, (2) the cost of adjusting machine tools or assembly lines for the new production run, and (3) the clerical and computer processing costs connected with the new production run.

7.4   DETERMINISTIC INVENTORY PROBLEMS

Suppose that the demand for an item during a specified period is known in advance and the lead time is either zero or a known constant. Then we have what is called a *deterministic inventory management problem*.

It is true that these assumed conditions do not quite obtain in most actual inventory management situations. Nevertheless, there is a class of inventory management problems for which these assumptions are quite adequate, for example when the item in question is used as raw material for a stable production process. Furthermore, it has been found in practice that deterministic inventory models are quite helpful in controlling the stocks of many regularly used low-value items.

We shall devote the remainder of this chapter to deterministic inventory problems.

7.5   ECONOMIC ORDER QUANTITY

We pointed out earlier that solving an inventory management problem consists in answering the questions (1) how often to order and (2) how much to order every time. In deterministic inventory management problems, however, the answers to these two questions are not independent of each other. If we know, for example, how much to order every time, then we must also know how often we have to order, since the total quantity needed for a specified period is assumed to be a known constant. Thus an inventory management problem may be considered solved when an optimal order quantity has been determined. Such an optimal order quantity is sometimes called an *economic order quantity*. We shall now describe a procedure that can be used to determine the economic order quantity. The procedure is sometimes known as the *EOQ* formula.

Example 1. Watchmaker's Problem   Let us consider an inventory management problem of Lorex Watches, a producer of very fine watches. The company uses platinum in making an alloy for its lines of very expensive watches. According to its production plan, the company will need 1000 lb of platinum for the next year. Since the watches are made by a small group of highly skilled craftsmen, the rate of production remains stable from day to day, so that the rate of platinum use is also fairly constant.

The company has signed a contract with a platinum producer, whereby the latter will supply 1000 lb of platinum during the next year for $3000/lb. The contract stipulates that Lorex has the option to choose the order size, but the supplier will charge $2000 for the processing of every order, which amount is designed to cover the costs of packaging, insurance, and other security meas- ures against theft during transit. Since the platinum is shipped by air, the lead time is negligible.

Lorex Watches considers the cost of money to be 12% per year, so that the capital cost of one pound of platinum held in inventory is $360 per year. Holding a pound of platinum will cost an additional $40 in insurance, storage, handling, and so on.

What is the order size that will minimize the total cost to the company of satisfying the platinum requirements for the next year? The company does not want to run out of platinum at any time.

We observe that for Lorex Watches (1) the total platinum requirement for the next year is known, (2) the daily rate of platinum use is fairly constant, and (3) the lead time is negligible. Under these conditions the order size that will minimize the total cost of inventory control may be ascertained rather simply.

Model of Decision Situation

As a first step toward solving the problem, we let

$$
\begin{aligned}
d &= \text{demand (total platinum need per year)}, \\
q &= \text{order quantity (size of each order)}, \\
n &= \text{order number (number of orders per year)}.
\end{aligned}
$$

It is apparent that d, q, and n are related. Given that the demand is 1000 lb per year, if the order size is 100 lb, for example, then the company will have to place the order ten times during the year. Thus

$$
n = \frac{d}{q} = \frac{1000}{q}.
$$

There are three types of cost which must be incorporated into any analysis of the Lorex Watches problem. First, there is the $2000 handling cost charged by the supplier for each order. We will call this the *unit order cost*. Second, there is the cost of platinum, which is $3000/lb. We will call this the *unit variable cost*. Finally, there is the holding cost: $400/lb of platinum held in the inventory per year, $360/lb capital cost, and $40 for other holding costs. We will call this the *unit holding cost*. We let

$$
\begin{aligned}
f &= \text{unit order cost}, \\
v &= \text{unit variable cost}, \\
h &= \text{unit holding cost}.
\end{aligned}
$$

If T is the total cost of satisfying the demand for the year, then it is the sum of the total order cost, the total variable cost, and the total holding cost. Each of these three cost components may be determined as follows.

Total Order Cost   The total order cost is the unit order cost times the order number:

$$
nf.
$$

But $n = d/q$. Therefore, the total order cost may also be expressed as

$$(d/q)f$$

If the order size is 100 lb, for example, then the total order cost is:

$$\left(\frac{d}{q}\right)f = \left(\frac{1000}{100}\right)2000 = 20,000.$$

The Total Variable Cost The total variable cost is equal to the unit variable cost times the demand:

$$vd, \quad \text{tot. var. cost.}$$

and

$$vd = (3000)(1000) = 3,000,000.$$

Total Holding Cost The total holding cost is equal to the unit holding cost times the average level of inventory holding for the year. We already defined the unit holding cost. So let us now describe how we may ascertain the average level of inventory holding for the year.

We recall our assumption that the rate of inventory depletion is constant during the year, which is to say the inventory level will fluctuate as shown in Figure 7.2. The diagram indicates that as soon as the inventory level reaches zero, a new order arrives, at which point the inventory level is equal to the size of the order. Then the inventory level steadily declines until it reaches zero, when another order arrives, again raising the inventory level. This pattern will repeat itself over and over again during the year.

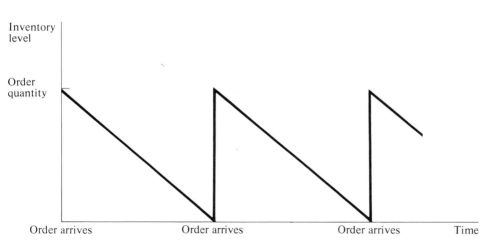

Figure 7.2

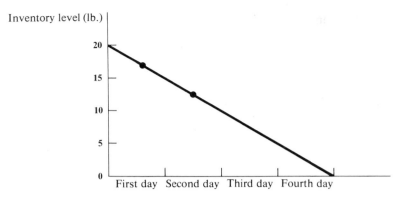

Figure 7.3

Suppose that we define an *inventory cycle* as the time span between a fresh replenishment of inventory and the complete depletion of this inventory. Then since the pattern of inventory level variation is identical for all inventory cycles, the average inventory level must be the same for all cycles. Hence the average inventory level for the entire year is also the same as the average inventory level for one inventory cycle, so that all we need to do to determine the average inventory level for the year is to find the average inventory level for just one inventory cycle.

Suppose that the order size of platinum is 20 lb. Then Lorex Watches will have to place the same order 50 times during the year. If we further assume that the company works 200 days during the year, then each inventory cycle consists of four days. The variation in inventory level during one such cycle is illustrated in Figure 7.3.

Note that the inventory level during the first day changes from 20 lb to 15 lb so that the average level on the first day is 17.5 lb. Similarly, the average inventory levels on the remaining three days are 12.5 lb, 7.5 lb, and 2.5 lb, respectively. The average inventory level during the entire cycle is

$$\frac{17.5 \text{ lb} + 12.5 \text{ lb} + 7.5 \text{ lb} + 2.5 \text{ lb}}{4} = \frac{40 \text{ lb}}{4} = 10 \text{ lb}$$

Note, however, that 10 lb is one-half of the order quantity. Thus if we denote the average inventory level by i, then

$$i = 0.5q.$$

Returning to the problem of ascertaining the total inventory holding cost, we note that by definition the total holding cost is hi. But since $i = 0.5q$, the total inventory holding cost is

$$0.5hq.$$

The Total Cost   The total cost T of satisfying the demand for the year is the sum of the total order cost, the total variable cost, and the total holding cost:

\# ndus $n = \dfrac{d}{q}$

$$T = pf + vd + hi$$
$f\frac{d}{q}$ $\frac{1}{2}hq$ $i = \frac{1}{2}q$

order quantity
size of each order

Since $n = d/q$ and $i = 0.5q$,

$$T = (d/q)f + vd + 0.5hq.$$

If we wish, we can now portray the problem of inventory management by the diagram in Figure 7.4. Given this model, the problem is to find the value of q that will minimize the value of T. This value of q is called the *economic order quantity*.

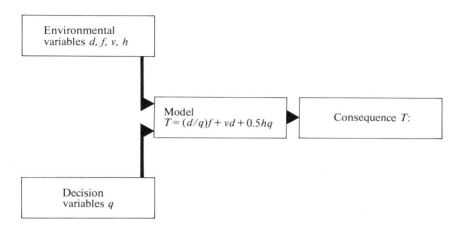

Figure 7.4

Graphic Approximation

We observe in Figure 7.4 that the total variable cost vd is not affected by the order quantity q. Therefore, if we define t as the *adjusted total cost*, where

$$t = (d/q)f + 0.5hq,$$

then the value of q which minimizes t will also minimize T. Note that t is the sum of the total order cost and the total holding cost.

We shall now illustrate how we may graphically determine the value of q that will minimize the value of t. We recall that for Lorex Watches, $d = 1000$, $f = 2000$, and $h = 400$. The values of t for some value of q can be obtained as shown in Table 7.1 and graphed in Figure 7.5.

In a graph such as shown in Figure 7.5 the lowest value of the adjusted total cost will always be at the point on the order quantity axis where the total order cost and the total holding cost cross each other. We note that in Figure 7.5 the two costs cross each other at the point where $q = 100$. Thus the adjusted total cost is minimized at $q = 100$, which is the economic order quantity, in pounds of platinum, for Lorex Watches.

Table 7.1

q	d/q	(d/q)f	0.5hq	t
20	50	100,000	4,000	104,000
40	25	50,000	8,000	58,000
60	16.67	33,340	12,000	45,340
80	12.50	25,000	16,000	41,000
100	10.00	20,000	20,000	40,000
120	8.33	16,660	24,000	40,660
140	7.14	14,280	28,000	42,280

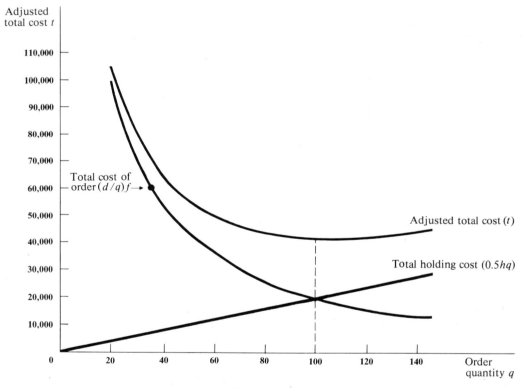

Figure 7.5

EOQ Formula

There is a simpler way of calculating the economic order quantity than using graphic approximations. Consider again the adjusted total cost

$$t = (d/q)f + 0.5hq.$$

Let q^* denote the value of q that will minimize the value of t. Then by using calculus, we can show that

$$q^* = \sqrt{2fd/h}.$$

This equation is called the EOQ formula.

Returning to the problem of Lorex Watches, since $f = 2000$, $d = 1000$, and $h = 400$, we have

$$q^* = \sqrt{\frac{2 \times 2000 \times 1000}{400}} = 100,$$

which indicates that the economic order quantity is 100 lb of platinum—the same answer as was obtained by graphic approximation.

7.6 SENSITIVITY OF EOQ

One of the frequently used arguments for not making use of the EOQ formula is that it is too difficult to determine the exact values of the costs required by the formula. However, one nice feature of the EOQ formula is that, even if the cost figures used are slightly off, we will nevertheless obtain a reasonably good approximation of what the economic order quantity should be. This is due to the fact that the economic order quantity is not too sensitive to any small variations in the cost figures.

In the case of Lorex Watches a unit order cost of $2000 and a unit holding cost of $400 yield an economic order quantity of 100 lb. Let us now examine how this figure will change with changing cost figures.

Varying the Unit Order Cost

The following table provides the economic order quantity for different assumed values of the unit order cost. The unit holding cost is still assumed to be $400 per pound per year.

Unit order cost	Economic order quantity
1000	70.7
1500	86.6
2000	100.0
2500	111.8
3000	122.5

Now suppose that the actual unit order cost is $3000 instead of $2000. Then, according to this table, the economic order quantity is 122.5 lb rather than 100 lb. A difference of $1000 in the unit order cost effects only a 22.5-lb change in the economic order quantity. We observe that a 50-percent change in the unit order cost brought only a 22.5-percent change in the economic order quantity.

Varying the Unit Holding Cost

Now assuming the unit order cost to be $2000, we find that the following table gives the economic order quantity for different values of the unit holding cost.

Unit holding cost	Economic order quantity
300	115.5
350	106.9
400	100.0
450	94.3
500	89.4

If now the unit holding cost is $500 instead of $400, then the economic order quantity becomes 89.4 lb rather than 100 lb. Again a difference of $100 in the unit holding cost effects only a 10.6-lb change in the economic order quantity. We observe that a 25-percent change in the unit holding cost brought only a 10.6-percent change in the economic order quantity.

7.7   QUANTITY DISCOUNTS

Frequently some sort of quantity discounts are offered by suppliers to induce buyers to place larger orders. Then any straightforward application of the EOQ formula may lead to erroneous decisions.

Returning to the problem of Lorex Watches, suppose that the supplier of platinum offers the following quantity discount option: the price of platinum will be reduced from $3000/lb to $2900/lb for orders of 500 lb or more.

Without the discount, the optimal order size is 100 lb, entailing a total cost per year of $3,040,000:

Total variable cost	$3000 × 1000	= $3,000,000
Total order cost	$2000 × 10	= 20,000
Total holding cost	$400 × 0.5 × 100 =	20,000
Total cost		$3,040,000

On the other hand, with the discount, if each order is for 500 lb, then the cost of platinum will be $2900/lb, or $2,900,000 for 1000 lb. In the event, the company will make exactly two orders per year, with a total order cost of $4000: two times $2000.

The calculation of the total holding cost is somewhat more involved. Since the unit price of platinum is $2900, the capital cost per pound of platinum is $2900 times 12 percent, or $348. Suppose that the insurance and storage costs remain at $40. Then the unit holding cost becomes $388 instead of $400, and the total holding cost becomes $97,000, or $388 times one-half of the order size. Then the total cost is $3,001,000:

Total variable cost	$2900 × 1000	= $2,900,000
Total order cost	$2000 × 2	= $4,000
Total holding cost	$388 × 0.5 × 500 =	$97,000
Total cost		$3,001,000

Thus, with the discount, Lorex Watches can save $39,000 in total cost by ordering 500 lb of platinum each time.

One may wonder at this point whether, since the company can save $39,000 by increasing the order size from 100 lb per order to 500 lb per order, it can save even more by further increasing the order size, for example to 1000 lb.

Our intuition suggests that, even with the quantity discount, there must be some cost advantage to staying as close to the economic order quantity of 100 lb as possible if the other considerations remain the same. We can verify this intuition by an actual calculation of the total cost associated with ordering 1000 lb at once:

Total variable cost	$2900 × 1000	= $2,900,000
Total order cost	$2000 × 1	= 2,000
Total holding cost	$388 × 0.5 × 1000	= 194,000
Total cost		$3,096,000

Ordering 1000 lb at once will mean a total cost even higher than that of not taking advantage of the quantity discount but staying with the economic order quantity.

7.8 EOQ ALLOWING SHORTAGES

In the preceding sections we assumed that a shortage in the inventory holding is not to be allowed. In practice, however, when the demand is known by its probability distribution only, we will invariably have to allow for the possibility of incurring a shortage. Still, it may appear that if the demand is known with certainty, there is really no reason to deliberately allow a shortage to occur. But this is not true, as we shall illustrate in this section.

Example 2. Let us now incorporate the following assumption into the problem of Lorex Watches: whenever the company runs out of platinum, it can borrow the metal from other local watch producers at $5/lb per day. Thus, since it is assumed that there are 200 working days in a year, the company can borrow one pound of platinum for an entire year for $1000.

Given this potential for borrowing, we have a new inventory model, as shown in Figure 7.6. We let

p = stock-out cost per unit of shortage per year,

s = total shortage for an inventory cycle,

r = order quantity minus total shortage for an inventory cycle.

Figure 7.6 shows that as soon as the order q arrives, the quantity s will be used immediately to pay back the borrowing. Then we may consider $r = q - s$ to be the beginning inventory and $-s$ to be the end inventory of an inventory cycle.

Now there are three decision variables in our inventory management problem. They are the order quantity q, the beginning inventory level r, and the

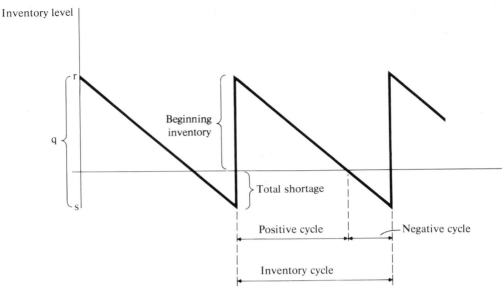

Figure 7.6

maximum allowable shortage s. The problem is then to find the values of q, r, and s that will minimize the total cost of satisfying the demand during the year; in other words, to find the total cost as a function of q, r, and s.

Let us now consider the various cost components.

The Total Order Cost

We recall that the number of orders per year is d/q so that the total order cost for the year is

$$(d/q)f.$$

This is not changed by the new assumption.

The Total Holding Cost

The total holding cost is the average inventory level for the year times the unit holding cost. The average inventory level during a positive inventory cycle is $0.5r$. During an entire inventory cycle it is equivalent to

$$\left(\begin{array}{c}\text{average level during}\\ \text{positive cycle}\end{array}\right)\left(\frac{\text{duration of positive cycle}}{\text{duration of entire cycle}}\right).$$

But if the rate of platinum use is constant, then

$$\left(\frac{\text{duration of positive cycle}}{\text{duration of entire cycle}}\right) = \frac{r}{q}.$$

Thus the average level of inventory during the entire cycle may be given by

$$(0.5r)(r/q) = 0.5r^2/q,$$

which is also the average inventory level for the entire year. Multiplying the above expression by the unit holding cost, we have

$$h(0.5r)(r/q) = 0.5hr^2/q, \qquad hc$$

which is the total holding cost for the year.

The Total Stock-Out Cost

The total stock-out cost is the average level of shortage for the year times the unit stock-out cost. The average shortage during a negative cycle is $0.5s$. For the entire cycle it is

$$(0.5s)\left(\frac{\text{duration of negative cycle}}{\text{duration of entire cycle}}\right),$$

which can be expressed as

$$(0.5s)(s/q) = 0.5s^2/q.$$

This is also the average level of shortage for the year. Multiplying the above expression by the unit stock-out cost p, we have

$$p(0.5s)(s/q) = 0.5ps^2/q, \qquad s\cdot o\ c$$

which is the total stock-out cost for the year.

The Adjusted Total Cost

We let t be the adjusted total cost, which is the sum of the total order cost, the total holding cost, and the total stock-out cost. Then

$$t = \left(\frac{d}{q}\right)f + \frac{0.5hr^2}{q} + \frac{0.5ps^2}{q}.$$

But by definition $s = q - r$. Substituting this expression into the above equation and collecting the terms, we obtain

$$t = \left(\frac{d}{q}\right)f + \frac{0.5(h + p)r^2}{q} - pr + 0.5pq.$$

We now have an expression for the adjusted total cost as a function of the two decision variables q and r. We must now find the values of q and r that will minimize the value of t.

Optimal-Values Formula

Let q^* and r^* be the values of q and r, respectively, that will minimize the value of t. By using calculus we can show that

$$q^* = \sqrt{2fd/h}\sqrt{(h + p)/p}, \qquad r^* = \sqrt{2fd/h}\sqrt{p/(h + p)}.$$

We note that the first term in each of these two equations is the EOQ formula already described.

Now we can solve the inventory management problem of Lorex Watches as given in Example 2. We recall that the platinum borrowing cost is $1000/lb per year: $1000 is the stock-out cost per unit of shortage per year, or $p = 1000$. Substituting this value into our equations, we have

$$q^* = \sqrt{\frac{2fd}{h}} \sqrt{\frac{h + p}{p}} = \sqrt{\frac{2 \times 2000 \times 1000}{400}} \sqrt{\frac{400 + 1000}{1000}} = 118.3,$$

$$r^* = \sqrt{\frac{2fd}{h}} \sqrt{\frac{p}{h + p}} = \sqrt{\frac{2 \times 2000 \times 1000}{400}} \sqrt{\frac{1000}{400 + 1000}} = 84.5,$$

and

$$s^* = q^* - r^* = 118.3 - 84.5 = 33.8,$$

where s^* is the optimal value of s.

Lorex Watches should order 118.3 lb of platinum each time and borrow as much as 33.8 lb during each inventory cycle. The total cost of this kind of operation can be ascertained as follows: Since the order size is 118.3 lb, the company will be ordering 8.45 times during the year: $1000/118.3 = 8.45$. The total order cost, therefore, is $16,900: $2000 \times 8.45 = 16,900$. The average inventory holding is 30.18: $(0.5)(84.5)(84.5/118.3) = 30.18$. The total holding cost is then $12,072: $400 \times 30.18 = 12,072$. The average level of shortage is 4.83: $(0.5)(33.8)(33.8/118.3) = 4.83$. The total stock-out cost is therefore $4830: $1000 \times 4.83 = 4830$. In summary we have:

Total order cost	$2000 \times 8.45 =$	$16,900
Total holding cost	$400 \times 30.18 =$	12,072
Total stock-out cost	$1000 \times 4.83 =$	4,830
Adjusted total cost		$33,802

The reader may recall that the adjusted total cost for Lorex Watches is $40,000 if we do not allow borrowing. By allowing borrowing, however, at the given borrowing price, we can bring down the adjusted total cost by $6198 to $33,802. This reduction is of course partially due to the reduction in the total order cost by $3100 from $20,000 to $16,900. The remaining $3098 difference is attributable to the fact that the sum of the total holding and stock-out costs is only $16,902 when we allow borrowing, whereas it is $20,000 when borrowing is not allowed.

At this point, the reader may ask, "How can Lorex Watches bring down the sum of the total holding and stock-out costs by borrowing platinum for $1000/lb per year, when it will cost only $400/lb per year to hold platinum in inventory?" Suppose, however, Lorex Watches does not borrow any platinum. Then the average inventory level will be 59.15 lb, one-half of the order quantity. On the other hand, the sum of the average inventory and average borrowing is only 35.01 lb. This is where the secret to the savings lies.

A Sensitivity Analysis

Table 7.2 lists the values of q^*, r^*, and s^* for some assumed values of p for Lorex Watches.

Table 7.2

p	q^*	r^*	s^*	r^*/q^*
1	2003	5	1998	0.003
10	640	15	625	0.024
100	224	45	199	0.200
1,000	118	84	34	0.714
10,000	102	98	4	0.962

We recall that when shortage is not allowed the optimal order size is 100 lb. Table 7.2 shows that when the shortage is allowed, the optimal order quantity approaches 100 lb as the unit stock-out cost p becomes larger and larger. This character of the optimal quantity is not surprising, since not allowing any shortage is to implicitly assume that the unit stock-out cost p is infinitely large, and for this value of p the table will show the optimal order quantity to be 100 lb.

The last column of Table 7.2 gives the ratio r^*/q^*, the proportion of time that Lorex Watches will have positive inventory of platinum. We note that this ratio approaches zero as the unit stock-out cost p becomes smaller and smaller. It will in fact become zero when the value of p is zero. This, too, is not surprising, since if the borrowing cost is zero, then there is really no reason for Lorex Watches to hold an inventory at any time.

EXERCISES

1. Kopper Ware Company will need 1,000,000 lb of copper during the next year to produce its cooking utensils. The production rates of the different utensils are expected to be fairly stable during the year. Thus the rate of copper use will also be constant during the year.

The company signed a contract with a supplier whereby the latter will provide for all the company's copper requirements for 70¢/lb during the next year. The cost of money is considered to be 10% for the company. The cost of holding a pound of copper in inventory for a year is estimated to be the capital cost plus 3¢ for storage and insurance. The clerical and other costs associated with placing an order are estimated at $80.

    a. Use a graph to determine the economic order quantity.
    b. Determine the economic order quantity by means of the EOQ formula.
    c. If the company orders the quantity suggested in (a) and (b), how many times will it order during the year?
    d. What will be the sum of the total order and inventory holding costs if the company follows the ordering policy suggested by the EOQ formula?

2. The supplier will give Kopper Ware of Exercise 1 a penny discount per pound if the size of order exceeds 100,000 lb. For Kopper Ware the order cost will remain at $80 per order, and the inventory holding cost will still be the capital cost plus 3¢/lb of copper per year.

    a. Would it be advantageous to Kopper Ware to accept the discount option and order at least 100,000 lb each time? Why?

b. Suppose the supplier offers a penny discount per pound if the order size exceeds 500,000 lb. Would it be advantageous to Kopper Ware to accept this discount option? Why?

3. Staying with the Kopper Ware problem of Exercises 1 and 2:

a. Suppose the inventory holding cost per pound of copper per year is equal to the capital cost plus 5¢ for storage and insurance. What is the economic order quantity? Compare this quantity with that obtained for Exercise 1(a).

b. Suppose the cost of placing an order is $100. What is the economic order quantity? Compare this quantity with that obtained for Exercise 1(a).

4. K-n-K Candy Company will need 10,000,000 lb of industrial sugar during the next year. The rate of sugar use is expected to be constant during the year.

Industrial sugar is sold in 100-lb bags. A sugar producer has agreed to provide K-n-K Candy with 100,000 bags of sugar during the next year for $20 per bag, which includes the transportation costs.

The cost of money is considered to be 10%. Storage, insurance, and other costs of holding one 100-lb bag in inventory are estimated to be $1 per year. The company estimates that clerical and other costs associated with placing an order will total $240.

a. Determine the economic order quantity.

b. If the company orders the quantity suggested by your last answer, how many times will it have to order during the year?

c. What, then, will be the sum of the total order and inventory holding costs?

5. The supplier will give K-n-K Candy of Exercise 4 a discount of 50¢ per bag of sugar whenever an order exceeds 10,000 bags. For K-n-K Candy the order cost will remain at $240, and the inventory holding cost will still be capital cost plus $1 per bag per year.

a. Would it be advantageous to K-n-K Candy to accept the discount option and order at least 10,000 bags each time? Why?

b. Suppose the supplier offers 50¢ per bag discount only if an order exceeds 50,000 bags. Would it be advantageous to K-n-K Candy to accept this discount option? Why?

6. Again consider the situation of K-n-K Candy of Exercise 4.

a. Suppose the inventory holding cost is equal to the capital cost plus $2 per bag for storage and insurance. What is the economic order quantity? Compare this figure with the answer obtained for Exercise 4(a).

b. Suppose that the cost of placing an order is $375. What is the economic order quantity? Compare your answer with that obtained for Exercise 4(a).

7. Albertson Equipment is a manufacturer of sophisticated industrial equipment. It buys certain parts of the equipment from an outside supplier. The company needs 40 units of one of these parts every day during the coming year. There are 250 work days in a year.

The cost of the part in question is $300 per unit. Albertson Equipment considers the cost of money to be 10%. The storage, insurance, and other costs of holding one unit of this part is estimated to be $10 per year. The cost of placing an order is estimated to be $500.

a. Determine the optimal order quantity.

b. How many times will the company have to order during the year if it stays with this optimal quantity?

c. What, then, will be the sum of the total ordering and holding cost for the year?

8. The parts manufacturer offers Albertson Equipment of Exercise 7 the following discount options: (A) a price discount of 1% when the order exceeds 1000 units; (B) a price discount of 2% whenever the order exceeds 5000 units.

Assuming that the other costs remain the same as in Exercise 7, should Albertson Equipment take advantage of either of the discount options? Why?

9. Fast Mail Order Company expects to sell 10,000 units of a certain item during the next year. The sales of this item are expected to be quite stable during the coming year.

The unit cost of the item is $8. The cost of money is considered to be 10% for the company. The storage, insurance, and other holding costs will total 20¢ per unit per year. The order cost is estimated to be $200 per order.

The company is known to fill its customer orders very promptly. Its present policy is to fill incoming orders on the same day they are received. This means that the item in question must not be allowed to run out during the year.

a. Determine the optimal order quantity.

b. How many times will the company have to order during the year if each order is for the optimal quantity?

c. What, then, will be the sum of the total ordering and holding costs for the year?

10. Again take Fast Mail Order Company. Suppose the company is willing to allow the stock to run out. Customer orders will be filled within a day so long as there is an inventory of this item on hand. Otherwise, they will be filled immediately after the inventory has been replenished.

The delay in filling orders, of course, will entail some loss of customer goodwill. The company figures that a delay of one day in filling a customer's order will mean a penny loss in customer goodwill. The company works 250 days a year. Thus a delay of one year in filling a customer's order is equivalent to $2.50 loss in customer goodwill.

a. Determine the optimal order quantity for Fast Mail Order Company.

b. What is the maximum level of shortage that the company should allow during an inventory cycle?

c. Determine the total ordering cost, total inventory holding cost, total stock-out cost due to loss of customer goodwill for the inventory management policy proposed in parts (a) and (b).

11. Quality Construction Company has signed a contract to build a small office building. The contract stipulates that the owner will pay the entire contract price to Quality Construction upon completion of the building.

The company plans to complete the building within the next 12 months. In the meantime it will require for operating expenses $100,000 every month. A local bank has made the following commitment to the company: the bank will (1) transfer periodically an agreed sum to the checking account of Quality Construction, (2) charge $3000 as a loan fee for each such transfer, and (3) charge an annual interest rate of 8% on the funds transferred to the account of Quality Construction. The interest charge is calculated as follows if, for example, the bank transfers $600,000 at a time:

First transfer: 8% on $600,000 for the year	$48,000
Second transfer: 8% on $600,000 for the last six months	24,000
Total interest charge	$72,000

a. Where Quality Construction is concerned, what is the optimal sum of every transfer?

b. If this sum is selected, how many times will the bank transfer funds to the account of Quality Construction during the next 12 months?

c. What, then, will be the total loan fees paid by Quality Construction?

d. What, then, will be the total interest paid by Quality Construction for the next 12 months? Of this amount, how much is just for holding funds idle in its bank account?

12. Again consider Quality Construction Company. Suppose the bank offers the following option: Quality Construction may overdraw on its bank account, but the bank will charge an annual interest of 12% for the amounts overdrawn during the year.

a. Given this option, what is the optimal sum of each transfer?

b. Should Quality Construction overdraw on its bank account? If so, what is the maximum amount it should overdraw?

c. Assuming that the company will adhere to the policy suggested by your answers to parts (a) and (b), what, for the next 12 months, will be (1) the total loan fees paid, (2) the total amount of interest paid on funds transferred into Quality Construction's checking account, (3) the total amount of interest paid on funds held idle in the checking account, and (4) the total amount of interest paid for overdrawing?

CHAPTER

8

PROBABILISTIC INVENTORY MANAGEMENT

In our discussion of the optimal order quantities in the preceding chapter, we assumed that the demand is a known constant and the lead time is zero. In many situations, however, these conditions do not hold. Often the demand and lead time are variable quantities, so that we know at best only their probability distributions.

If we assume that both the demand and lead time are random variables, the analysis of inventory management problems will become very complex. It has been found, however, that reasonably good solutions can be obtained for many practical inventory management problems by assuming that the lead time is a known constant. Therefore, in this chapter we shall assume that the demand is a random variable but the lead time is constant. In a later chapter we will nevertheless show how inventory management problems where both the demand and lead time are assumed to be random variables, can be solved.

8.1 AGGREGATING DEMAND DISTRIBUTIONS

When the demand is assumed to be a random variable, one of the first steps in inventory management analysis is to ascertain the probability distribution of the demand, which we will call the *demand distribution,* for the period under consideration. Frequently this will require an aggregation of the demand distributions for shorter periods. For example, we may obtain the demand distribution for a month by aggregating the daily demand distributions and similarly obtain the demand distribution for a year by aggregating the monthly demand distributions.

The following statistical proposition is very important in such an aggregation process.

Proposition Let $x_1, \ldots, x_n$ be statistically independent and identically distributed random variables with mean and standard deviation μ_x and σ_x, respectively. Let $y = x_1 + \cdots + x_n$. Then the mean and standard deviation of y are given by

$$\mu_y = \mu_x n, \qquad \sigma_y = \sigma_y \sqrt{n}.$$

Furthermore, according to a well-known statistical theorem called the *central-limit theorem*, the probability distribution of y may be approximated by a normal probability distribution if y is a sum of a large number of such random variables $x_1, \ldots, x_n$.

The following problem will illustrate the significance of this statistical proposition.

Example 1. Forecasting Demand The quantity of all orders received by Valley Wholesale Liquor from retail liquor stores for a certain brand of Scotch whiskey varies from one week to another. However, the mean of the weekly quantities of order is 40 cases, with a standard deviation of 10 cases. Valley Wholesale Liquor wants to forecast the demand for this particular brand of whiskey for the next 25 weeks.

We assume that the demand in one week is not influenced by that of any preceding week. This is also the assumption that the weekly demands are statistically independent. Next, we assume that the demand distribution for one week is not likely to be materially different from that of any other week. (This assumption may not be true; for example, Christmas sales tend to be heavy.) In any case, it implies that the weekly demands have an identical distribution.

Let $x_1, \ldots, x_{25}$ be the random variable weekly demands. Then by assumption $\mu_x = 40$ and $\sigma_x = 10$. Furthermore, these random variables are statistically independent and identically distributed. Now we let $y = x_1 + \cdots + x_{25}$. Then y is the random variable total demand for the next 25 weeks. By the preceding proposition, therefore,

$$\mu_y = \mu_x n = (40)(25) = 1000,$$

$$\sigma_y = \sigma_x \sqrt{n} = (10)\sqrt{25} = 50.$$

Thus the mean and standard deviation of the demand for the next 25 weeks are 1000 cases and 50 cases, respectively. Furthermore, by the central-limit theorem, the probability distribution of y may be approximated by a normal

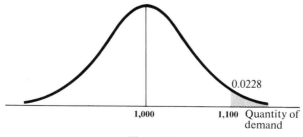

Figure 8.1

probability distribution. The demand distribution for the next 25 weeks is now the normal probability distribution as shown in Figure 8.1. The diagram shows that the probability of the demand during the next 25 weeks exceeding 1100 cases, for example, is 0.0228.

Suppose Valley Wholesale Liquor actually has in stock 1100 cases of this whiskey. Then the probability that its inventory holding will satisfy the demand during the next 25 weeks is 0.9772, that is 1.0000 minus 0.0228. Alternatively, the probability of running out of stock during the period is 0.0228 even if the store does not receive any more of this whiskey in the duration.

8.2 DETERMINING ORDER SIZE OR ORDER FREQUENCY

In Chapter 7 we showed that, if the demand d, the unit order cost f, and the unit holding cost h are given, then the optimal order size q^* is

$$q^* = \sqrt{2fd/h}.$$

Since by definition $n = d/q$, where n is the order frequency, the optimal order frequency n^* is

$$n^* = \frac{d}{\sqrt{2fd/h}} = \sqrt{dh/2f}.$$

Thus when the demand d is assumed to be a known constant, we can utilize one of these two formulas to determine either the optimal order size or the optimal order frequency.

However, a straightforward application of these formulas is not possible when the demand is assumed to be a random variable. Nevertheless, it has been found that we can still obtain a reasonably good approximation of either the optimal order size or frequency if the mean demand quantity, μ_d, is substituted for the demand. Thus

$$q^* = \sqrt{2f\mu_d/h}, \qquad n^* = \sqrt{\mu_d h/2f}$$

are good approximations of the optimal order quantity and the optimal order frequency when d is a random variable.

Example 2. Mail Order Problem   On the average Fast Mail Order Company receives orders for 40 units of a certain item a day, with a standard deviation of 10 units. The cost to the company of placing an inventory order is $300, and the unit inventory holding cost is 80¢ per year. There will be 300 working days in the coming year.

Since there will be 300 working days in the year, the expected demand for the item during the year is 12,000 units. We let $\mu_d = 12,000$ for the year. Hence

$$q^* = \sqrt{\frac{2f\mu_d}{h}} = \sqrt{\frac{2 \times 300 \times 12,000}{0.8}} = 3000,$$

$$n^* = \sqrt{\frac{\mu_d h}{2f}} = \sqrt{\frac{12,000 \times 0.8}{2 \times 300}} = 4.$$

That is, a reasonably good inventory management policy is to order 3000 units at a time, or alternatively order four times during the year.

8.3 SELECTING AN ORDERING POLICY

When the demand is a known constant, to know the optimal order quantity is also to know the order frequency, and vice versa. But this is no longer true when the demand is a random variable. Thus in the case of Example 2, the fact that the Fast Mail Order Company decides to order 3000 units at a time does not necessarily mean that it will be ordering exactly four times during the year, as our calculations seem to imply. Suppose that the company in fact orders 3000 units at a time. Then it will order exactly four times if the demand turns out to be for exactly 12,000 units; otherwise, how many times it will place this order is contingent on the demand. Suppose, on the other hand, that the company decides to place four orders during the year. Then, unless the demand turns out to be for exactly 12,000 units, the average size of the orders may be more or less than 3000 units.

Accordingly, Fast Mail Order Company is likely initially to select one of the following two decision alternatives:

1. Order 3000 units at a time and let the actual demand determine the order frequency.
2. Order 4 times during the year and let the actual demand determine the average order size.

An inventory management system based on the first of these two alternatives may be called the *fixed-order-size system* or simply the *fixed-quantity system*. One based on the second alternative may be called the *fixed-order-frequency system* or simply the *fixed-frequency system*.

Moreover, if Fast Mail Order decides on the fixed-frequency system and orders four times a year, then given 300 working days during the year, it will order once every 75 days. Thus this system may also be called the *fixed-order-period system* or simply the *fixed-period system*.

8.4 THE FIXED-QUANTITY SYSTEM

It was pointed out that if the fixed-quantity system is adopted, the order frequency must be allowed to vary to account for the variation in demand during the anticipated period. This means that such an inventory management system should have a built-in control device that will raise the order frequency in periods of high demand and lower the order frequency when the demand is low.

One way of controlling the inventory is to continuously monitor the inventory level so that a new order is placed only when the inventory level has reached a predetermined level. For obvious reasons such a control system is known as the *continuous-review system* or the *alarm-ring system* (see Section 7.2).

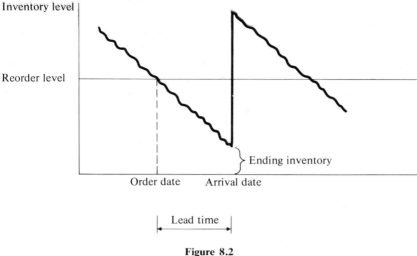

Figure 8.2

The critical decision that must be made for the continuous-review system is to fix the reorder level—the level of inventory at which a new order must be placed. Too high a reorder level will result in a high ending inventory at the time the new order arrives (see Figure 8.2). But too low a reorder level will entail shortage before the arrival of the new order (Figure 8.3).

The decision on reorder level must, therefore, take into account both the inventory holding costs and the stock-out cost. While we may well decide to undertake an explicit analysis of these two costs in order to arrive at the

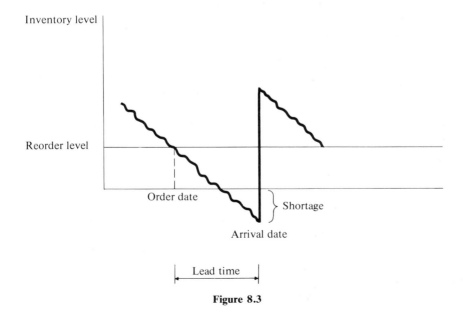

Figure 8.3

optimal reorder level, we shall choose to describe a procedure, based on a heuristic approach, that takes into account the two costs only implicitly.

Suppose the inventory holding cost is low but the stock-out cost is high. Then we would most likely want a very low stock-out probability and therefore a relatively high reorder level. On the other hand, suppose the inventory holding cost is high but the stock-out cost is low. Then we would be more willing to accept a relatively large stock-out probability, resulting in a relatively low reorder level. The procedure we shall describe here is based on the assumption that, after weighing the two types of costs, we have arrived at a relatively low maximum acceptable stock-out probability, say 0.05 or 0.01.

Example 3. Let us return to the problem of Fast Mail Order, as given in Example 2, and assume that the company has decided on the fixed-quantity system of inventory replacement. Calculations reveal that the company should order 3000 units at a time.

The problem still to be solved by the company is the determination of the reorder level. We recall that in Example 2 the lead time was given to be 25 days and the mean and the standard deviation of the daily demand were 40 units and 10 units, respectively. Let x_i be the demand on the ith day. Then

$$y = x_1 + \cdots + x_{25}$$

is the demand during the lead time. The mean and standard deviation of this demand are

$$\mu_y = \mu_x(25) = (40)(25) = 1000,$$

$$\sigma_y = \sigma_x\sqrt{25} = (10)(\sqrt{25}) = 50.$$

Since y is the sum of a large number of daily demands, we can assume it to be approximately normally distributed.

We observe that the mean lead time demand is 1000 units. Thus, if an order is placed whenever the inventory level is at 1000 units, then the expected inventory level at the end of the lead time is zero. On the other hand, the stock-out probability during the lead time is 0.5, since there is a 0.5 probability of the actual lead time demand exceeding the mean value of 1000 units.

Suppose Fast Mail Order wants to accept no more than 0.01 stock-out probability. Then it should have more than 1000 units in stock at the time of reorder. The number of units in excess of 1000 that Fast Mail Order decides to carry in its inventory at the time of reorder is called the safety stock. Thus, if r is the reorder level and μ_y is the expected demand during the lead time, then the safety stock is $r - \mu_y$, where $r > \mu_y$.

Let us now calculate the reorder level that will give us a stock-out probability during the lead time of at most 0.01. Assume that the lead time demand is in fact normally distributed. Then since the standard deviation of the demand during the period is 50 units, we can use the table of normal probability distribution to find that the probability of a demand in excess of 1116 units is only 0.01 (Figure 8.4). Thus the desired reorder level is 1116 units— 116 units more than the mean demand which, therefore, is the safety stock.

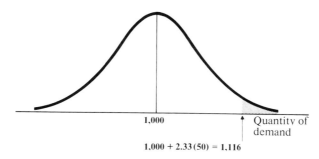

1,000

↑ Quantity of
demand

1,000 + 2.33(50) = 1,116

Figure 8.4

Behavior of the System

Assume now that Fast Mail Order places inventory orders whenever the inventory level reaches 1116 units. Since the expected demand during the lead time is 1000 units, the expected inventory level at the end of the period will be 116 units, which is the safety stock. However, the actual demand will fluctuate around 1000 units, which means that the actual inventory level at the end of the period will also fluctuate around 116 units.

The inventory variation characteristic of the fixed-quantity ordering system is illustrated in Figure 8.5. The diagram shows that the inventory level at the end of the lead time fluctuates around the safety-stock value, also that the inventory level goes up by 3000 units every time the new order arrives. Suppose we define an *inventory cycle* as the time span between the dates of two consecutive orders. Then the length of the inventory cycle is likely to vary from one cycle to the next, which variation is also shown in the diagram.

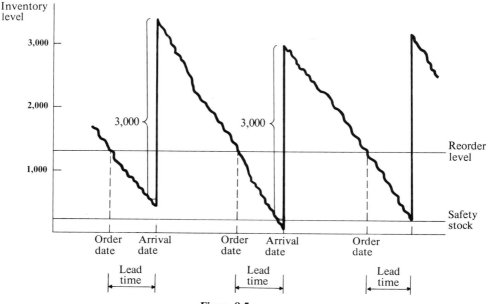

Figure 8.5

8.5   THE FIXED-PERIOD SYSTEM

Let us now examine the fixed-period system of inventory replacement, in which reordering is done at constant intervals. Since the lengths of the inventory cycles are all the same and the actual demands during the various cycles are not likely to be the same, the order size must be allowed to vary. One way of allowing the order size to vary with the demand is the following:

1. Estimate the maximum probable demand for the lead time plus one inventory cycle.
2. Check the inventory level at the time of order.
3. Order the difference between the maximum demand and the inventory level at the time of order.

Now, since the maximum probable demand will remain the same from one order date to the next and the inventory level on a particular order date will be low when the immediately preceding inventory cycle is characterized by high demand, an inventory cycle of high demand will tend to increase the size of the subsequent order. Similarly, an inventory cycle of low demand tends to reduce the size of the subsequent order.

Example 4.   Assume that the Fast Mail Order Company of Example 2 has decided on the fixed-period system. Our earlier calculations showed that the company should order four times during the year, or every 75 working days, since there are 300 working days; 75 working days thus constitute an inventory cycle.

Assume that on a given order date Fast Mail Order has already reviewed its inventory holding. To decide on the order size, the company can proceed as follows. Since the lead time is 25 days and the inventory cycle is 75 days, the next order will arrive 100 days from today. Therefore, the inventory of the item on hand today and the quantity which will arrive 25 days from today will have to meet the demand for the next 100 days. Let y be the demand for the next 100 days, and let $x_1, \ldots, x_{100}$ be the daily demands. Since the daily demands have a mean of 40 with a standard deviation of 10,

$$\mu_y = \mu_x(100) = (40)(100) = 4000,$$

$$\sigma_y = \sigma_x\sqrt{100} = (10)\sqrt{100} = 100.$$

Thus the mean and standard deviation of the demand for the next 100 days are 4000 units and 100 units, respectively. Furthermore, according to the central-limit theorem, the distribution of the demand for the next 100 days may be approximated by a normal distribution with a mean and a standard deviation of 4000 and 100, respectively. This means that the probability of the demand for the next 100 days exceeding, for example, 4233 units is 0.01 (Figure 8.6). Suppose Fast Mail Order wants to be at least 99 percent sure that its present inventory holding plus the present order, which will arrive at the end of the lead time, will be adequate to meet the demand for the next 100 days. Then its present order should be for 4233 units less the present inventory holding. For

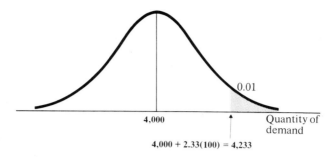

Figure 8.6

example, if its present inventory holding is 1200 units, then it should order 3033 units.

Suppose we identify 4233 units as the *maximum probable demand* for the next 100 days. Then the order size of 3033 units is obtained by subtracting the inventory holding on the date of order from the maximum probable demand for a lead time and an inventory cycle. This procedure for ascertaining the appropriate size is exactly what we outlined at the beginning of this section.

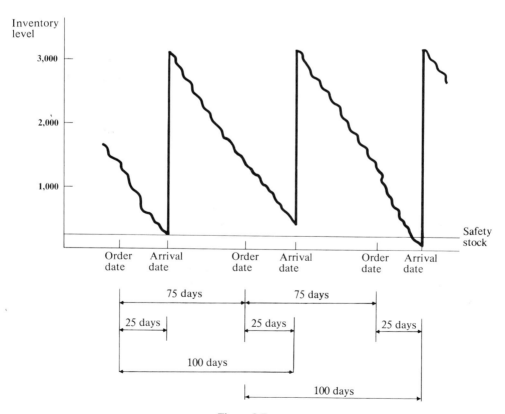

Figure 8.7

Suppose now Fast Mail Order actually orders 3033 units. Then with 1200 units on hand, there will be a total of 4233 units available to meet the demand for the next 100 days. However, as we have already shown, the mean or expected demand for this period is 4000 units. Therefore, the difference of 233 units may be regarded as the safety stock.

Character of the System

Suppose that the above procedure is used over several inventory cycles. Then the expected inventory level at the end of a lead time is 233 units, which is the safety-stock value. But the actual inventory level at the end of this period is likely to fluctuate around 233 units, since the actual demand for the entire period of lead time plus inventory cycle is likely to fluctuate around 4000 units.

The variation in inventory associated with the fixed-period system of inventory replacement may now be illustrated (Figure 8.7). This figure shows that the inventory level at the end of each time period fluctuates around the safety-stock value. It also shows that the lengths of the inventory cycles are the same but that the quantities which arrive at different arrival dates are not the same.

8.6   COST COMPARISONS

One way to compare the two types of inventory management systems described above is to compare some of the relevant costs associated with the two systems.

The Fixed-Quantity System

Assume that q^* is the quantity of each order in a fixed-quantity system. Then the expected number of orders per year is μ_d/q^*, where μ_d is the mean demand for the year, and $f(\mu_d/q^*)$ is the expected total order cost for the year.

In the case of Fast Mail Order, we have $f = 300$, $\mu_d = 12,000$, and $q^* = 3000$. Thus the expected number of orders is $12,000/3000 = 4$, and the expected total order cost is $\$300 \times 4 = \$1200$.

Since the expected inventory level at the end of the lead time is the safety stock, it is also the expected lowest inventory level for the inventory cycle. If the daily demand is fairly stable with only minor variations, then the average inventory holding for the year may be approximated by $0.5q^* + s$, where s is the safety stock. The expected total inventory holding cost is then $h(0.5q^* + s)$, where h is the unit inventory holding cost.

Since $h = 0.8$ for Fast Mail Order and $s = 116$ for the fixed-quantity system, the average inventory holding for the year is

$$0.5 \times 3000 + 116 = 1616$$

and the expected inventory holding cost is

$$\$0.8 \times 1616 = \$1292.80.$$

The cost calculations for the company may be summarized as follows:

Expected total order cost	$300 × 4	= $1200.00
Expected total holding cost	$0.8 × 1616	= $1292.80
Sum		$2492.80

The Fixed-Period System

Assume that n^* is the order frequency for the year in a fixed-period system. Then the total order cost for the year is fn^*. In the case of Fast Mail Order $fn^* = \$300 \times 4 = \$1200$ since $n^* = 4$.

As with the fixed-quantity system, the expected lowest inventory level for an inventory cycle is the safety stock value. And the average inventory level for the year is $0.5(\mu_d/n^*) + s$, where μ_d/n^* is the average order size. Thus the expected total inventory holding cost is $h[0.5(\mu_d/n^*) + s]$.

Since in the case of Fast Mail Order $s = 233$ for the fixed-period system, the average inventory holding for the year is $0.5(12,000/4) + 233 = 1733$, so that the expected total inventory holding cost for the year is $\$0.8 \times 1733 = \$1386.40$.

The cost calculations for the company may be summarized as follows:

Expected total order cost	$300 × 4	= $1200.00
Expected total holding cost	$0.8 × 1733	= $1386.40
Sum		$2586.40

A Comparison

We observe that, for Fast Mail Order, the expected total order cost is $1200 when either system of inventory replacement is adopted. However, the expected total inventory holding cost is $1292.80 for the fixed-quantity system and $1386.40 for the fixed-period system. The difference of $93.60 is attributable to the fact that the safety stock has to be larger by 117 units for the fixed-period system.

8.7 OTHER CONSIDERATIONS

Our illustration above suggests that the inventory holding cost tends to be higher with a fixed-period system of inventory replacement than with a fixed-quantity system, because the former involves a larger safety stock. Therefore, the fixed-period system is likely to be less desirable than the fixed-quantity system in a situation where the unit order cost is low but the unit inventory holding cost is high.

On the other hand, the fixed-quantity system requires a continuous monitoring of the inventory level, so that if the cost of monitoring the inventory is very high, the overall cost of adopting a fixed-quantity system may actually be higher than that of a fixed-period system.

Frequently several items can be ordered from one supplier. Then it would not only be convenient but cheaper to order all such items at the same time. A fixed-period system is likely to be more suitable than a fixed-quantity system in such a situation or where the orders are processed in batches in a computerized inventory management system.

EXERCISES

1. The average quantity of daily shipments of one canned-food item from the warehouse of Save-a-Way Foods to its stores is 20 cases, with a standard deviation of 5 cases. The cost of holding a case of this item is 30¢ per year. The cost of placing an order for this item with the canning company is $100. The warehouse operates 300 days in a year.

    a. Suppose the warehouse were to adopt a fixed-quantity system of inventory replacement. Then what should the order size be?
    b. Suppose the warehouse adopts a fixed-period system. Then what should the order frequency be? What is the length of an inventory cycle?

2. Assume that the warehouse of Exercise 1 adopts the fixed-quantity system of inventory replacement. The lead time is 36 days, and the warehouse manager is willing to accept a 0.01 stock-out probability during the lead time.

    a. What should the reorder level be?
    b. How large should the safety stock be?

3. Assume that the warehouse of Exercise 1 adopts the fixed-period system of inventory replacement. The lead time is still 36 days, and the warehouse manager is willing to accept a 0.01 stock-out probability during an inventory cycle.

    a. How should the warehouse determine the order size?
    b. How large should the safety stock be?
    c. Suppose that, on a given order date, the inventory holding is 1000 cases. How many cases should be ordered?

4. Calculate the expected total order cost and expected inventory holding cost for the warehouse of Exercise 1:

    a. assuming that the fixed-quantity system of Exercise 2 is adopted;
    b. assuming that the fixed-period system of Exercise 3 is adopted.

5. Albertson Equipment is a manufacturer of sophisticated industrial equipment. It buys certain parts of the equipment from an outside supplier. The average daily requirement for one special part is 40 units, with a standard deviation of 10 units. The company works 250 days in a year. The cost of placing an order is $500, and the cost of carrying one unit of this part is $10 per year.

    a. Suppose the company adopts a fixed-quantity system of inventory replacement. What should the order quantity be?
    b. Suppose the company adopts a fixed-period system. Then what should the order frequency and the length of an inventory cycle be?

6. Assume that Albertson Equipment of Exercise 5 adopts the fixed-quantity system of inventory replacement. The lead time is 9 days, and the demand during this period is normally distributed. The company wants to accept no more than 0.001 stock-out probability during the period.

   a. What should the reorder level be?
   b. What should the safety-stock value be?
   c. What are the expected total order cost and expected total inventory holding cost for the year?

7. Assume that Albertson Equipment of Exercise 5 adopts the fixed-period system of inventory replacement. The lead time is 9 days, and the company wants to accept no more than a 0.001 stock-out probability during an inventory cycle.

   a. How should the company determine the order size?
   b. How large should the safety stock be?
   c. What are the expected total order cost and the expected inventory holding cost for the year?

CHAPTER

9

LINEAR PROGRAMMING: FORMULATIONS

One of the most important managerial decisions concerns the channeling of scarce resources to obtain their most productive uses. The resources in question may be raw materials, machinery and equipment, space, time, money, and men. They may be used to produce tangible commodities or intangible services. A most elegant analytical method for tackling resource allocation problems is the linear-programming method. We shall devote this and the next two chapters to the illustration of how this method may be applied.

9.1 BASIC PHILOSOPHY

Alpha Beta Manufacturing Company brings out two products, named Product 1 and Product 2, requiring two basic resources, alpha and beta:

	Input-output coefficients		Quantity of available resource
	Product 1	Product 2	
Alpha	1	1	600
Beta	2	1	1000
Selling price	$150	$100	

The selling price of Product 1 is $150, that of Product 2 is $100; 600 units of the resource alpha and 1000 units of resource beta are available for the production run. One unit of product 1 requires one unit of alpha and two units of beta; one unit of product 2 requires one unit each of alpha and beta. **107**

The company is trying to decide how best to allocate the use of alpha and beta.

Model Formulation

In actual production situations the quantities of available resources, the product prices, and the input-output coefficients are all likely to be variable quantities subject to some influence by the manufacturing companies. However, in our problem description we assume that the values of these variables are given and therefore not controllable by Alpha Beta Manufacturing, at least in the short run. They are, then, the environmental variables for the given decision problem.

The company must decide how to allocate the resources. Since the input-output coefficients are given and constant, if the company decides how many units of each product to manufacture, then it will also have decided on the allocation of the resources. Let x_1 and x_2, respectively be the quantities of Product 1 and Product 2 to be manufactured. Then x_1 and x_2 are in fact the decision variables for the problem. A decision regarding x_1 and x_2 will be called a *product mix* decision.

We are now ready to formulate a model for the decision problem of Alpha Beta Manufacturing. We recall that in this context a model will enable us to predict the consequences of choosing a specific decision alternative given the environmental variables. These consequences can then be evaluated for their desirability.

What are some of the consequences that Alpha Beta Manufacturing will need to know in order to evaluate a product mix decision? First, it needs to know the total revenue that can be generated by this product mix. Second, it needs to know whether it has enough of the resources to implement the decision.

We shall now formulate these consequences as functions of the environmental and decision variables. Let

$$f = 150x_1 + 100x_2$$

be the total revenue that will be generated by the product mix x_1 and x_2. Let

$$g = x_1 + x_2 - 600,$$

where, by reason of the input-output coefficients, $x_1 + x_2$ is the total quantity of alpha needed to implement the product mix decision and 600 is the total available quantity of alpha. Then g will tell us whether the company has enough of alpha to implement the decision. If g is positive, then

$$x_1 + x_2 > 600,$$

meaning that the company does not have enough of alpha for this product mix. Similarly, if

$$h = 2x_1 + x_2 - 1000,$$

then h will tell us whether the company has enough of beta for the decision.

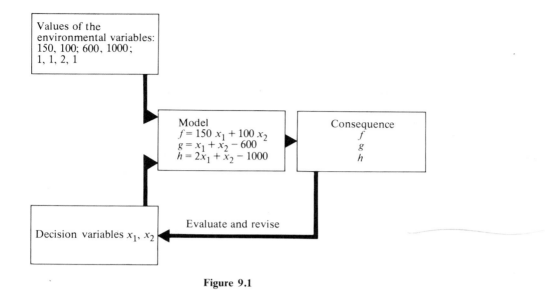

Figure 9.1

Our model may now be given in diagrammatic form as shown in Figure 9.1. We observe that all the consequences f, g, and h are linear functions of the decision and environmental variables. The model is, therefore, called a *linear model*.

Programming Approach

Having formulated a model such as given in Figure 9.1, Alpha Beta Manufacturing can proceed to solve its product mix decision, in the following way. First, decide on a tentative product mix plan. Then evaluate the consequences of implementing this plan. If the consequences are satisfactory, then the plan can be adopted. If the consequences are not satisfactory, then another plan must be formulated and evaluated. The process can be repeated until a satisfactory product mix plan is found.

Such a trial-and-error approach of arriving at a product mix decision is probably not an uncommon practice, but it is often time-consuming, whereas time is precious to a business manager. Thanks to the advent of the computers, however, much of the trial-and-error routines can now be carried by machines.

If a computer is to produce an acceptable product mix plan, it must be given a specific set of guidelines for determining whether a particular plan is acceptable or not. One possible set of guidelines is:

A product mix plan is acceptable if and only if it maximizes the total revenue without violating any resource constraints.

Usually it is easier to feed the above guidelines in mathematical notations. In the case of Alpha Beta Manufacturing the instruction to maximize the total revenue may be specified as follows:

objective func. $$\max f = 150x_1 + 100x_2,$$

where max is an abbreviation for "maximize" and f is the total revenue. We note that the revenue function f is in a sense the objective underlying the problem. Therefore, it is called the *objective function.*

The instruction that the total use of the resource alpha in a particular product mix should not exceed 600 can be specified as

$$x_1 + x_2 \leq 600;$$

and that the total use of beta should not exceed 1000 may be specified as

structural constraints $$2x_1 + x_2 \leq 1000.$$

These two constraints will be called the *structural constraints.*

It is quite obvious that neither x_1 nor x_2 must be allowed to take on a negative value. Thus it is necessary to further specify

nonnegativity constraints $$x_1 \geq 0, \qquad x_2 \geq 0,$$

which are called the *nonnegativity constraints.*

Summarizing our instruction to the computer, we have

$$\max f = 150x_1 + 100x_2,$$
$$x_1 + x_2 \leq 600,$$
$$2x_1 + x_2 \leq 1000,$$
$$x_1, x_2 \geq 0.$$

This set of mathematical expressions is called a *linear-programming* formulation of the product mix decision problem—it is a *programming* formulation because if a computer is to solve the problem, it must be programmed to follow a given set of solution steps; the programming is *linear* because both the objective function and the constraints are linear expressions.

9.2 RESOURCE ALLOCATION PROBLEMS

Let us now describe a few typical resource allocation problems. For the sake of expository clarity we shall make our problems very simple. Actual problems tend to be more complex, but usually because they have larger dimensions rather than because their structures are fundamentally different.

Example 1. Machine Allocation Precision Lens Company produces three types of lenses for industrial use: low intensity, medium intensity, and high intensity. The lenses must go through three machine processes: blowing, grinding, and polishing.

The following table shows the hourly production rates of the machines for the different types of lenses:

	Blowing	Grinding	Polishing
Low intensity	50	40	25
Medium intensity	40	20	20
High intensity	25	10	10

The hourly costs of running the machines are $500 (blowing), $400 (grinding), and $200 (polishing). The costs per lens of material are $10 (low intensity), $12 (medium intensity), and $15 (high intensity). The company sells the low-intensity lenses for $50 per lens, medium-intensity lenses for $80 per lens, the high-intensity lenses for $130 per lens. It wants to allocate the machine hours in such a way as to maximize the hourly profit.

A model for the decision problem of Precision Lens may be formulated as follows. Let x_1, x_2, and x_3, respectively, be the quantities of the low-intensity, medium-intensity, and high-intensity lenses produced. Let c_1, c_2, and c_3, respectively, be their unit profit margins. Then the objective function may be written:

$$\max f = c_1 x_1 + c_2 x_2 + c_3 x_3,$$

where f is the total profit.

Still to be calculated are the profit margins c_1, c_2, and c_3, which may be obtained as follows. Since the blowing machine can blow 50 low-intensity lenses per hour and it costs $500 per hour to run the machine, the cost of blowing a low-intensity lens is $10. Similarly, it costs $10 to grind and $8 to polish a low-intensity lens. If we add the material cost of $10, we find that the total unit cost of a low-intensity lens is $38. Since the selling price is $50, the unit profit margin is $12. The unit profit margins of the other lenses may be calculated in a similar way. Thus Table 9.1 shows the breakdown of cost, price, and profit.

Table 9.1

	Low intensity	Medium intensity	High intensity
Machine cost			
blowing	$10.00	$12.50	$20.00
grinding	10.00	20.00	40.00
polishing	8.00	10.00	20.00
Material cost	10.00	12.00	15.00
Total cost	38.00	54.50	95.00
Selling price	50.00	80.00	130.00
Profit margin	12.00	25.50	35.00

The objective function for the problem may now be expressed as

$$\max f = 12.00x_1 + 25.50x_2 + 35.00x_3.$$

[handwritten margin notes: "100% = % of max needed by the product", "# blown/hr", "100/50 = 2", "100/40 = 2.5", "100/25 = 4"]

There remain the structural constraints. First, note that not more than 100 percent of the blowing machine capacity can be utilized. Since the blowing machine can blow 50 low-intensity lenses, one low-intensity lens requires 2 percent of the capacity of this machine. Similarly, one medium-intensity lens requires 2.5 percent and one high-intensity lens requires 4 percent of the hourly capacity of the blowing machine. Thus

$$0.020x_1 + 0.025x_2 + 0.040x_3$$

represents the percentage of the total hourly capacity of the blowing machine utilized by a given product mix. The restriction for the blowing machine may then be expressed as

$$0.020x_1 + 0.025x_2 + 0.040x_3 \leq 1.$$

Similarly, the capacity restrictions for the two other machines are:

$$0.025x_1 + 0.050x_2 + 0.100x_3 \leq 1,$$
$$0.040x_1 + 0.050x_2 + 0.100x_3 \leq 1.$$

Adding the nonnegative constraints $x_1 \geq 0$, $x_2 \geq 0$, and $x_3 \geq 0$, we have completed our model formulation. Following is a tabular summary of the structural constraints and the objective function:

x_1	x_2	x_3		
0.020	0.025	0.040	$\leq$	1
0.025	0.050	0.100	$\leq$	1
0.040	0.050	0.100	$\leq$	1
12.00	25.50	35.00	$=$	f

[handwritten labels: "structural constraints" bracketing first three rows; "obj. func" labeling last row]

Example 2. Cargo Plane Capacity Allocation A cargo airplane has two compartments, the front and the rear. The loading capacities in weight and spatial dimensions are as follows:

	Weight limit	Space limit
Front	20,000 lb	15,000 ft³
Rear	25,000 lb	20,000 ft³

The following cargos are available for transport, and the plane may carry all or any part of each commodity:

Commodity	Amount (lb)	ft³/lb	Revenue/lb
1	30,000	1	$1.00
2	15,000	2	$1.50

The carrier company wants to accept the commodities in such proportions as to maximize the total revenue, subject of course to weight and space limitations.

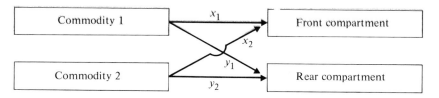

Figure 9.2

The nature of the problem may be diagramed as in Figure 9.2. Let x_1 and y_1 respectively denote the weights of commodity 1 accepted for the front and rear compartments, and x_2 and y_2 the weights of commodity 2 accepted for the front and rear compartments. The objective function for the problem may be expressed as

$$\max f = 1.0x_1 + 1.5x_2 + 1.0y_1 + 1.5y_2,$$

where f is the total revenue.

There are three types of structural constraints: weight limitations of the compartments, space limitations of the compartments, and supply limitations of the commodities. The weight limitations are

$$x_1 + x_2 \leq 20{,}000, \qquad y_1 + y_2 \leq 25{,}000,$$

and the supply limitations are

$$x_1 + y_1 \leq 30{,}000, \qquad x_2 + y_2 \leq 15{,}000.$$

Finally, the space limitations are

$$x_1 + 2x_2 \leq 15{,}000, \qquad y_1 + 2y_2 \leq 20{,}000.$$

We can summarize these structural constraints and the objective function in the following table:

x_1	x_2	y_1	y_2		
1	1			$\leq$	20,000
		1	1	$\leq$	25,000
1		1		$\leq$	30,000
	1		1	$\leq$	15,000
1	2			$\leq$	15,000
		1	2	$\leq$	20,000
1.0	1.5	1.0	1.5	$=$	f

Adding the nonnegativity constraints, we have completed the formulation of the model.

9.3   OTHER LINEAR-PROGRAMMING MODELS

The structural constraints in resource allocation problems which we have thus far described pertain only to the scarce resources. In actual resource allocation problems, however, there are usually also other constraints. Nevertheless, we may still be able to use the linear-programming technique.

Before proceeding to Examples 3 and 4, however, we note that even though solving resource allocation problems constitutes an important application of linear programming, many other types of problem can also be solved by this method. We shall consider a number of such applications in Examples 5, 6, and 7.

Example 3. Aviation Gasoline Blending   Pure Oil Company sells two grades of aviation gasoline, premium and regular. Each must meet certain specifications such as maximum allowable vapor pressure and the minimum required octane rating. These specifications, along with some other relevant information, are provided below.

Aviation gasoline	Maximum vapor pressure	Minimum octane rating	Maximum weekly demand (barrels)	Price per barrel
Premium	6	100	10,000	$9.00
Regular	7	95	50,000	8.00

Two types of blending gasoline are used to produce the marketed products. They have the following characteristics:

Blending gasoline	Vapor pressure	Octane rating	Maximum supply (barrels)	Cost per barrel
Type A	8	105	20,000	$7.00
Type B	5	90	30,000	6.00

The company wants to maximize the weekly profit from the combined sales of the two grades of gasoline.

The nature of the problem faced by Pure Oils is similar to the air cargo problem of Example 2. Figure 9.3 shows a diagram of this problem.

Let x_1 and y_1, respectively, be the quantities of blending gasoline A allocated to the production of the regular and the premium, and similarly x_2 and y_2 be the analogous quantities of blending gasoline B. Then the profit

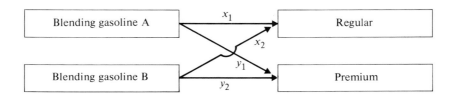

Figure 9.3

margin for x_1 may be ascertained as follows. We note that blending gasoline A costs $7.00 per barrel and the regular gasoline is sold at $8.00 per barrel. Thus a barrel of blending gasoline A allocated to the regular will yield $1.00 profit, which is the profit margin for x_1. The profit margins for y_1, x_2, and y_2 can be calculated in the same way. The following table summarizes these figures.

| | Cost | Profit margin if used in | |
		Regular	Premium
Type A	$7	$1	$2
Type B	6	2	3
Selling price		8	9

Using the information thus obtained, we can formulate our objective function as

$$\max f = 1x_1 + 2x_2 + 2y_1 + 3y_2.$$

Next let us indicate the restrictions that at most 20,000 barrels of blending gasoline A and 30,000 barrels of blending gasoline B are available per week:

$$x_1 + y_1 \le 20{,}000, \qquad x_2 + y_2 \le 30{,}000.$$

Also the company cannot sell more than 50,000 barrels of regular and 10,000 barrels of premium per week (note that these restrictions do not arise from the scarcity of resources):

$$x_1 + x_2 \le 50{,}000, \qquad y_1 + y_2 \le 10{,}000.$$

Moreover, the blended gasoline must satisfy the vapor pressure and octane rating specifications. The general rule is that the vapor pressure and the octane rating of a blended gasoline are each the sum of the respective contributions of the blending gasolines; and the contribution of a blending gasoline in vapor pressure or octane rating is a function of the proportional volume of this blending gasoline in the mixture. Thus, if one barrel of blending gasoline A and one barrel of blending gasoline B are mixed, and given the vapor pressures of A and B, the vapor pressure of the blended gasoline is the sum of vapor pressure of A times $\frac{1}{2}$ and vapor pressure of B times $\frac{1}{2}$, or $8(\frac{1}{2}) + 5(\frac{1}{2}) = 6.5$. Similarly, the octane rating of this blended gasoline is $105(\frac{1}{2}) + 90(\frac{1}{2}) = 97.5$.

Let us now consider the restriction that the vapor pressure of the regular gasoline must not exceed 7. The vapor pressure of the regular gasoline is

$$\frac{8x_1 + 5x_2}{x_1 + x_2}.$$

Therefore, the restriction is

$$\frac{8x_1 + 5x_2}{x_1 + x_2} \le 7.$$

Similarly, the vapor pressure restriction on the premium gasoline is

$$\frac{8y_1 + 5y_2}{y_1 + y_2} \le 6.$$

Modifying the two restrictions, we have

$$x_1 - 2x_2 \leq 0, \qquad 2y_1 - y_2 \leq 0.$$

The regular gasoline must also have a minimum octane rating of 95. The formula for the octane rating of the regular gasoline is

$$\frac{105x_1 + 90x_2}{x_1 + x_2},$$

so that the octane rating requirement reads:

$$\frac{105x_1 + 90x_2}{x_1 + x_2} \geq 95,$$

which may be converted to

$$10x_1 - 5x_2 \geq 0.$$

Similarly, the octane rating requirement for the premium is

$$\frac{105y_1 + 90y_2}{y_1 + y_2} \geq 100$$

or

$$5y_1 - 10y_2 \geq 0.$$

Here is a tabular summary of our formulation:

x_1	x_2	y_1	y_2		
1		1		$\leq$	20,000
	1		1	$\leq$	30,000
1	1			$\leq$	50,000
		1	1	$\leq$	10,000
1	-2			$\leq$	0
	2		-1	$\leq$	0
10	-5			$\geq$	0
		5	-10	$\geq$	0
1	2	2	3	$=$	f

This formulation is completed by the addition of the nonnegativity constraints.

Example 4. Transportation problem Good Food Company has pineapple canning plants in Hawaii and the Philippines. The production capacities and production costs for the two plants are:

	Capacity	Cost/can
Hawaii	2 million cans	15¢
Philippines	4 million cans	12¢

The American market has been divided into two regions: the western region, which is supplied through the Los Angeles port; and the eastern region, which is supplied through the port of New York.

The shipping costs per can are shown below.

To From	Los Angeles	New York
Hawaii	2¢	5¢
Philippines	6¢	7¢

The prices charged per can at these two ports, as well as the demand in the two regions, are:

	Demand	Price/can
Western	3 million cans	20¢
Eastern	3 million cans	22¢

The company wants to maximize the total profit from its canning operations.

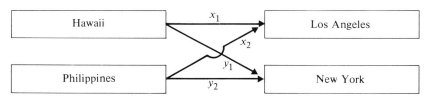

Figure 9.4

The nature of the problem is diagramed in Figure 9.4. Since a can of pineapple shipped from Hawaii to Los Angeles costs 15¢ for production, 2¢ for transportation, and sells for 20¢, the profit margin per can is 3¢ in the western market. The profit margins for the cans shipped from the two producing plants to the two marketing regions are given in the following table, where the corresponding total costs are shown in parentheses.

To From	Los Angeles	New York
Hawaii	$(15 + 2 = 17)$ $20 - 17 = 3$	$(15 + 5 = 20)$ $22 - 20 = 2$
Philippines	$(12 + 6 = 18)$ $20 - 18 = 2$	$(12 + 7 = 19)$ $22 - 19 = 3$

Now we let x_1 and y_1, respectively, be the quantities shipped from Hawaii to Los Angeles and to New York; and let x_2 and y_2, respectively, be the quantities shipped from the Philippines to Los Angeles and to New York. Then the objective function is

$$\max f = 3x_1 + 2x_2 + 2y_1 + 3y_2,$$

where f is the profit.

The capacity constraints for the plants are:

$$x_1 + y_1 \leq 2,000,000,$$
$$x_2 + y_2 \leq 4,000,000.$$

The demand constraints are

$$x_1 + x_2 \leq 3,000,000,$$
$$y_1 + y_2 \leq 3,000,000.$$

And we can summarize our formulation as follows:

x_1	x_2	y_1	y_2		
1		1		$\leq$	2,000,000
	1		1	$\leq$	4,000,000
1	1			$\leq$	3,000,000
		1	1	$\leq$	3,000,000
3	2	2	3	$=$	f

Adding the nonnegativity constraints will complete the formulation of the problem.

Example 5. Trim Problem   Quality Lumber Company has to fill the following orders:

Lumber dimensions	Quantity to be shipped
1 in. × 2 in. × 8 ft	1000
1 in. × 4 in. × 8 ft	800
2 in. × 2 in. × 8 ft	500

All these orders have to be filled by cutting the standard-size lumber, whose dimensions are 2 in. × 4 in. × 8 ft. The company wants to minimize the total number of pieces of the standard-size lumber used to satisfy the orders.

The possible patterns of cutting the standard-size lumber are shown in Figure 9.5. Let $x_1, x_2, x_3, x_4,$ and x_5, respectively, be the numbers of the standard-size lumber cut according to the five patterns shown in the figure. Then the objective function may be written:

$$\min f = x_1 + x_2 + x_3 + x_4 + x_5.$$

Note that the pattern corresponding to x_1 will yield 4 units of 1″ × 2″ × 8′ (where ″ stands for inches and ′ stands for feet), that corresponding to x_3 will yield 2 units of 1″ × 2″ × 8′, and that corresponding to x_4 will yield 2 units of 1″ × 2″ × 8′. Thus the total requirement for 1″ × 2″ × 8′ may be expressed as

$$4x_1 + 2x_3 + 2x_4 \geq 1000.$$

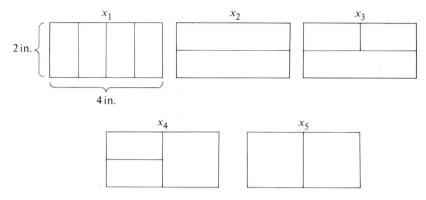

Figure 9.5

Similarly, the requirements for $1'' \times 4'' \times 8'$ and $2'' \times 2'' \times 8'$ may be expressed as

$$2x_2 + x_3 \geq 800, \qquad x_4 + 2x_5 \geq 500,$$

respectively. Summarizing our formulations, we can obtain the following table:

x_1	x_2	x_3	x_4	x_5		
4		2	2		$\geq$	1000
	2	1			$\geq$	800
			1	2	$\geq$	500
1	1	1	1	1	$=$	f

Adding the nonnegativity constraints will complete the formulation of the problem.

Example 6. Production Planning Name Your Brand Appliance is committed to delivering 1000 units of a certain model of appliance this year and another 1000 units next year to a large mail order house chain. The company can produce as many as 1500 units of this model in a year. The unit production cost is $100 this year, but it is expected to rise to $150 next year. Any unit produced this year but not delivered during the year will incur a $20 holding cost. The manufacturer does not have any inventory of this model and does not want to have any ending inventory of the model at the end of the second year. How should its production be scheduled so as to minimize the total cost of meeting the delivery requirements?

We can let

$$x_1 = \text{quantity produced this year,}$$
$$x_2 = \text{quantity produced next year,}$$
$$y_0 = \text{inventory at the beginning of this year,}$$
$$y_1 = \text{inventory at the end of this year,}$$
$$y_2 = \text{inventory at the end of next year.}$$

Since $y_0 = 0$ and $y_2 = 0$, the objective function may be written:

$$\min f = 100x_1 + 20y_1 + 150x_2.$$

As to the constraints, first, we must specify that the inventory at the beginning of this year, plus the quantity produced during the year, less the ending inventory, be equal to the delivery requirement for the year:

$$y_0 + x_1 - y_1 = 1000.$$

Similarly, for the second year we have

$$y_1 + x_2 - y_2 = 1000.$$

Since $y_0 = 0$ and $t_2 = 0$, the following is a tabular summary of the preceding formulation:

why not 2 for demand

x_1	y_1	x_2		
1	−1		=	1000
	1	1	=	1000
100	20	150	=	f

Adding the nonnegativity constraints will complete the formulation.

Example 7. Automobile Generator Problem
The maintenance division of Speedy Taxi Company needs the following quantities of automobile generators for the next three months:

Month	Generator requirement
1	100
2	150
3	200

It can purchase a new generator for $40 or have a used generator rebuilt by an outside firm for $25. In the latter case the outside firm picks up the used generators at the beginning of the month and returns the rebuilt generators at the beginning of the following month. The taxi company has 120 used generators in stock, but the used generators will not have any salvage value at the end of three months. If possible, the company want to avoid storing any used generators. How can the taxi company minimize the total cost of meeting the generator requirements for the three-month period?

Let x_1, x_2, x_3 be the quantities of new generators purchased in the first, second, and third months, respectively, and y_1, and y_2 be the quantities of used generators sent out for rebuilding at the beginnings of the first and second months, respectively. Note that there is no need to have a y_3, since a generator sent out at the beginning of the third month cannot be returned for use in that month. The objective function may be expressed as

$$\min f = 40x_1 + 40x_2 + 40x_3 + 25y_1 + 25y_2.$$

There are two types of structural constraints for this problem. First, the rebuilt generators returned at the beginning of a month plus the new generators purchased during the month must satisfy the requirement for that month. Since there are not any rebuilt generators at the beginning of the first month, the constraint for this month is

$$x_1 \geq 100.$$

Since y_1 units of rebuilt generators will be returned at the beginning of the second month, the requirement for this month will be met so long as

$$y_1 + x_2 \geq 150.$$

For the third month we have

$$y_2 + x_3 \geq 200.$$

The second type of structural constraints is that the quantity of used generators sent out at the beginning of a month cannot exceed the quantity available at that time. Therefore, for the first month

$$y_1 \leq 120.$$

Also during the first month $120 - y_1$ units of used generators will still be on hand after a batch has been sent for rebuilding. In addition, another 100 generators will become used ones during the month. Thus the constraint for the second month is

$$y_2 \leq 120 - y_1 + 100.$$

Summarizing our formulation, we have the table:

x_1	y_1	x_2	y_2	x_3		
1					$\geq$	100
	1	1			$\geq$	150
			1	1	$\geq$	200
	1				$\leq$	120
	1		1		$\leq$	220
40	25	40	25	40	$=$	f

Adding the nonnegativity constraints will complete the formulation.

9.4 GRAPHIC SOLUTION

In practice the application of linear programming to managerial decision-making will invariably require the services of computers to carry out the mechanics of the solution. Therefore, a manager need not be familiar with the solution process. Nevertheless, knowing the rudiments of the solution process cannot but help the manager in his application of the linear-programming technique. Certainly it will help him to better understand the nature of his decision problem. Also it will help him in interpreting the particular solutions generated by computers. Therefore, we shall undertake to describe how a linear-programming formulation may be solved. Let us reconsider the first problem in Section 9.1:

$$\max f = 150x_1 + 100x_2,$$

$$x_1 + x_2 \leq 600$$

$$2x_1 + x_2 \leq 1000$$

$$x_1, x_2 \geq 0.$$

This problem is simple enough that we can solve it graphically.

Let the two axes of the diagram in Figure 9.6 stand for the feasible solution values of x_1 and x_2. Any set of values for x_1 and x_2 that satisfies all of the constraints is said to be a *feasible solution.*

The nonnegativity constraints $x_1 \geq 0$ and $x_2 \geq 0$ indicate that any feasible solution will be in the first quadrant, where both x_1 and x_2 have nonnegative values. Adding the structural constraint

$$x_1 + x_2 \leq 600,$$

we find that the allowable solutions must fall within the shaded triangular area in Figure 9.7. And, finally, those solutions which satisfy *all* the constraints fall within the shaded polygon in Figure 9.6. This polygon may therefore be called the *feasible solution space* for the given linear-programming problem.

Since there are infinitely many points in the shaded polygon, there must also be an infinite number of feasible solutions for the given linear-programming problem. The next question is then, How do we determine which of these solutions is optimal for the problem?

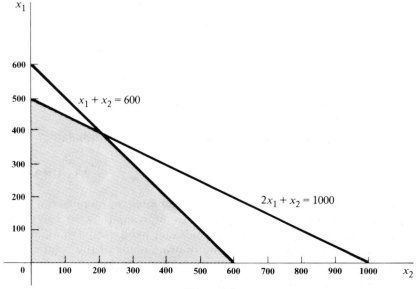

Figure 9.6

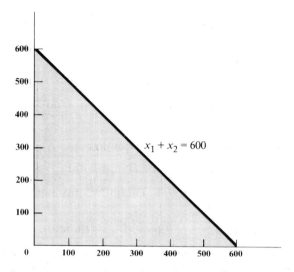

Figure 9.7

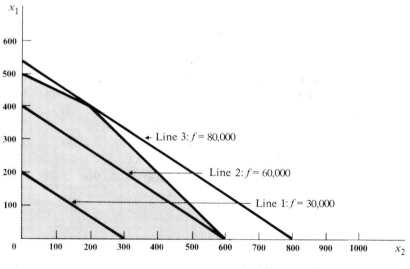

Figure 9.8

To answer the question, we present the feasible solution space again, as shown in Figure 9.8, and examine the objective function

$$f = 150x_1 + 100x_2.$$

Suppose we assign an arbitrary value of f, for example $f = 30{,}000$. Then the equation

$$150x_1 + 100x_2 = 30{,}000$$

is represented by line 1 in Figure 9.8; any point on the line will yield the value $f = 30,000$. We note that $x_1 = 200$ and $x_2 = 0$ is on this line:

$$150x_1 + 100x_2 = (150 \times 200) + (100 \times 0) = 30,000$$

The points with (x_1, x_2) values corresponding to

$$(200, 0), \qquad (100, 150), \qquad (0, 300)$$

are also on the line.

Now if we let $f = 60,000$, then the equation

$$150x_1 + 100x_2 = 60,000$$

is represented by line 2 in Figure 9.8. Therefore, any point on this line 2 will yield $f = 60,000$; for example

$$(400, 0), \qquad (200, 300), \qquad (0, 600).$$

It is obvious that any point on line 2 represents a better solution than any on line 1. The two lines 1 and 2 also suggest that the farther the line is from the point of origin, the higher will be the value of f. Thus an optimal solution for the given linear-programming problem may be obtained by drawing the line, parallel to lines 1 and 2, which is farthest from the point of origin and yet contains at least one point in the feasible solution space. Such line is shown in Figure 9.8 as line 3, corresponding to the equation

$$150x_1 + 100x_2 = 80,000$$

We observe that this line contains only one point of the feasible solution space, namely $x_1 = 400$ and $x_2 = 200$. Thus we may conclude that the optimal feasible solution is

$$x_1 = 400, \qquad x_2 = 200,$$

and therefore the maximum value of f is

$$f = (150)(400) + (100)(200) = 80,000$$

EXERCISES

1. Plush Furniture Company produces four types of desks for home use. The desks are assembled in the carpentry shop and then finished in the finishing shop. The numbers of labor hours required for the several types of desk in each shop are given below.

	Type 1	Type 2	Type 3	Type 4
Carpentry shop	4	9	7	10
Finishing shop	1	1	3	6
Profit	$25	$50	$45	$80

The limitations in plant capacity are such that no more than 6000 labor hours in the carpentry shop and 4000 labor hours in the finishing shop can be expected during a year.

The company wants to plan its desk production so as to maximize its total profit. Formulate a linear-programming model for the production decision.

2. Storex manufactures three types of storage disk packs for computers, with the brand names Mod 1, Mod 2, and Mod 3. Each disk must go through four production processes: (1) cutting, (2) cleaning and coating, (3) testing, and (4) assembly.

The hours per disk pack required by each type of processing for the three types of disk packs are shown below.

	Mod 1	Mod 2	Mod 3	*availability*
Cutting	0.1	1.0	2.0	10×160 = 1600
Cleaning and coating	0.5	3.0	8.0	30×160 = 4800
Testing	0.1	0.8	2.0	10 × 160 = 1600
Assembly	0.5	1.0	2.0	30 × 160 = 4800

There are 10 cutting units, 30 cleaning and coating machines, 10 testing stations, and 30 assembly stations. The plant operates on a five-day, four-shift basis. Even though each machine or station can work 168 hours per week, the productive work hours are assumed to be 160 hours per week.

The prices of the disk packs are established by the industry's leader. On the basis of the prevailing price structure the calculated profit margins for the disk packs are:

Disk packs	Profit margin
Mod 1	$50
Mod 2	$150
Mod 3	$200

The company wants to schedule its production so as to maximize the total weekly profit. Formulate the linear-programming model for this decision problem.

3. ABC Manufacturing produces three products named X, Y, and Z. Each product must go through some or all of three manufacturing processes, named A, B, and C (Figure 9.9). The per hour capacities of the three processes are shown in the table below.

		Process	
Product	A	B	C
X		50	40
Y	40	50	20
Z	50	25	
Running cost	$500	$1000	$800

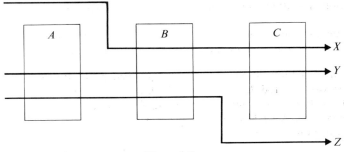

Figure 9.9

The cost of material and the selling price of each product are:

Product	Material cost	Selling price
X	$10	$75
Y	$20	$120
Z	$15	$80

The company wants to plan the production so as to maximize the total profit. Formulate a linear-programming model for this decision problem.

4. Long Life Bearing Company produces bearings for various uses. The bearings are made of white metal, which is an alloy. The composition of the alloy varies according to the purpose for which the bearing is designed. Usually the alloy consists of tin, antimony, copper, and lead. After the bearings have been machined, the swarf is collected and remelted. The salvaged white metal from this and other operations is cast in batches, whose compositions are determined by chemical analysis. The recovered batches may be combined with other recovered melts and with quantities of virgin metals to produce a new white metal for a production run of bearings. On the other hand, the recovered melts may be sold.

To start a production run, the company needs 100 lb of alloy with the following composition: 50% tin, 15% antimony, 20% copper, and 15% lead.

There are three different melts on hand, with the following compositions and prices, and in these quantities:

Melt	Composition				Available quantity	Price per pound
	Tin	Antimony	Copper	Lead		
1	0.60	0.10	0.20	0.10	30 lb	$2.70
2	0.70	0.10	0.10	0.20	40 lb	$3.10
3	0.10	0.20	0.20	0.50	20 lb	$4.10

The prices of virgin metals are: $2.00/lb (tin), $4/lb (antimony), $3/lb (copper), and $5/lb (lead).

The company wants to minimize the cost of a new production run for the alloy. Formulate a linear-programming model for this decision problem.

5. Tasty Meat Packing is a small meat-packing house. On the average it slaughters 2000 hogs a day. The company always has the problem of deciding what proportion of hams, bellies, and picnic hams should be processed for sale as smoked products and what proportion should be sold fresh or green.

The average weight of the hogs is 240 lb. Usually the daily input of 2000 hogs will yield the following amounts (in hundreds of pounds) of fresh meat product: hams 564, bellies 504, and picnics 264.

The critical operation in obtaining smoked products is pumping. The plant capacity (in hundreds of pounds) for this operation is as follows: ham 150, bellies and picnics 450.

All the costs that can be directly charged to the product, such as labor, packaging materials, fuel for smoke ovens, electricity for freezing rooms, and storage charges, are shown below (per hundred pounds):

	Smoked product	**Green product**
Hams	$5.20	$0.50
Bellies	$4.70	$0.47
Picnics	$5.70	$0.52

The difference per hundred pounds between the selling prices of smoked and green hams is $6.00, that between smoked and green bellies is $5.00, and that between smoked and green picnics is $6.00.

Formulate a linear-programming model that will help the packing house maximize its daily profit.

6. Groovy Textile Company is trying to decide on its weekly production of differently styled fabrics. Three styles A, B, and C, are under consideration. Table 9.3 contains the information required for the decision.

Table 9.3

	Fabric Styles			Weekly mill
	A	**B**	**C**	**capacity**
Profit per 100 yd.	4.00	3.70	2.80	
Machine hours needed (per 100 yds.)				
carding	2	3	3	30,000
roving	37.50	25	20	250,000
spinning	720	640	800	8,000,000
weaving	32	28	24	400,000

The sales requirements and restrictions are:

	Minimum	**Maximum**
A	20,000 yd.	50,000 yd.
B	15,000 yd.	40,000 yd.
C	10,000 yd.	20,000 yd.

The company wants to schedule its production in such a way as to maximize its total profit. Formulate a linear-programming model for this decision problem.

7. Fresh Grown Fryers, a poultry farm, is trying to decide on the least costly feed mix for its chicken stock. Any mixture of feeds that the company decides on must satisfy the following requirements and constraints: (1) the protein content of the mixture must be at least 25%! (2) the fat content of the mixture must be at least 4%, (3) the fiber content of the mixture must not exceed 3%.

The available feed stocks, with their protein, fat, and fiber contents, and prices per ton are shown in Table 9.4.

Table 9.4

	Fish meal	Meat and bone mix	Poultry by-products	Soybean mix	Alfafa mix	Yellow corn
Percentage of protein	60	50	65	45	20	10
Percentage of fat	13	10	13	1	4	3
Percentage of fibre	0	0	0	3	20	2
Price per ton	$130	$80	$75	$70	$50	$40

Formulate a linear-programming model for this decision problem.

8. No-Flat Tire is contractually obliged to supply the following numbers of tires to an automobile manufacturer during the next six months:

Month	Quantity	Unit cost	Month	Quantity	Unit cost
1	100,000	$20.00	4	100,000	$21.00
2	80,000	$18.00	5	140,000	$21.50
3	120,000	$19.50	6	160,000	$22.50

Due to fluctuations in various cost components, the unit production cost will change from month to month, as indicated above. The storage and other costs of holding a tire are $1.00 per month.

The company wants to schedule its production of tires so as to minimize the total production and holding costs. Formulate a linear-programming model for this problem.

9. California Atlantic Paper manufactures paper in reels of a standard width (180 in.). The company regularly receives orders for paper of narrower widths. The present batch of such orders is given in the table below:

Width (inches)	Order quantity (reels)
80	2000
60	1400
50	1000

The narrower reels must be cut from standard-size reels.

The company wants to minimize the number of standard-size reels used to satisfy these orders. Formulate a linear programming model for this decision problem.

10. Spicy Ketchup Company manufactures ketchup in three different plants in the United States and distributes to four different warehouses. There is always the problem of how best to distribute the ketchup from the plants to the warehouses. A key element in the decision is that the freight cost is different for different shipping routes, as shown below (from plants A, B, C to warehouses I, II, III, and IV, per ton of ketchup):

Plants	I	II	III	IV
		Warehouses		
A	$20	$15	$18	$22
B	18	21	20	14
C	15	18	24	20

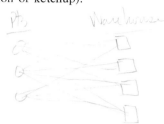

The daily requirements, in tons, of the warehouses are: 200(I), 100(II), 300(III), and 400(IV).

The company wants to minimize the total freight cost. Formulate a linear-programming model for this decision problem.

11. The plant capacities of Spicy Ketchup Company of Exercise 10 and its production costs per ton are:

Plant	Capacity	Production costs (per ton)
A	500	$30
B	400	$35
C	500	$32
	1400	

The requirements in tons and the average revenues per ton of the four warehouses are:

Warehouse	Requirement	Revenue
I	200	$53
II	300	$55
III	300	$54
IV	400	$54
	1200	

The freight costs are the same as given in Exercise 10.

Formulate a linear-programming model to help the company maximize the total revenue.

12. Gourmet Delicatessen does catering service. Its napkin requirements for the coming week are as follows:

Monday	2000
Tuesday	1500
Wednesday	2500
Thursday	1000
Friday	3000
Saturday	8000
Sunday	4000

New napkins cost $12.00 per 100. Used napkins can be laundered for $5.00 per 100. They are picked up every morning by a laundry service truck and returned two mornings later, when they can be used on the same day. On this Monday morning the inventory of napkins consists of 1000 fresh napkins and 1500 used ones. The delicatessen does not want to wind up with an inventory of more than 4000 napkins at the end of the week.

Formulate a linear-programming model to help the delicatessen meet its napkin requirements and minimize the total cost.

13. Solve the following linear-programming problem graphically:

$$\max f = 10x_1 + 10x_2,$$
$$x_1 + 2x_2 \leq 8000,$$
$$3x_1 + 2x_2 \leq 12{,}000,$$
$$x_1, x_2 \geq 0.$$

14. Solve the following linear-programming problem graphically:

$$\max f = 20x_1 + 30x_2,$$
$$3x_1 + x_2 \leq 12{,}000,$$
$$x_1 + x_2 \leq 600,$$
$$x_1 + 2x_2 \leq 1000,$$
$$x_1, x_2 \geq 0.$$

CHAPTER

10

LINEAR PROGRAMMING: COMPUTATIONS

Even though we can solve relatively simple linear-programming problems graphically, as shown in Chapter 9, nearly all actual linear-programming problems cannot be solved graphically; they must be solved by some other method.

10.1 THE SIMPLEX METHOD: FUNDAMENTAL REASONING

The most elegant method of solving linear-programming problems was originally proposed by George Dantzig in the 1940s; he named it the *simplex method*. Since then several variations of the original simplex method have been developed. Here we shall describe what is known as the *primal simplex method*.

Let us again consider the linear-programming problem of Alpha Beta Manufacturing (Section 9.1):

$$\max f = 150x_1 + 100x_2,$$
$$x_1 + x_2 \leq 600, \qquad 2x_1 + x_2 \leq 1000,$$

with the nonnegativity constraints $x_1 \geq 0$ and $x_2 \geq 0$, where x_1 and x_2 are respectively the quantities of product 1 and product 2, and the two structural constraints pertaining to the raw materials alpha and beta.

We note that the inequality

$$x_1 + x_2 \leq 600$$

may be converted into an equation by introducing a *slack variable* x_3:

$$x_1 + x_2 + x_3 = 600.$$

Similarly, the inequality

$$2x_1 + x_2 \leq 1000$$

may be converted into an equation by introducing another slack variable x_4:

$$2x_1 + x_2 + x_4 = 1000.$$

Thus we have the *modified system* of structural constraints:

$$x_1 + x_2 + x_3 \quad\;\; = 600,$$
$$2x_1 + x_2 + \quad\;\; x_4 = 1000.$$

What exactly are slack variables? Suppose we were to decide not to produce either product 1 or product 2. Then

$$x_1 = 0 \quad\text{and}\quad x_2 = 0,$$

and we would have 600 units of unused alpha, and 1000 units of unused beta. And the only way the system of structural-constraints equations could be solved is to let

$$x_3 = 600, \quad x_4 = 1000.$$

Thus the slack variable x_3 represents the unused quantity of alpha, and x_4 represents the unused quantity of beta.

These unused quantities of alpha and beta, however, contribute nothing to the company's revenue. Therefore, the coefficients of x_3 and x_4 in the objective function are zero; that is, $c_3 = 0$ and $c_4 = 0$. The objective function for the modified system thus remains as it was:

$$\max f = 150x_1 + 100x_2.$$

Basic Solution

Let us assume that the modified system of structural constraints for a linear-programming problem consists of *m* number of equations and *n* number of variables. Typically *n* will be larger than *m*, in which case there are infinitely many solutions. Obviously even a computer cannot evaluate so many solutions.

We now propose the following definition:

A solution for the modified system is said to be a basic solution if it is solved for any set of m variables by assigning zero to the remaining n − m variables.

                                     # Variables − #equations

We observe that in our illustration above $n = 4$ and $m = 2$ so that $n - m = 2$. Therefore, any solution that involves assigning zero to two of the four variables is a basic solution.

For example, we can let $x_2 = 0$ and $x_4 = 0$. Then the basic solution is obtained by solving the system of equations for x_1 and x_3. Since $x_2 = 0$ and $x_4 = 0$, we can ignore the terms containing these two variables and obtain

$$x_1 + x_3 = 600, \quad 2x_1 = 1000.$$

Now we have two equations with two variables, so that the system has a unique solution. Dividing the second equation by 2, we have

$$x_1 = \frac{1000}{2} = 500.$$

Substituting this value of x_1 into the first equation and rearranging the terms, we have

$$x_3 = 600 - 500 = 100.$$

The whole solution is therefore

$$x_1 = 600, \qquad x_2 = 0, \qquad x_3 = 100, \qquad x_4 = 0.$$

This is a basic solution, since it was obtained by assigning zero to $n - m$ variables.

We can obtain another basic solution for this system of equations by letting $x_2 = 0$ and $x_3 = 0$. Then we can solve the equations for x_1 and x_4. Ignoring the x_1 and x_3 terms, we have

$$x_1 = 600, \qquad 2x_1 + x_4 = 1000.$$

Substituting the value of x_1, given by the first equation, into the second equation and transposing, we have

$$x_4 = 1000 - 2(600) = -200.$$

Thus our second basic solution is

$$x_1 = 600, \qquad x_2 = 0, \qquad x_3 = 0, \qquad x_4 = -200.$$

The other basic solutions may be obtained in a similar way. Altogether there are six basic solutions for this system of equations. We name them B_i, $i = 1, \ldots, 6$:

B_1:	$x_1 = 0$	$x_2 = 0$	$x_3 = 600$	$x_4 = 1000$ ✓
B_2:	$x_1 = 0$	$x_2 = 600$	$x_3 = 0$	$x_4 = 400$ ✓
B_3:	$x_1 = 0$	$x_2 = 1000$	$x_3 = -400$	$x_4 = 0$
B_4:	$x_1 = 400$	$x_2 = 200$	$x_3 = 0$	$x_4 = 0$ ✓
B_5:	$x_1 = 500$	$x_2 = 0$	$x_3 = 100$	$x_4 = 0$ ✓
B_6:	$x_1 = 600$	$x_2 = 0$	$x_3 = 0$	$x_4 = -200$

Note that in each of these solutions two variables assume zero value, because $n - m = 2$, and the remaining two variables ($m = 2$) have nonzero values. However, as we will show later in the chapter, while at least $n - m$ variables must assume zero value in a basic solution, not all of the remaining m variables must have nonzero values.

Basic Feasible Solution

Let us now reexamine the six basic solutions listed above. We observe, for example, that B_3 involves a negative value for one variable. This cannot be allowed, since, as we noted earlier, a negative value in a solution is meaningless in linear programming, it being incapable of implementation. Therefore, we must add the following definition:

A basic solution is said to be feasible if all the solution values are nonnegative.
Such a solution will also be called a basic feasible solution.

Reexamining the set of basic solutions listed above, we now find that B_1, B_2, B_4, and B_5 are basic feasible solutions.

Our next task is to describe the geometric properties of basic feasible solutions. The feasible solution space for our illustrative problem, including the basic feasible solutions B_1, B_2, B_4, and B_5, is depicted in Figure 10.1. We note that B_2 is in a sense a corner point of the polygon representing the feasible solution space. Such a point is called an *extreme point* of the feasible solution space. An extreme point of a two-dimensional feasible solution space is a point where two boundary lines intersect. An extreme point of a three-dimensional feasible solution space is one where three boundary planes intersect.

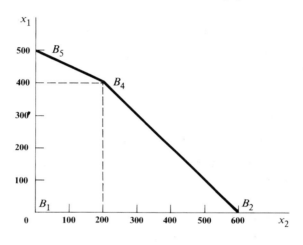

Figure 10.1

We note further that in Figure 10.1 all four basic feasible solutions correspond to extreme points of the feasible solution space. Therefore a basic feasible solution is also called an *extreme-point solution*.

A Fundamental Proposition

What is the significance of extreme-point solutions? To answer this question, we must return to the graphic method illustrated in the preceding chapter. We pointed out in connection with Figure 9.8 that an optimal solution may be obtained by drawing a line depicting the objective function in such a way that the line is farthest from the point of origin and yet contains at least one point belonging to the feasible solution space.

Let us now examine the following two feasible solution spaces. They are drawn somewhat arbitrarily to illustrate our next proposition. In Figure 10.2 only B_4 is an optimal feasible solution. But in Figure 10.3 any point between B_4 and B_5 is an optimal feasible solution. These two figures illustrate the following fundamental proposition in linear programming:

If a linear-programming problem has an optimal feasible solution, then at least one such optimal solution must be an extreme-point solution.

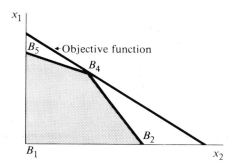

Figure 10.2

The validity of this proposition is apparent when we examine Figures 10.2 and 10.3. When the line representing the objective function is moved as far as possible from the point of origin so that it nevertheless contains at least one feasible point, this point, if it is unique, must be an extreme point, such as B_4 in Figure 10.2, or if it is not unique, must be on the line segment joining two extreme points, such as a point between B_4 and B_5 in Figure 10.3.

The proposition does not say that an optimal feasible solution is necessarily an extreme-point solution, merely that if there is an optimal feasible solution which is not an extreme-point solution, then we can always find an optimal feasible solution which is also an extreme-point solution.

This proposition is very important from the computational standpoint for the following reason. It implies that there is really no reason for us to examine any feasible solution which is not an extreme-point solution. Thus we can confine our search for an optimal feasible solution only among those solutions which correspond to the extreme points. Therefore, we can solve a linear-programming problem by just examining the basic feasible solutions, since every basic feasible solution is equivalent geometrically to an extreme-point solution.

The simplex method is based on a reasoning such as we have just described. A rough sketch of the method is given by the flow chart in Figure 10.4.

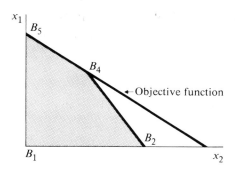

Figure 10.3

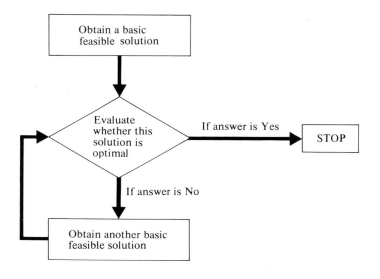

Figure 10.4

10.2 THE SIMPLEX METHOD: MECHANICS

We now proceed to the mechanics of the simplex method. Let us consider again the modified linear-programming formulation:

$$\max f = 150x_1 + 100x_2,$$
$$x_1 + x_2 + x_3 \quad\quad = 600,$$
$$2x_1 + x_2 + \quad\quad x_4 = 1000,$$

where the nonnegativity constraints are assumed. Since

$$f = 150x_1 + 100x_2$$

can be rearranged to read

$$f - 150x_1 - 100x_2 = 0,$$

we can express the modified linear-programming formulation as follows:

$$f - 150x_1 - 100x_2 = 0,$$
$$x_1 + x_2 + x_3 \quad\quad = 600,$$
$$2x_1 + x_2 + \quad\quad x_4 = 1000,$$

where it is assumed that f is to be maximized. Aligning the variables and moving x_3 and x_4 to the left, we have

$$f \quad\quad\quad - 150x_1 - 100x_2 = 0,$$
$$x_3 \quad + \quad x_1 + \quad x_2 = 600,$$
$$x_4 + \quad 2x_1 + \quad x_2 = 1000,$$

which can be expressed in the form:

f	x_3	x_4	x_1	x_2		
1	0	0	-150	-100	=	0
0	1	0	1	1	=	600
0	0	1	2	1	=	1000

Let us now examine the columns containing the coefficients of the first three variables f, x_3, and x_4. In the case of f, the first coefficient is 1 and the remaining coefficients are 0. In the case of x_3, the second coefficient is 1 and the remaining coefficients are 0. In the case of x_4, the third coefficient is 1 and the remaining coefficients are 0. A system of equations with such a set of characteristics is called a *canonical system* of equations. That is, a system of m linear equations is a canonical system if and only if among the first m variables in the equations the ith variable has a unit coefficient in the ith equation and zero coefficients in all other equations.

Initial Solution

One nice feature of a canonical system of equations is that the system will readily yield a basic feasible solution. In the case of the given canonical system, let us assign zero to the variables x_1 and x_2. Then the resulting equations are

$$f = 0, \qquad x_3 = 600, \qquad x_4 = 1000,$$

which is a basic feasible solution for the given linear-programming problem.

We recall that in obtaining our initial basic feasible solution, we arbitrarily assigned zero to x_1 and x_2. Such variables will be called *nonbasis variables*. The remaining variables, x_3 and x_4 in the given solution, will be called the *basis variables*. Together the basis variables will be referred to as a *basis*.

This initial basic feasible solution clearly cannot be optimal, since it specifies that resources alpha and beta remain entirely unused. But even though we do not need any elaborate analysis to know that this particular solution is not optimal, we will nevertheless carry out a systematic analysis to show that the solution is indeed not optimal.

We observe that the value of the objective function f for the solution is zero since the solution calls for no output of either Product 1 or Product 2. The solution cannot be optimal if some positive output of either Product 1 or Product 2 will increase the value of f.

To evaluate the impact of producing one unit of either Product 1 or Product 2, let us first rearrange our canonical system of equations as follows:

$$f = \quad 0 + 150x_1 + 100x_2,$$
$$x_3 = \quad 600 - \quad x_1 - \quad x_2,$$
$$x_4 = 1000 - \quad 2x_1 - \quad x_2.$$

This rearranged system of equations will readily tell us what will happen if we produce one unit of Product 1 or one unit of Product 2. Suppose, for example, we are to produce one unit of Product 1 and none of Product 2. Then $x_1 = 1$ and $x_2 = 0$. Substituting these values into our equations, we obtain

$$f = \quad 0 + 150(1) + 100(0) = 150,$$
$$x_3 = \quad 600 - \quad (1) - \quad (0) = 599,$$
$$x_4 = 1000 - \quad 2(1) - \quad (0) = 988,$$

which show that the value of f will increase by 150, the value of x_3 will decrease from 600 to 599, and that of x_4 will decrease from 1000 to 998.

Suppose, on the other hand, we are to produce none of Product 1 and one unit of Product 2. Then $x_1 = 0$ and $x_2 = 1$. Substituting these values into the equations, we obtain

$$f = \quad 0 + 150(0) + 100(1) = 100,$$
$$x_3 = \quad 600 - \quad (0) - \quad (1) = 599,$$
$$x_4 = 1000 - \quad 2(0) - \quad (1) = 999,$$

which show that the value of f will increase by 100, that of x_3 will decrease by 1 to 599, and that of x_4 will decrease by 1 to 999.

The obvious significance of our analysis is that we can improve our initial basic feasible solution by producing some units of either Product 1 or Product 2. Therefore, the present solution cannot be optimal.

Second Solution

According to the above analysis one unit of Product 1 will increase the value of f by 150, whereas one unit of Product 2 will increase the value of f by 100. Therefore, it seems sensible that we should produce some units of Product 1 before producing any of Product 2.

Let us assume that we have decided to produce some units of Product 1. Since the value of f will increase by 150 for each unit of Product 1 produced, we are inclined to produce as many units of Product 1 as possible. However, since one unit of Product 1 will use one unit of alpha and two units of beta, 600 units of Product 1 will exhaust the supply of alpha. But we cannot even produce 600 units of Product 1, because that would require 1200 units of beta where only 1000 units are available. Indeed, the maximum number of Product 1 that can be produced is 500 units.

This conclusion can be reached in a more systematic manner. Consider again the equations

$$f = \quad 0 + 150x_1,$$
$$x_3 = \quad 600 - \quad x_1,$$
$$x_4 = 1000 - \quad 2x_1.$$

The second equation indicates that the value of x_3 will become negative if x_1 is allowed to exceed 600. The third equation indicates that the value of x_4 will become negative if x_1 is allowed to exceed 500. Since neither x_3 nor x_4 can assume a negative value, the value of x_1 must not be allowed to exceed 500:

$$x_1 = \min \left\{ \tfrac{600}{1} = 600, \tfrac{1000}{2} = 500 \right\} = 500,$$

where the numerators of the ratios are the solution values of the basis variables and the denominators 1 and 2 are the coefficients in the x_1 column of the canonical system of equations.

Let us now substitute $x_1 = 500$ into the preceding equations. Then

$$
\begin{aligned}
&\quad\quad\quad\quad\quad\quad\quad \text{Solution} \\
&\quad\quad\quad\quad\quad\quad\quad \text{values} \\
&\quad\quad\quad\quad\quad\quad\quad \text{of } x_1 \\
&\quad\quad\quad\quad\quad\quad\quad\quad\downarrow \\
f &= \quad 0 + 150(500) = 75{,}000, \\
x_3 &= \quad 600 - \quad 1(500) = 100, \\
x_4 &= 1000 - \quad 2(500) = 0.
\end{aligned}
$$

Old solution values   New solution values

The above equations tell how our second basic feasible solution is related to the initial basic feasible solution. That is, if $x_1 = 0$, then $x_1, x_2 = 0$

$$f = 0, \quad\quad x_3 = 600, \quad\quad x_4 = 1000,$$

which is our initial basic feasible solution. On the other hand, if $x_1 = 500$, then $x_2, x_4 = 0$

$$f = 75{,}000, \quad\quad x_1 = 500, \quad\quad x_3 = 100,$$

which turns out to be our second basic feasible solution.

Before proceeding any further, let us review what we have done so far. We started out with an initial basic feasible solution,

$$f = 0, \quad x_1 = 0, \quad x_2 = 0, \quad x_3 = 600, \quad x_4 = 1000,$$

and determined that it was not optimal. We then obtained our second basic feasible solution,

$$f = 75{,}000, \quad x_1 = 500, \quad x_2 = 0, \quad x_3 = 100, \quad x_4 = 0.$$

Our next task is therefore to evaluate whether the second solution is optimal. This evaluation is readily done if we have the canonical system of equations for this solution.

Obtaining the New Canonical System

The canonical system of equations for the second basic feasible solution can be obtained from that of the initial basic feasible solution by a number of simple algebraic operations. First, we take the initial canonical system

$$
\begin{aligned}
f \quad\quad\quad &- 150x_1 - 100x_2 = 0, \\
x_3 \quad + \quad & x_1 + \quad x_2 = 600, \\
x_4 + \quad & 2x_1 + \quad x_2 = 1000,
\end{aligned}
$$

and rearrange it as follows:

$$f \qquad\qquad - 150x_1 \qquad\quad - 100x_2 = 0,$$
$$x_3 \quad + \quad x_1 \quad + \qquad x_2 = 600,$$
$$2x_1 + x_4 + \qquad x_2 = 1000.$$

In this new arrangement the positions of the x_1- and x_4-terms are switched so that x_1 will replace x_4 as the new basis variable.

It is an axiom of algebra that what are called *elementary row operations* do not affect an equation system. The following are elementary row operations:

1. Multiply an equation by a nonzero constant.
2. Add to an equation a nonzero multiple of another equation.

These elementary row operations can be used to solve an equation system. Indeed, they can also be used to obtain the canonical system for the new basic feasible solution. Thus we shall multiply the third equation in the rearranged system by 0.5:

$$f \qquad\qquad - 150x_1 \qquad\quad - 100x_2 = 0,$$
$$x_3 + \quad x_1 \qquad + \qquad x_2 = 600,$$
$$x_1 + 0.5x_4 + 0.5x_2 = 500.$$

Then multiplying the third equation again by 150 and adding the resulting equation to the first equation, we obtain

$$f \qquad\qquad + 75x_4 - 25x_2 = 75,000,$$
$$x_3 + x_1 \qquad\quad + \qquad x_2 = 600,$$
$$x_1 + 0.5x_4 + 0.5x_2 = 500.$$

Multiplying the third equation again by -1 and adding the resulting equation to the second equation, we have

$$f \qquad\qquad + 75x_4 - 25x_2 = 75,000,$$
$$x_3 \qquad - 0.5x_4 + 0.5x_2 = 100,$$
$$x_1 + 0.5x_4 + 0.5x_2 = 500.$$

Now the system of equations is in canonical form. If we let $x_4 = 0$ and $x_2 = 0$, then

$$f = 75,000, \qquad x_3 = 100, \qquad x_1 = 500,$$

which is our second basic feasible solution.

Evaluating Optimality

We shall now check to see whether our second basic feasible solution is optimal. First, let us rearrange our second canonical system as follows:

$$f = 75,000 - 75x_4 + 25x_2,$$
$$x_3 = \qquad 100 + 0.5x_4 - 0.5x_2,$$
$$x_1 = \qquad 500 - 0.5x_4 - 0.5x_2.$$

This rearranged system of equations will tell us what will happen if we let $x_4 = 1$ or $x_2 = 1$.

Suppose we let $x_2 = 1$ and $x_4 = 0$. Substituting these values into our equation, we have

$$f = 75,000 - 75(0) + 25(1) = 75,025,$$
$$x_3 = 100 \quad 0.5(0) - 0.5(1) = 99.5,$$
$$x_1 = 500 - 0.5(0) - 0.5(1) = 499.5,$$

which show that the value of f will increase by 25, that of x_3 will decrease by 0.5, and that of x_1 will also decrease by 0.5.

A similar analysis will show that if we let $x_2 = 0$ and $x_4 = 1$, the value of f will decrease by 75, that of x_3 will increase by 0.5, and that of x_1 will decrease by 0.5.

The solution is obviously not optimal, since a unit positive output of Product 2 will increase the total revenue by \$25.

Third Solution

Since producing one unit of Product 2 will increase the value of f by \$25, producing more than one unit of Product 2 should increase the value of f even more. But we have already pointed out that 1 unit of Product 2 will reduce the output of Product 1 by 0.5 unit and at the same time use up 0.5 unit of alpha. Consequently, we cannot produce an arbitrarily large quantity of Product 2. To determine the upper limit of x_2, let us consider again the system of equations

$$f = 75,000 + 25x_2,$$
$$x_3 = 100 - 0.5x_2,$$
$$x_1 = 500 - 0.5x_2.$$

The second equation indicates that the value of x_3 will become negative if x_2 exceeds 200. The third equation indicates that the value of x_1 will become negative if x_2 exceeds 1000. Therefore, the maximum allowable value of x_2 for the third solution is 200:

$$x_2 = \min\{100/0.5 = 200, 500/0.5 = 1000\} = 200.$$

Here again the numerators of the ratios are the solution values of the basis variables, and the denominators are the corresponding coefficients of the x_2 column in the canonical system of equations for the second solution.

Substituting $x_2 = 200$ into the above equations, we have

Solution
value of
x_2
↓

$$f = 75,000 + 25(200) = 80,000,$$
$$x_3 = 100 - 0.5(200) = 0,$$
$$x_1 = 500 - 0.5(200) = 400.$$

       ↑   ↑_____↑

Old   New
solution   solution
values   values

The above system of equations reveals that our third basic feasible solution is: $x_3, x_4 = 0$

$$f = 80{,}000, \quad x_1 = 400, \quad x_2 = 200, \quad x_3 = 0, \quad x_4 = 0.$$

The value of the objective function may also be arrived at as follows:

$$f = 150x_1 + 100x_2 = 150(400) + 100(200) = 80{,}000.$$

Obtaining the Third Canonical System

Before checking to see whether our third solution is optimal, let us first obtain the canonical system for this solution. Rearranging the canonical system for the second solution, we have

$$
\begin{aligned}
f - 25x_2 \quad\quad + 75x_4 \quad\quad &= 75{,}000, \\
+ 0.5x_2 \quad\quad - 0.5x_4 + x_3 &= 100, \\
+ 0.5x_2 + x_1 + 0.5x_4 \quad\quad &= 500.
\end{aligned}
$$

Multiplying the second equation by 50 and adding the resulting equation to the first equation, we have

$$
\begin{aligned}
f \quad\quad\quad + 50x_4 + 50x_3 &= 80{,}000, \\
0.5x_2 \quad\quad - 0.5x_4 + \quad x_3 &= 100, \\
0.5x_2 + x_1 + 0.5x_4 \quad\quad &= 500.
\end{aligned}
$$

Multiplying the second equation by -1 and adding it to the third equation, we have

$$
\begin{aligned}
f \quad\quad\quad + 50x_4 + 50x_3 &= 80{,}000, \\
0.5x_2 \quad\quad - 0.5x_4 + \quad x_3 &= 100, \\
x_1 \quad\quad x_4 - \quad x_3 &= 400.
\end{aligned}
$$

Finally, multiplying the second equation by 2, we have

$$
\begin{aligned}
f \quad\quad\quad + 50x_4 + 50x_3 &= 80{,}000, \\
x_2 \quad\quad - \quad x_4 + 2x_3 &= 200, \\
x_1 + \quad x_4 - \quad x_3 &= 400.
\end{aligned}
$$

which are in canonical form.

Evaluating Optimality

We observe that in this canonical system the first coefficient of x_3 is 50. This means that if we let $x_3 = 1$, then the value of f will decrease by 50. Similarly, the value of f will decrease by 50 if we let $x_4 = 1$. Therefore the solution is an optimal solution for the given linear-programming problem.

If we now return to the graphic analysis of the preceding chapter, we will find that our third basic feasible solution is indeed the same as the optimal solution obtained there.

10.3 A REVIEW OF THE PROCEDURE

Let us now review the mechanics of the simplex method as presented in Section 10.2. First, we obtained a canonical system of equations for a basic feasible solution. Then we checked the solution for optimality by examining the coefficients of the nonbasis variables in the top row of the canonical system and discovered that the solution was not optimal because the coefficient was negative. The incoming variable was then found to have the smallest coefficient in the top row. Next, the outgoing variables were determined by dividing the solution values of the basis variables by the corresponding coefficients of the incoming variable in the canonical system of equations. The smaller of these ratios turned out to be the outgoing variable. Then we obtained the canonical system of equations for the new basic feasible solution.

Once we obtained the canonical system for the new solution, we repeated the same sequence of steps to determine whether the solution was optimal. And since the solution was again not optimal, still another canonical system was obtained for a third solution, and the same steps were repeated. This procedure eventually led to an optimal solution.

In proceeding as we did, however, we overlooked an important detail in connection with the determination of the outgoing variables. Suppose the following canonical system is an abstraction of a basic feasible solution of a linear-programming problem:

$$
\begin{aligned}
f \qquad\qquad\quad -100x_5 \quad &\qquad\qquad = 200{,}000, \\
x_1 \qquad\quad + 2x_5 \quad &\text{Columns} \qquad = 800, \\
x_2 \quad\; - 4x_5 \quad &\text{for the} \qquad = 200, \\
x_3 \; + 0x_5 \quad &\text{remaining} \quad = 500, \\
x_4 + 3x_5 \quad &\text{variables} \qquad = 600.
\end{aligned}
$$

The top coefficient -100 of x_5 indicates that the solution can be improved by bringing x_5 into the basis. Consider now the following rearrangement of the canonical system:

$$
\begin{aligned}
f &= 20{,}000 + 100x_5, \\
x_1 &= 800 - 2x_5, \\
x_2 &= 200 + 4x_5, \\
x_3 &= 500 - 0x_5, \\
x_4 &= 600 - 3x_5.
\end{aligned}
$$

The third row of this system shows that the value of x_2 will actually increase by 4 per unit increase of x_5, and the fourth row shows that the value of x_3 will remain the same as we increase the value of x_5. Consequently, we do not have to worry about the values of x_2 and x_3 becoming negative with increasing values of x_5. The values of x_1 and x_4 can, however, become negative if x_5 becomes sufficiently large. The largest allowable value of x_5 is:

$$
x_5 = \min \left\{ \tfrac{800}{2} = 400, \tfrac{600}{3} = 200 \right\} = 200.
$$

Note that the denominators of the two ratios are both positive. Thus in the process of determining the value of the outgoing variable, we can ignore the zero and negative coefficients in the incoming-variable column.

10.4   SIMPLEX TABLEAU

The computations in the simplex method can be made even more systematic by using the so-called *simplex tableau,* which is a table containing all the relevant information on a basic feasible solution of a linear-programming problem.

Consider again the linear-programming problem of Alpha Beta Manufacturing:

$$\max f = 150x_1 + 100x_2,$$
$$x_1 + x_2 + x_3 = 600,$$
$$2x_1 + x_2 + x_4 = 1000,$$

where x_1 and x_2 are respectively the quantities of Product 1 and Product 2, and x_3 and x_4 are respectively the slack variables indicating the unused quantities of alpha and beta.

Initial Simplex Tableau

We assume now that our initial basic feasible solution is given by

$$x_3 = 600, \quad x_4 = 1000, \quad x_1 = 0, \quad x_2 = 0.$$

The simplex tableau for this solution is as follows:

Basis variables	Basis prices	x_1	x_2	x_3	x_4	Solution values
x_3	0	1	1	1	0	600
x_4	0	2	1	0	1	1000
Increased revenues		-150	-100	0	0	0

We note that this tableau is merely a rearrangement of the canonical system of equations for the initial basic feasible solution. The canonical system for this solution is

$$f \qquad - 150x_1 - 100x_2 = 0,$$
$$x_3 \quad + \quad x_1 + \quad x_2 = 600,$$
$$x_4 + \quad 2x_1 + \quad x_2 = 1000.$$

Bringing down the first row to the bottom, we have

$$x_3 \quad + \quad x_1 + \quad x_2 = 600,$$
$$x_4 + \quad 2x_1 + \quad x_2 = 1000,$$
$$f \qquad - 150x_1 - 100x_2 = 0.$$

Moving the variables x_3 and x_4 to the right, we have

$$x_1 + \quad x_2 + x_3 \quad\quad = 600,$$
$$2x_1 + \quad x_2 \quad\quad + x_4 = 1000,$$
$$f \quad - 150x_1 - 100x_2 \quad\quad = 0,$$

which arrangement corresponds to the arrangement of the coefficients in the simplex tableau.

Tableau Headings

Headings are used in the simplex tableau so that we can easily associate the coefficients with the variables in the tableau. We see in the first column that x_3 and x_4 are the basis variables for the initial solution. The next column shows that the prices for the basis variables are zero. The last column indicates that the solution values of the basis variables are

$$x_3 = 600, \quad\quad x_4 = 1000,$$

and that the value of the objective function is zero:

$$f = 0.$$

Now let us consider the x_1 column. The first two entries show that if we increase the value of x_1 by 1, then the values of x_3 and x_4 will decrease by 1 and 2, respectively. The bottom entry indicates that the value of f will increase by 150 with a unit increase of x_1. These are the same conclusions as we reached earlier by examining the equations

$$x_3 = \quad 600 - \quad\quad x_1,$$
$$x_4 = 1000 - \quad\quad 2x_1,$$
$$f = \quad\quad 0 - (-150)x_1.$$

The x_2, x_3, and x_4 columns lend themselves to similar interpretations.

Increased Revenues

Let us now reexamine the bottom row of the simplex tableau. It was pointed out that the -150 corresponding to the x_1 column implies that the f will increase by 150 when x_1 is increased by 1. Since f stands for total revenue, we will call this -150 the *increased revenue* associated with x_1. Indeed, all the bottom-row entries in the nonbasis variable columns will be called increased revenues.

What is meant by increased revenues, however, requires careful considera-tion. As we pointed out earlier, if f is the total revenue and the increased revenue is negative for a particular variable, then the total revenue will increase when the variable in question increases in value. But if the increased revenue is positive, then the total revenue will actually decrease with increas-ing values of the variable in question.

If, on the other hand, f is the total cost instead, then the bottom-row coefficients will indicate how the total cost will be affected by changing the solution values of the variables. Therefore, the coefficients are sometimes also called the *reduced costs*. We will always call them increased revenues, however.

In the initial solution the increased revenues are equal to the prices of the same variables, but the economic meanings are of course not the same.

Now let us assume that x_1 is increased from 0 to 1, meaning that the output in the form of Product 1 will increase from 0 to 1. Since the unit price of Product 1 is \$150, one unit of Product 1 will obviously generate \$150 in revenue. However, the total revenue f will also increase by \$150 only if there is no compensating decrease in the total revenue caused by the production of one unit of Product 1.

To determine whether there are such compensating decreases in the value of f, we must consider the adjustments that have to be made to accommodate the change in x_1. For example, we pointed out earlier that the value of x_3 will decrease by 1 and that of x_4 will decrease by 2 with a unit increase in x_1. But x_3 and x_4 represent the unused quantities of alpha and beta with a zero price. So if we let z_1 be the loss of revenue due to the adjustments required by the production of 1 unit of Product 1, then since the prices for x_3 and x_4 are zero, we have

$$z_1 = (c_3 \times 1) + (c_4 \times 2)$$
$$= (0 \times 1) + (0 \times 2) = 0.$$

Therefore,

$$c_1 - z_1 = 150 - 0 = 150$$

is the net increase in the value of f when x_1 increases from 0 to 1. Recalling that the increased revenue for x_1 is -150, we can define this increased revenue as $z_1 - c_1$:

$$z_1 - c_1 = 0 - 150 = -150.$$

Similarly, the increased revenue for x_2 is defined as

$$z_2 - c_2 = 0 - 100 = -100,$$

where

$$z_2 = (c_3 \times 1) + (c_4 \times 1)$$
$$= (0 \times 1) + (0 \times 1) = 0.$$

The increased revenues for the remaining variables are:

$$z_3 - c_3 = (c_3 \times 1) + (c_4 \times 0) - c_3$$
$$= (0 \times 1) + (0 \times 0) - 0 = 0,$$
$$z_4 - c_4 = (c_3 \times 0) + (c_4 \times 1) - c_4$$
$$= (0 \times 0) + (0 \times 1) - 0 = 0.$$

Evaluating Optimality

Now let us assume that in a given basic feasible solution the increased revenue for a nonbasis variable is negative. Then, according to the preceding discussion, the value of f can be further increased by letting the nonbasis variable in question assume some positive value. For example, in the initial basic feasible solution

$$z_1 - c_1 = -150 \quad \text{and} \quad z_2 - c_2 = -100$$

imply that the value of f can be increased by letting either x_1 or x_2 assume some positive values.

If a given solution shows that the value of f can be further increased, then that solution cannot be optimal, which in turn suggests that a solution cannot be optimal if the increased revenue for any variable is negative in that solution. Therefore, once we have obtained the simplex tableau for a solution, we can determine whether the solution is optimal by rather mechanical means. If all the increased revenues, found in the bottom row of the tableau, are nonnegative, then the solution is optimal. However, if any nonbasis variable has a negative increased revenue, then we can improve on the solution by bringing that variable into the basis.

Incoming Variable

We observe that our initial basic feasible solution can be improved on by bringing either x_1 or x_2 into the basis. We note, however, that one unit of x_1 will increase the value of f by 150, whereas one unit of x_2 will increase the value of f by 100. Since one unit of x_1 will increase the value of f by a greater amount than a unit of x_2, it is better to bring x_1 into the basis. Thus we make x_1 the *incoming variable* and call the x_1 column the *pivot column*.

Therefore, given a simplex tableau where some increased revenues are negative, we will let that column be the pivot column which has the smallest increased revenue, that is, the increased revenue with the largest absolute value.

Outgoing Variable

We decide to bring x_1 into the basis; then, since a basic feasible solution can have only two variables in the basis, we must remove one variable from the original basis. Which variable should be removed may be determined in the following manner.

In the preceding chapter we obtained the following maximum possible value of x_1:

$$x_1 = \min \{ \tfrac{600}{1} = 600, \tfrac{1000}{2} = 500 \} = 500.$$

The numerators of the two ratios in this equation belong in the solution values column, whereas the denominators are elements in the pivot column. For this equation we can write:

Basis variables	x_1	Solution values	Ratios
x_3	1	600	$\frac{600}{1} = 600$
x_4	2	1000	$\frac{1000}{2} = 500 \leftarrow$ pivot row

$$\uparrow$$
pivot
column

We note that the ratio $\frac{100}{2} = 500$ corresponds to x_4 in the basis variable column, indicating that x_4 is the variable which must be removed from the basis. The row corresponding to x_4 will be called the *pivot row*, and x_4 will be called the *outgoing variable*.

In general, the pivot row of a simplex tableau may be determined according to the following rule:

Divide the positive coefficients of the pivot column, excluding the increased revenue, into the corresponding elements in the solution values column. The pivot row is that which has the smallest of the resulting ratios.

Obtaining a New Solution

Since a simplex tableau contains all the relevant information on a solution, any new solution which is obtained can be evaluated by means of a corresponding simplex tableau. Another advantage of having a simplex tableau is that one simplex tableau contains all relevant information needed to construct the simplex tableau for a new solution.

For easy reference we present again the simplex tableau for our initial solution:

Basis variables	Basis prices	x_1	x_2	x_3	x_4	Solution values	Ratios
x_3	0	1	1	1	0	600	600
x_4	0	②	1	0	1	1000	500 ← pivot row
Increased revenues		−150	−100	0	0	0	

pivot↑
column

The fact that the pivot column here corresponds to x_1 implies that x_1 should be brought into the basis, and the fact that the pivot row corresponds to x_4 implies that x_4 should be removed from the basis.

Note that the circled number 2 is an element in the pivot column as well as an element in the pivot row. Such a number will be called the *pivot element* and will play a useful role in the subsequent computations.

The replacement of x_4 in the present basis by a new basis variable x_1 must be reflected in the rest of the simplex tableau. Thus it will lead to an entirely new tableau. We shall begin the construction of this simplex tableau by writing:

Basis variables	Basis prices	x_1	x_2	x_3	x_4	Solution values
x_3	0					
x_1	150					
Increased revenues						

Our next task is to make the numerical calculations for the remaining parts of the new simplex tableau. The calculations may be divided into two stages.

First-Stage Calculations   *First, we divide the elements in the pivot row of the original simplex tableau by its pivot element. The resulting values constitute the corresponding row for the new simplex tableau.*

Thus we have:

Basis variables	Basis prices	x_1	x_2	x_3	x_4	Solution values
x_3	0					
x_1	150	1	0.5	0	0.5	500
Increased revenues						

Second-Stage Calculations   We let

E_{ij} = the element of the old tableau in row i and column j,

E_{ij}^* = the element of the new tableau in row i and column j,

E_{ip} = the ith element in the pivot column of the old simplex tableau,

E_{pj}^* = the jth element in the pivot row of the new simplex tableau.

Then the remaining elements of the new simplex tableau may be ascertained by the rule:

$$E_{ij}^* = E_{ij} - E_{ip}E_{pj}^*.$$

To illustrate how we can apply this rule, let us first use the initial simplex tableau to clarify our use of the notation E_{ij}:

	Basis variables	Basis prices	x_1	x_2	x_3	x_4	Solution values
pivot row →	x_3	0	$E_{1p} = 1$	$E_{12} = 1$	$E_{13} = 1$	$E_{14} = 0$	$E_{15} = 600$
	x_4	0	$E_{2p} = 2$	$E_{22} = 1$	$E_{23} = 0$	$E_{24} = 1$	$E_{25} = 1000$
	Increased revenues		$E_{3p} = 150$	$E_{23} = 100$	$E_{33} = 0$	$E_{34} = 0$	$E_{35} = 0$

↑
pivot
column

The first-stage calculations yielded this much of the new tableau:

Basis variables	Basis prices	x_1	x_2	x_3	x_4	Solution values
x_3	0					
x_1	150	$E_{p1}^* = 1$	$E_{p2}^* = 0.5$	$E_{p3}^* = 0$	$E_{p4}^* = 0.5$	$E_{p5}^* = 500$
Increased revenues						

We can now proceed to complete the new tableau as follows. Let us first obtain E_{11}^*:

$$E_{11}^* = E_{11} - E_{1p}E_{p1}^* = 1 - (1)(1) = 0.$$

As to the rest, we have

$$E_{12}^* = E_{12} - E_{1p}E_{p2}^* = 1 - (1)(0.5) = 0.5,$$
$$E_{15}^* = E_{15} - E_{1p}E_{p5}^* = 600 - (1)(500) = 100.$$

The completed tableau for the new solution is:

Basis variables	Basis prices	x_1	x_2	x_3	x_4	Solution values
x_3	0	0	0.5	1	-0.5	100
x_1	150	1	0.5	0	0.5	500
Increased revenues		0	-25	0	75	75,000

↑
pivot
column

Second Simplex Tableau

Let us now examine our second simplex tableau closely. The last column shows that the solution values of the variables and the objective function are:

$$x_1 = 500, \quad x_2 = 0, \quad x_3 = 100, \quad x_4 = 0, \quad f = 75,000.$$

Suppose we want to increase the solution value of x_2 from 0 to 1 unit. Then the first two elements of the x_2 column indicate that an optimal adjustment will require that we reduce the solution values of the current basis variables x_1 and x_3 by 0.5 unit each.

We can justify these adjustments as follows. Our second basic feasible solution calls for 500 units of Product 1. Producing 500 units of Product 1, however, will exhaust all the available supplies of beta. Thus the only way that we can produce 1 unit of Product 2 is to reduce the output of Product 1 by 0.5 unit. This is what is meant by the value of x_1 having to decrease by 0.5 when that of x_2 is increased by 1.

There is another adjustment which will have to be made to our second basic feasible solution when the output of Product 2 is to be increased by one unit. To produce one unit of Product 2, we will need one unit of alpha. However, when the output of Product 1 is reduced by 0.5 unit, 0.5 unit of alpha will also be released. Consequently, the net requirement of alpha per unit of Product 1 is only 0.5 unit. This is what is meant by the conclusion that if we let $x_2 = 1$, then the value of x_3 will decline by 0.5.

The bottom row of the simplex tableau indicates that the increased revenue for x_2 is -25, meaning that the value of f will increase by 25 if that of x_2 is increased by 1. How can this be so in light of the fact that the unit price of Product 2 is \$100? We recall that in order to produce one unit of Product 2, we must reduce the output of Product 1 by 0.5 unit. Since the price of Product

1 is \$150, the loss in revenue caused by the reduction in output of Product 1 is \$75. Thus the net increase in the total revenue is only \$25.

If z_2 is the loss of revenue due to the adjustments in the present solution occasioned by one unit of Product 2, then

$$z_2 = (c_3 \times 0.5) + (c_1 \times 0.5)$$
$$= (0 \times 0.5) + (150 \times 0.5) = 75.$$

Therefore, the increased revenue for x_2 is

$$z_2 - c_2 = 75 - 100 = -25,$$

as shown by the bottom element of the x_2 column.

The increased revenues for the other variables are obtained in a similar way.

Evaluating Optimality Again

Having obtained our second simplex tableau, we can evaluate the new solution for optimality by just examining the bottom row. We note that

$$z_2 - c_2 = -25.$$

Since this quantity is negative, we conclude that the solution is not optimal.

A New Iteration Phase

Since the solution given by the second simplex tableau is not optimal, we must repeat the whole procedure to obtain a third simplex tableau.

The pivot column in the above simplex tableau indicates to us which variable is to be brought into the basis. The process of determining the pivot row and therefore the variable to be removed from the present basis is illustrated below.

Basis variables	x_2	Solution values	Ratios	
x_3	(0.5)	100	$100/0.5 = 200$ ←	pivot row
x_1	0.5	500	$500/0.5 = 1000$	
	↑ pivot column			

We see that x_3 is the outgoing variable. The pivot element in our second simplex tableau is the circled number.

Having identified the pivot element, we can now proceed to the first-stage calculations in the construction of our third simplex tableau. Dividing the elements of the pivot row by the pivot element, we obtain

Basis variables	Basis prices	x_1	x_2	x_3	x_4	Solution values
x_2	100	0	1	2	-1	200
x_1	150					
Increased revenues						

The rest of the tableau is obtained by the second-stage calculations. For example,

$$E^*_{13} = E_{13} - E_{1p}E^*_{p3} = 0 - (0.5)(2) = -1,$$
$$E^*_{33} = E_{33} - E_{3p}E^*_{p3} = 0 - (25)(2) = -50$$

complete the column for x_3, and

$$E^*_{25} = E_{25} - E_{2p}E^*_{p5} = 500 - (0.5)(200) = 400,$$
$$E^*_{35} = E_{35} - E_{3p}E^*_{p5} = 75,000 - (25)(200) = 80,000$$

complete the solution values column. The completed tableau is presented below.

Basis variables	Basis prices	x_1	x_2	x_3	x_4	Solution values
x_2	100	0	1	2	-1	200
x_1	500	1	0	-1	1	400
Increased revenues		0	0	50	50	80,000

We observe that our third basic feasible solution is optimal, since the increased revenues are all nonnegative. This solution, as given by the above simplex tableau, is

$$x_1 = 400, \quad x_2 = 200, \quad x_3 = 0, \quad x_4 = 0,$$

with $f = 80,000$.

10.5 MULTIPLE OPTIMA

Our illustrative programming problem was designed to have a unique optimal solution. Other linear-programming problems, however, may each have more than one optimal solution.

Consider, for example, the following linear-programming problem:

$$\max f = 150x_1 + 100x_2 + 250x_3,$$
$$x_1 + x_2 + 2x_3 \le 600,$$
$$2x_1 + x_2 + 3x_3 \le 1000,$$

with the usual nonnegativity constraints. The following tableau depicts a basic feasible solution for this problem.

Basis variables	Basis prices	x_1	x_2	x_3	x_4	x_5	Solution values	Ratios
x_3	250	0	1	1	2	-1	200	200
x_1	150	1	-1	0	-3	2	200	
Increased revenues		0	0	0	50	50	80,000	

We note that the increased revenues are nonnegative for all variables. Therefore, the solution is optimal. On the other hand, $z_2 - c_2 = 0$, which means that the value of f will remain the same even if we bring x_2 into the basis. We will then have the following simplex tableau.

Basis variables	Basis prices	x_1	x_2	x_3	x_4	x_5	Solution values
x_2	100	0	1	1	2	−1	200
x_1	150	1	0	1	−1	1	400
Increased revenues		0	0	0	50	50	80,000

Here again all the increased revenues are nonnegative, so that the solution is optimal.

The two optimal solutions can be summarized as follows:

First optimal solution	Second optimal solution
$x_1 = 200$	$x_1 = 400$
$x_3 = 200$	$x_2 = 200$
$f = 80,000$	$f = 80,000$

10.6 OTHER COMPUTATIONAL ISSUES

Now let us examine some of the unusual problems that might confront us in simplex iterations.

Degeneracy

We have assumed that we can always determine uniquely the variable that must be removed from a basis, but this is not always true. Consider the following linear-programming problem:

$$\max f = 4x_1 + 3x_2,$$
$$2x_1 + x_2 + x_3 = 100,$$
$$x_1 + x_2 + x_4 = 500,$$

with the usual nonnegativity constraints. The initial basic feasible solution is given by the following tableau:

Basis variables	Basis prices	x_1	x_2	x_3	x_4	Solution values	Ratios
x_3	0	②	1	1	0	1000	$\frac{1000}{2} = 500$
x_4	0	1	1	0	1	500	$\frac{500}{1} = 500$
Increased revenues		−4	−3	0	0		

The tableau indicates that x_1 should be brought into the basis. The last column, however, shows that the minimum ratio is not unique, which means that we can remove either x_3 or x_4 from the basis.

Since x_3 and x_4 are, in a sense, tied, the procedure for deciding which of the two variables to remove from the basis may be called a *tie-breaking procedure*. One very simple way is to remove the variable having the smallest subscript. In the above example, then, x_3 would be removed from the basis, yielding the following simplex tableau:

Basis variables	Basis prices	x_1	x_2	x_3	x_4	Solution values	Ratios
x_1	4	1	0.5	0.5	0	500	1000
x_4	0	0	0.5	−0.5	1	0	0
Increased revenues		0	−1	2	0	2000	

We observe that one of the basis variables, namely x_4, assumes zero value in the solution. Such a solution is called a *degenerate solution*. Suppose that now we obtain another new solution by bringing x_2 into the basis. Then as indicated by the entries in the ratio column above, the value of x_2 will be zero in the new solution, which will therefore also be degenerate.

It is possible that once we have obtained a degenerate solution, all of the succeeding solutions will turn out to be degenerate. This will happen if the same sequence of the basic feasible solutions is obtained over and over, that is, when the simplex iterations are said to be in a *cycle*.

If the simplex iterations get trapped in such a cycle, obviously we cannot obtain an optimum solution even though it exists. A number of very elaborate tie-breaking procedures have been devised to prevent the simplex iterations from cyclical entrapment. However, it has been found that in actual application problems the simplex iterations rarely fall into cycles. Therefore, we really do not have to be concerned with elaborate tie-breaking procedures.

Unbounded Solution

Let us now consider the following linear-programming problem:

$$\max f = x_1 + 2x_2,$$
$$x_1 - x_2 \leq 1,$$
$$x_1 \leq 4,$$

with the usual nonnegativity constraints. The following tableau depicts a basic feasible solution obtained in terms of the slack variables x_3 and x_4.

Basis variables	Basis prices	x_1	x_2	x_3	x_4	Solution values
x_3	0	1	−1	1	0	1
x_4	0	1	0	0	1	4
Increased revenues		−1	−2	0	0	0

We note that the increased revenue for x_2 is -2, indicating that an improved solution can be obtained by bringing x_2 into the basis. On the other hand, the remaining coefficients in the x_2 column are all nonpositive, meaning that x_2 can become infinitely large without x_3 and x_4 becoming negative. Therefore, f can become infinitely large; that is, f has no upper bound. A solution of a linear-programming problem in which f has no upper bound is said to be an *unbounded solution*. And as suggested by our illustration, a linear-programming problem has an unbounded solution if at any stage during simplex iterations a column appears all of whose elements are nonpositive.

An unbound solution, however, is too good to be true in reality. What is likely to have happened is that some pertinent constraints were overlooked in the formulation of the linear-programming problem.

EXERCISES

1. Formulate the modified system of constraints for the following linear-programming problem:

$$\max f = 3x_1 + 2x_2,$$
$$x_1 + 2x_2 \leq 80,$$
$$2x_1 + x_2 \leq 100,$$
$$x_1 \geq 0, \quad x_2 \geq 0.$$

Then obtain all the basic solutions for the modified system.

2. Which among the basic solutions obtained in Exercise 1 are also feasible? Which among the basic feasible solutions is the optimal solution?

3. Depict the feasible solution space of the linear-programming problem in Exercise 1 in a graph. Indicate on the graph the basic feasible solutions obtained in Exercise 2, including the optimal solution.

4. Formulate the modified system of constraints for the following linear-programming problem:

$$\max f = 10x_1 + 5x_2,$$
$$x_1 + x_2 \leq 300,$$
$$2x_1 + x_2 \leq 500,$$
$$x_1 \geq 0, \quad x_2 \geq 0.$$

Then obtain all the basic solutions for the modified system.

5. Among the basic solutions obtained in Exercise 4, which are also feasible? Which is the optimal solution among the basic feasible solutions?

6. Graphically depict the feasible solution space of the linear-programming problem of Exercise 4. Indicate on this graph the basic feasible solutions obtained in Exercise 5, as well as the optimal solution.

7. Given the linear-programming problem

$$\max f = 2x_1 + 3x_2,$$
$$x_1 + x_2 + x_3 = 40,$$
$$x_1 + 2x_2 + x_4 = 60,$$

find all the basic feasible solutions. Then obtain the optimal basic feasible solution.

8. Solve the following linear-programming problem by means of the simplex method and using canonical formulations:

$$\max f = 3x_1 + 2x_2,$$
$$x_1 + 2x_2 \leq 80,$$
$$2x_1 + x_2 \leq 100,$$
$$x_1, x_2 \geq 0.$$

9. Solve the following linear-programming problem by means of the simplex method and using canonical formulations:

$$\max f = 10x_1 + 5x_2,$$
$$x_1 + x_2 \leq 300,$$
$$2x_1 + x_2 \leq 500,$$
$$x_1, x_2 \geq 0.$$

10. Solve the following linear-programming problem by means of the simplex method and using canonical formulations:

$$\max f = 2x_1 + x_2 + 3x_3,$$
$$x_1 + x_2 + 2x_3 \leq 400,$$
$$2x_1 + x_2 + x_3 \leq 500,$$
$$x_1, x_2, x_3 \geq 0.$$

11. Solve the following linear-programming problem by means of the simplex method and using canonical formulations:

$$\max f = 3x_1 + 2x_2,$$
$$x_1 + 2x_2 \leq 100,$$
$$x_1 + x_2 \leq 60,$$
$$2x_1 + x_2 \leq 100,$$
$$x_1, x_2 \geq 0.$$

12. Solve the following linear-programming problem by means of simplex tableaus:

$$\max f = 3x_1 + 2x_2,$$
$$x_1 + 2x_2 \leq 80,$$
$$2x_1 + x_2 \leq 100,$$
$$x_1, x_2 \geq 0.$$

13. Solve the following linear-programming problem by means of simplex tableaus:

$$\max f = 10x_1 + 5x_2,$$
$$x_1 + x_2 \le 300,$$
$$2x_1 + x_2 \le 500,$$
$$x_1, x_2 \ge 0.$$

14. Solve the following linear-programming problem by means of simplex tableaus:

$$\max f = 2x_1 + x_2 + 3x_3,$$
$$x_1 + x_2 + 2x_3 \le 400,$$
$$2x_1 + x_2 + x_3 \le 500,$$
$$x_1, x_2, x_3 \ge 0.$$

15. Solve the following linear-programming problem by means of simplex tableaus:

$$\max f = 3x_1 + 2x_2,$$
$$x_1 + 2x_2 \le 100,$$
$$x_1 + x_2 \le 60,$$
$$2x_1 + x_2 \le 100,$$
$$x_1, x_2 \ge 0.$$

16. Solve the linear-programming problem given in Exercise 15 with the difference that

$$\max f = 2x_1 + 3x_2.$$

17. We are given the linear-programming problem

$$\max f = 8x_1 + 10x_2 + 14x_3,$$
$$x_1 + x_2 + 2x_3 + x_4 = 200,$$
$$x_1 + 2x_2 + x_3 + x_5 = 300,$$

with the usual nonnegativity constraints, and the following optimal simplex tableau:

Basis variables	Basis prices	x_1	x_2	x_3	x_4	x_5	Solution values
x_1	8	1	0	3	2	-1	100
x_2	10	0	1	-1	-1	1	100
Increased revenues		0	0	0	6	2	1800

Does the problem have another optimum solution? If so, what is the corresponding simplex tableau?

18. We are given the linear programming problem

$$\max f = 10x_1 + 6x_2 + 16x_3,$$
$$x_1 + x_2 + 2x_3 + x_4 = 400,$$
$$2x_1 + x_2 + 3x_3 + x_5 = 500,$$

with the usual nonnegativity constraints, and the following optimal simplex tableau:

Basis variables	Basis prices	x_1	x_2	x_3	x_4	x_5	Solution values
x_1	10	1	0	1	-1	1	100
x_2	6	0	1	1	2	-1	300
Increased revenues		0	0	0	2	4	2800

Does the problem have another optimal solution? If so, what is the corresponding simplex tableau?

19. We are given the linear programming problem

$$\max f = 4x_1 + 5x_2,$$
$$x_1 + x_2 + x_3 = 200,$$
$$2x_1 + x_2 + x_4 = 400,$$

with the usual nonnegativity constraints, and the following simplex tableau for the initial solution:

Basis variables	Basis prices	x_1	x_2	x_3	x_4	Solution values
x_3	0	1	1	1	0	200
x_4	0	2	1	0	1	400
Increased revenues		-4	-5	0	0	0

Obtain a new solution by bringing x_1 into the basis. Show that the resulting solution is degenerate. Continue with the simplex iterations until an optimal solution is obtained. Is the optimal solution degenerate?

20. By means of simplex iterations show that the following linear-programming problem has an unbounded solution:

$$\max f = x_1 + 2x_2,$$
$$x_1 - x_2 \le 2, \qquad 0 \le x_1 \le 5, \qquad x_2 \ge 0.$$

21. Give a graphic explanation of why the problem in Exercise 20 has an unbound solution.

11

LINEAR PROGRAMMING: ANALYSIS

In addition to providing the optimal solution, an optimal simplex tableau also contains other information that is useful in managerial decisions. In this chapter we shall examine some of this information.

11.1 SHADOW PRICES

Let us consider the optimal simplex tableau for the problem of Alpha Beta Manufacturing:

Basis variables	Basis prices	x_1	x_2	x_3	x_4	Solution values
x_2	100	0	1	2	-1	200
x_1	150	1	0	-1	1	400
Increased revenues		0	0	50	50	80,000

Here x_3 represents the unused quantity of alpha. That the increased revenue for x_3 is

$$z_3 - c_3 = 50$$

implies that if the unused quantity of alpha is increased from 0 to 1, then f will decrease by \$50. Increasing the unused quantity of alpha by one unit, however, is equivalent to reducing the total supply of alpha from 600 units to 599 units. Thus $z_3 - c_3 = 50$ also implies that if the supply of alpha is reduced by one unit, from 600 to 599, then the optimal value of f will be reduced by \$50, from \$80,000 to \$79,950, for the following reason.

The x_3 column in the tableau shows that if the supply of alpha is reduced **159** by one unit, then the quantity of Product 1 must increase by one unit and the quantity of Product 2 must increase by two units for optimal readjustment. Thus the optimal solution, when the supply of alpha is 599, is

$$x_1 = 401, \qquad x_2 = 198,$$
$$f = (150)(401) + (100)(198) = 79,950.$$

The value of f has decreased by $50.

Now, if the value of f will decrease by $50 when the supply of alpha is reduced by one unit, then the value of f should increase by $50 when the supply of alpha is increased by one unit. Therefore, let us assume that the supply of alpha is to be increased to 601 from 600.

Then the optimal solution is

$$x_1 = 399, \qquad x_2 = 402,$$
$$f = (150)(399) + (100)(202) = 80,050.$$

The preceding analysis shows that $z_3 - c_3 = 50$, in a sense, depicts the incremental revenue that can be generated by a marginal unit of alpha. Thus the $50 can be considered to be the value of a marginal unit of alpha; it is sometimes called the *shadow price* of alpha.

Next we note that $z_4 - c_4 = 50$. But since x_4 depicts the unused quantity of beta, the $50 is also the shadow price of β. Let us assume that a linear-programming problem is formulated in such a way that there is a slack variable for each resource. Then the optimal simplex tableau for the problem will indicate a shadow price for every given resource equivalent to the increased revenue corresponding to the slack variable in question.

Shadow prices play a very significant role in managerial decisions. In the linear-programming problem above, for example, we may wish to evaluate the possibility of increasing the supply of alpha. That the shadow price of alpha is $50 means that a marginal unit of alpha is worth only $50. Consequently, if it costs more than $50 per unit to expand the supply of alpha, then the expansion is obviously not worth the price.

11.2 EVALUATING THE ADDITION OF A NEW VARIABLE

Once we have the shadow prices, we can evaluate the addition of a new variable without having to solve the whole problem again. In the case of Alpha Beta Manufacturing let us assume that the company has been following the product mix plan suggested by the optimal linear-programming solution given in Section 11.1. Suppose that now the company is debating whether to produce a new product, which we will call Product n. One unit of Product n will require 3 units of alpha and 2 units of beta and will sell for $220 per unit. Let x_n be the quantity of Product n to be produced. One way of evaluating the desirability of producing this new product is to formulate a model:

$$\max f = 150x_1 + 100x_2 + \qquad\qquad 220x_n,$$
$$x_1 + \quad x_2 + x_3 + \qquad 3x_n = 600,$$
$$2x_1 + \quad x_2 + \qquad x_4 + 2x_n = 1000,$$
$$x_1, \ldots, x_n \geq 0.$$

Solving this problem, we will find that the optimal simplex tableau is:

Basis variables	Basis prices	x_1	x_2	x_3	x_4	x_n	Solution values
x_2	100	0	1	2	-1	4	200
x_1	150	1	0	-1	1	-1	400
Increased revenues		0	0	50	50	30	80,000

which indicates that the optimal solution is still

$$x_1 = 400, \qquad x_2 = 200, \qquad f = 80,000.$$

Thus it will not be profitable for the company to produce Product n. The simplex tableau also shows that one unit of Product n will bring about a \$30 decrease in the total revenue: $z_n - c_n = 30$.

We could, however, have reached the very same conclusion without reformulating the problem and solving the new problem all over again. We recall that the shadow prices of alpha and beta are both \$50, meaning that given the present product mix plan, a reduction of one unit in either alpha or beta will reduce the total revenue by \$50. On the other hand, one unit of Product n will need 3 units of alpha and 2 units of beta. Therefore, a production of one unit of Product n will reduce the total revenue by \$250: $3 \times \$50 + 2 \times \$50 = \$250$. That is, it will use up quantities of alpha and beta that are presently contributing \$250 towards the total revenue. If one unit of Product n will sell for more than \$250, then the company will benefit by producing Product n. But the selling price of \$220 will mean a net loss in revenue of \$30 per unit of Product n produced. Thus the company should not produce Product n.

In this instance the use of shadow prices eliminated the need to reformulate the entire linear-programming problem.

Let us now reexamine the preceding analyses. The optimal simplex tableau for the reformulated problem showed that

$$z_n - c_n = 30;$$

that is, one unit of Product n would reduce the total revenue by \$30. We note that

$$z_n = (c_2 \times 4) + [c_1 \times (-1)] = (100 \times 4) + [150 \times (-1)] = 250$$

and

$$z_n - c_n = 250 - 220 = 30.$$

The same result was obtained by simple calculations with shadow prices. The two methods of evaluation are equivalent and will always yield the same conclusion about the desirability of adding a new product.

Let us now formalize the second method in notations. Let λ_a and λ_b, respectively, be the shadow prices of alpha and beta. Then

$$z_n = (\lambda_a \times 3) + (\lambda_b \times 2) = (50 \times 3) + (50 \times 2) = 250$$

and

$$z_n - c_n = 250 - 220 = 30.$$

Example 1   Alpha Beta Manufacturing is considering another product, called Product m. One unit of Product m will require 2 units of alpha and 4 units of Beta. The company wants to know the minimum unit selling price of Product m that will make the production of Product m beneficial to the company.

This problem can be handled in the following way. First, we calculate the amount of revenue loss caused by channeling the available supply of alpha and beta to produce one unit of Product m:

	Shadow price	Quantity used	Total amount
alpha	$50	2	$100
beta	$50	4	$200
		Total:	$300

In effect, the unit cost of producing Product m, in terms of rechanneling available resources, is $300. Therefore, the selling price of Product m must be greater than $300 if the introduction of Product m is to benefit the company.

11.3   RESOURCE RANGING

Let us again consider the optimal simplex tableau for Alpha Beta Manufacturing:

Basis variables	Basis prices	x_1	x_2	x_3	x_4	Solution values
x_2	100	0	1	2	−1	200
x_1	150	1	0	−1	1	400
Increased revenues		0	0	50	50	80,000

Since x_3 is the slack variable for alpha, $z_3 - c_3 = 50$ is the shadow price of alpha. It is also the meaning of this shadow price that an addition of one unit of alpha to the present supply of 600 units will increase the total revenue by $50. Are we then to conclude that an additional 100 units will increase the total revenue by $5000, an additional 1000 units will increase the total revenue by $50,000, etc.? The answer is "not necessarily."

To understand this, let us consider again how an increase of $50 in total revenue can be brought about by one additional unit of alpha. The x_3 column in the above simplex tableau indicates that, if we are to use one additional unit of alpha in the most beneficial manner, we must

increase the production of Product 2 by two units, and
decrease the production of Product 1 by one unit.

An increase of two units of Product 2 will increase the total revenue by $200, and a reduction of one unit of Product 1 will reduce the total revenue by $150. The net increase, therefore, is $50, which is the shadow price.

The optimal solution before adding the unit of alpha specifies that we produce

200 units of Product 2,
400 units of Product 1.

Therefore, the optimal new solution after adding one unit of alpha must be to produce

202 units of Product 2,
399 units of Product 1.

This means that, if the supply of alpha is increased by 100 units, then the optimal solution will be to produce:

400 units of Product 2,
300 units of Product 1;

and if the supply of alpha is increased by 400 units to 1000, then the optimal solution will be to produce

1000 units of Product 2,
0 units of Product 1.

In the latter case the total revenue will be

$$f = (\$150 \times 0) + (\$100 \times 1000) = \$100,000,$$

which is $20,000 more than the total revenue obtainable with 600 units of alpha. Since this increase in revenue can be brought about by 400 additional units of alpha, we can say that each additional unit of alpha between 600 units and 1000 units will contribute $50 in additional revenue.

Now suppose we are to increase the supply of alpha from 1000 units to 1001 units. If this additional unit were to contribute $50 in additional revenue, we must

increase the production of Product 2 by two units, and
decrease the production of Product 1 by one unit.

But the optimal output in Product 1 is already zero when the supply in alpha is 1000 units. There can be no further reduction in the production of Product 1. Therefore, once the supply of alpha has reached 1000 units, the shadow price of alpha is no longer $50 for any further increase in the supply of alpha. The quantity of 1000 units is the *upper limit* of a range within which the previous pattern of optimal adjustment in production can be made.

Now consider the problem of reducing the supply of alpha. Reviewing the beginning situation of optimal product mix, we see that if the supply of alpha is reduced by one unit, then the necessary optimal adjustment is to

reduce the production of Product 2 by two units, and
increase the production of Product 1 by one unit.

Such an adjustment will result in a $50 decrease in total revenue.

Since the optimal product mix before the marginal reduction of one unit of alpha was to produce

200 units of Product 2,
400 units of Product 1,

a reduction by 100 units in the supply of alpha from 600 units to 500 units will require the optimal adjustment in production to

0 units of Product 2,
500 units of Product 1.

There can be no further reduction in the production of Product 2. Therefore, the present pattern of optimal adjustment in product mix to reductions in the supply of alpha cannot be maintained beyond the supply level of 500 units of alpha. That is, the shadow price of alpha is no longer $50 when the supply of alpha is reduced below 500 units. In this case the quantity 500 units is the *lower limit* of the range within which the suggested optimal adjustment can be made.

The preceding discussion may be summarized by the diagram in Figure 11.1. This diagram shows that so long as the supply of alpha is not increased beyond 1000 units or reduced to less than 500 units, the solution based on the present basis variables is feasible. The determination of these upper and lower limits of supply is called *supply ranging* or *resource ranging*.

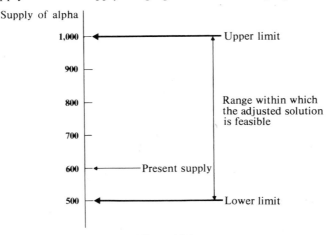

Figure 11.1

Let us now describe the procedure of resource ranging in general form. Assume that the following is an abstraction of the simplex tableau for an optimal solution:

Basis variables	Basis prices	$x_1 \cdots x_k \cdots x_n$	Solution values
1		p_1	y_1
2		p_2	y_2
.		.	.
.		.	.
.		.	.
m		p_m	y_m
Increased revenues			

Assume further that x_k is the slack variable for the kth resource. If we let d_k be the present supply of the kth resource and $d_k(U)$ and $d_k(L)$ be the respective upper and lower limits of the range within which the optimum solution based on the present basis variables is feasible,

$$d_k(U) = d_k - \max\{y_i/p_i\} \qquad \text{for all } p_i < 0,$$
$$d_k(L) = d_k - \min\{y_i/p_i\} \qquad \text{for all } p_i > 0.$$

Illustration 1. Let us assume that an optimum solution for a linear-programming problem with five structural constraints is

$$
\begin{aligned}
p_1 &= 1, & y_1 &= 300, \\
p_2 &= -2, & y_2 &= 500, \\
p_3 &= 0, & y_3 &= 100, \\
p_4 &= 4, & y_4 &= 800, \\
p_5 &= -3, & y_5 &= 600,
\end{aligned}
$$

and that $d_k = 1000$. Then

$$d_k(U) = 1000 - \max\left\{\frac{y_2}{p_2} = \frac{500}{-2} = -250, \frac{y_5}{p_5} = \frac{600}{-3} = -200\right\}$$
$$= 1000 - \max\{-250, -200\}$$
$$= 1000 + 200 = 1{,}200.$$

(Note that the denominators of the two ratios are both negative numbers.) Next we have

$$d_k(L) = 1000 - \min\left\{\frac{y_1}{p_1} = \frac{300}{1} = 300, \frac{y_4}{p_4} = \frac{800}{2} = 400\right\}$$
$$= 1000 - \min\{300, 400\}$$
$$= 1000 - 300 = 700.$$

(Note that the denominators of the two ratios here are both positive.)

Illustration 2. Let us now return to the optimal simplex tableau for Alpha Beta Manufacturing. We can establish the upper and lower limits for alpha as follows. From the optimal simplex tableau we obtain

$$p_1 = \quad 2, \quad y_1 = 200,$$
$$p_2 = -1, \quad y_2 = 400,$$

and $d_1 = 600$ since the initial supply of alpha is 600 units. Then

$$d_1(U) = 600 - \max \left\{ \frac{400}{-1} \right\} = 1000,$$

$$d_1(L) = 600 - \min \left\{ \frac{200}{2} \right\} = \quad 500.$$

These upper and lower limits of the range for alpha are the same as what we obtained before.

What about the upper and lower limits of the range for beta? From the x_4 column and the solution values column in the optimal simplex tableau we obtain:

$$p_1 = -1, \quad y_1 = 200,$$
$$p_2 = \quad 1, \quad y_2 = 400.$$

Since $d_2 = 1000$, we have

$$d_2(U) = 1000 - \max \left\{ \frac{200}{-1} \right\} = 1200,$$

$$d_2(L) = 1000 - \min \left\{ \frac{400}{1} \right\} = \quad 600.$$

Thus the upper and lower limits of beta are, respectively, 1200 units and 600 units.

11.4 PRICE RANGING

Let us again consider the optimal simplex tableau for the product mix problem of Alpha Beta Manufacturing:

Basis variables	Basis prices	x_1	x_2	x_3	x_4	Solution values
x_2	100	0	1	2	-1	200
x_1	150	1	0	-1	1	400
Increased revenues		0	0	50	50	80,000

This optimal solution is based on the assumption that the prices of the variables are $c_1 = 150$, $c_2 = 100$, $c_3 = 0$, and $c_4 = 0$. In this section we shall examine how the optimality of this solution may be affected by changing the price of a variable. The determination of the extent to which we can change a price without affecting the optimality of a solution is called *price ranging*.

In a given optimal solution the nonbasis prices are $c_3 = 0$ and $c_4 = 0$, meaning that the unused alpha and beta have no value. But suppose Alpha Beta Manufacturing can sell its unused alpha for some positive price, $c_3 > 0$. What, then, is the increased revenue for x_3? We have

$$z_3 - c_3 = (100)(+2) + (150)(-1) - c_3$$
$$= 50 - c_3.$$

So long as the value of c_3 is 50 or less, $z_3 - c_3$ will be nonnegative, meaning that the given solution is still optimal. However, if the value of c_3 is greater than 50, then $z_3 - c_3$ will become negative, meaning that the given solution is no longer optimal, since it can be improved on by bringing x_3 into the basis. Thus c_3 can rise to 50 without affecting the optimality of the given solution.

Similarly, we can determine that c_4 can rise to as much as 50 without affecting the optimality of the given solution.

On the basis of the preceding illustrations, we now propose the following rule:

Let x_k be a certain nonbasis variable and $z_k - c_k = k$. Then the extent to which the value of c_k can be increased without affecting the optimality of the given solution is k.

In the given optimal solution the basis prices are $c_1 = 150$ and $c_2 = 100$. If the value of c_2 is increased by 50 then

$$z_3 - c_3 = (c_2 + 50)(2) + (c_1)(-1) - c_3$$
$$= (100 + 50)(2) + (150)(-1) - 0 = 150,$$
$$z_4 - c_4 = (c_2 + 50)(-1) + (c_1)(1) - c_4$$
$$= (100 + 50)(-1) + (150)(1) - 0 = 0.$$

The value of $z_3 - c_3$ will increase from 50 to 150, whereas that of $z_4 - c_4$ will decrease from 50 to 0. If the value of c_1 is increased any further, $z_4 - c_4$ will become negative. For example, if we increase the value of c_2 by 51 instead of 50, then

$$z_4 - c_4 = (c_2 + 51)(-1) + (c_1)(1) - c_4$$
$$= (100 + 51)(-1) + (150)(1) - 0 = -1.$$

But, as we pointed out earlier, a solution is not optimal whenever any increased revenue, such as $z_4 - c_4$, is negative. Thus the value of c_1 cannot be increased beyond 150 without making the given solution nonoptimal.

If we now decrease the value of c_2 by 25, then we will have

$$z_3 - c_3 = (c_2 - 25)(2) + (c_1)(-1) - c_3$$
$$= (100 - 25)(2) + (150)(-1) - 0 = 0,$$
$$z_4 - c_4 = (c_2 - 25)(-1) + (c_1)(1) - c_3$$
$$= (100 - 25)(-1) + (150)(1) - 0 = 75.$$

Thus the value of $z_3 - c_3$ will decrease from 50 to 0, whereas that of $z_4 - c_4$ increased from 50 to 75. This suggests that if the value of c_2 is decreased by more than 25, $z_3 - c_3$ will become negative. Therefore, the value of c_2 cannot fall below 75 without making the given solution nonoptimal.

We have shown, therefore, that 150 and 75 are the upper and lower limits of the range within which the basis price c_2 can fluctuate without affecting the optimality of the given solution.

Ranging Procedure

Ranging a basis price is much more involved than ranging a nonbasis price. We shall now describe a ranging procedure for a basis price. Assume that the following is an abstraction of the simplex tableau for an optimal solution:

Basis variables	Basis prices	x_1	x_2	$\cdots$	x_n	Solution values
1	c_1					
.	.					
.	.		*only for non basis qs*			
.	.					
k	c_k	q_1	q_2	$\cdots$	q_n	
.	.		$\longrightarrow$			
.	.					
.	.					
m	c_m					
Increased revenues		$z_1 - c_1$	$z_2 - c_2$	$\cdots$	$z_n - c_n$	

Assuming that c_k is the basis price whose upper and lower limits we wish to determine, we let $c_k(U)$ and $c_k(L)$ be the upper and lower limits of c_k within which the given optimal solution will remain optimal. Then

$$c_k(U) = c_k - \max \left\{ \frac{z_i - c_i}{q_i} \right\} \quad \text{for all nonbasis } q_i < 0,$$

$$c_k(L) = c_k - \min \left\{ \frac{z_i - c_i}{q_i} \right\} \quad \text{for all nonbasis } q_i > 0.$$

Illustration 1. Let us assume that the following tableau is an abstraction of the simplex tableau for an optimal linear-programming solution:

Basis variables	Basis prices	x_1	x_2	x_3	x_4	x_5	x_6	Solution values
x_2	200	-1	1	2	0	-2	1	
x_4								
Increased revenues		60	0	200	0	100	40	

Here $c_2 = 200$. The upper limit of c_2 is therefore

$$c_2(U) = 200 - \max\left\{\frac{z_1 - c_1}{q_1} = \frac{60}{-1} = -60 \frac{z_5 - c_5}{q_5} = \frac{100}{-2} = -50\right\}$$

$$= 200 - \max\{-60, -50\} = 250.$$

And the lower limit of c_2 is

$$c_2(L) = 200 - \min\left\{\frac{z_3 - c_3}{q_3} = \frac{200}{2} = 100, \frac{z_6 - c_6}{q_6} = \frac{40}{1} = 40\right\} \quad why\ not\ \frac{0}{1}$$

$$= 200 - \min\{100, 40\} = 160.$$

Illustration 2. Let us again return to the optimal solution for Alpha Beta Manufacturing. We shall reestablish the upper and lower limits of the price of Product 2. From the simplex tableau we obtain

$$q_1 = 0, \quad z_1 - c_1 = 0,$$
$$q_2 = 1, \quad z_2 - c_2 = 0,$$
$$q_3 = 2, \quad z_3 - c_3 = 50,$$
$$q_4 = -1, \quad z_4 - c_4 = 50,$$

where x_1 and x_2 are the basis variables and $c_2 = 100$. Then

$$c_2(U) = 100 - \max\left\{\frac{50}{-1}\right\} = 150,$$

$$c_2(L) = 100 - \min\left\{\frac{50}{2}\right\} = 75.$$

These are the same upper and lower limits that we obtained before.
What about the upper and lower limits of the price range of **Product 1**? From the optimal simplex tableau we obtain

$$q_1 = 1, \quad z_1 - c_1 = 0,$$
$$q_2 = 0, \quad z_2 - c_2 = 0,$$
$$q_3 = -1, \quad z_3 - c_3 = 50,$$
$$q_4 = 1, \quad z_4 - c_4 = 50,$$

and $c_1 = 150$. Therefore,

$$c_1(U) = 150 - \max\left\{\frac{50}{-1}\right\} = 200, \quad c_1(L) = 150 - \min\left\{\frac{50}{1}\right\} = 100.$$

Thus the upper and lower limits of the range are $200 and $100, respectively.

11.5   MINIMIZATION PROBLEMS

The primal simplex method which we have described so far is specifically designed to handle only objective functions of the form

$$\max f = c_1 x_1 + \cdots + c_n x_n.$$

Suppose that now we need to solve a linear-programming problem of the form

$$\min f = c_1 x_1 + \cdots + c_n x_n.$$

The method we have described is still usable once a very simple modification has been made in the structure of the problem.

Consider the following three numbers:

$$a = 1, \qquad b = 2, \qquad \text{and} \qquad c = 3.$$

We can write the smallest of these as

$$\min \{a = 1, b = 2, c = 3\} = a.$$

Note, however, that

$$\max \{-a = -1, -b = -2, -c = -3\} = -a.$$

Thus we can find the smallest number among a, b, and c by first finding the largest number among $-a$, $-b$, and $-c$ and then taking the negative of the resulting number.

Therefore, to find the minimum value of f, we can first find the maximum value of $-f$ and then discard the minus sign. We can write

$$\max -f = -c_1 x_1 - \cdots -c_n x_n$$

and then apply the simplex method described above to find the solution that maximizes $-f$.

11.6 ARTIFICIAL VARIABLES

We have shown that we can modify a linear-programming formulation by adding slack variables. We will now introduce another type of variable called the *artificial variables*, which are added to a linear-programming formulation to facilitate the computations for the simplex method.

Example 2. Production Planning   Name Your Brand Appliance is committed to deliver 1000 units of a certain model this year and another 1000 units next year to a large mail order house chain. The company's production capacity this year is 1500 units, but the limitation will no longer exist next year. The unit production cost is \$100 this year, but it will rise to \$150 next year. Any unit produced this year but not delivered during the year will result in a \$20 holding cost. The manufacturer does not have any beginning inventory and does not wish to have any ending inventory at the end of the second year. It wants to minimize the total cost of meeting the delivery requirements.

This is a slightly modified version of the production planning problem in Example 6 of Chapter 9. If we let

$$x_1 = \text{quantity produced this year,}$$

$$x_2 = \text{quantity produced next year,}$$

$$y_1 = \text{inventory at the end of this year,}$$

then the problem may be formulated as follows:

$$\max -f = -100x_1 - 20y_1 - 150x_2,$$
$$x_1 - y_1 = 1000,$$
$$y_1 + x_2 = 1000,$$
$$x_1 \leq 1500.$$

Adding the slack variable s_1 for the third constraint, we may rewrite the problem as

$$\max -f = -100x_1 - 20y_1 - 150x_2,$$
$$x_1 - y_1 = 1000,$$
$$y_1 + x_2 = 1000,$$
$$x_1 + s_1 = 1500.$$

The first step in the application of the simplex method is to find a basic feasible solution. But the above formulation of the problem is such that we cannot easily find a basic feasible solution.

Suppose that now we modify the system of the structural constraints to read:

$$x_1 - y_1 + \alpha_1 = 1000,$$
$$y_1 + x_2 + \alpha_2 = 1000,$$
$$x_1 + s_1 = 1500.$$

where α_1 and α_2 are two arbitrarily added variables. Then we can obtain a basic feasible solution very easily:

$$s_1 = 1500, \quad x_1 = 0,$$
$$\alpha_1 = 1000, \quad y_1 = 0,$$
$$\alpha_2 = 1000, \quad x_2 = 0.$$

Note that the variables α_1 and α_2 were added purely to facilitate the finding of an initial basic solution that is feasible. Therefore, these variables do not have any meaning in the context of the real problem confronting the manufacturer. They are thus called *artificial variables*, whereas in this instance x_1, x_2, y_1, and s_1 are called *real variables*.

Since the artificial variables in a basis are not meaningful, we should try to remove them from the basis in the subsequent iterations. This can be done by simply applying the simplex method already described.

Suppose that we assign a very large cost coefficient, say M, where M approaches infinity, to the artificial variables. Then we can write the objective function as

$$\min f = 100x_1 + 20y_1 + 150x_2 + M\alpha_1 + M\alpha_2$$

or

$$\max -f = -100x_1 - 20y_1 - 150x_2 - M\alpha_1 - M\alpha_2.$$

If the cost coefficients for the artificial variables are incomparably larger than those of the real variables, then routine simplex iterations will force the variables out of the basis.

To be more specific, let us now return to our initial basic feasible solution whose basis contains the artificial variables α_1 and α_2. The simplex tableau for this solution is:

Basis variables	Basis price	x_1	y_1	x_2	s_1	α_1	α_2	Solution values
α_1	$-M$	1	-1	0	0	1	0	1000
α_2	$-M$	0	1	①	0	0	1	1000 ← pivot row
s_1	0	1	0	0	1	0	0	1500
Increased revenues		$-M + 100$	20	$-M + 150$	0	0	0	$-2000M$

↑
pivot
column

Since M is infinitely large, the increased revenues $-M + 100$ and $-M + 150$ must be negative numbers, which mean that the solution is not optimal. Thus, if we assign M to be the cost coefficient of the artificial variables, then some increased revenues will be negative wherever one or more artificial variables are in a basis, thereby signaling that the basis is not optimal.

The above simplex tableau thus shows that either x_1 or x_2 should be brought into the basis. But $-M + 100 < -M + 150$. Therefore, we should bring x_1 into the basis. But, instead, we shall bring x_2 into the basis, for reasons that are primarily pedagogical.

The circled number in the above simplex tableau is the pivot element. Therefore, we can obtain a new tableau:

Basis variables	Basis prices	x_1	y_1	x_2	s_1	α_1	α_2	Solution values	Ratios
α_1	$-M$	①	-1	0	0	1	0	1000	⟨1000⟩ ← pivot row
x_2	-150	0	1	1	0	0	1	1000	
s_1	0	1	0	0	1	0	0	1500	1500
Increased revenues		$-M+100$	$M-130$	0	0	0	$M-150$	$-1000M$ $-150,000$	

↑
pivot
column

This is still not a meaningful solution, since it still has the artificial variable α_1 in the basis. But we see that the increased revenue for x_1 is $-M + 100$, which is a negative number. Therefore, we will bring x_1 into the basis, and the ratio column shows that the artificial variables α_1 should be removed from the basis. The pivot element thus determined is indicated by the circle in the above simplex tableau.

The simplex tableau for the next solution is:

Basis variables	Basis prices	x_1	y_1	x_2	s_1	α_1	α_2	Solution values	Ratios
x_1	-100	1	-1	0	0	1	0	1000	
x_2	-150	0	1	1	0	0	1	1000	1000
s_1	0	0	①	0	1	-1	0	500	(500)
Increased revenues		0	-30	0	0	$M-100$	$M-150$	$-250,000$	

Now the basis of the solution does not contain any artificial variables, and the value of the objective function is:

$$-f = (-100 \times 1000) + (-150 \times 1000) + (0 \times 500) = -250,000.$$

This is the first meaningful solution we have obtained, and it says that if the company produces 1000 units this year and another 1000 units next year, then the total cost for the two years will be $250,000. Nevertheless, it is still not an optimal solution. This is signified by the increased revenue for y_1:

$$[-100 \times (-1)] + (-150 \times 1) + (0 \times 1) - (-20) = -30,$$

suggesting that we should bring y_1 into the basis. The ratio column shows that s_1 should be removed from the basis.

The simplex tableau for the new solution is:

Basis variables	Basis prices	x_1	y_1	x_2	s_1	α_1	α_2	Solution values
x_1	-100	1	0	0	1	0	0	1500
x_2	-150	0	0	1	-1	1	1	500
y_1	-20	0	1	0	1	-1	0	500
Increased revenues		0	0	0	30	$M-130$	$M-150$	$-235,000$

Finally, we have an optimal solution, since the increased revenues are all nonnegative. The solution indicates that the optimal policy is to (1) produce 1500 units this year, (2) store 500 units at the end of this year, and (3) produce only 500 units next year. The cost for the two years will then be only $235,000.

Example 3. Feed Mix Problem   Assume that a dairy cow must be fed at least 30 units of nutritional element A and at least 40 units of nutritional element B per day. The dairy farmer is considering two different types of feed, which we will call feed 1 and feed 2. One pound of feed 1 contains one unit of A and one unit of B, whereas one pound of feed 2 contains one unit of A and two units of B. Feed 1 costs 3¢/lb and feed 2 5¢/lb. The farmer wants to mix the two types of feed in such proportions as to minimize the total cost of feeding a cow.

We let x_1 and x_2, respectively, be the quantities of feed 1 and feed 2 to be fed to a cow. Then the problem may be formulated as follows:

$$\min f = 3x_1 + 5x_2,$$
$$x_1 + x_2 \geq 30,$$
$$x_1 + 2x_2 \geq 40,$$

with the nonnegativity constraints $x_1 \geq 0$ and $x_2 \geq 0$.

The system of constraints may be converted into a system of equations:

$$x_1 + x_2 - x_3 = 30,$$
$$x_1 + 2x_2 - x_4 = 40,$$

where x_3 and x_4 are called *negative slack variables* or *surplus variables*.

These *surplus variables* may be explained as follows. Suppose, for example, the farmer decides to use 40 lb of feed 1 and none of feed 2. A cow will then receive just enough of B but 10 extra units of A. We can consider these 10 units as the surplus amount of A for the cow. The proposed feed mix may be written:

$$x_1 = 40, \quad x_2 = 0, \quad x_3 = 10, \quad x_4 = 0.$$

Here x_3 represents the surplus amount of A which is being fed to the cow.

Since such a surplus quantity will not entail any additional cost to the farmer, we can let the cost coefficients for x_3 and x_4 be zero. Then the modified problem may be given by

$$\max -f = -3x_1 - 5x_2,$$
$$x_1 + x_2 - x_3 = 30,$$
$$x_1 + 2x_2 - x_4 = 40,$$

with the nonnegativity constraints.

We can see that a basic feasible solution is not readily available. Therefore, we shall again add artificial variables:

$$\max -f = -3x_1 - 5x_2 - M\alpha_1 - M\alpha_2,$$
$$x_1 + x_2 - x_3 + \alpha_1 = 30,$$
$$x_1 + 2x_2 - x_4 + \alpha_2 = 40.$$

Then we can get a simplex tableau for the initial solution, with the artificial variables α_1 and α_2 in the basis:

	Basis variables	Basis prices	x_1	x_2	x_3	x_4	α_1	α_2	Solution values	Ratios
	α_1	$-M$	1	1	-1	0	1	0	30	30
pivot row $\rightarrow$	α_2	$-M$	1	②	0	-1	0	1	40	⑳
	Increased revenues		$-2M + 3$	$-3M + 5$	M	M	0	0	$-70M$	

$$\uparrow$$
pivot
column

This tableau shows that $z_1 - c_1 = -2M + 3$ and $z_2 - c_2 = -3M + 5$. Therefore, we should bring x_2 into the basis, and the ratio column indicates that α_2 should be removed from the present basis. The pivot element is circled in the tableau.

The next simplex tableau we get is:

Basis variables	Basis prices	x_1	x_2	x_3	x_4	α_1	α_2	Solution values	Ratios
α_1	$-M$	⓪.5	0	-1	0.5	1	-0.5	10	㉒
x_2	-5	0.5	1	0	-0.5	0	0.5	20	40
Increased revenues		$-0.5M + 0.5$	0	M	$-0.5M + 2.5$	0	$0.5M - 2.5$	$-10M - 100$	

Here we find that $z_1 - c_1 = -0.5M + 0.5$ and $z_4 - c_4 = -0.5M + 2.5$. Therefore, we should bring x_1 into the basis, and the ratio column indicates that α_1 should be removed from the basis. Again the pivot element is circled.

The simplex tableau for the new solution is:

Basis variables	Basis prices	x_1	x_2	x_3	x_4	α_1	α_2	Solution values
x_1	-3	1	0	-2	1	2	-1	20
x_2	-5	0	1	1	-1	-1	1	10
Increased revenues		0	0	1	2	$M - 1$	$M - 2$	-110

We observe that the basis in this solution does not contain any artificial variables. Therefore, it is a meaningful solution. Moreover, all the increased revenues are nonnegative. Therefore, the solution is also an optimal solution. It indicates that the dairy farmer should feed 20 lb of feed 1 and 10 lb of feed 2 to each cow, at a cost of $1.10.

11.7 UNFEASIBLE PROBLEM

Let us assume that a linear-programming problem which we want to solve has at least one feasible solution and that we have added some artificial variables into the formulation to help us begin our computations. Then one of two possibilities will obtain when we find the simplex tableau all of whose increased revenues are nonnegative: (1) all artificial variables have already been removed from the basis; (2) one or more artificial variables still remain in the basis, but their solution values are zero. In either case, the solution thus obtained is an optimal feasible solution for the given linear-programming problem. The solution is optimal, because the increased revenues are all nonnegative. It is feasible, because the basis does not contain any artificial variable which assumes a positive value in the solution.

Suppose that we began our computations after having added some artificial variables to a linear-programming problem and that we have obtained a simplex tableau where all the increased revenues are nonnegative but at least one artificial variable still remains in the basis with a positive solution value. Then there is nothing more we can do, according to the simplex method, since the fact that all the increased revenues are nonnegative implies that the solution is optimal. Yet the solution is not feasible, since the basis contains at least one more artificial variable with a positive solution value.

What should we make of this situation? We should conclude that the problem has either no feasible solution or no solution whatever, as illustrated in our next example.

Example 4 Consider the following linear-programming problem:

$$\max f = 10x_1 + 4x_2,$$
$$2x_1 + x_2 = 10,$$
$$2x_1 + x_2 = 20,$$

with the usual nonnegativity constraints. It is clear that the two structural constraints are inconsistent with each other. Therefore, the problem does not have any solution whatever.

Let us assume that we are not aware the problem does not have any solution and want to solve it. Adding the artificial variables, we obtain

$$\max f = 10x_1 + 4x_2 - M\alpha_1 - M\alpha_2,$$
$$2x_1 + x_2 + \alpha_1 = 10,$$
$$2x_1 + x_2 + \alpha_2 = 20,$$

where α_1 and α_2 are the artificial variables. Then the simplex tableau for the initial solution is:

Basis variables	Basis prices	x_1	x_2	α_1	α_2	Solution values	Ratio
α_1	$-M$	②	1	1	0	10	⑤
α_2	$-M$	2	1	0	1	20	10
Increased revenues		$-4M - 10$	$-2M - 4$	0	0	$-30M$	

Removing α_1 and bringing x_1 into the basis, we obtain a new solution with the following simplex tableau:

Basis variables	Basis prices	x_1	x_2	α_1	α_2	Solution values
x_1	10	1	0.5	0.5	0	5
α_2	$-M$	0	0	-1	1	10
Increased revenues		0	1	$2M + 5$	0	$-10M + 50$

This tableau satisfies the optimality requirements, since the increased revenues are all nonnegative. On the other hand, the solution value of α_2 is 10. There is no solution to the problem, at least no feasible solution.

11.8 SHADOW PRICES AGAIN

In Section 11.1 we explained the significance of shadow prices and illustrated how they may be obtained from a simplex tableau. The shadow prices with which we were concerned in Section 11.1, however, pertained only to the scarce resources. We shall now consider other kinds of shadow prices.

Let us first return to the production planning problem of Name Your Brand Appliance (Example 2). Consider the constraint

$$x_1 - y_1 = 1000,$$

which means that the quantity produced during the first year, less the quantity stored at the end of the year, should be equal to the quantity delivered to the mail order house chain during that year, namely 1000 units.

Suppose that the quantity to be delivered is increased by 1 unit to 1001 units, while all other factors remain the same. This additional unit will obviously increase the total cost of meeting the delivery requirements. But by how much?

We recall that the optimal policy, without this additional unit, is to produce 1500 units during the first year, of which 1000 units will be delivered during the year, store 500 units at the end of the first year, and ship them during the second year together with an additional 500 units produced during the second year.

Since the production capacity is 1500 units for the first year, if 1001 must be shipped during the first year, then there will be only 499 units to be stored at the end of the first year. This also means that 501 units will have to be produced during the second year. The incremental cost for the additional unit to be delivered during the first year may then be calculated as follows:

cost of producing one additional unit during the second year	$150
less saving in storage cost at the end of the first year	$ 20
net increase in cost	$130

Therefore, $130 is the shadow price for the marginal addition of one unit in delivery requirement for the first year. This shadow price, however, can be obtained directly from a simplex tableau. Let us now return to the optimal simplex tableau on p. 173. We note that the increased revenue corresponding to α_1 is $M - 130$. The variable α_1, however, is the artificial variable inserted into the constraint expressing the delivery requirement for the first year. It can be shown that the increased revenue corresponding to α_1 less the quantity M is in fact the shadow price for the marginal unit increase in delivery requirement for the first year. Thus the shadow price in question is -130. The minus sign indicates that the marginal unit increase in delivery requirement will entail an additional cost to the company.

Similarly, we note that the increased revenue corresponding to α_2 is $M - 150$, where α_2 is the artificial variable inserted into the constraint expressing the delivery requirement for the second period. Therefore, the shadow price for the marginal unit increase in delivery requirement for the second period is -150, which implies that the marginal unit cost is \$150.

Let us now return to the feed mix problem of Example 3. In the optimal simplex tableau for the problem we find that the increased revenue corresponding to α_1 is $M - 1$ and that corresponding to α_2 is $M - 2$, where α_1 and α_2 are respectively the artificial variables inserted into the constraints expressing the two nutritional requirements. Thus the shadow price for a marginal unit of nutritional element A is 1¢ and that of B is 2¢.

These shadow prices can be useful information to the dairy farmer in the following respects. Suppose the farmer wants to evaluate the effect of increasing the requirement for nutritional element A from 30 units to 31 units. Then, since the shadow price for A is 1¢, the total cost of feeding a cow will increase by 1¢.

11.9 DUAL FORMULATION

Let us now consider a linear-programming formulation

$$\max f = c_1 x_1 + \cdots + c_n x_n,$$
$$a_{11} x_1 + \cdots + a_{1n} x_n \leq d_1,$$
$$a_{21} x_1 + \cdots + a_{2n} x_n \leq d_2,$$
$$\cdot \qquad\qquad\qquad \cdot$$
$$\cdot \qquad\qquad\qquad \cdot$$
$$\cdot \qquad\qquad\qquad \cdot$$
$$a_{m1} x_1 + \cdots + a_{mn} x_n \leq d_m,$$

with the usual nonnegativity constraints. We will call this formulation the *primal* formulation of a linear-programming problem. But there is also another way of formulating this problem, called the *dual* formulation.

The primal formulation of the linear-programming problem given above can be presented in tabular form as follows:

Primal variables	x_1	x_2	$\cdots$	x_n
Primal constraints	a_{11}	a_{12}	$\cdots$	$a_{1n} \leq d_1$
	a_{21}	a_{22}	$\cdots$	$a_{2n} \leq d_2$
	$\cdot$	$\cdot$		$\cdot$ $\quad$ $\cdot$
	$\cdot$	$\cdot$		$\cdot$ $\quad$ $\cdot$
	$\cdot$	$\cdot$		$\cdot$ $\quad$ $\cdot$
	a_{m1}	a_{m2}	$\cdots$	$a_{mn} \leq d_m$
Primal objective function	c_1	c_2		$c_n = f$ (max.)

Then the dual formulation may be written as:

Dual variables	Dual constraints				Dual objective function
w_1	a_{11}	a_{12}	$\cdots$	a_{1n}	d_1
w_2	a_{21}	a_{22}	$\cdots$	a_{2n}	d_2
$\cdot$	$\cdot$	$\cdot$		$\cdot$	$\cdot$
$\cdot$	$\cdot$	$\cdot$		$\cdot$	$\cdot$
$\cdot$	$\cdot$	$\cdot$		$\cdot$	$\cdot$
w_m	a_{m1}	a_{m2}	$\cdots$	a_{mn}	d_m
	$\lVert\!\vee$	$\lVert\!\vee$		$\lVert\!\vee$	$\lVert$
	c_1	c_2		c_n	g (min)

Completely written out, the dual formulation is

$$\min g = d_1w_1 + d_2w_2 + \cdots + d_mw_m,$$
$$a_{11}w_1 + a_{21}w_2 + \cdots + a_{m1}w_m \geq c_1,$$
$$a_{12}w_1 + a_{22}w_2 + \cdots + a_{m2}w_m \geq c_2,$$
$$\cdot$$
$$\cdot$$
$$\cdot$$
$$a_{1n}w_1 + a_{2n}w_2 + \cdots + a_{mn}w_m \geq c_n,$$

with the nonnegativity constraints $w_1, \ldots, w_m \geq 0$.

We note that here the primal formulation is to maximize the objective function with coefficients $c_1, c_2, \ldots, c_n$, whereas the dual formulation is to minimize the objective function with coefficients $d_1, d_2, \ldots, d_m$. But it is not necessary that the primal formulation maximize the objective function; it may minimize its objective function, in which case the dual formulation must maximize its objective function.

Example 5. Material Allocation   Let us now return to the material allocation problem of Alpha Beta Manufacturing of Section 9.1. Let the primal formulation of this problem be:

$$\max f = 150x_1 + 100x_2,$$
$$x_1 + x_2 \leq 600,$$
$$2x_1 + x_2 \leq 1000,$$

with the nonnegativity constraints $x_1 \geq 0$ and $x_2 \geq 0$. Then the dual formulation is

$$\min g = 600w_1 + 1000w_2,$$
$$w_1 + 2w_2 \geq 150,$$
$$w_1 + w_2 \geq 100,$$

with the nonnegativity constraints $w_1 \geq 0$ and $w_2 \geq 0$.

Example 6. Trim Problem   Let us return to the trim problem of Example 5, Chapter 9. The problem was formulated as follows:

$$\min f = x_1 + x_2 + x_3 + x_4 + x_5,$$
$$4x_1 + 2x_3 \geq 500,$$
$$4x_1 + 2x_3 + 2x_4 \geq 1000$$
$$2x_2 + x_3 \geq 800,$$
$$x_4 + 2x_5 \geq 500,$$

with the nonnegativity constraints. We note that here the inequality signs in the structural constraints are of the form $\geq$. This direction of inequality can be reversed by simply multiplying each structural constraint by -1. Thus an equivalent linear-programming problem is:

$$\min f = x_1 + x_2 + x_3 + x_4 + x_5,$$
$$-4x_1 - 2x_3 \leq -500,$$
$$-4x_1 - 2x_3 - 2x_4 \leq -1000$$
$$-2x_2 - x_3 \leq -300, -800$$
$$-x_4 - 2x_5 \leq -200, -2000.$$

If this formulation of the problem is primal, then the dual formulation is:

$$\max g = -500w_1 - 300w_2 - 200w_3,$$
$$-4w_1 \geq 1,$$
$$-2w_2 \geq 1,$$
$$-2w_1 - w_2 \geq 1,$$
$$-2w_1 - w_3 \geq 1,$$
$$-2w_3 \geq 1,$$

where $w_1, w_2, w_3 \geq 0$.

Example 7. Production Planning   In Example 2 of this chapter we formulated a production planning problem as follows:

$$\min f = 100x_1 + 20y_1 + 150x_2,$$
$$x_1 - y_1 = 1000,$$
$$y_1 + x_2 = 1000,$$
$$x_1 \leq 1500,$$

with the nonnegativity constraints $x_1 \geq 0$, $y_1 \geq 0$, and $x_2 \geq 0$.

In all the primal formulations we examined before, the structural constraints had inequality signs of the form $\leq$. But here the first two structural constraints are equations. Therefore, we now introduce a new rule for formulating the dual problems:

If the i-th primal structural constraint is an inequality of the form $\leq$, then the ith dual variable must be nonnegative. But if the ith primal structural constraint is an equation, then the ith dual variable can be positive, zero, or negative.

In Examples 5 and 6, all structural constraints in the primal formulations were inequalities of the form $\leq$. Therefore, the corresponding dual problems must have nonnegative dual variables. In the present problem, however, the first two dual variables can have positive, zero, or negative values since the first two structural constraints are equations. Thus the dual problem is:

$$\max g = 1000w_1 + 1000w_2 + 1500w_3,$$
$$w_1 + w_3 \geq 100,$$
$$-w_1 + w_2 \geq 20,$$
$$w_2 \geq 150,$$

where $w_3 \geq 0$ but w_1 and w_2 are unrestricted in sign. This formulation is called a *generalized dual formulation*.

11.10 PRIMAL-DUAL RELATIONS

In the preceding section we illustrated the formulation of dual problems without explaining why we might wish to attempt such formulations in the first place. In this section we shall provide some of the reasons, first, by presenting the *duality theorem*, which states the relation between the solutions of the primal and the dual formulations.

Duality Theorem A   Let the primal problem be to maximize f and the dual problem to minimize g. Then $f \leq g$.

The significance of this theorem may be described as follows. Suppose we have obtained an arbitrary feasible solution for the primal problem with f as the solution value of the objective function and similarly, a feasible solution for the dual problem with g as the solution value of the objective function. Then, according to duality theorem A, we can always be sure that f is equal to or less than g.

Duality Theorem B   Assume that we have obtained an optimal feasible solution for a primal problem with a finite solution value, f, for the objective function. Then there exists a corresponding feasible solution for the dual problem, and if the solution value of the dual objective function is g, then $g = f$. Conversely, if we have an optimal feasible solution for a dual problem with a finite solution value, g, for the objective function, then there exists a corresponding feasible solution for the primal problem with a solution value, f, for the primal objective function such that $f = g$.

The significance of the two duality theorems may be explained as follows. Assume that we have obtained an optimal feasible solution for the primal problem with a finite solution value, f, for the objective function. Then duality theorem B says that the corresponding solution for the dual problem not only is feasible but also has a value, g, for the objective function which is equal to f. But since theorem A says that $f \leq g$, the solution for the dual problem is not only feasible, as stated by duality theorem B, but must also be optimal since the value of the objective function, g, being equal to f, is as low as it can possibly be. Similarly, if we have an optimal feasible solution for the dual problem and the solution value, g, is finite, then there exists a corresponding solution, f, for the primal problem that is also an optimal feasible solution, where $g = f$.

According to these theorems, therefore, if we know the precise relation between the solutions of the primal and dual problems, then we may be able to obtain an optimal feasible solution for a primal problem by solving its dual problem, or vice versa. This relation is described by duality theorem C.

Duality Theorem C   Let the primal objective function be to maximize f and the dual objective function be to maximize $-g$. Then in any optimal feasible solution for the primal problem the solution value of the kth dual variable is equal to the increased revenue for the kth slack variable in the primal problem; and in any optimal solution for the dual problem the solution value of the kth primal variable is equal to the increased revenue for the kth surplus variable in the dual problem.

To illustrate this theorem, let us return to our linear-programming problem of Section 9.1. The primal problem is:

$$\max f = 150x_1 + 100x_2,$$
$$x_1 + x_2 \le 600,$$
$$2x_1 + x_2 \le 1000,$$

with $x_1 \ge 0$ and $x_2 \ge 0$. The dual problem, then, is

$$\min g = 600w_1 + 1000w_2,$$
$$w_1 + 2w_2 \ge 150,$$
$$w_1 + w_2 \ge 100,$$

with $w_1 \ge 0$ and $w_2 \ge 0$.

Adding the slack variables x_3 and x_4 to the primal problem and the surplus variables w_3 and w_4 to the dual problem, we can convert the two problems into the following forms:

Primal

$$\max f = 150x_1 + 100x_2$$
$$x_1 + x_2 + x_3 = 600$$
$$2x_1 + x_2 + x_4 = 1000$$
$$x_1, \ldots, x_4 \ge 0$$

Dual

$$\max (-g) = -600w_1 - 100w_2$$
$$w_1 + 2w_2 - w_3 = 150$$
$$w_1 + w_2 - w_4 = 100$$
$$w_1, \ldots, w_4 \ge 0$$

The corresponding optimal simplex tableaus are:

Optimal Primal Tableau

Basis variables	Basis prices	x_1	x_2	x_3	x_4	Solution values
x_2	100	0	1	2	−1	200
x_1	150	1	0	−1	1	400
Increased revenues		0	0	50	50	80,000

Optimal Dual Tableau

Basis variables	Basis prices	w_1	w_2	w_3	w_4	Solution values
w_1	−500	1	0	1	−2	50
w_2	−1000	0	1	−1	1	50
Increased revenues		0	0	400	200	−80,000

According to the first tableau, the optimal feasible solution for the primal problem is

$$x_1 = 400, \qquad x_2 = 200.$$

But this solution can also be obtained from the optimal simplex tableau for the dual problem. The bottom row of this tableau shows that the increased revenue for the first surplus variable w_3 is 400 and that for the second surplus variable w_4 is 200. According to duality theorem C, then,

$$x_1 = 400, \qquad x_2 = 200.$$

The second tableau shows that the optimal feasible solution for the dual problem is

$$w_1 = 50, \qquad w_2 = 50.$$

But this solution can also be obtained from the optimal simplex tableau for the primal problem. The bottom row of this tableau shows that the increased revenue for the first slack variable x_3 is 50 and that for the second slack variable x_4 is 50. Thus, according to duality theorem C,

$$w_1 = 50, \qquad w_2 = 50.$$

We have now shown that any given linear-programming problem can be solved by means of either the primal or the dual formulation. But why should we be concerned at all with the dual formulation? The reason is primarily computational. A large number of constraints usually present more computational difficulties than do a large number of variables. Thus if a given linear-programming problem is such that its primal formulation has a large number of constraints but fewer variables, then the same problem can be more efficiently solved by means of the dual formulation, since in the dual problem the relative numbers of constraints and variables are exactly reversed.

EXERCISES

1. Alpha Beta Manufacturing produces two products, named Product 1 and Product 2, with two basic resources, alpha and beta. The following information is available for the solution of the company's product mix problem:

	Input-output coefficients		Quantities of available resources
	Product 1	Product 2	
Alpha	10	20	800,000
Beta	20	10	1,000,000
Profit margins	$300	$200	

Let x_1 and x_2, respectively, be the quantities of Product 1 and Product 2 to be produced, and x_3 and x_4 be the slack variables corresponding to alpha and beta. The simplex tableau for the optimal solution is given below:

Basis variables	Basis prices	x_1	x_2	x_3	x_4	Solution values
x_2	200	0	1	0.0667	−0.0333	20,000
x_1	300	1	0	−0.0333	0.0667	40,000
Increased revenues		0	0	3.3333	13.3333	16,000,000

a. What are alpha and beta's shadow prices?
b. Suppose the company is considering a new product, called Product Y, one unit of which will require 15 units of alpha and 25 units of beta. The profit margin for the product is estimated to be $350. Should the previously obtained optimal product mix plan be revised?
c. Suppose the company can produce another new product, called Product W, one unit of which will require 30 units of alpha and 20 units of beta. What should the minimum profit margin on this product be if its introduction into the product mix is to be beneficial to the company?

2. Storex manufactures three types of computer storage disk packs: Mod 1, Mod 2, and Mod 3. Each disk pack must go through four different production phases: cutting, cleaning and coating, testing, and assembly. We have the following set of information with which to make a product mix decision for the company (see also Exercise 2 of Chapter 5):

	Processing hours			Total hours available per week
	Mod 1	Mod 2	Mod 3	
Cutting	0.2	1.2	2.4	3200
Cleaning and coating	0.8	2.3	5.0	8000
Testing	0.2	0.8	1.2	2400
Assembly	0.3	1.0	2.0	4800
Profit margin	$50	$150	$320	

Let x_1, x_2, and x_3, respectively, be the quantities of Mod 1, Mod 2, and Mod 3 to be produced, and let x_4, x_5, x_6, and x_7, respectively, be the slack variables representing the unused hours of the cutting, cleaning and coating, testing, and assembly facilities. The simplex tableau for an optimum solution of the problem is given below:

Basis variables	Basis prices	x_1	x_2	x_3	x_4	x_5	x_6	x_7	Solution values
x_3	320	0	0	1	0.776	0.345	−2.155	0	68.97
x_1	50	1	0	0	−5.344	2.069	2.069	0	4413.79
x_2	150	0	1	0	0.172	−1.034	3.965	0	1793.10
x_7	0	0	0	0	−0.121	−0.276	−0.276	1	1544.83
Increased revenues		0	0	0	6.896	58.621	8.621	0	511,724

a. What are the shadow prices of the four production processes? What do these shadow prices mean?

b. A competitor has just introduced a sophisticated new disk pack. If Storex is to bring out a similar disk pack, each unit of this disk pack will require 3 hours of cutting, 5 hours of cleaning and coating, 3 hours of testing, and 4 hours of assembly. The profit margin on this new disk pack will be $350. Should Storex bring out the new type of disk pack?

3. ABC Manufacturing produces three products X, Y, and Z. Each product must go through some or all of three manufacturing processes A, B, and C. We are given the following set of information with which to make a product mix decision for the company:

	Weekly production capacity		
	X	Y	Z
A		50,000	40,000
B	40,000	50,000	20,000
C	50,000	25,000	
Profit margin	$2.00	$3.00	$2.40

A linear-programming formulation of the above problem is

$$\max f = 2.0x_1 + 3.0x_2 + 2.4x_3,$$
$$0.00002x_2 + 0.000025x_3 \le 1,$$
$$0.000025x_1 + 0.00002x_2 + 0.00005x_3 \le 1,$$
$$0.00005x_1 + 0.00004x_2 \le 1,$$

where x_1, x_2, and x_3, respectively, represent the quantities of X, Y, and Z. An optimal simplex tableau is shown below where x_4, x_5, and x_6 are the slack variables for A, B, and C, respectively.

Basis variables	Basis prices	x_1	x_2	x_3	x_4	x_5	x_6	Solution values
x_4	0	0	0	0	1	−0.5	−0.25	0.25
x_3	2.4	0.3	0	1	0	20,000	−10,000	10,000
x_2	3.0	0.5	1	0	0	0	25,000	25,000
Increased revenues		0.22	0	0	0	48,000	51,000	99,000

a. What is the composition of the optimal product mix? How much profit will be generated by this product mix?

b. What are the shadow prices and what do the shadow prices mean?

c. Suppose that the company is considering a new product W. The weekly production capacity of the A and C facilities for W are 40,000 units and 50,000 units, respectively. This product does not have to go through process B. The profit margin of W is $1.50. Should the company introduce this product?

d. At present the facilities for B consist in 100 production machines. The company can add another machine to this group at a cost of $400. Will an additional machine be beneficial to the company?

4. We are given the linear-programming problem

$$\max f = 150x_1 + 120x_2 + 160x_3 + 160x_4 + 160x_5,$$

$$10x_1 + 10x_2 + 20x_3 + 30x_4 + 20x_5 + x_6 = 100,000,$$

$$10x_1 + 20x_2 + 10x_3 + 10x_4 + 20x_5 + x_7 = 200,000,$$

$$30x_1 + 20x_2 + 20x_3 + 10x_4 + 10x_5 + x_8 = 280,000,$$

with the usual nonnegativity constraints. An optimal simplex tableau for this problem is:

Basis variables	Basis prices	x_1	x_2	x_3	x_4	x_5	x_6	x_7	x_8	Solution values
x_1	150	1	0	−2	−5	−3	−0.2	0	0.1	8,000
x_2	120	0	1	4	8	5	0.3	0	−0.1	2,000
x_7	0	0	0	−50	−100	−50	−4.0	1	1.1	80,000
Increased revenues		0	0	20	50	50	6.0	0	3	1,440,000

a. For each structural constraint establish the upper and lower limits of the solution value within which the given basis will remain feasible.

b. Establish the extent to which the price of x_3 and x_4 can each be increased without affecting the optimality of the given solution.

c. Establish the upper and lower limits of the prices of x_1 and x_2 within which the given solution will remain feasible.

5. Using the information provided in Exercise 1 by the optimal simplex tableau for the Alpha Beta Manufacturing problem,

a. establish for each resource the upper and lower limits within which the given basis will remain feasible;

b. establish for each nonbasis variable the extent to which the price can be increased without affecting the optimality of the given solution;

c. establish for each basis price the upper and lower limits within which the given solution will remain optimal.

6. Utilizing the information provided by the optimal simplex tableau in Exercise 2,

a. establish for each storex production process the upper and lower limits of total use within which the given basis will remain feasible;

b. establish the price range for each type of disk pack within which the given solution will remain optimal.

7. Utilizing the information provided by the optimal simplex tableau for ABC Manufacturing in Exercise 3,

a. establish the upper and lower limits of the solution value for each structural constraint and interpret the significance of these limits;

b. establish for each product the profit range within which the given solution will remain optimal.

8. Convert the following linear-programming problem,

$$\min f = 10x_1 + 6x_2,$$
$$2x_1 + x_2 \geq 4000,$$
$$x_1 + x_2 \geq 3000,$$
$$x_1, x_2 \geq 0,$$

into a maximizing problem. Then solve the new problem by the simplex method.

9. Convert the following linear-programming problem,

$$\min f = 10x_1 + 6x_2 + 8x_3,$$
$$x_1 + x_2 + 2x_3 \geq 6000,$$
$$4x_1 + x_2 + x_3 \geq 10,000,$$

with the usual nonnegativity constraints, into a maximizing problem. Then solve the new problem by the simplex method.

10. Solve the following linear programming problem by the simplex method:

$$\max f = x_1 + 2x_2 + x_3,$$
$$2x_1 + x_2 + x_3 = 300,$$
$$x_1 + x_2 + 2x_3 = 200,$$
$$x_1, x_2, x_3 \geq 0.$$

11. Solve the following linear-programming problem by the simplex method:

$$\max f = 2x_1 + x_2,$$
$$x_1 + x_2 \leq 10,$$
$$x_1 + x_2 \geq 5,$$
$$x_1, x_2 \geq 0.$$

12. Apply the simplex method to the following problem to show that the problem has no feasible solution:

$$\max f = 2x_1 + 3x_2,$$
$$x_1 + x_2 \leq 10,$$
$$x_1 + x_2 \geq 20,$$
$$x_1, x_2 \geq 0.$$

13. Show that the following problem does not have a solution by applying the simplex method:

$$\max f = x_1 + 2x_2,$$
$$x_1 + x_2 = 10,$$
$$2x_1 + 2x_2 = 30,$$
$$x_1, x_2 \geq 0.$$

14. Healthy Vitamin uses two substances, M1 and M2, to produce vitamin pills. Each pill must contain 30 units of vitamin A and 20 units of vitamin B. From one unit of M1 can be extracted 20 units of vitamin A and 10 units of vitamin B. From one unit of M2 can be extracted 10 units of vitamin A and 10 units of vitamin B. The unit costs are 3¢ for M1 and 2¢ for M2. The company wants to mix the two substances in such proportions as to minimize the total cost of a vitamin pill.

Let x_1 and x_2, respectively, be the quantities of M1 and M2 used in a pill. Then the problem may be initially formulated as follows:

$$\min f = 3x_1 + 2x_2,$$
$$20x_1 + 10x_2 \geq 30,$$
$$10x_1 + 10x_2 \geq 20,$$
$$x_1, x_2 \geq 0.$$

After converting the above into a maximizing problem and adding the surplus variables x_3 and x_4 and the artificial variables x_5 and x_6, we can obtain the following optimal simplex tableau:

Basis variables	Basis prices	x_1	x_2	x_3	x_4	x_5	x_6	Solution values
x_1	−3	1	0	−0.1	0.1	0.1	−0.1	1
x_2	−2	0	1	0.1	−0.2	−0.1	0.2	1
Increased revenues		0	0	0.1	0.1	$M - 0.1$	$M - 0.1$	−5

a. What are the shadow prices of vitamins A and B?

b. Suppose the vitamin A requirement in a pill is increased by one unit. How will the unit cost of the pill be affected?

c. Suppose the company can purchase vitamin B in pure form at a cost of 3¢ per 10 units. Should it use any vitamin B in pure form? Explain your answer.

d. The company can use another substance, say Y. From one unit of Y can be extracted 10 units of A and 20 units of B. The cost of Y is 4¢ per unit. Should the company use any of this substance in its vitamin production? Why?

15. Fresh Grown Fryers can use fish meal and yellow corn in its chicken feed mix, but the mix must contain at least 20% protein and 5% fat. The protein and fat contents of fish meal and yellow corn are:

	Fish meal	Yellow corn
Protein	60%	10%
Fat	13%	3%

The costs per ton are $130 for fish meal and $40 for yellow corn, and the company wants to minimize the total cost of its feed mix.

Let x_1 and x_2 be the respective percentages of fish meal and yellow corn in the mix. Then the problem can be formulated as follows:

$$\min f = 130x_1 + 40x_2,$$
$$60x_1 + 10x_2 \geq 20,$$
$$13x_1 + 3x_2 \geq 5,$$
$$x_1 + x_2 = 1,$$

with the usual nonnegativity constraints. An optimal simplex tableau for the problem is:

Basis variables	Basis prices	x_1	x_2	x_3	x_4	x_5	x_6	x_7	Solution values
x_1	130	1	0	-0.02	0	0.02	0	-0.2	0.2
x_6	0	0	0	0.2	-1	-0.2	1	-1.0	0
x_2	40	0	1	0.02	0	-0.02	0	1.2	0.8
Increased revenues		0	0	1.8	0	$M-1.8$	0	$M-22$	-58.0

Here x_3 and x_4 are, respectively, the surplus variables for the first two constraints, and x_5, x_6, and x_7 are the artificial variables.

a. What are the shadow prices and what do they mean?
b. Suppose the minimum protein requirement is increased from 20% to 21%. How will the cost of the mix be affected?
c. Suppose the minimum fat requirement is increased from 5% to 6%. How will the cost of the mix be affected?

16. No-Flat Tire manufactures tires for automobile companies. The delivery commitments, production capacities, and unit production costs for the next three months are:

Month	Delivery requirement	Production capacity	Unit cost
1	100,000	150,000	20.00
2	140,000	150,000	21.50
3	180,000	150,000	22.50

The holding cost is $1 per tire per month. The company wants to minimize the total cost of meeting the quarterly delivery commitment. There is no beginning inventory and there must not be any end inventory.

Let x_i and y_i, respectively, be the quantity of production and the end inventory for each period i. Then the problem may be formulated as follows:

x_1	y_1	x_2	y_2	x_3	s_1	s_2	s_3	
1	-1							= 100,000
	1	1	-1					= 140,000
			1	1				= 180,000
1					1			= 150,000
		1				1		= 150,000
				1			1	= 150,000
20.00	1	21.50	1	22.50				= f (min)

Table 11.1

Basis variables	Basis prices	x_1	y_1	x_2	y_2	x_3	s_1	s_2	s_3	α_1	α_2	α_3	Solution values
x_1	−20.0	1	0	0	0	0	1	0	0	0	0	0	150,000
x_2	−21.5	0	0	1	0	0	0	1	0	0	0	0	150,000
x_3	−22.5	0	0	0	0	1	−1	−1	0	1	1	1	120,000
y_1	−1.0	0	1	0	0	0	1	0	0	−1	0	0	50,000
y_2	−1.0	0	0	0	1	0	1	1	0	−1	−1	0	60,000
s_3	0	0	0	0	0	0	1	1	1	−1	−1	−1	30,000
Increased revenues		0	0	0	0	0	0.5	0	0	$M - 20.5$	$M - 21.5$	$M - 22.5$	9,035,000

Here s_i is the unused production capacity during the period i.

After converting the problem into a maximizing problem and adding the artificial variables α_1, α_2, and α_3, respectively, for the first three constraints, we can obtain the optimal simplex tableau in Table 11.1.

a. What is the optimal production plan for the next three months?

b. What are the shadow prices and what do they mean?

c. Suppose the company can increase its production capacity during the first month by one unit. How will the total cost of meeting the delivery requirement be affected?

d. Suppose the delivery requirement for the first month is increased by one unit. How will the total cost of meeting the delivery requirement be affected?

17. Formulate the dual of the following primal linear-programming problem:

$$\max f = 2x_1 + x_2,$$
$$x_1 + 2x_2 \le 400,$$
$$x_1 + x_2 \le 300,$$
$$2x_1 + x_2 \le 500,$$
$$x_1, x_2 \ge 0.$$

18. Given the following dual linear-programming problem,

$$\min g = 100w_1 + 200w_2,$$
$$w_1 + 2w_2 \ge 2,$$
$$w_1 + w_2 \ge 1,$$
$$2w_1 + w_2 \ge 3,$$
$$w_1, w_2 \ge 0,$$

formulate the primal problem.

19. Given the following primal linear-programming problem,

$$\max f = 3x_1 + 2x_2 + 4x_3,$$
$$2x_1 + x_2 + x_3 = 400,$$
$$x_1 + x_2 + 2x_3 = 400,$$
$$x_1, x_2, x_3 \ge 0,$$

formulate the dual problem.

20. Given the following linear-programming problem,

$$\min f = 3x_1 + 2x_2,$$
$$2x_1 + x_2 \ge 100,$$
$$x_1 + x_2 = 80,$$
$$x_1 + 2x_2 \ge 120,$$
$$x_1, x_2 \ge 0,$$

formulate the dual problem.

21. Given the following dual linear-programming problem,

$$\min g = 200w_1 + 300w_2 + 400w_3,$$
$$w_1 + 2w_2 + w_3 \geq 2,$$
$$2w_1 + w_2 + 2w_3 \geq 3,$$
$$w_1, w_3 \geq 0,$$

where w_2 is unrestricted in sign, formulate the primal problem.

CHAPTER

12

NETWORK MODELS

Some linear-programming problems possess a special mathematical structure called a *network*. They are then called *network models*. Two reasons motivate us to study network models. First, there are many important practical problems which can be formulated in terms of network models. If we are familiar with the mathematical structure of network models, then the solution of these problems will certainly be made easier for us. Second, a number of computational procedures are specifically designed for solving network models. Consequently, some linear-programming problems possessing network structures may be solved more easily than others for which we have only the general procedure for solving all linear-programming problems.

12.1 NETWORK

We are familiar with such expressions as "transportation network," "communications network," and "transmission network." Here we shall describe the mathematical structure of a network.

A network is a collection of *nodes* and *arcs* where each node is connected with one or more of the other nodes by arcs. Figure 12.1, for example, shows a

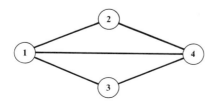

Figure 12.1

network. In this figure a circle with a number depicts a node and a line connecting two circled numbers depicts the arc connecting the two nodes. A sequence of arcs joining any two node is called a *chain*. Thus in Figure 12.1,

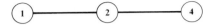

‚is one of the chains connecting nodes 1 and 4. Another such chain is:

A chain of arcs connecting a node to itself is called a *loop*. One example of a loop in the network of Figure 12.1 is:

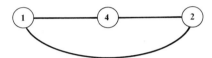

A network which does not contain any loop and in which every node is connected to every other node by a chain of arcs is called a *tree*. An example of a tree is:

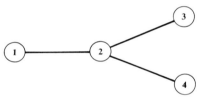

If an arc is drawn as an arrow, for example

it is said to be *directed*, in this case from 1 to 2. The arc ① → ② is then considered to be different from the arc ② → ① even though both connect nodes 1 and 2.

Network models may be divided into the following three categories according to their applications:

1. maximum-flow models,
2. shortest-path models,
3. activity network models.

In this chapter we shall describe maximum-flow and shortest-path models. Subsequently we shall devote an entire chapter to activity network models.

12.2 MAXIMUM-FLOW PROBLEMS

Let us examine the network with directed arcs shown in Figure 12.2. Assume that a certain commodity flows into the network at the node labeled *source*

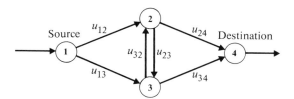

Figure 12.2

through the network along the directed arcs and out of the network at the node labeled *destination*. The capacities of the arcs are indicated by u_{ij}.

Then the maximum-flow problem connected with this network is to determine the quantities of flow along each arc that will maximize the total flow through the network. We may formulate a model for the problem as follows. There are two types of constraints: one on the arcs and the other on the nodes.

Let x_{ij} be the quantity of flow to be allowed in the directed arc from i to j. Then the constraints on the arcs are:

$$0 \leq x_{12} < u_{12}, \qquad 0 \leq x_{13} \leq u_{13}, \qquad o \leq x_{23} \leq u_{23},$$

$$0 \leq x_{32} \leq u_{32}, \qquad 0 \leq x_{24} \leq u_{24}, \qquad 0 \leq x_{34} \leq u_{34},$$

which simply specify that the actual quantity of flow through any arc from i to j cannot exceed the capacity of that arc.

Next we let f be the quantity of flow into node 1. From there the flow must continue into either node 2 or node 3. Therefore,

$$x_{12} + x_{13} = f$$

is another constraint, called a *material-balance equation* for the simple reason that it says the sum of the material that flows into a node must be equal to the sum of the material that flows out from that node. The remaining material-balance equations for Figure 12.2 are:

$$x_{12} + x_{32} = x_{23} + x_{24} \qquad \text{(node 2)},$$

$$x_{13} + x_{23} = x_{32} + x_{34} \qquad \text{(node 3)},$$

$$x_{24} + x_{34} = f \qquad \text{(node 4)}.$$

These four constraints, then, pertain to the nodes.

We note that the second material-balance equation may be rearranged to read:

$$-x_{12} + x_{23} + x_{24} - x_{32} = 0.$$

The second and third equations may also be rearranged so that the whole set of constraints for the nodes becomes:

$$
\begin{aligned}
x_{12} + x_{13} && &= f, \\
-x_{12} && + x_{23} + x_{24} - x_{32} &= 0, \\
&- x_{13} - x_{23} && + x_{32} + x_{34} = 0, \\
&&- x_{24} && - x_{34} = -f.
\end{aligned}
$$

Now we can summarize the four material-balance equations in the form of a table:

Arcs

$$
\begin{array}{c}
\text{Nodes} \\
\end{array}
\begin{array}{c}
\\
1 \\
2 \\
3 \\
4 \\
\end{array}
\begin{array}{c}
\begin{array}{cccccc}
x_{12} & x_{13} & x_{23} & x_{24} & x_{32} & x_{34} \\
\end{array} \\
\left[
\begin{array}{cccccc}
1 & 1 & & & & \\
-1 & & 1 & 1 & -1 & \\
& -1 & -1 & & 1 & 1 \\
& & & -1 & & -1 \\
\end{array}
\right]
\end{array}
\begin{array}{l}
= f \\
= 0 \\
= 0 \\
= -f \\
\end{array}
$$

The brackets indicated that the table is in the form of a *matrix*. In this case it is called a *node-arc incidence matrix*. (A unique property of the node-arc incidence matrix is that every element in the matrix is either 1 or -1.)

The maximum-flow problem is then solved by maximizing f, subject to the constraints of the node-arc incidence matrix and the arc flow capacity constraints $0 \leq x_{ij} \leq u_{ij}$.

It is obvious that we can apply the network models, for example, to the calculation of maximum rate of traffic flow between two cities, or the maximum rate of flow in a natural gas transmission network between two terminals, or the maximum amount of electric power that can be transmitted from a generating station to a given geographic region. We note that all of these problems involve **genuine networks**.

There are, however, also problems without genuine networks that can nevertheless be formulated as maximum-flow problems in networks. Consider the following examples.

Example 1. Transportation Problem Gamma Manufacturing produces its product at two different plants, labeled 1 and 2. The product must be shipped to two warehouses, labeled 3 and 4. We are given the following information on plant production and warehouse requirements:

	Warehouses		Quantities
	3	**4**	**produced**
Plant 1	p_{13}	p_{14}	300
Plant 2	p_{23}	p_{24}	400
Quantities required	500	200	

Here p_{13}, for example, is the unit profit margin of an item shipped from plant 1 to warehouse 3, after taking into account the transportation cost.

Assume that Gamma Manufacturing wants to allocate the commodity produced at the two plants to the warehouses in such a way as to maximize the total profit. Then we have what is called a *transportation problem*.

We remember having formulated such a problem in Chapter 9. Here we shall reformulate the problem to show that the mathematical model portraying the problem in fact has a network structure.

Let x_{ij} be the quantity to be shipped from plant i to warehouse j. Then the objective function is

$$\max f = p_{13}x_{13} + p_{14}x_{14} + p_{23}x_{23} + p_{24}x_{24},$$

and the constraints are

x_{13}	x_{14}	x_{23}	x_{24}		
1	1			=	300
		1	1	=	400
1		1		=	500
	1		1	=	200

or

x_{13}	x_{14}	x_{23}	x_{24}		
1	1			=	300
		1	1	=	400
-1		-1		=	-500
	-1		-1	=	-200

We note that this set of four equations amounts to a node-arc incidence matrix. If we add the constraints that $x_{ij} \geq 0$, then we have completed a formulation of the transportation problem. The structure of this problem can also be diagramed as shown in Figure 12.3.

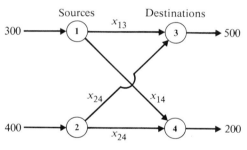

Figure 12.3

One may ask in what sense the given transportation problem is a maximum-flow problem. In regular maximum-flow problems we try to maximize the total quantity of flow. In the transportation problem, however, we are maximizing a value generated by the flow.

Example 2. Transshipment Problem   The following table gives the components of the transportation costs of Delta Manufacturing:

| | Warehouses | | Quantity |
	3	4	produced
Plant 1	c_{13}	c_{14}	500
Plant 2	c_{23}	c_{24}	500
Quantities required	600	400	1000

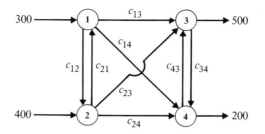

Figure 12.4

Here c_{13}, for example, is the transportation cost of shipping a unit from plant 1 to warehouse 3. Assuming that Delta Manufacturing wants to ship the products of the two plants to the two warehouses in such quantities as to minimize the total transportation cost, we can obviously formulate the problem in the form of the transportation model given in Example 1.

Suppose, however, that shipments between plants and between warehouses are also possible at the following costs:

	Between plants			Between warehouses	
	1	2		3	4
1		c_{12}	3		c_{34}
2	c_{21}		4	c_{43}	

Figure 12.4 shows a network allowing such transshipments. The constraint for node 1, then, is

$$300 + x_{21} = x_{12} + x_{13} + x_{14}.$$

Rearranging the terms and formulating similar constraints for the other nodes, we have

Nodes	x_{12}	x_{13}	x_{14}	x_{21}	x_{23}	x_{24}	x_{34}	x_{43}		
1	1	1	1	-1					$=$	300
2	-1			1	1	1			$=$	400
3		-1			-1		1	-1	$=$	-500
4			-1			-1	-1	1	$=$	-200

which is a node-arc incidence matrix.

The objective function for the problem is therefore

$$\min f = c_{13}x_{13} + c_{14}x_{14} + c_{23}x_{23} + c_{24}x_{24} + c_{12}x_{12} + c_{21}x_{21} + c_{34}x_{34} + c_{43}x_{43}.$$

Example 3. Assignment Problem   Easy-to-Learn Textbook Company has divided California into two sales territories, say 1 and 2. Two salesmen want to be assigned to California. The problem is to assign the right salesman to the right sales territory. Let s_{ij} be the sales that can be generated by salesman

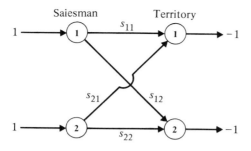

Figure 12.5

i in territory j. Then the problem can be shown as a network, as in Figure 12.5.

This is called an *assignment problem*. An assignment problem is a special case of the transportation problem, with the following properties:

a. If there are m sources, then there must also be m destinations.
b. The flow into any source or out of any destination is 1.
c. If x_{ij} is the flow through the arc from i to j, then x_{ij} is either 1 or 0.

The node-arc incidence matrix and the coefficients of the objective function are then given as follows:

x_{11}	x_{12}	x_{21}	x_{22}		
1	1			$=$	1
		1	1	$=$	1
-1		-1		$=$	-1
	-1		-1	$=$	-1
s_{11}	s_{12}	s_{21}	s_{22}	$=$	f (min.).

We note again that the node-arc incidence matrix exhibits a network structure.

Example 4. Production Planning Problem The delivery commitments, production capacities, and unit production costs for the next three production periods of No-Flat Tire Company are:

Period	Delivery commitments	Production capacities	Unit production cost
1	100,000	150,000	$20.00
2	140,000	150,000	21.50
3	180,000	150,000	22.50

The holding cost is $1 per tire per month.

Assuming that there is no inventory at the beginning of period 1 and the company does not want any inventory left over at the end of period 3, how should the company plan its production so as to minimize the total cost of meeting its delivery commitments for the three periods.

For each of the three periods the following material-balance equation must hold:

$$\underset{\text{inventory}}{\text{Beginning}} + \underset{\text{produced}}{\text{Quantity}} - \underset{\text{delivered}}{\text{Quantity}} = \underset{\text{inventory,}}{\text{End}}$$

which may be written

$$\underset{\text{inventory}}{\text{Beginning}} + \underset{\text{produced}}{\text{Quantity}} - \underset{\text{inventory}}{\text{End}} = \underset{\text{delivered.}}{\text{Quantity}}$$

Let x_i and y_i be respectively the quantity produced and the end inventory of period i. Then the material-balance equation for the first period may be expressed as

$$y_0 + x_1 - y_1 = 100,000,$$

where $y_0 = 0$ by assumption. Those for the succeeding two periods are

$$y_1 + x_2 - y_2 = 140,000,$$
$$y_2 + x_3 - y_3 = 180,000,$$

where $y_3 = 0$ by assumption.

The production capacity constraints for the three periods are:

$$x_1 \leq 150,000, \qquad x_2 \leq 150,000, \qquad x_3 \leq 150,000.$$

The constraint $x_1 \leq 150,000$, however, is equivalent to $-x_1 \geq -150,000$.

Summarizing the constraints and adding the objective function, we have:

x_1	y_1	x_2	y_2	x_3		
1	-1				$=$	100,000
	1	1	-1		$=$	140,000
			1	1	$=$	180,000
-1					$\geq$	$-150,000$
		-1			$\geq$	$-150,000$
				-1	$\geq$	$-150,000$
20.0	1.0	21.50	1.0	22.5	$=$	f (min.).

Again we have a model with a network structure.

12.3 SHORTEST-PATH PROBLEMS

Let us consider the network in Figure 12.6, where c_{12}, for example, is the distance between node 1 and node 2. We may wish to find a chain between the source and the destination which constitutes the shortest path between the two nodes. The chain having the shortest distance is called the *shortest path* between the two nodes, and the problem of finding the shortest path is called the *shortest-path problem*.

Finding the shortest path between the source and the destination, however,

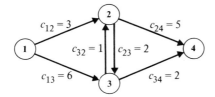

Figure 12.6

is only a special example of shortest-path problems. Some examples are finding:

1. the shortest path between any two nodes,
2. the shortest path from one node to all the other nodes in a network,
3. the shortest path between every pair of nodes in a network.

Let us now reexamine the problem of the shortest path between the source and destination. The problem can be solved by means of a linear-programming model. One way to construct such a model is to consider the shortest-path problem as one of transshipment where one unit of an item flows into the source and out of the destination and nodes 2 and 3 are merely transshipment points. Then the node-arc incidence matrix is:

Nodes	x_{12}	x_{13}	x_{23}	x_{24}	x_{32}	x_{34}		
				Arcs				
1	1	1					=	1
2	−1		1	1	−1		=	0
3		−1	−1		1	1	=	0
4				−1		−1	=	−1.

And the objective function is

$$\min f = c_{12}x_{12} + c_{13}x_{13} + c_{23}x_{23} + c_{24}x_{24} + c_{32}x_{32} + c_{34}x_{34},$$

with the nonnegative constraints $x_{12}, \ldots, x_{34} \geq 0$.

There are many practical problems which have the character of shortest-path problems. One very obvious example is a driver's search for the shortest path between two cities. Another is finding the cheapest among several shipping routes between two points. A somewhat less obvious example is an airplane pilot's determination of the flight path in terms of altitude and plane velocity that will minimize the time required for the plane to climb from an initial altitude and velocity to a prescribed final altitude and velocity.

There are, however, also many practical problems, not essentially shortest-path problems, that can nevertheless be converted into shortest-path problems. Some examples follow.

Example 5. Replacement Problem Reliable Machine Shop will need a certain piece of equipment for the next three years. It can buy the equipment and use it for three years, replace the equipment every year, or take up some other combination of purchase and replacement. The net costs of the various options are indicated in Figure 12.7, where, for example, the net cost of buying the equipment now and using it for two years is shown to be $20,000. The machine shop wants to plan the equipment replacement schedule so as to minimize the total cost for the three-year period.

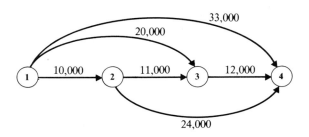

Figure 12.7

The problem is simple enough that we can solve it without formulating a mathematical model. A careful examination of Figure 12.7 will show that there are only four feasible replacement schedules with the following total costs:

Schedules	Total cost
$1 \rightarrow 4$	$33,000
$1 \rightarrow 3 \rightarrow 4$	32,000
$1 \rightarrow 2 \rightarrow 4$	34,000
$1 \rightarrow 2 \rightarrow 3 \rightarrow 4$	33,000

Obviously the optimum schedule is to use the first equipment for two years and a second piece of equipment for one year, at a total cost of $32,000.

While we have solved the replacement problem by enumeration, the problem might have been more complex, in which case we would have had to formulate a model. We will therefore formulate a mathematical model for the given replacement problem.

Suppose that the net cost c_{ij} is really the distance between nodes i and j. Then the equipment problem in question becomes a shortest-path problem. Thus we let

$$x_{ij} = \begin{cases} 1 & \text{if the replacement schedule calls for} \\ & \text{buying at time } i \text{ and replacing} \\ & \text{it at time } j, \\ 0 & \text{if the schedule does not call} \\ & \text{for buying at time } i \text{ and} \\ & \text{replacing it at time } j. \end{cases}$$

Then the node-arc incidence matrix is:

Nodes	x_{12}	x_{13}	x_{14}	x_{23}	x_{24}	x_{34}	
1	1	1	1				= 1
2	−1			1	1		= 0
3		−1		−1		1	= 0
4			−1		−1	−1	= −1
	10,000	20,000	33,000	11,000	24,000	12,000	f

where the coefficients of the objective function are in the bottom row. The optimum solution for this problem is:

$$x_{13} = 1, \qquad x_{34} = 1, \qquad \text{all other } x_{ij} = 0,$$
$$f = 20{,}000x_{13} + 12{,}000x_{34} = 32{,}000.$$

Example 6. Reliability Problem   Let us consider the following simple reliability problem. We need to choose one system from the two shown in Figure 12.8. System 1 consists of components A and B with reliability factors of 0.8 and 0.7, respectively. System 2 consists of components C and D with reliability factors of 0.9 and 0.6, respectively. In each case both components must work if the system is to work. The problem is to select the system with the larger reliability factor.

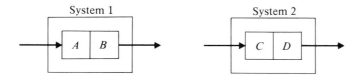

Figure 12.8

We can again solve this problem without formulating a mathematical model. Let us assume that the components in each system work independently of each other. Then the reliabilities of the systems are:

System 1 $P(A)P(B) = (0.8)(0.7) = 0.56$
System 2 $P(C)P(D) = (0.9)(0.6) = 0.54$

System 1 is evidently more reliable.

The same problem, however, can be transformed into a shortest-path problem. First, let us construct the network characterization of the problem, as

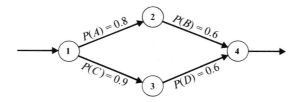

Figure 12.9

shown in Figure 12.9. Then what we want is the path between nodes 1 and 4 with the highest reliability factor.

According to probability laws, the reliability factor associated with a path is the product of the reliability coefficients in that path. We know, however, that if

$$y = A \times B,$$

then

$$\log y = \log A + \log B.$$

Thus we can add the logarithms of the appropriate reliability coefficients to obtain the reliability factor for a path. The logarithmic coefficients for the above network are shown in Figure 12.10, yielding the following reliability calculations:

	Log of reliability	Antilog
System 1	$-0.0969 - 0.1549 = -0.2518$	0.56
System 2	$-0.0458 - 0.2218 = -0.2676$	0.54

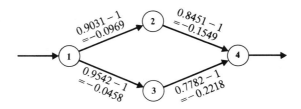

Figure 12.10

We note that since a reliability coefficient must be between zero and one, its logarithmic coefficient is always negative. Thus we can ignore the minus signs in our calculations. And we observe that the path with the larger reliability is the one with the smaller absolute value of the logarithmic reliability coefficient. Thus the problem amounts to finding the shortest path between source and destination. A model for this problem is as follows.

Node	Arcs			
	x_{12}	x_{13}	x_{24}	x_{34}
1	1	1		1
2	-1		1	0
3		-1		1	0
4			-1	-1	-1
	0.0969	0.1549	0.0458	0.2218 f

The optimal solution is:

$$x_{12} = 1, \quad x_{13} = 0, \quad x_{24} = 1, \quad x_{34} = 0,$$
$$f = 0.0969x_{12} + 0.1549x_{24} = 0.2518.$$

12.4 NETWORK ALGORITHMS

Even though all the network problems that we have so far examined have rather similar mathematical structures, the differences must not be overlooked, because they mean the use of different types of computational algorithms. Consider the maximum-flow problems. They lend themselves to the following classifications:

1. maximum-flow problems with capacitated networks,
2. transportation problems,
3. assignment problems.

There are well-known computational algorithms for each of these types of problems.

While it would be worthwhile to study all the different types of network algorithms, their detailed discussion is beyond the scope of this book. We shall describe just one such algorithm in the following section as an illustration of how a network algorithm might differ from the general linear-programming algorithm. For other types of algorithms the reader may consult the references listed at the end of this chapter.

12.5 A SHORTEST-PATH ALGORITHM

Consider the network shown in Figure 12.11. The distances between the nodes are given by members accompanying the directed arcs. The problem is to find the shortest path from node 1 to node 4. We note that all the distances are nonnegative.

Several well-known algorithms are available for this problem. We shall describe only one. Let d_{ij} be the direct distance between nodes i and j. For example, $d_{11} = 0$ and $d_{12} = 3$. Since nodes 1 and 4 are not directly connected, we may write $d_{14} = \infty$. The direct distances between the nodes are shown in the

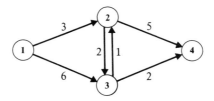

Figure 12.11

matrix below. The fact that the node 2, for example, cannot be reached directed from node 4 is indicated by $d_{42} = \infty$.

	1	2	3	4
1	0	3	6	∞
2	∞	0	2	5
3	∞	1	0	2
4	∞	∞	∞	0

Now we let y_j be the shortest distance between nodes 1 and j. Thus y_4 is the shortest distance between nodes 1 and 4. Then our problem is solved once we have determined the path from node 1 to node 4 that yields y_4. Needless to say, the problem is also solved when we know the paths which yield y_2, y_3, as well as y_4.

Let Y_j^0 be a tentative value for y_j. Initially we assign a very large value to Y_j^0 so that y_j cannot exceed Y_j^0. This can be done by letting $Y_2^0 = \infty$, $Y_3^0 = \infty$, and $Y_4^0 = \infty$. Then we say that the jth node has been *temporarily labeled*.

Having assigned the initial tentative values Y_j^0, we can calculate new tentative values, Y_j^1, as follows:

$$Y_j^1 = \min_{j=2,3,4}\{Y_j^0, y_1 + d_{1j}\},$$

where $y_1 = 0$. Then we will have:

$$Y_2^1 = \min\{Y_2^0, y_1 + d_{12}\} = \min\{\infty, 0 + 3\} = 3,$$
$$Y_3^1 = \min\{Y_3^0, y_1 + d_{13}\} = \min\{\infty, 0 + 6\} = 6,$$
$$Y_4^1 = \min\{Y_4^0, y_1 + d_{14}\} = \min\{\infty, 0 + \infty\} = \infty.$$

Now Y_3^1, for example, is 6. It may not be the shortest distance between nodes 1 and 3, but it is the actual distance of one possible path from node 1 to node 3. Consequently, the shortest distance from node 1 to node 3 cannot be larger than Y_3^1.

Similarly, we can argue that the shortest distance from node 1 to node 2 cannot exceed Y_2^1, which is 3, and that from node 1 to node 4 cannot exceed Y_4^1, which is ∞.

Now we let

$$Y^1 = \min\{Y_2^1, Y_3^1, Y_4^1\} = \min\{3, 6, \infty\} = 3.$$

We observe that Y_2^1 is the smallest of the actual distances from node 1 to the remaining three nodes. Our intuition also suggests that the node that is closest to node 1 should be directly reachable from node 1, so that $Y^1 = 3$ is the actual distance from node 1 to that node which is closest to it.

Since $Y^1 = Y_2^1$, we may conclude that node 2 is closest to node 1. Furthermore, since $Y^1 = Y_2^1 = 3$ is the direct distance between nodes 1 and 2, it must also be the shortest distance between nodes 1 and 2.

The significance of our results so far is that at least one among Y_2^1, Y_3^1, and Y_4^1 is no longer a tentative value, since Y_2^1 is in fact the actual shortest distance from node 1 to node 2. We will indicate the fact that $Y_2^1 = 3$ is no longer a tentative value by writing $y_2 = Y_2^1 = 3$. We say that node 2 has been *permanently labeled*.

Next we proceed in the same way with the other temporarily labeled nodes: for example,

$$Y_j^2 = \min_{j=3,4}\{Y_j^1, y_2 + d_{2j}\},$$

so that

$$Y_3^2 = \min\{Y_3^1, y_2 + d_{23}\} = \min\{6, 3 + 2\} = 5,$$
$$Y_4^2 = \min\{Y_4^1, y_2 + d_{24}\} = \min\{\infty, 3 + 5\} = 8.$$

The shortest distance from node 1 to node 3 cannot exceed $Y_3^2 = 5$, and that from node 1 to node 4 cannot exceed 8. Now,

$$Y^2 = \min\{Y_3^2, Y_4^2\} = \min\{5, 8\} = 5.$$

Therefore, $Y^2 = 5$ must be the shortest distance from node 1 to that node which is second closest to it. But $Y^2 = Y_3^2$ implies that node 3 is this node, and $Y_3^2 = 5$ means that the shortest distance between nodes 1 and 3 is 5. Thus we can permanently label node 3 by writing $y_3 = 5$.

Proceeding to the remaining temporarily labeled node, we have

$$Y_j^3 = \min_{j=4}\{Y_j^3, y_3 + d_{3j}\},$$

so that

$$Y_4^3 = \min\{Y_4^2, y_3 + d_{34}\} = \min\{8, 5 + 2\} = 7.$$

We can further ascertain that

$$Y^4 = \min\{Y_4^3\} = \min\{7\} = 7.$$

Thus $Y^3 = Y_4^3 = 7$ is the shortest distance from node 1 to that node which is third closest to it. Hence we write $y_4 = 7$, completing the permanent labeling of all the nodes in the network, as shown in Figure 12.12.

Now if we want to determine the composition of the arcs making up the shortest path from node 1 to node 4, we can do so as follows. We observe that y_4 must be equal to either $y_2 + 5$ or $y_3 + 2$. But y_4 cannot be $y_2 + 5$ since $y_4 = 7$ and $y_2 + 5 = 8$. Thus $y_4 = y_3 + 2 = 7$, so that the path must contain the arc from node 3 to node 4.

Next we observe that y_3 must be equal to either $y_0 + 6$ or $y_2 + 2$. But y_3

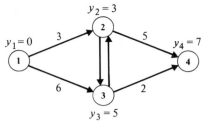

Figure 12.12

cannot be $y_0 + 6 = 6$ since $y_3 = 5$. Thus $y_3 = y_2 + 2 = 5$, which in turn suggests that the shortest path from node 1 to node 3 must contain the arc between nodes 2 and 3.

Finally, we observe that the shortest path from node 1 to node 2 must contain the arc directly connecting the two nodes. Thus, retracing our steps, we find that the shortest path from node 1 to node 4 consists of the following arcs:

The shortest path from node 1 to any other node may be determined in the same way.

Example 7. Consider the network shown in Figure 12.13. The calculations for the shortest paths are summarized in Table 12.1, where permanent labeling is indicated by the circled distances. Using the information in the table, we can find the shortest path from the source to any other node in the network, as shown in Figure 12.14.

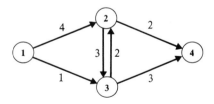

Figure 12.13

Table 12.1

	0	1	2	3
Y_1^i	①	0	0	0
Y_2^i	∞	min $\{\infty, 0 + 4\} = 4$	min $\{4, 1 + 2\} = $ ③	3
Y_3^i	∞	min $\{\infty, 0 + 1\} = $ ①	1	1
Y_4^i	∞	min $\{\infty, 0 + \infty\} = \infty$	min $\{\infty, 1 + 3\} = 4$	min $\{4, 3 + 2\} = $ ④

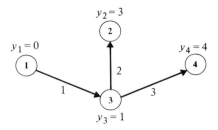

Figure 12.14

Example 8. The shortest-path algorithm described in this section will not work, however, whenever there is an arc having a negative distance. Consider the network, shown in Figure 12.15. The calculations for the shortest paths are summarized in Table 12.2, which indicates that the shortest path from node 1 to node 3 is ① → ③ with a distance of 1. But an examination of the network will reveal that the path that is actually shortest is ① → ② → ③, which has a distance of −1.

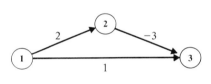

Figure 12.15

Table 12.2

	0	1	2
Y_1^i	⓪	0	0
Y_2^i	∞	min $\{\infty, 0 + 2\} = 2$	②
Y_3^i	∞	min $\{\infty, 0 + 1\} = $ ①	1

While we shall not describe them here, there are also algorithms for finding the shortest paths in networks with negative arc distances.

EXERCISES

1. In the network shown in Figure 12.16 the number accompanying an arrow indicates the flow capacity of that arc. Formulate a network model that will maximize the total flow for the network.

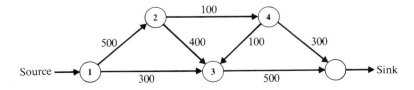

Figure 12.16

2. There are two pipelines from the oil fields in northern Alaska to two ports in southern Alaska. The pipeline to Port A has a daily capacity of 800,000 barrels, and that to Port B has a capacity of 500,000 barrels a day. There is a pipeline between Port A and Port B with a capacity of 200,000 barrels a day in either direction.

Crude oil must be carried from the two ports to the west coast of the continental United States by tankers. Port A can accommodate 500,000 barrels a day, whereas Port B can accommodate 800,000 barrels a day. Formulate a network model for maximizing the total flow of crude oil from the Alaskan North Slope to the west coast of the United States.

3. Rich Oil Company has two refineries in the United States with the following production costs and capacities:

Refinery	Production cost (per gallon)	Production capacity (gallons per day)
1	$0.20	3,000,000
2	0.22	5,000,000

The company has divided the United States into three marketing areas with the following characteristics:

Market area	Wholesale price (per gallon)	Daily demand (gallons)
1	$0.35	2,000,000
2	0.32	4,000,000
3	0.34	3,000,000

The transportation costs per gallon from the refineries to the marketing areas are:

Refinery	Market area 1	2	3
1	$0.04	$0.06	$0.05
2	0.05	0.03	0.01

Formulate a network model for allocating the gasoline from the refineries to the marketing areas in such a way as to maximize the total daily company profit.

4. Tar-Free Tobacco Company has arrived at the following estimates of sales of a particular brand of cigar for the next three months:

Month	Estimated sales
1	2,000,000
2	2,000,000
3	4,000,000

The company's production facilities can be operated on two shifts, if desired. The production cost per 1000 cigars and the daily production capacity of each shift are:

Shift	Cost/1000 cigars	Capacity
Regular	$100	250,000
Overtime	120	100,000

The cost of storing 1000 cigars per month is $5.

There is no inventory of these cigars at the moment, and the company does not want any left-over inventory at the end of the third month.

Formulate a network model for minimizing the total cost of satisfying the sales requirements for the next three months.

5. World Transport has a cargo plane at each of the following four airports: Buenos Aires, Capetown, Honolulu, and Sydney. These airplanes must be sent empty to the following four airports: Chicago, Los Angeles, London, and Tokyo. The distances in miles between the airports are given below:

	Chicago	Los Angeles	London	Tokyo
Buenos Aires	5,600	6,200	6,900	11,400
Capetown	8,500	10,000	6,000	9,200
Honolulu	4,300	2,600	7,200	3,900
Sydney	9,200	7,500	10,500	4,900

The company wants to dispatch the empty cargo planes in such a way as to minimize the total distance traveled by four cargo planes. Formulate a model for the problem. Show that the model has a network structure.

6. Global Oceanliner serves the five ports shown in Figure 12.17. Since Yokohama and San Francisco export more than they import, they are constantly in need of empty freighters. On the other hand, Capetown, La Plata, and Sydney import more than they export, so that empty ships must be sent from these ports to the ports that need them. Because of refueling considerations, any ship leaving Capetown for San Francisco must stop over either at Yokohama, La Plata, or Sydney. The number of days required for a ship to travel from one port to another is indicated by the number accompanying the connecting line in this figure. The average monthly requirements for the empty ship tonnages are indicated by the negative numbers (in thousand tons) in the brackets, and the average supplies of empty ship tonnages are indicated by the positive numbers in

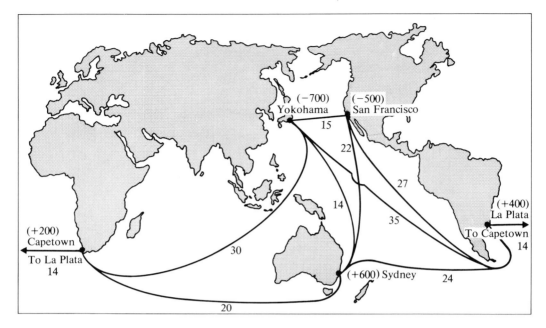

Figure 12.17

brackets. The cost of a voyage between any two ports is assumed to be proportional to the number of days required for the voyage times the empty tonnage of a ship.

Formulate a model for minimizing the total cost of the monthly dispatches of empty ships that will meet the demand and supply requirements.

7. Hanson Equipment Company has to meet the following delivery schedule for the next three periods:

Period	Requirement
1	3
2	3
3	5

There is no beginning inventory, and the company can produce the equipment in any period and make delivery at the end of the period. Any undelivered equipment at the end of a period will involve a handling cost of $30,000. The company does not want more than 2 units of end inventory in any period. The unit production costs of the equipment are estimated to be:

Period	Unit cost
1	$100,000
2	140,000
3	150,000

The company wants to schedule the production for the three periods so as to minimize the total cost. Formulate the problem in a network framework.

8. The delivery requirements of the next four quarters for a certain model of computer manufactured by Computex Company are:

Quarter	Requirement
1	1
2	2
3	4
4	3

There is no beginning inventory, and the company, which cannot produce more than three computers in any one quarter, does not want any left-over inventory at the end of the fourth quarter. The unit manufacturing costs of the four quarters are:

Quarter	Unit cost
1	$200,000
2	170,000
3	240,000
4	210,000

The holding cost of undelivered computers is $20,000 per computer per quarter.

Formulate a network model for the company to schedule the production of the computers during the next four quarters so as to minimize the total cost.

Table 12.3

Flight number	From	Departure time	To	Arrival time
1	San Francisco	9:00 AM	New York	5:00 PM
2	San Francisco	1:00 PM	New York	9:00 PM
3	San Francisco	11:00 AM	Miami	6:00 PM
4	New York	9:45 AM	San Francisco	1:00 PM
5	New York	5:00 PM	San Francisco	7:00 PM
6	New York	10:00 AM	Miami	1:00 PM
7	New York	2:00 PM	Miami	6:00 PM
8	Miami	8:00 AM	New York	11:00 AM
9	Miami	2:00 PM	New York	7:00 PM
10	Miami	4:00 PM	San Francisco	8:00 PM

9. The daily flight schedule of Eastwest Airlines is given in Table 12.3. The layover cost per stop is proportional to the layover time. But refueling, maintenance, and the boarding of passengers make it necessary for each arriving airplane to be on the ground for at least five hours.

The airline wants to match the arriving and departing flights in such a way as to minimize the total layover cost. Formulate a model for the problem and show that it has a network structure.

10. Errorless Typing provides typing service to university students. The assignments may be classified as ordinary, statistical, and mathematical. Ordinary materials do not contain any statistical tables or mathematical notations. Statistical materials contain many statistical tables. Mathematical materials contain many mathematical notations.

Errorless Typing charges $1.00 per page for ordinary materials, $1.60 for statistical materials, and $2.00 for mathematical materials. At present it employs three typists, Ann, Barbara, and Carol. The average numbers of pages per hour typed by the three typists for each type of material are:

	Ordinary	Statistical	Mathematical
Ann	6	2	3
Barbara	4	3	2
Carol	5	2	1

Errorless Typing wants to assign each typist to just one kind of material. Formulate a model for Errorless Typing to make the optimal assignments.

11. Nationwide Movers have contracted to move the household items of a family from Los Angeles to Boston. The moving van can take any one of several different routes, as shown in Figure 12.18 with the distances in miles. Formulate a model for minimizing the total distance traveled by the moving van. Show that the model has a network structure.

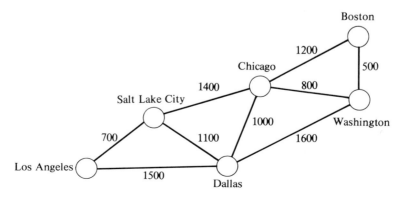

Figure 12.18

12. Brown Cab plans to enlarge its taxi fleet. The company wants to work out a replacement schedule for each new taxi cab for the next five years. An auto manufacturer has agreed to sell a particular model of four-door sedan to Brown Cab for a unit price of $4000 during the next five years. The estimated annual maintenance costs for cars of different ages are:

Age of car	Maintenance cost
0–1	$200
1–2	300
2–3	500
3–4	800
4-5	700

The resale value of a car varies with its age as follows:

Age of car	Resale value
1	$2800
2	2000
3	1200
4	600
5	100

The company wants to minimize the total cost of operating each additional cab for the next five years. Formulate a model for this problem.

13. An overseas telephone call originating from a city designated as node 1 must reach the city designated as node 6. The call, however, must go through intermediate points, as indicated in Figure 12.19. The coefficients along the arcs indicate the probabilities

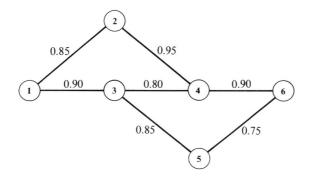

Figure 12.19

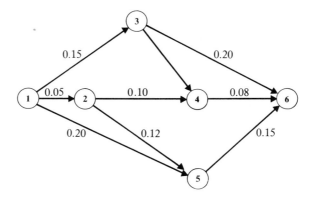

Figure 12.20

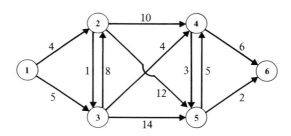

Figure 12.21

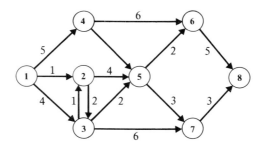

Figure 12.22

that the circuits between the given nodes are open. The telephone operator wants to try the route with the highest probability of successful connection between nodes 1 and 6. Formulate a model for this problem.

14. A nuclear submarine must leave the point designated as node 1 and arrive at the point designated as node 6. There are four alternative intermediate points: nodes 2, 3, 4, and 5 (see Figure 12.20). The coefficients shown in the figure are the probabilities that the submarine will be detected while in transit along the respective paths. Assuming that the probability of detection in any path is not influenced by those in the other paths, formulate a model for minimizing the probability of detection while the submarine travels from node 1 to node 6.

15. Utilizing the algorithm described in Section 12.5, find the shortest path from node 1 to node 6 in the network shown in Figure 12.21.

16. Using the algorithm described in Section 12.5, find the shortest path between node 1 and node 8 of the network shown in Figure 12.22.

13

ACTIVITY NETWORK ANALYSIS

It is not uncommon that when a project requires the completion of a number of separate activities, the activities must be performed in some specified sequence; that is, some activities must be completed before some other activities can begin. The managers of such projects must carefully plan the work in order that the project be completed within either a specific time limit or a budget limit. A very important quantitative tool for this type of planning is the *activity network analysis.*

13.1 ACTIVITY NETWORK

Let us assume that a project consists of five separate activities, *A*, *B*, *C*, *D*, and *E*, and describe these activities by a network such as shown in Figure 13.1. The network is said to be an *activity network* if it gives (1) the time requirement of each activity, that is, *activity time*, and (2) the precedence relations among the activities. Precedence relations are usually indicated by arrows. Thus Figure 13.2 shows that activity *A* must be completed before activities *D* and *C* can be started. Figure 13.3, on the other hand, shows that activities *C* and *B* must be completed before activity *E* can commence.

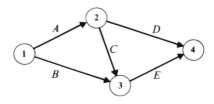

Figure 13.1

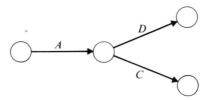

Figure 13.2

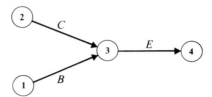

Figure 13.3

Precedence relations among the activities in a project are often due to technological considerations governing the project. For example, if the project is to build a house and if we let A correspond to laying the foundation and B to construction of the frame, then A must precede B:

Here by convention the activities are represented by the directed arcs in a network. Then the nodes in the network are said to depict the *events*, where an event represents a state of progress in the entire sequence of activities. For example, the beginning and end of an activity are two events connected by that activity. Strictly speaking, completing 50 percent of an activity is also an event, but in our discussion of activity networks we are interested only in the events depicting beginnings and ends of activities. Therefore, a node in an activity network invariably represents the beginning or end of one or more activities.

Sometimes we may wish to indicate that a certain event cannot occur until another event has occurred even though there is no work done between the two events. The precedence relation between the two events must then be indicated by a *dummy activity* with zero activity time. Consider the precedence relations among the following four activities:

Activity	Immediate predecessor
A	
B	
C	A
D	A, B

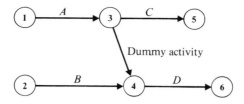

Figure 13.4

Activity C cannot start until A has been completed, whereas activity D cannot start until A and B have been completed. A network representation of these precedence relations is given in Figure 13.4. Note that here a dummy activity has been placed between events 3 and 4 to indicate that activity D cannot start until both A and B have been completed.

The events in an activity network are usually identified by numbers. We also adhere to the convention that the number for an event must be greater than those of preceding events.

13.2 EXAMPLES OF NETWORK PROBLEM

Many different types of projects can be depicted by activity networks. We shall give two examples.

Example 1. House Construction The activities involved in building a house are listed in Table 13.1 together with the activity times and precedence relations. A network description of the activities is shown in Figure 13.5. For the most part the information contained in the table and the network diagram should be self-evident. But we shall briefly elaborate on one point.

Table 13.1 House-Building Activities

Activity	Description	Immediately preceding activity	Activity time (days)
A	Foundation		6
B	Frame		4
C	Siding	B	5
D	Plumbing	B	6
E	Wiring	B	4
F	Roof	C	3
G	Plaster	D, E	10
H	Finishing	G	12
I	Painting	F, H	4

According to Table 13.1, wiring and plumbing can be started only after the frame has been completed, and plastering can start only after both wiring and plumbing have been completed. These precedence relations are shown in

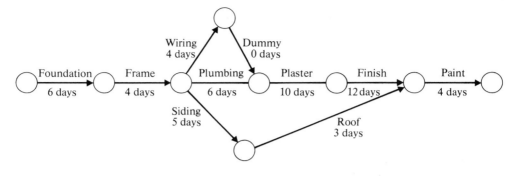

Figure 13.5

Figure 13.6. Note that two activities originate from node 3 and both end at node 5. By convention, however, we do not allow a network to have more than one directed arc from any node to another node. Therefore, in situations such as we have here, we add a dummy activity, in this case between nodes 4 and 5 (Figure 13.7), which nevertheless preserves the proper precedence relations. Thus in Figure 13.7 plastering still cannot start until both wiring and plumbing have been done. Also, since the dummy activity has zero activity time, the total time required to complete both the wiring and the dummy activity is still 4 days.

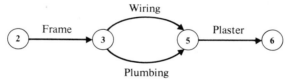

Figure 13.6

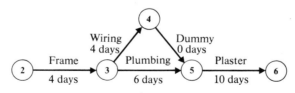

Figure 13.7

Example 2. Manufacturing Operation Bay Area Electronics Company is planning to start a manufacturing operation in a Far Eastern country. Some of the activities needed to get the manufacturing operations started are:

A, negotiation with that country's government;
B, building the plant;
C, shipping the equipment from California to that country;
D, recruiting workers;

E, installing the equipment in the plant;
F, training the workers in the use of the equipment;
G, pilot manufacturing operation.

The activity times and precedence relations are listed in Table 13.2, and the activity network for this whole project is shown in Figure 13.8. Note that the arcs between nodes 4 and 3 and between nodes 4 and 5 represent dummy activities.

Table 13.2

Activity	Description	Immediately preceding activity	Completion time (in months)
A	Negotiation		4
B	Plant-building	A	6
C	Shipping of equipment	A	4
D	Recruiting workers	A	3
E	Installing equipment	B, C	3
F	Training of workers	C, D	2
G	Pilot run	E, F	1

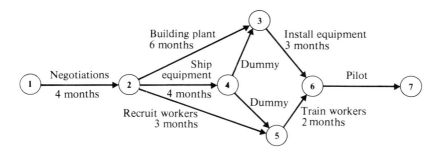

Figure 13.8

13.3 CRITICAL PATH

Let us assume that a project consists of five separate activities: *A*, *B*, *C*, *D*, and *E*. The time required for these activities as well as the precedence relations among them are listed below:

Activity	Activity time	Activity that must already be completed
A	8 weeks	none
B	9 weeks	none
C	7 weeks	A
D	9 weeks	A
E	5 weeks	B, C

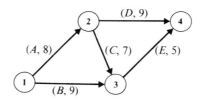

Figure 13.9

These activities and their precedence relations are represented by the network in Figure 13.9. The notation $(A, 8)$, for example, indicates that the arc in question represents activity A, whose completion time is 8 weeks.

For the purpose of our subsequent discussions we define a sequence of arcs connecting two nodes as a *path*. For example,

is a path between nodes 1 and 3, and

is a path between the nodes 1 and 4.

Critical Path

Figure 13.9 shows that activity B will be completed at the end of the first nine weeks but activity E cannot commence immediately thereafter because activity C will not have been completed at this time. Indeed, activity E cannot commence until after the fifteenth week. The end of the fifteenth week is the earliest time that event 3 can occur.

Suppose that we want to determine how soon at the earliest the project can be completed. The answer must correspond to the earliest that both D and E can be completed or the earliest time that event 4 can occur. We note that D can be completed at as early as the end of the seventeenth week, whereas E can be completed by the end of the twentieth week. Consequently, at the earliest, the entire project cannot be completed until after the twentieth week.

An examination of the network diagram will show that the twenty weeks represent the longest path between nodes 1 and 4, which is called the *critical path* for the following reason. Suppose we want to expedite some of the activities in order to reduce the total completion time of twenty weeks. Then we must reduce the completion time of some of the activities lying on the critical path. Thus, if we expedite C so as to reduce its completion time to two weeks, then we can reduce the completion time of the whole project by two weeks; whereas reducing the completion time of D by two days will leave unchanged the twenty weeks needed to complete the project. This also means that unforeseen delays in the activities not on the critical path may not adversely affect the completion time of the entire project. Any delay in the activities on the critical path, on the other hand, will definitely lengthen the completion time of the project.

13.4 MATHEMATICAL MODEL

If we wish, we may reduce the problem of finding the critical path to a mathematical model. Let t_2, for example, be the earliest time that event 2 can occur. We note that t_2 must be at least eight weeks from the time that any work on the project got started. This constraint can be written:

$$t_2 \geq 8.$$

The constraint for event 3 are:

$$t_3 \geq 9, \qquad t_3 \geq t_2 + 7,$$

where the second inequality means that the earliest that event 3 can occur is at least seven weeks, the completion time for activity C, after the occurrence of event 2. Similarly, the constraints for event 4 are:

$$t_4 \geq t_2 + 9, \qquad t_4 \geq t_3 + 5.$$

Rearranging the constraints, we have

t_2	t_3	t_4	
1			≥ 8
	1		≥ 9
-1	1		≥ 7
-1		1	≥ 9
	-1	1	≥ 5

which represent the whole set of constraints for the critical path.

What is the objective function? If the project manager wants to find the earliest time at which t_4 can occur, then the objective function is

$$\min t_4.$$

Now we note that t_2, t_3, and t_4 may be represented by points on a line representing time. There is no reason to insist that these points be on the positive half of the line, so that t_2, t_3, and t_4 will be allowed to assume either positive or negative values.

We can now formulate the dual problem of the above mathematical formulation:

$$\max f = 8x_{12} + 9x_{13} + 7x_{23} + 9x_{24} + 5x_{34},$$

$$x_{12} \qquad\qquad - x_{23} - x_{24} \qquad = 0,$$

$$x_{13} + x_{23} \qquad\qquad - x_{34} = 0,$$

$$x_{24} + x_{34} = 1.$$

Adding the three constraints, we obtain

$$x_{12} + x_{13} = 1.$$

Even though this constraint is redundant, if we add it to the set of constraints, then we have the following complete dual formulation:

Nodes			Arcs		
	x_{12}	x_{13}	x_{23}	x_{24}	x_{34}	
t_1	-1	-1				$= -1$
t_2	1		-1	-1		$= 0$
t_3		1	1		-1	$= 0$
t_4				1	1	$= 1$
	8	9	7	9	5	$= f(\text{max})$

Thus, the dual problem is really one of finding the longest path in the network. But this is exactly how we defined the critical path.

Solving the problem, for example, by means of a linear-programming technique, we will find that the optimal solution is:

$$x_{12} = 1, \quad x_{13} = 0, \quad x_{23} = 1, \quad x_{24} = 0, \quad x_{34} = 1,$$
$$f = 8x_{12} + 7x_{23} + 5x_{34} = 20,$$

exactly what we obtained earlier by mere enumeration.

13.5 EARLIEST EVENT TIMES

Let us now reexamine the activity network shown in Figure 13.10. We assume that the earliest that work on the project can start is the beginning of the first week; that is, the earliest time at which event 1 can occur is the end of zeroth week. This assumption is indicated by the boxed 0 next to node 1 in the figure.

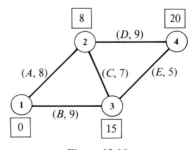

Figure 13.10

Since the activity time for A is 8 weeks, the earliest that event 2 can occur is at the end of the 8th week, indicated by the boxed 8 next to node 2. The number 8 in the square will be called the *earliest time* for event 2.

What is the earliest time for event 3? We note that event 3 cannot occur until after B and C have been completed. The earliest that B can be completed is the earliest time for event 1 plus the activity time for B:

$$0 + 9 = 9.$$

And the earliest that C can be completed is the earliest time for event 2 plus the activity time for C:

$$8 + 7 = 15.$$

Since event 3 cannot occur until after both B and C have been completed, the earliest that event 3 can occur is at the end of the 15th week, as indicated by the boxed 15 next to node 3 in the figure.

A general procedure for finding the earliest time for any given event may now be described:

Find the set of events that immediately precede the given event. To the earliest time of each immediately preceding event add the time required for the activity that links the given event to the immediately preceding event in question. Then take the highest value among the sums thus obtained.

Now let us examine event 4 in our activity network. The immediately preceding events are events 2 and 3. For event 2 we have

$$8 + 9 = 17,$$

and for event 3 we have

$$15 + 5 = 20.$$

The earliest time for event 4 is the higher of the two sums, which is 20. Thus we write 20 in the box next to node 4.

The procedure illustrated above can be expressed in algebraic notations. Such notations, while not necessary for the above example, can be useful, as when we want to write a computer program for the procedure.

First, we define

E_j = the earliest time for event j,
t_{ij} = the time required for the activity that connects
  the events i and j.

Then we can use the following convention to calculate E_j:

1. Let $E_0 = 0$.
2. Let the succeeding events be

$$E_j = \max_{i \in x}\{E_i + t_{ij}\},$$

where x is the set of indices for the events immediately preceding event j.

Thus we have:

$E_1 = 0,$
$E_2 = \max\{E_1 + t_{12}\} = \max\{0 + 8\} = 8,$
$E_3 = \max\{E_1 + t_{13}, E_2 + t_{23}\} = \max\{0 + 9, 8 + 7\} = 15,$
$E_4 = \max\{E_2 + t_{24}, E_3 + t_{34}\} = \max\{8 + 9, 15 + 5\} = 20,$

which are the same as the results obtained earlier.

13.6   EARLIEST START AND FINISH TIMES

In planning and coordinating the activities in a network, we may want to know the earliest possible time at which an activity can start, called the *earliest start time* of an activity. The earliest start times of the activities, however, can be obtained from the earliest event times. For example, the earliest time for event 2 in the network of Figure 13.10 is the end of the 8th week. But activities *C* and *D* cannot start until event 2 has occurred. Thus the earliest start times of activities *C* and *D* are both the end of the 8th week.

If we add the activity time to the earliest start time of an activity, then we will have the earliest possible time at which an activity can be completed, called the *earliest finish time* of an activity. Again in the network of Figure 13.10 the earliest start time of *D* is the end of the 8th week, and since the activity time of *D* is 9 weeks, the earliest finish time of *D* is the end of the 17th week.

The earliest start and finish times of the activities in Figure 13.10 are now summarized in the table below:

Events	Activity	Activity time	Earliest start	Earliest finish
1, 2	A	8	0	8
1, 3	B	9	0	9
2, 3	C	7	8	15
2, 4	D	9	8	17
3, 4	E	5	15	20

13.7   LATEST EVENT TIMES

Figure 13.11 shows the same network as Figure 11.10 with one difference: the square boxes have been replaced by triangular boxes. Earlier we found that the *earliest time* at which event 4 can occur is the end of the 20th week. Let us assume that the latest that we are willing to allow event 4 to occur is the end of the 20th week. This requirement is indicated by the number 20 in the triangular box next to node 4, which number will be called the *latest time* for event 4.

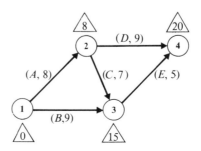

Figure 13.11

If the latest time for event 4 is to be the end of the 20th week, then the latest time for event 3 must be no later than the end of the 15th week, since the activity time of E is 5 weeks. The latest time for event 3 is therefore indicated by the number in the triangular box next to node 3.

Now, as to the latest time for event 2, since the activity time of D is 9 weeks, D can begin as late as the end of the 11th week, and can be finished by the end of the 20th week. But the latest allowable starting time of C is the end of the 8th week if C is to be completed by the end of the 15th week. Thus the latest time for event 2 is the end of the 8th week, as indicated by the number 8 in the triangular box next to node 2.

Here, then, is the procedure for finding the latest time of an event:

Find the set of events that immediately follow the given event. From the latest time of each immediately succeeding event subtract the time of the activity that links the given event to the immediately succeeding event in question. Then take the lowest value among the differences thus obtained.

Let us examine event 1 in this activity network. The immediately succeeding events are 2 and 3. For event 2 we have

$$8 - 8 = 0,$$

and for event 3 we have

$$15 - 9 = 6.$$

The latest time for event 1 is then the smaller of the two differences, which is 0. Thus we write 0 in the triangular box next to node 1.

We shall express the procedure of finding the latest event times in algebraic notation. Let L_i be the latest time for event i. Then we adopt the following convention:

1. Let $L_i = E_i$ for the last node in the network.
2. Let the preceding nodes be

$$L_i = \min_{j \in y} \{L_j - t_{ij}\},$$

where y is the set of indices for the events which immediately follow event i.

Thus we have:

$$L_4 = 20,$$
$$L_3 = \min\{L_4 - t_{34}\} = \min\{20 - 5\} = 15,$$
$$L_2 = \min\{L_3 - t_{23}, L_4 - t_{24}\} = \min\{15 - 7, 20 - 9\} = 8,$$
$$L_1 = \min\{L_2 - t_{12}, L_3 - t_{13}\} = \min\{8 - 8, 15 - 9\} = 0,$$

which are the same as the results obtained earlier.

The reader may have noted that in the case of the given network the earliest and latest times are the same for each event. However, this is a coincidence, not a rule. In more complicated networks, such equality does not usually obtain.

13.8 LATEST START AND FINISH TIMES

One very useful piece of information in planning and coordinating the activities in a network is the latest time that an activity can finish without delaying the completion time of the entire project. It is called the *latest finish time* of the activity.

This information, however, can be obtained from the latest event times. For example, the latest time for event 3 is the end of the 15th week. But event 3 cannot occur until *B* and *C* are finished. Thus the latest finish times for *B* and *C* are both the end of the 15th week.

If we subtract the activity time from the latest finish time of an activity, then we will have the latest time at which an activity can start without delaying the completion time of the entire project; it will be called the *latest start time* of an activity. For example, the latest start time of *D* is the end of the 6th week, since the latest finish time of *B* is the end of the 15th week and the activity time of *B* is 9 weeks.

The latest start and finish times of the activities in the network of Figure 13.11 are summarized below:

Events	Activity	Activity time	Latest start	Latest finish
1, 2	*A*	8	0	8
1, 3	*B*	9	6	15
2, 3	*C*	7	8	15
2, 4	*D*	9	11	20
3, 4	*E*	5	15	20

13.9 SLACK TIMES

The information which we have obtained for the illustrative network may now be summarized in Table 13.3. We note that acticity *D*, for example, can start as early as the end of the 8th week, and as late as the end of the 11th week without affecting the completion time of the entire project. The difference between the earliest and the latest starting times is called the *slack time*. We note that the difference between the earliest and the latest finish times is also equal to the slack time. The slack times for the various activities in this network are listed in the "slack" column in the table.

Table 13.3

Events	Activity	Activity time	Start time Earliest	Start time Latest	Finish time Earliest	Finish time Latest	Slack	Critical path
1, 2	*A*	8	0	0	8	8	0	*
1, 3	*B*	9	0	6	9	15	6	
2, 3	*C*	7	8	8	15	15	0	*
2, 4	*D*	9	8	11	17	20	3	
2, 5	*E*	5	15	15	20	20	0	*

The slack times tell us the extent to which we can delay the start or the finish of various activities without causing a delay in the completion of the entire project.

On the other hand, activities A, C, and E have no slack times, meaning that any delay in starting any of these activities will cause a delay in the completion of the entire project. The reader may recall, however, that these three activities constitute the critical path of the project. Therefore, it is not surprising that their slack times should be zero. The activities belonging to the critical path are indicated by the asterisks in the right-hand column of Table 13.3.

13.10 CRASHING THE ACTIVITIES

If we wish to reduce the completion time of an entire project, we must reduce the completion times for some of the constituent activities. Such an action is called *crashing the activities*. It is obvious, however, that crashing those activities that do not belong to the critical path will not reduce the completion time of the entire project. Thus, if an activity is to be crashed at all, it should be on the critical path.

When there are many activities on the critical path, it may be difficult to decide which activity to crash and by how much. Any decision of this nature, however, must take into account the following considerations:

1. How much will it cost to speed up the activity?

2. How much difference will the contemplated reduction in activity time make to the completion time of the entire project?

Let us return to the network we have been studying, presented again in Figure 13.12. The critical path in this network is indicated by the bold arrows. As before, the diagram shows that the project will be completed in 20 weeks.

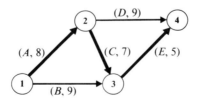

Figure 13.12

Suppose we can crash activities A or C by 4 weeks at identical cost. If we crash activity C by 4 weeks, then we have a new critical path as shown by bold arrows in Figure 13.13, with a length of 17 weeks. Therefore, even though the completion of activity C has been speeded up by 4 weeks, the completion time of the entire project is reduced only by 3 weeks.

On the other hand, if we crash activity A by 4 weeks. Then the new critical path is indicated by the bold arrows in Figure 13.14; its length is 16 weeks. Thus the completion time of the entire project is reduced by 4 weeks when the completion of activity A is speeded up by 4 weeks.

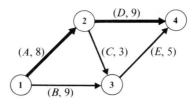

Figure 13.13

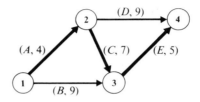

Figure 13.14

13.11 PERT

The prevailing assumption in our preceding analysis is that each activity in the network is a known constant. In practice, however, the exact time requirements of the various activities are usually not known. Consequently, it is more realistic to assume that the activity times are uncertain quantities. One way to incorporate this assumption explicitly into activities network analysis is to treat activity times as random variables. This method is known as program evaluation and review technique or PERT.

13.12 PROBABILISTIC TIME ESTIMATE

Assuming that the activity time is a random variable, we should nevertheless be able to determine the expected activity time, as well as its variance and standard deviation, if we can specify its exact probability distribution. One assumption most frequently made is that activity time has a beta distribution—an assumption that enables us to calculate the expected activity time and its standard deviation by means of a very simple procedure.

For the purpose at hand we have three different estimates of the completion time of an activity:

$$a = \text{the most optimistic estimate of activity time,}$$
$$m = \text{the most likely estimate of activity time,}$$
$$b = \text{the most pessimistic estimate of activity time.}$$

If μ and σ are respectively the expected value and the standard deviation of the activity time, then

$$\mu = \frac{a + (4 \times m) + b}{6}, \qquad \sigma = (b - a)/6.$$

We shall illustrate the use of these formulas in the following example.

Example 3. Assume that the following three estimates have been made of the time required to complete a given activity in a network:

> most optimistic estimate, 4 weeks;
> most likely estimate, 5 weeks;
> most pessimistic estimate, 10 weeks.

Then

$$\mu = \frac{a + (4 \times m) + 6}{6} = \frac{4 + (4 \times 5) + 10}{6} = 5.67 \text{ weeks},$$

$$\sigma = \frac{b - a}{6} = \frac{10 - 4}{6} = 1 \text{ week}.$$

The relations among the estimates are illustrated in Figure 13.15. We note that there are six standard deviations between the most optimistic and the most pessimistic estimates.

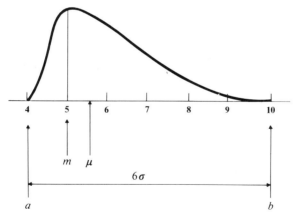

Figure 13.15

13.13 ADDING THE PROBABILISTIC ESTIMATES

Consider the following simple network diagram:

$$\begin{array}{ccc} & \text{Activity } A & & \text{Activity } B \\ \textcircled{1} \longrightarrow & \textcircled{2} \longrightarrow & \textcircled{3} \\ \mu_A = 15, \ \sigma_A = 3 & & \mu_B = 20, \ \sigma_B = 4 \end{array}$$

It shows, for example, that the activity A has an expected activity time of 15 weeks with a standard deviation of 3 weeks.

$$\mu_T = \mu_A + \mu_B = 15 + 20 = 35,$$

$$\sigma_T = \sqrt{\sigma_A^2 + \sigma_B^2} = \sqrt{3^2 + 4^2} = 5.$$

We note that $\sigma_T^2 = \sigma_A^2 + \sigma_B^2$. Thus the expected completion time for this path is the sum of the expected activity times of the activities constituting the path. The variance of the completion time for this path is the sum of the variances of the activity times of the activities in the path.

We may now generalize our conclusion: Let μ_A, $\mu_B, \ldots, \mu_G$ and σ_A^2, $\sigma_B^2, \ldots, \sigma_G^2$, respectively, be the expected activity times and the variances of the activity times of the activities in a path. Assuming that the time required for one activity is not influenced by those of the others, then the expected completion time, μ_T, and the variance of the completion time, σ_T^2, for the path are:

$$\mu_T = \mu_A + \mu_B + \cdots + \mu_G,$$

$$\sigma_T^2 = \sigma_A^2 + \sigma_B^2 + \cdots + \sigma_G^2.$$

13.14 EXPECTED EVENT TIMES

Let us now examine the network in Figure 13.16. The expression $(A, 12, 4)$, for example, indicates that the arc in question corresponds to activity A, whose expected completion time is 12 weeks, with a standard deviation of 4 weeks.

Let us now define the *expected earliest event time* as the expected value of the earliest time at which an event can occur. The calculations for this value are quite similar to those of the earliest event time. We simply substitute in the calculations the expected activity times for the activity times.

In the case of the given network let us assume that the earliest time for event 1 is zero, as indicated by the number in the square box next to node 1. Then the expected earliest time for event 2 is $0 + 12 = 12$, where the first 12 represents the expected activity time of A. Then the expected earliest time for event 3 may be obtained as

$$\max \{0 + 30, 12 + 20\} = 32,$$

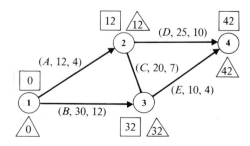

Figure 13.16

and that for event 4 is

$$\max \{12 + 25, 32 + 10\} = 42.$$

The expected earliest times of the events are given in the square boxes next to the nodes corresponding to those events.

Next let us define the *expected latest event time* as the expected value of the latest time at which an event can occur without delaying the expected latest time of the final event in a PERT network. The calculations for the expected latest event times are similar to those for the latest event times, except that we substitute expected activity times for activity times.

Let us, therefore, assume that the latest time for event 4 is 42, as indicated in the triangular box next to node 4 in our network. Then the expected latest time for event 3 must be 30, which is obtained by subtracting the expected activity time of E from 42. Then the expected latest time for event 2 is

$$\min \{32 - 20, 42 - 25\} = 12,$$

and that for event 1 is

$$\min \{12 - 12, 32 - 30\} = 0.$$

The expected latest times of the events are indicated by the numbers in the triangular boxes next to the nodes corresponding to those events.

13.15   EXPECTED START AND FINISH TIMES

Let us now define the *expected earliest start time* of an activity as the expected value of the earliest time at which an activity can be started. This value can be obtained from the earliest event times. For example, the earliest time for event 2 is 12. But activities C and D cannot start until after event 2 has occurred. Thus the expected earliest start times of both C and D are 12.

If we add the expected activity time to the expected earliest start time of an activity, then we will have the *expected earliest finish time* of that activity. For example, the expected earliest finish time of D is 37, which is the sum of the expected earliest start time and the expected activity time of D.

Next we can define the *expected latest finish time* of an activity as the expected value of the latest time at which an activity can be finished without delaying the expected value of the completion time for the entire project. Again this value can be obtained from the latest event times. For example, the latest time for event 3 is 32. But event 3 cannot occur until B and D are completed. Thus the expected latest finish times of both B and C are 32.

If we subtract the expected activity time from the expected latest finish time of an activity, then we will have the *expected latest start time*, which is the expected value of the latest time at which an activity can be started without delaying the expected completion of the entire project. For example, the expected latest start time of D is 17, which is the expected latest finish time of D minus the expected activity time of D.

Various expected start and finish times of the activities in the given PERT network are summarized in Table 13.4.

Table 13.4

Events	Activity	Expected activity time	Expected start time		Expected finish time		Slack	Critical path
			Earliest	Latest	Earliest	Latest		
1, 2	A	12	0	0	12	12	0	*
1, 3	B	30	0	2	30	32	2	
2, 3	C	20	12	12	32	32	0	*
2, 4	D	25	12	17	37	42	5	
2, 5	E	10	32	32	42	42	0	*

13.16   PROBABILISTIC CRITICAL-PATH ANALYSIS

If we examine Table 13.4, we will note that activities A, C, and E have no expected slacks. Thus the path containing these activities has the longest expected completion time. As before, we call it the *critical path* in the network.

Also the expected completion time for the critical path is 42 weeks. The standard deviation for this path is

$$\sigma_T = \sqrt{\sigma_A^2 + \sigma_C^2 + \sigma_E^2} = \sqrt{4^2 + 7^2 + 4^2} = 9 \text{ weeks.}$$

Suppose we ask, What is the probability that the activities in the critical path will be completed, for example, within 60 weeks of the start of the project? If the path contains a large number of activities, then the probabilistic analysis called for can be done by assuming that the completion time for the critical path is normally distributed.

Even though the network we have been using as example contains only three activities in the critical path, let us nevertheless assume that the completion time for the path is normally distributed in order to illustrate the application of the normal probability distribution to the problem. Since the completion time for the path has an expected value of 42 weeks with a standard deviation of 9 weeks, then the probability is 0.9772 that the activities in the path will be completed within 60 weeks. The manner in which we can obtain this probability coefficient is illustrated in Figure 13.17.

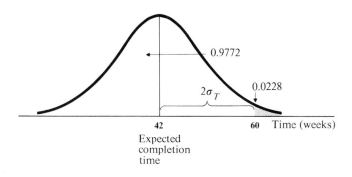

Figure 13.17

Such probabilistic analyses of the completion time for critical paths obviously can be useful in planning and coordinating the activities in a project.

13.17 PROJECT PROBABILISTIC ANALYSIS

In the planning and coordination of a project, such as can be described by the network diagram we have been discussing, we may have to take into account a completion deadline. Suppose, for example, we have to complete the entire project within 60 weeks of the start of the project. What is the probability that the entire project can be completed within the prescribed period? It may appear, on the basis of our probabilistic analysis of the critical path, that the probability in question is 0.9772. But this is not true. Since the time required for each activity is variable, when the entire project is completed the actual critical path may turn out to be different from the expected one. For example, suppose the actual completion times of the activities turn out to be as indicated in Figure 13.18. Then the longest path is the one involving activities B and E, not A, C, and E as expected.

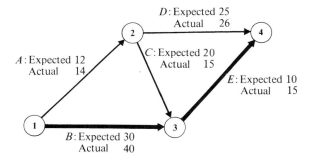

Figure 13.18

For this reason the probability of the entire project being completed within a specified period is quite difficult to calculate. If it must be obtained, then we usually resort to the technique of *simulation*, which we shall illustrate in a later chapter.

In the critical-path analysis where we assumed the activity times to be constant, we argued for the need to carefully monitor the progress of only those activities belonging to the critical path. But this argument is no longer valid when we assume that the completion times of the activities are variable.

Suppose again that we want to complete the entire project of the given network in 60 weeks. We have already shown that the probability of the activities on the critical path being completed within 60 weeks is 0.9772. Let us now examine the path consisting of B and E. The expected completion time of the path is 40 weeks, 2 weeks shorter than the critical path. The corresponding

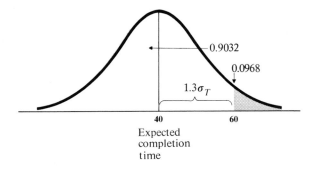

Figure 13.19

standard deviation is

$$\sigma_T = \sqrt{\sigma_B^2 + \sigma_E^2} = \sqrt{15^2 + 4^2} \cong 15.5 \text{ weeks.}$$

As illustrated in Figure 13.19, the probability of this path being completed within the 60 weeks is only 0.9000. Thus, if the project is not completed within 60 weeks, the delay is more likely to have been caused by delays in completing activities B and E rather than in activities A, B, and C.

EXERCISES

1. The activities to be completed for a project are shown in Table 13.5, together with their precedence relations. Draw a network diagram for the project.

Table 13.5

Activity	Immediately preceding activity
A	
B	
C	A
D	A, B
E	B, C
F	D
G	D
H	F, G

2. Table 13.6 lists the activities which need to be completed for a project, together with the time required for each and the various precedence relations.

　　a. Draw a network diagram for the project.
　　b. Calculate the earliest times at which the various events can occur.
　　c. Calculate the earliest start and finish times of the activities.

Table 13.6

Activity	Immediately preceding activity	Activity time (weeks)
A	None	5
B	None	10
C	None	8
D	A	6
E	A	12
F	B, D	7
G	C	4
H	E, F, G	6
I	C	10

d. Calculate the latest times at which the events can occur.
e. Calculate the latest start and finish times of the activities.
f. What are the slack times of the various activities?
g. What does the critical path for the network consist of?
h. On the basis of the preceding calculations determine the minimum number of weeks required to complete the project.

3. Given the activity network of Exercise 2, determine the impact of each of the following proposed changes in the critical path, on the completion time for the entire project:

a. Reduce the activity time of B from 10 weeks to 8 weeks.
b. Reduce the activity time of D from 6 weeks to 3 weeks.
c. Reduce the activity time of F from 7 weeks to 3 weeks.

4. Reputable Construction Company has won a bid to construct a small industrial plant in the outskirts of a city. The area has not been developed previously, so it will be necessary for the company to clear the area, bring in utility lines, drill a well, and install a water tower before plant construction can begin. The activities which need to be completed before starting construction are listed in Table 13.7, together with the precedence relations and activities times.

a. Draw a network diagram for the project.
b. Calculate the earliest and latest start times and the earliest and latest finish times.
c. Calculate the slack times.
d. Determine the critical path.

5. If Reputable Construction Company of Exercise 4 finds that the well-drilling or sewer installation can be speeded up by as many as 3 days at the same cost, which of the two activities should be expedited? Explain your answer.

6. Easy Learning Textbook Company has received the final manuscript for a textbook. The activities involved in bringing out the textbook, together with their precedence relations and required times, are listed in Table 13.8.

Table 13.7

Activity	Description	Immediately preceding activity	Activity time (weeks)
A	Clear site		2
B	Survey	A	2
C	Rough grade	B	1
D	Drill well	C	6
E	Install water pump	D	2
F	Install water pipes	E	4
G	Excavate sewer	C	3
H	Install sewer	G	6
I	Set utility poles	C	2
J	Excavate for electrical manholes	C	3
K	Install manholes	J	4
L	Install electrical ducts	H, K	4
M	Pull in power feeder	L, K	2

Table 13.8

Activity	Description	Immediately preceding activity	Activity time (weeks)
A	Copy-editing	None	4
B	Artwork	A	6
C	Check artwork	B	4
D	Make blocks	C	8
E	Check block pulls	D	2
F	Compose the text	A	10
G	Check galleys	F	12
H	Correct type	G	2
I	Design cover	A	3
J	Prepare binding cases	I	9
K	Paginate	E, H	3
L	Index	K	4
M	Check page proofs	K	4
N	Printing	L, M	6
O	Binding	J, N	5

a. Draw a network diagram for the project.
b. Calculate the earliest and latest start times and the earliest and latest finish times.
c. Calculate the slack times.
d. Determine the critical path for the network.
e. What is the minimum time required to bring out the textbook?

7. The present plans call for composing the entire textbook of Exercise 6 before sending the galleys to the author for proofreading, but the company can actually send the galleys of one chapter at a time to the author for proofreading. Such a procedure will reduce the total time required for composition, checking the galleys, and correction of typing, from 24 weeks to 16 weeks. By how much can this procedure reduce the total time required to bring out the textbook?

8. Table 13.9 lists the activities to be completed for a project, together with the relevant information on these activities.

Table 13.9

Activity	Immediately preceding activity	Estimated Activity Time Most optimistic	Most likely	Most pessimistic
A		4	6	10
B		3	4	6
C	A	5	8	14
D	A	8	12	20
E	B, C	6	10	15

a. Calculate the expected value and the standard deviation of the completion time for each activity in the network.
b. Draw a network diagram for the project. Then ascertain the expected start and finish times of the various events, as well as the expected latest start and finish times of the events.
c. Ascertain the expected latest start and finish times of the activities.
d. Ascertain the expected slack times for the activities.
e. Determine the critical path.

9. Tynix Computer is planning to develop and market a new kind of mini computer. The activities that must go into the development and marketing of this computer are listed in Table 13.10 along with other relevant information.

Table 13.10

Activity	Description	Immediately preceding activity	Completion Time (months) Mean	Standard deviation
A	Design hardware		24	6
B	Manufacture hardware	A	16	4
C	Design software	A	20	6
D	Test and integrate	B, C	12	3
E	Develop marketing plan		20	5
F	Produce technical manuals	D	8	2
G	Advertise	D, E	16	3

Assuming that the completion times are normally distributed:

a. Draw a PERT network diagram for the project and ascertain all the possible paths from the first node to the last node in the network.
b. Calculate the expected value and standard deviation of the total time required to complete all the activities in each of the paths obtained in part (a).
c. Calculate the probability of all the activities being completed within 60 days of the start of the project, for each path obtained in (a).

CHAPTER

14

INTEGER PROGRAMMING: FORMULATION

Let us return to the following linear-programming problem:

$$\max f = c_1 x_1 + \cdots + c_n x_n,$$

$$a_{11} x_1 + \cdots + a_{1n} x_n \leq d_1,$$

$$\vdots \qquad\qquad \vdots$$

$$a_{m1} x_1 + \cdots + a_{mn} x_n \leq d_m,$$

$$x_1, \ldots, x_n \geq 0.$$

In the formulation of this problem we have assumed that the decision variables $x_1, \ldots, x_n$ can assume any nonnegative real values. However, there are situations where we should allow some of $x_1, \ldots, x_n$ to assume only integer values. A linear-programming problem requiring all the variables $x_1, \ldots, x_n$ to assume integer values is called an *all-integer* programming problem. If the problem calls for some of these variables to assume integer values and the remaining variables to assume any nonnegative values, then the problem is called the *mixed-integer programming* problem.

Among the integer programming problems there are some which require the variables $x_1, \ldots, x_n$ to be either zero or one. These problems are called *zero-one programming* problems.

Integer programming is obviously needed when we have a linear-programming problem involving indivisibility of units. For example, suppose that the variables $x_1, \ldots, x_n$ of a linear-programming problem represent the different quantities in a product mix problem. Then it may not be meaningful to let $x_1, \ldots, x_n$ assume fractional values, since a fraction of a unit of some product is usually of no commercial use. Therefore, if we reexamine the linear

243

programming examples in Chapter 9, we will find that many of them are really integer programming problems.

Some integer programming problems, however, may not appear on the surface to be amenable to integer programming formulation. We will describe these problems in the sections that follow.

14.1 KNAPSACK PROBLEMS

Consider an old-fashioned hiker who carries all the supplies he needs for the hiking trip in a sack. Assume that there are n items that he wants to put in the sack but he does not want the total weight of the sack to exceed, say, d pounds. We let a_i be the weight of the ith item on the list and c_i be the relative value of that item. Suppose the hiker wants to select the items to be taken on the trip in such a way as to maximize the total value of the items in the sack without exceeding the weight limitation. Then he may well formulate his problem as follows.

Let

$$x_i = \begin{cases} 1 & \text{if } i\text{th item is included,} \\ 0 & \text{if } i\text{th item is not included.} \end{cases}$$

Then the model for the problem is

$$\max f = c_1 x_1 + \cdots + c_n x_n,$$
$$a_1 x_1 + \cdots + a_n x_n \leq d,$$
$$x_1, \ldots, x_n \text{ be either 0 or 1.}$$

This is called a *knapsack problem*, which, we note, is a zero-one programming problem.

Some other practical problems may also possess the structure of a knapsack problem.

Example 1. Cargo-Loading Problem   A cargo plane has a weight capacity of 10,000 lb. For one particular flight there is a choice of four kinds of items to be carried by the plane with the following characteristics:

Item	Weight (lb)	Total profit
1	1000	$1000
2	2000	2500
3	3000	4000
4	4000	6000

Then the problem of maximizing the total profit for this flight may be formulated as follows. Let x_i be the decision variables so that

$$x_i = \begin{cases} 1 & \text{if } i\text{th item is to be carried,} \\ 0 & \text{if } i\text{th item is not to be carried.} \end{cases}$$

The model for the problem is then

$$\max f = 1000x_1 + 2500x_2 + 4000x_3 + 6000x_4,$$
$$1000x_1 + 2000x_2 + 3000x_3 + 4000x_4 \leq 10{,}000,$$
$$x_1, \ldots, x_4 \text{ be either 1 or 0.}$$

Example 2. Budgeting Capital Spending   Assume that Alpha and Omega are confronted with the following four investment proposals, each calling for allocation of funds for the next two years:

Project	First-year requirement	Second-year requirement	Present value of the project
1	$3 million	$2 million	$8 million
2	2 million	2 million	5 million
3	1 million	2 million	5 million
4	2 million	1 million	4 million

Assume that the company can allocate $5 million in each of the next two years for capital investment.

If the company wants to select the projects so as to maximize the total present value, then the problem can be formulated as follows. Let

$$x_i = \begin{cases} 1 & \text{if project } i \text{ is chosen,} \\ 0 & \text{if project } i \text{ is not chosen.} \end{cases}$$

The model for the problem is then

$$\max f = 8x_1 + 5x_2 + 5x_3 + 4x_4,$$
$$3x_1 + 2x_2 + x_3 + 2x_4 \leq 5,$$
$$2x_1 + 2x_2 + 2x_3 + x_4 \leq 5,$$
$$x_1, \ldots, x_4 \text{ be either 1 or 0.}$$

14.2   FIXED-CHARGE PROBLEM

In our formulation of linear-programming problems we have assumed that the objective function is of the form

$$f = c_1 x_1 + \cdots + c_n x_n.$$

Figure 14.1 shows a graph of $c_1 x_1$, for example, where c_1 is the slope of the line $c_1 x_1$. Now, if the objective function is a cost function, then only the variable costs are associated with the decision variables $x_1, \ldots, x_n$.

As we will illustrate below, however, in some situations it is more appropriate to assume that the cost function for a given decision variable has a graph such as is shown in Figure 14.2. Here there is a fixed cost f_1 associated with letting x_1 assume any positive value at all, f_1 still being zero when x_1 is zero. Then we have a *fixed-charge problem*.

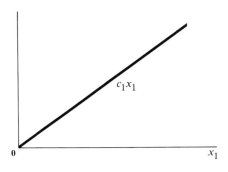

Figure 14.1

A fixed-charge problem has a mathematical model of the following form. If we let

$$y_i = \begin{cases} 1 & \text{if } x_i > 0, \\ 0 & \text{if } x_i = 0, \end{cases}$$

then the linear-programming formulation of the problem is:

$$\max f = (f_1 y_1 + c_1 x_1) + \cdots + (f_n y_n + c_n x_n),$$
$$a_{11}x_1 + \cdots + a_n x_n \leq d_1$$
$$\vdots \qquad \qquad \vdots \; \cdot$$
$$a_{m1}x_1 + \cdots + a_{mn}x_n \leq d_m$$
$$y_i = \begin{cases} 1 & \text{if } x_i > 0, \\ 0 & \text{if } x_i = 0, \end{cases}$$
$$x_1, \ldots, x_n \geq 0.$$

We note that a fixed-charge problem is a mixed-integer programming problem, since y_i must assume only integer values whereas x_i need not do so.

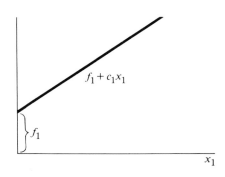

Figure 14.2

Example 3. Transportation Problem   Whitex Washing Machine Company must make deliveries of washing machines from its two warehouses to two department stores. The available quantities at the warehouse are:

Warehouse	Available quantity
1	50
2	50

And the delivery requirements are:

Store	Delivery requirement
1	60
2	40

The company utilizes the services of a moving company to make the deliveries. The moving company charges a fixed amount for dispatching a truck from a warehouse to a department store. This cost is not dependent on the number of washing machines carried by the truck. However, the moving company does charge an insurance premium for each washer. For example, it charges a fixed amount of $1000 for delivery from warehouse 1 to department store 1, plus $2 per washer for insurance. The cost schedule for making deliveries is:

Warehouse	Department Store 1		Department Store 2	
	Fixed charge	Unit insurance premium	Fixed charge	Unit insurance premium
1	$1000	$2	$600	$5
2	500	6	800	4

Each truck can carry at least 60 washers. What is needed is a delivery schedule that will minimize the total cost of meeting the delivery requirements.

We let x_{ij} be the number of washers shipped from warehouse i to department store j. Then

$$1000 + 2x_{11}$$

is the total cost of shipping x_{11} units from warehouse 1 to department store 1.

An initial formulation of the problem is:

$$\min f = (1000 y_{11} + 2x_{11}) + (600 y_{12} + 5x_{12})$$
$$+ (500 y_{21} + 6x_{21}) + (800 y_{22} + 4x_{22}),$$
$$x_{11} + x_{12} = 50, \qquad x_{21} + x_{22} = 50,$$
$$x_{11} + x_{21} = 60, \qquad x_{12} + x_{22} = 40,$$
$$y_{ij} = \begin{cases} 1 & \text{if } x_{ij} > 0, \\ 0 & \text{if } x_{ij} = 0, \end{cases}$$
$$x_{11}, \ldots, x_{22} \geq 0.$$

While this is a correct formulation of the problem, it is difficult to handle the constraints

$$y_{ij} = \begin{cases} 1 & \text{if } x_{ij} > 0, \\ 0 & \text{if } x_{ij} = 0, \end{cases}$$

in computations. Therefore, we shall formulate another model which avoids these difficulties.

We note that y_{ij} is 1 if the solution calls for x_{ij} to be a positive number and y_{ij} is zero if the solution calls for x_{ij} to be zero. These are the constraints requiring reformulation.

We let u_{ij} be an arbitrarily large number so that $x_{ij} \le u_{ij}$. In the given problem suppose we let $u_{11} = 100$, then since x_{11} cannot be larger than 50, we have $x_{11} \le u_{11}$. Then the following set of constraints,

$$\begin{cases} 0 \le y_{ij} \le 1, \\ y_{ij} \text{ be an integer}, \\ x_{ij} - u_{ij} y_{ij} \le 0, \end{cases}$$

is equivalent to the constraints

$$y_{ij} = \begin{cases} 1 & \text{if } x_{ij} > 0, \\ 0 & \text{if } x_{ij} = 0, \end{cases}$$

for the following reasons. Suppose that a solution to the problem calls for x_{ij} to be positive and at the same time y_{ij} to be zero. Then the constraint $x_{ij} - u_{ij} y_{ij} \le 0$ will be violated. Thus x_{ij} cannot be positive when y_{ij} is zero. On the other hand, if x_{ij} is positive and at the same time $y_{ij} = 1$, then the constraint $x_{ij} - u_{ij} y_{ij} \le 0$ is not violated, since by assumption $x_{ij} \le u_{ij}$. Thus x_{ij} cannot be positive without at the same time y_{ij} being 1. Consequently, we can use the new set of constraints to take the place of the original constraints on y_{ij}.

Of course, the new set of constraints will not prevent y_{ij} from being 1 when $x_{ij} = 0$. But since we will be minimizing $f_{ij} y_{ij} + c_{ij} x_{ij}$, the integer programming algorithm will ensure that $y_{ij} = 0$ whenever $x_{ij} = 0$.

In summary, then, the transportation problem may be formulated as follows:

x_{11}	x_{12}	x_{21}	x_{22}	y_{11}	y_{12}	y_{21}	y_{22}	
1	1							= 50
		1	1					= 50
−1		−1						= −60
	−1		−1					= −40
1				−100				≤ 0
	1				−100			≤ 0
		1				−100		≤ 0
			1				−100	≤ 0
2	5	6	4	1000	600	500	800	= f

where y_{ij} is either 0 or 1.

Example 4. Plant Location Problem Ohio Electronics has television manufacturing plants in Tokyo and Los Angeles. Many of the components used in
the television sets are presently manufactured in Japan, but the company is
planning to do some component assembly in countries where wages are lower
than in Japan. Three possible locations are under consideration: Hong Kong,
Manila, and Seoul.

The total requirements for this component during the next five years are:

Television plants	Components required
Tokyo	30 million
Los Angeles	10 million

The initial cost of building the assembly plant, as well as the unit assembly cost
and total plant capacity, are listed below for each location:

	Initial building cost	Unit assembly cost	Assembly capacity
Hong Kong	$20 million	$3.00	15 million units
Manila	40 million	2.00	25 million
Seoul	30 million	2.50	20 million

The components will be shipped by air to Tokyo and Los Angeles. The unit air
freight costs are:

From \ To	Tokyo	Los Angeles
Hong Kong	$0.50	$1.00
Manila	0.40	1.20
Seoul	0.20	0.80

Ohio Electronics wants to meet its component needs for the next five years at
the minimum total cost. Where should it locate the new plant?

The structure of this problem is quite similar to that of the transportation
problem with fixed cost. We let x_{HT} and x_{HL}, respectively, be the total number
of components to be shipped from Hong Kong to Tokyo, and from Hong Kong
to Los Angeles in the event that the plant is built in Hong Kong. Let $y_H = 1$ if
the plant is built in Hong Kong and $y_H = 0$ otherwise. We note that the unit
delivery costs from Hong Kong are $3.50 to Tokyo and $4.00 to Los Angeles.
Thus the total cost of shipping the components from Hong Kong to Tokyo and
Los Angeles is:

$$f_H = 20{,}000{,}000 y_H + 3.50 x_{HT} + 4.00 x_{HL},$$

where

$$y_H = \begin{cases} 0 & \text{if } x_{HT} + x_{HL} = 0, \\ 1 & \text{if } x_{HT} + x_{HL} > 0. \end{cases}$$

Similarly, the total cost of shipping the component from Manila is

$$f_M = 40,000,000y_M + 2.40x_{MT} + 3.20x_{ML},$$

where

$$y_M = \begin{pmatrix} 0 & \text{if } x_{MT} + x_{ML} = 0, \\ 1 & \text{if } x_{MT} + x_{ML} > 0. \end{pmatrix}$$

And in the case of Seoul,

$$f_S = 30,000,000y_S + 2.70x_{ST} + 3.30x_{SL},$$

where

$$y_S = \begin{cases} 0 & \text{if } x_{ST} + x_{SL} = 0, \\ 1 & \text{if } x_{ST} + x_{SL} > 0. \end{cases}$$

The objective function is:

$$\min f = f_H + f_M + f_S.$$

We have defined y_H so that $y_H = 1$ if $x_{HT} + x_{HL} > 0$ and $y_H = 0$ otherwise. This definition may be expressed in the form of a constraint. We note that the maximum capacity of the Hong Kong plant is 15,000,000 units. Suppose that we specify

$$x_{HT} + x_{HL} \leq 15,000,000y_H.$$

Then $x_{HT} + x_{HL}$ cannot be positive without at the same time y_H being 1. We can also write for Manila and Seoul:

$$x_{MT} + x_{ML} \leq 25,000,000y_M,$$
$$x_{ST} + x_{SL} \leq 20,000,000y_S.$$

The preceding three constraints accomplish the following objectives.

1. They say that the total quantity to be shipped from a plant, in the event that it is built, cannot exceed the plant's capacity.
2. They ensure that the computer program used to solve the problem will assign the value of 1 to y_H, for example, *only* if the plant is constructed in Hong Kong.

Next we must obtain the constraints to ensure that the total component requirements at Tokyo and Los Angeles are satisfied. These requirements may be specified as

$$x_{HT} + x_{MT} + x_{ST} \geq 30,000,000$$

for Tokyo and

$$x_{HL} + x_{ML} + x_{ST} \geq 10,000,000$$

for Los Angeles.

Summarizing our formulation and rearranging the terms, we have Table 14.1. Adding the constraints $x_{HT}, \ldots, x_{SL} \geq 0$ and $y_H = 0$ or 1, $y_M = 0$ or 1, and $y_S = 0$ or 1 will complete the formulation of the problem.

Table 14.1

x_{HT}	x_{HL}	x_{MT}	x_{ML}	x_{ST}	x_{SL}	y_H	y_M	y_S	
1	1					$-15{,}000{,}000$			≤ 0
		1	1				$-25{,}000{,}000$		≤ 0
				1	1			$-20{,}000{,}000$	≤ 0
-1		-1		-1					$\le -30{,}000{,}000$
	-1		-1		-1				$\le -10{,}000{,}000$
3.50	4.00	2.40	3.20	2.70	3.30	$20{,}000{,}000$	$40{,}000{,}000$	$30{,}000{,}000$	$= f$

14.3   TRAVELING SALESMAN PROBLEM

Consider a traveling salesman who must visit various cities, starting from his hometown, and finally return to his hometown. He must decide which city to visit first, which to visit second, etc. He may want to plan his route so as to minimize the total distance of his travel or to minimize either the total cost or the total time required for the travel.

If we assume that there are only two cities to visit, then there are only two possible routes for the salesman. If there are three cities, then there are six possible routes. In general, if there are n cities to visit, then there are $n!$ (read "n factorial") possible routes, where $n! = n(n - 1)(n - 2) \cdots 1$. Thus if·he must visit ten cities, he must choose from 10! or 3,628,800 different routes. It is practically impossible to find the best route by enumerating all the possible routes. We shall, therefore, illustrate how such problems can be formulated in terms of mathematical models.

Example 5. Delivery Truck Problem   A bakery delivery truck in San Jose must make daily deliveries to a store in Los Gatos and another store in Cupertino during the morning rush hours. The traveling times in minutes during the rush hours between the different cities are indicated in Figure 14.3. The driver wants to select his morning delivery route so as to minimize the driving time, including the return to his San Jose bakery.

With only two possible routes the problem is almost trivial and requires no elaborate model formulation. If he takes the route

$$\text{San Jose} \rightarrow \text{Los Gatos} \rightarrow \text{Cupertino} \rightarrow \text{San Jose}$$

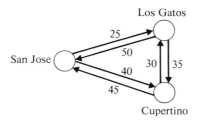

Figure 14.3

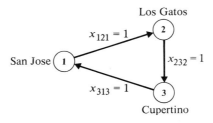

Figure 14.4

he will incur 105 minutes of driving time, but if he takes the route

$$\text{San Jose} \to \text{Cupertino} \to \text{Los Gatos} \to \text{San Jose}$$

the driving time will be 120 minutes. Thus he will want to take the first route.

While in this case the solution is easily available without resorting to mathematical formulation, a delivery truck may well have to visit, say, ten different stores. Then a model will become almost indispensable. We shall illustrate the formulation of a model by using our simplified problem.

Let us define

$$x_{ijk}$$

as the variable which assumes the value 1 if the truck goes from point i to point j on its kth leg of the trip. For example, if the truck takes the route shown in Figure 14.4, then $x_{121} = 1$ indicates that the truck goes from San Jose to Los Gatos on the first leg of its trip.

It is implicit here that there are other variables which assume zero value, as shown in Figure 14.5. For example, the San Jose-to-Los Gatos route may be taken as the first or the third leg of the trip. If it is the first leg, then it cannot also be the third leg of the trip. Therefore,

$$x_{213} = 0,$$

as indicated in the diagram.

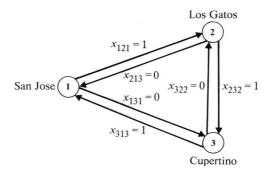

Figure 14.5

Also there are all together six variables in the model. At any given time only three of them can assume nonzero values in a solution.

If the truck takes the route San Jose → Los Gatos → Cupertino → San Jose, then the total time required for the trip is

$$25 + 35 + 45 = 105.$$

But this solution may also be obtained by first formulating the objective function

$$f = 25x_{121} + 50x_{213} + 35x_{232} + 30x_{322} + 40x_{131} + 45x_{313}$$

and then letting $x_{121} = 1$, $x_{213} = 0$, $x_{232} = 1$, $x_{322} = 0$, $x_{131} = 0$, and $x_{313} = 1$.

Having formulated the objective function, we must specify the constraints. We will divide the constraints into four categories.

a. One Leg From Each Node   Consider the predicament of the delivery truck of the San Jose bakery. It must head toward either Los Gatos or Cupertino but not toward both cities at the same time. This restriction can be expressed as:

$$x_{121} + x_{131} = 1.$$

Or, if the truck is in Los Gatos, the fact that it must head toward either San Jose or Cupertino may be expressed as:

$$x_{213} + x_{232} = 1.$$

Similarly, if it is in Cupertino, the constraint becomes:

$$x_{322} + x_{313} = 1.$$

In effect, each of these constraints specifies that only one leg of a trip can originate from a node.

b. One Leg to Each Node   Now consider how the delivery truck reaches, for example, the Los Gatos store: from San Jose on the first leg or from Cupertino on the second leg of its trip, but not from both cities simultaneously. This restriction may be expressed as:

$$x_{121} + x_{322} = 1.$$

Similar constraints for San Jose and Cupertino are:

$$x_{213} + x_{313} = 1,$$
$$x_{131} + x_{232} = 1.$$

These constraints specify that only one leg of a trip can end at any one node.

c. Sequencing the Legs   Suppose the delivery truck reaches Los Gatos on its first leg. Then the second leg of the trip must start from Los Gatos. On the other hand, suppose the truck reaches Los Gatos on its second leg. Then the third leg of the trip must start from Los Gatos. These constraints may be expressed as:

$$x_{121} = x_{232}, \qquad x_{322} = x_{213}.$$

Let us see how these equations work by examining the first one. Suppose the truck in fact reaches Los Gatos from San Jose on its first leg. Then by definition $x_{121} = 1$, so that by the first equation $x_{232} = 1$ also. But $x_{232} = 1$ implies that the second leg of the trip must start from Los Gatos. The two constraints together specify that if the kth leg of the trip ends at Los Gatos, then the $(k + 1)$th leg of the trip must start from Los Gatos. The similar constraints for Cupertino are:

$$x_{131} = x_{322}, \qquad x_{232} = x_{313}.$$

d. Only One of Each Leg   It is not difficult for us to see that there can be no more than one of the first leg, no more than one of the second leg, and so on. But the computer, for example, does not know this unless it is explicitly given this information. Therefore, we must specify for the first leg

$$x_{121} + x_{131} = 1,$$

and for the second and third legs

$$x_{322} + x_{232} = 1,$$
$$x_{213} + x_{313} = 1.$$

But we have already formulated the first of the these constraints as "one leg from each node" and also the third constraint as "one leg to each node."

Summary   Rearranging some terms, we can summarize the preceding formulation as Table 14.2. To complete the formulation, however, we must add that x_{ijk} must be either 0 or 1.

Table 14.2

Constraint type	x_{121}	x_{131}	x_{232}	x_{213}	x_{322}	x_{313}	
a	1	1					= 1
			1	1			= 1
					1	1	= 1
b				1		1	= 1
	1				1		= 1
		1	1				= 1
c	1		-1				= 0
				-1	1		= 0
		1			-1		= 0
			1			-1	= 0
d			1		1		= 1
Objective function	25	40	35	50	30	45	$= f$

Consider the optimal route San Jose → Los Gatos → Cupertino → San Jose. In notation this route is

$$x_{121} = 1, \quad x_{232} = 1, \quad x_{313} = 1,$$

with zero value for all other variables. Substituting these values into the above model, we will find that every constraint is satisfied.

Example 6. Machine Shop Scheduling A certain machine in Precision Machine Shop must do four different jobs. The set-up time for each job depends on the job that precedes it. The amount of time required to complete a job, on the other hand, is independent of the job that precedes it. What is wanted is to minimize the total set-up time by properly sequencing the jobs.

The structure of this problem is identical to that of the traveling salesman's problem. We let the nodes in the network shown in Figure 14.6 represent the jobs to be done, and let the coefficient c_{ij} be the set-up time for job j, given that job i precedes job j.

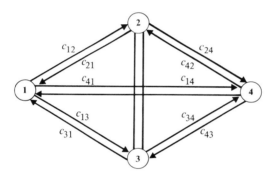

Figure 14.6

If we think of the nodes 1, 2, 3 and 4 as four different cities and c_{ij} as the time required to travel from city i to city j, then the machine shop scheduling problem becomes a traveling salesman's problem.

14.4 SET-COVERING PROBLEMS

Consider the network shown in Figure 14.7, where the arcs are not directed. Let N be the set of nodes and A the set of arcs in the network. A subset of A is said to have covered N if every node in N is incident to some arc in the

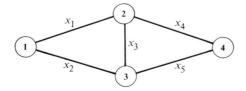

Figure 14.7

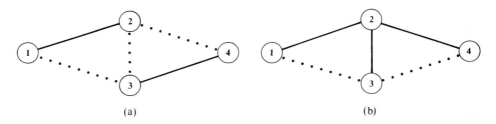

Figure 14.8

subset. Two examples of N-covering subsets of arcs are illustrated in Figure 14.8. In part (a) of the figure only two arcs cover N, whereas in part (b) three arcs cover N.

A *simple set-covering problem* is to find a minimum subset of arcs that will cover N. To formulate a model for such a problem, we let x_1 be 1 if the arc joining nodes 1 and 2 is included in the cover, and x_1 be 0 if the arc is not in the cover. The other variables are also indicated in Figure 14.7. Then the fact that node 1 should be covered may be specified by

$$x_1 + x_2 = 1.$$

That node 2 should be covered is specified by

$$x_1 + x_3 + x_4 = 1.$$

Similarly,

$$x_2 + x_3 + x_5 = 1, \qquad x_4 + x_5 = 1.$$

The objective function is

$$\min f = x_1 + x_2 + x_3 + x_4 + x_5.$$

The structure of the model is captured by Table 14.3.

Table 14.3

	x_1	x_2	x_3	x_4	x_5	
Constraints	1	1				≥ 1
	1		1	1		≥ 1
		1	1		1	≥ 1
				1	1	≥ 1
Objective function	1	1	1	1	1	$= f$

Now consider the zero-one programming problem:

$$\min f = c_1 x_1 + \cdots + c_n x_n,$$

$$a_{11} x_1 + \cdots + a_{1n} x_n \geq 1,$$

$$\vdots \qquad \qquad \vdots$$

$$a_{m1} x_1 + \cdots + a_{mn} x_n \geq 1.$$

Our set-covering problem was obtained by letting all c_j be 1, some a_{ij} be 1, and the remaining a_{ij} be 0. Such a set-covering problem is called a *simple set-covering problem*. In other problems it may be necessary to let c_j assume some other value besides 1 while letting a_{ij} be either 1 or 0. These are called *weighted set-covering problems.*

Example 7. Delivery Problem The warehouse of a large department store in San Jose must dispatch various items to four different customers. It uses the services of a common carrier. If the orders of more than one customer are dispatched in one batch, there can be savings in handling and shipping costs. But we will assume that the common carrier will not deliver a batch containing orders of more than three customers.

The delivery rates depend on the weight and volume of the batch, the number of stop-offs involved, and the routes and destinations.

The problem of the warehouse manager is to combine the four orders into batches in such a way as to minimize the total shipping costs.

To formulate a model for this problem, let us assume that the following combinations of orders are possible, with the indicated rates:

		Batch						
		1	2	3	4	5	6	7
Customer	1	1	1				1	
	2	1		1	1		1	1
	3		1	1		1	1	1
	4				1	1		1
Shipping cost		c_1	c_2	c_3	c_4	c_5	c_6	c_7

The orders for customers 1 and 4 cannot be combined into a batch.

Let x_j be 1 if the jth batch is included in the delivery scheme, 0 otherwise. Customer 1 can receive his order as part of batch 1, 2, or 6. To ensure that he receives his order, we must have a constraint:

$$x_1 + x_2 + x_6 = 1.$$

The constraint is an equation since a customer should not be served by more than one batch. The complete set of constraints for the problem is summarized in Table 14.4. The objective function is then:

$$\min f = c_1 x_1 + \cdots + c_7 x_7,$$

as shown in the table.

We can see now that the model for our delivery problem has the structure of a weighted set-covering problem.

Example 8. Airline Crew Scheduling Orient Airline maintains a daily flight for each of the routes shown in Figure 14.9. One crew can fly, for example, from San Francisco to Tokyo and then onto Hong Kong. However, one flight

Table 14.4

	x_1	x_2	x_3	x_4	x_5	x_6	x_7	
	1	1				1		= 1
Constraints	1		1	1		1	1	= 1
		1	1		1	1	1	= 1
				1	1		1	= 1
Objective function	c_1	c_2	c_3	c_4	c_5	c_6	c_7	= f

crew cannot make the flight from San Francisco to Tokyo and then back to San Francisco. The possible flights that can be assigned to any single crew are indicated below, along with the costs of the assignments:

	Flight assignment						
	1	2	3	4	5	6	7
S.F. to Tokyo	1	1					
Tokyo to H.K.		1	1		1		
H.K. to Tokyo				1	1	1	
Tokyo to S.F.						1	1
Cost	c_1	c_2	c_3	c_4	c_5	c_6	c_7

The problem for the airline is to assign the crews so as to minimize the total cost while at the same time meeting the daily flight schedules.

We let x_j be 1 if the jth assignment scheme is utilized, 0 otherwise. Note that the flight schedule from San Francisco to Tokyo can be met by either scheme 1 or scheme 2. Thus in order to ensure that this schedule is met, we must have the constraint

$$x_1 + x_2 = 1.$$

The remaining constraints are summarized in Table 14.5. The objective function is then

$$\min f = c_1 x_1 + \cdots + c_7 x_7,$$

also as shown in the table.

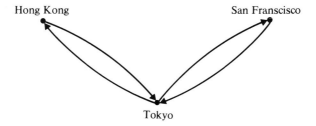

Figure 14.9

Table 14.5

	x_1	x_2	x_3	x_4	x_5	x_6	x_7	
Constraints	1	1						$= 1$
		1	1		1			$= 1$
				1	1	1		$= 1$
						1	1	$= 1$
Objective function	c_1	c_2	c_3	c_4	c_5	c_6	c_7	$= f$

Suppose, for example, instead of minimizing the total cost, the airline wants to minimize the total number of crews. Then we simply let $c_1 = 1, \ldots, c_7 = 1$ and formulate a simple set-covering model.

EXERCISES

1. Pacific Air Transport Company has scheduled a flight by cargo plane from Oakland to a Far Eastern city. The plane will have a weight capacity of 30,000 lb, and a volume capacity of 25,000 ft³. There are four different commodity lots awaiting shipment from Oakland to the Far Eastern city, with the following characteristics:

Lot	Amount (lb)	Volume (ft³/)lb	Revenue/lb
1	10,000	1.0	0.80
2	12,000	1.2	1.00
3	18,000	1.5	1.20
4	7,000	2.0	1.50

The plane must carry all or none of a given lot. The company wants to select the lots in such a way as to maximize the total revenue from the flight. Formulate a model for this problem.

2. The finance committee of the board of directors of Brown Manufacturing Company screens the major capital expenditure projects for the company. The projects under consideration, with their fund requirements and present values in millions, are shown below:

	Fund Requirements			
Projects	1st year	2nd year	3rd year	Present value
1	$4	$3	$5	$18
2	5	4	6	24
3	2	5	8	22
4	6	6	2	20

The finance committee is agreed that the company should not expend more than $15 million in any of the three years and wants to determine the set of projects which will maximize the sum of the present values. Formulate a model for this problem.

3. Rich Oil Company plans to import additional crude oil from the Persian Gulf and the Caribbean areas. It expects to import 150 million additional barrels from the Persian Gulf, and 50 million additional barrels from the Caribbean during each of the next ten years. To accommodate these additional imports, the company must build one or more refineries. Three locations in the United States under consideration are: the East Coast, Gulf Coast, and West Coast. The projected capacities and estimated initial costs for the refineries are:

Location	Annual capacity	Initial cost
East Coast	80 million barrels	$300 million
Gulf Coast	60 million barrels	200 million
West Coast	120 million barrels	400 million

The shipping costs per ton of crude oil are:

From \ To	East Coast	Gulf Coast	West Coast
Persian Gulf	$42	$40	$38
Caribbean	10	13	25

One ton of crude oil is approximately three barrels.

The company is trying to determine the locations for the refineries and the allocations of crude oil from the oil fields to the refineries in such a way as to minimize the total initial refinery construction costs and the total shipping costs for the next ten years. Formulate a model for this problem.

4. Every year Davis Motor Company awards one week of paid vacation and business trip to the top automobile salesmen of the year. During the week of vacation a number of formal and informal meetings are held between company executives and the vacationing salesmen for purposes of exchanging ideas.

Three possible vacation spots under consideration are: Acapulco, the Bahama Islands, and Honolulu. Because the company wants an informal atmosphere for the meetings, it does not want to have more than 100 salesmen at any one location. The cost figures for the three locations are:

Location	Fixed cost	Variable cost per salesman
Acapulco	$15,000	$250
Bahama Islands	10,000	350
Honolulu	20,000	300

The company will pay the round-trip charter fare for the salesmen and their wives from either San Francisco or New York to the vacation spots. The fares per couple are

From \ To	Acapulco	Bahamas	Honolulu
San Francisco	$200	$300	$250
New York	200	150	450

There will be 90 couples departing from San Francisco and 100 couples from New York.

The company wants to select the vacation spots and assign the salesmen to these places in such a way as to minimize the total cost. Formulate a model for this problem.

5. A machine in Precision Machine Shop of Example 6 is to perform operations A, B, C, and D, starting with A. After performing the remaining three operations, the machine will have to perform operation A again. The set-up times, in hours, are:

Completed operations	Starting operations			
	A	B	C	D
A		1.5	3.0	0.8
B	2.0		1.8	1.3
C	2.4	2.3		1.0
D	3.2	1.7	2.5	

The machine shop wants to sequence the operations in such a way as to minimize the total set-up time. Formulate a model for this problem.

6. Jim Brown is a vice president of an automobile manufacturer in charge of international operations. His office is in New York City and he is planning a trip to Buenos Aires, Capetown, Manila, and Paris, and then back to New York. The distances in air miles between the cities are:

	Capetown	Manila	New York	Paris
Buenos Aires	8,500	11,000	5,300	6,900
Capetown		7,500	7,800	5,800
Manila			8,500	6,700
New York				3,600

Jim Brown wants to visit all of these cities and return to his New York office so that the total distance in air miles travelled is held to the minimum. Formulate a model for this problem.

7. Given the network shown in Figure 14.10, formulate a model that will yield the smallest subset of arcs covering all of the nodes in the network.

8. Ford Manufacturing is exploring the possibility of establishing a production and

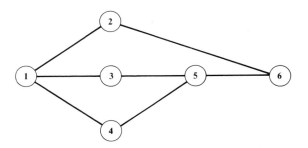

Figure 14.10

distribution center in the Far East. Before such a center can be established, however, the company must engage in extensive negotiations with the government of the host country. The selection of a team for these negotiations is now in process. The team must include at least one expert in each of the following areas: international finance, production, marketing, and government regulations. The candidates under consideration are listed below with their fields of expertise:

Candidates	Fields of expertise
J. Adams	International finance, marketing
K. Brown	Government regulations
L. Cox	Marketing, production
M. Davis	Government regulations, marketing, production
N. Edwards	Government regulations, marketing

Formulate a model with which the company can minimize the number of individuals chosen for the negotiating team.

15

INTEGER PROGRAMMING: COMPUTATIONS

In Chapter 14 we were concerned with the formulations of integer programming problems. Now we shall examine the computations in integer programming. Consider the following integer programming problem:

$$\max f = 10x_1 + 7x_2,$$

$$4x_1 + 3x_2 \leq 10,$$

$$x_1, x_2 \geq 0,$$

where x_1 and x_2 are integers. All the feasible solutions for this problem are indicated by the large dots on the diagram in Figure 15.1. There are all together

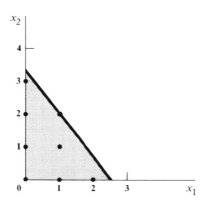

Figure 15.1

eight feasible solutions. By the following enumeration:

x_1	0	1	2	0	0	0	1	1
x_2	0	0	0	1	2	3	1	2
f	0	10	20	7	14	21	17	24

we can see that the optimal solution is

$$x_1 = 1, \qquad x_2 = 2, \qquad f = 24.$$

The complete enumeration of all feasible solutions, such as shown above, however, is probably the most inefficient way of solving an integer programming problem. When the problem is of even a modest size, this method will already require a tremendous amount of computer time. In the rest of this chapter we shall consider some well-known procedures for solving integer programming problems without complete enumerations.

15.1 LINEAR-PROGRAMMING APPROXIMATIONS

Let us first assume that the problem given above is really a linear-programming problem; that is, we drop the integer requirement. Then the solution space for the linear-programming problem is the shaded triangle in Figure 15.1, and the optimum solution is

$$x_1 = 2.5, \qquad x_2 = 0, \qquad f = 25$$

At this point we may round off the decimal and obtain

$$x_1 = 2, \qquad x_2 = 0, \qquad f = 20,$$

which is quite close to the actual optimal solution for the original problem.

In practice, obtaining an optimum linear-programming solution and rounding off the decimals will often yield a reasonably good solution for one or another integer programming problem. But in other integer programming problems such an approach may be quite unsatisfactory.

15.2 CUTTING THE SOLUTION SPACE

Let us now consider the following integer programming problem:

$$\max f = 10x_1 + 2x_2,$$
$$4x_1 + x_2 = 10,$$

where x_1, x_2 are integers. The set of feasible solutions are indicated by the large round dots in Figure 15.2. The optimum solution is

$$x_1 = 2, \qquad x_2 = 2, \qquad f = 24.$$

Suppose we drop the integer constraints in the problem. Then the solution

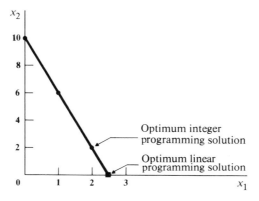

Figure 15.2

space for the resulting linear-programming problem is the line segment shown in the figure, with the following optimum solution:

$$x_1 = 2.5, \qquad x_2 = 0, \qquad f = 25,$$

also shown in the figure. In this case the solution contains a noninteger.

Now consider the following linear-programming problem:

$$\max f = 10x_1 + 2x_2,$$
$$4x_1 + x_2 = 10,$$
$$x_2 \geq 1,$$

which is merely the linear-programming problem we just solved with the additional constraint

$$x_2 \geq 1.$$

The solution space for this new linear-programming problem is the solid line segment shown in Figure 15.3.

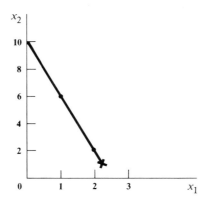

Figure 15.3

What is the significance of the constraint

$$x_2 \geq 1$$

to the original linear-programming problem? The constraint cuts off a segment from the solution space for the original linear-programming problem; in particular, the optimum solution for the original linear-programming problem is no longer feasible for the new problem. On the other hand, the constraint does not eliminate the integer solutions from the solution space. Thus the revised linear-programming problem has a different optimum solution than the original problem without the constraint.

Is the optimum solution for this new linear-programming problem feasible for the integer programming problem? We note that the new optimum linear-programming solution is

$$x_1 = 2.25, \qquad x_2 = 1, \qquad f = 24.5,$$

which obviously is not a feasible integer programming solution. On the other hand, had this solution turned out to be feasible for the integer programming problem, then it would also have been an optimum feasible solution for the integer programming problem.

The foregoing discussion suggests that a procedure such as is described by the flow chart in Figure 15.4 may be useful in solving integer programming problems.

15.3 GOMERY CUT

The procedure described by the flow chart in Figure 15.4 is rather intuitively motivated. There is no guarantee that repeated cutting of the solution space will indeed yield an optimum solution for an integer programming problem. Therefore, we may well ask, is it possible to obtain an optimum solution for an integer programming problem in a finite number of steps from an initial linear-programming solution? The answer is, Yes. Gomery, for example, devised just such a method, and it is called the *Gomery cut method*.

Consider the optimum solution for the original linear-programming problem

$$\max f = 10x_1 + 2x_2,$$
$$4x_1 + x_2 = 10.$$

The simplex tableau for the optimum solution is

Basis variables	Basis prices	x_1	x_2	Solution values
x_1	10	1	0.25	2.5
Increased revenues		0	0.50	25.0

We note that this is not an integer solution. But a Gomery cut can begin from here.

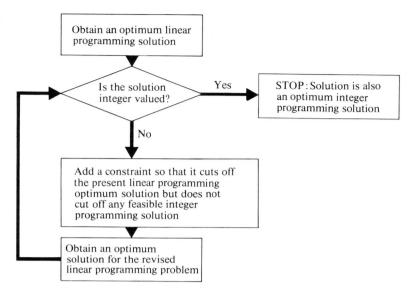

Figure 15.4

Let us change some of the notations in the simplex tableau so that it becomes:

Basis variables	Basis prices	x_1	x_2	Solution values
x_1	10	y_1	y_2	u
Increased revenues		0	0.5	25

On the basis of these two simplex tableaus we have

$$x_1 = u - y_2 x_2 = 2.5 - 0.25 x_2.$$

Now if we let

u^I be the largest integer less than u,

y_2^I be the largest integer less than y_2,

and

$$u^F = u - u^I, \qquad y_2^F = y_2 - y_2^I,$$

then

$$u^I = 2, \quad y_2^I = 0, \quad u^F = 0.5, \quad y_2^F = 0.25.$$

Moreover,

$$x_1 = (u^I + u^F) - (y_2^I + y_2^F)x_2$$

or, after a rearrangement of terms,

$$x_1 = (u^I - y_2^I x_2) + (u^F - y_2^F x_2).$$

Now assume that we plan to assign some positive integer to x_2 so that x_1

will also be an integer. We know, however, that $u^I - y_2^I x_2$ will be an integer so long as x_2 is an integer, since u^I and y_2^I are by definition integers. Therefore, if x_1 is an integer, then $u^F - y_2^F x_2$ is an integer. But $0 < u^F < 1$, since by assumption $u = u^I + u^F$ is not an integer. And since $0 \le y_2^F < 1$, we must have $y_2^F x_2 \ge 0$ for any positive integer x_2. Consequently, $u^F - y_2^F x_2$ cannot be a positive integer.

Thus if we want to obtain a new linear-programming solution so that x_1, which is currently not an integer, will be an integer, then the new solution must satisfy the constraint

$$u^F - y_2^F x_2 \le 0.$$

This constraint is called a *Gomery cut.*

To illustrate, let us return to our initial linear-programming solution. We note that $u^F = 0.5$ and $y_2^F = 0.25$ for this solution. Thus the constraint corresponding to the Gomery cut is

$$0.5 - 0.25x_2 \le 0$$

or

$$x_2 \ge 2.$$

The revised linear-programming problem is, then,

$$\max f = 10x_1 + 2x_2,$$
$$4x_1 + x_2 = 10,$$
$$x_2 \ge 2,$$

whose solution space is shown in Figure 15.5. The Gomery cut is also illustrated in the figure, by the dotted line. What has been cut from the solution space is the initial optimum linear-programming solution. But all the feasible solutions for the integer programming problem remain.

We may now propose the flow chart in Figure 15.6 for solving integer programming problems. An example of the application of the Gomery cut follows.

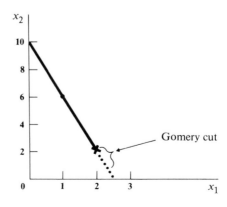

Figure 15.5

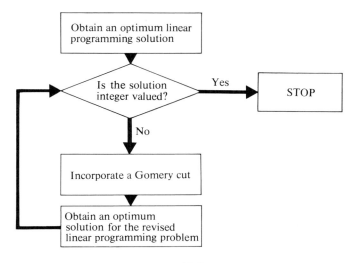

Figure 15.6

Example 1 Let us again consider the problem

$$\max f = 10x_1 + 7x_2,$$
$$4x_1 + 3x_2 \leq 10,$$

where x_1 and x_2 are nonnegative integers. The initial optimum linear-programming solution is provided by the following simplex tableau:

Basis variables	Basis prices	x_1	x_2	x_3	Solution values
x_1	10	1	0.75	0.25	2.5
Increased revenues		0	0.50	0	25.0

Here x_3 is the slack variable for the initial linear-programming problem. We note that x_1 is not integer valued. Therefore, we add the constraint

$$u^F - y_2^F x_2 - y_3^F x_3 \leq 0$$

or

$$0.5 - 0.75x_2 - 0.25x_3 \leq 0.$$

Then the new linear-programming problem is

$$\max f = 10x_1 + 7x_2,$$
$$4.00x_1 + 3.00x_2 + x_3 = 10,$$
$$-0.75x_2 - 0.25x_3 + x_4 \leq -0.5,$$

where x_4 is the slack variable for the new constraint. An optimal solution for the revised linear-programming problem is given by the following tableau:

Basis variables	Basis prices	x_1	x_2	x_3	x_4	Solution values
x_1	10	1	0	0	1	2
x_2	7	0	1	$\frac{1}{3}$	$-\frac{4}{3}$	$\frac{2}{3}$
Increased revenues		0	0	$2\frac{1}{3}$	$\frac{2}{3}$	$24\frac{2}{3}$

We note now that x_2 is not integer valued. On the basis of the coefficients in the row for x_2 we can incorporate a new constraint

$$\tfrac{2}{3} - \tfrac{1}{3}x_3 - \tfrac{2}{3}x_4 \leq 0.$$

Rearranging the terms in the new constraint and adding the constraint to the revised linear-programming problem, we have

$$\max f = 10x_1 + 7x_2,$$
$$4.00x_1 + 3.00x_2 + x_3 = 10,$$
$$-0.75x_2 - 0.25x_3 + x_4 = -0.5,$$
$$-\tfrac{1}{3}x_3 - \tfrac{2}{3}x_4 + x_5 = -\tfrac{2}{3},$$

where x_5 is the slack variable for the third constraint. The optimum solution for this problem is provided by the following tableau:

Basis variables	Basis prices	x_1	x_2	x_3	x_4	x_5	Solution values
x_1	10	1	0	-2	0	$\frac{3}{2}$	1
x_2	7	0	1	3	0	-2	2
x_4	0	0	0	2	1	$-\frac{3}{2}$	1
Increased revenues		0	0	1	0	1	24

Now all solution values of the variables are integers. Therefore, we have an optimum solution for the integer programming problem.

15.4   A COMPUTATIONAL SHORTCUT

The discussion in the last section may have left the impression that, once we have added a constraint for a Gomery cut, we must solve the new linear-programming problem all over again. This is not so. As a matter of fact, we can obtain an optimum solution for the new linear-programming problem with just one simplex iteration after we have incorporated the constraint for a Gomery cut.

Example 2   Consider the following integer programming problem:

$$\max f = 3x_1 + 6x_2 + 2x_3,$$
$$2x_1 + x_2 + 3x_3 \leq 10,$$
$$x_1 + 2x_2 + 3x_3 \leq 10,$$

where x_1, x_2, x_3 are nonnegative integers. An optimal linear-programming solution is given by the tableau

Basis variables	Basis prices	x_1	x_2	x_3	x_4	x_5	Solution values
x_1	3	1	0	1	$\frac{2}{3}$	$-\frac{1}{3}$	$\frac{10}{3}$
x_2	6	0	1	1	$-\frac{1}{3}$	$\frac{2}{3}$	$\frac{10}{3}$
Increased revenues		0	0	1	0	3	30

where x_4 and x_5 are the slack variables. We note that both x_1 and x_2 are noninteger valued. Therefore, we introduce a Gomery cut for either x_1 or x_2, say x_1. The constraint to be added is

$$-\tfrac{2}{3}x_4 - \tfrac{2}{3}x_5 + x_6 = -\tfrac{1}{3},$$

where x_6 is the slack variable for the new constraint.

We can now obtain an optimum solution for our revised linear-programming problem by solving it all over. But instead, suppose we add the new constraint to the simplex tableau of the previous optimal solution. Then we will have the new simplex tableau:

Basis variables	Basis prices	x_1	x_2	x_3	x_4	x_5	x_6	Solution values
x_1	3	1	0	1	$\frac{2}{3}$	$-\frac{1}{3}$	0	$\frac{10}{3}$
x_2	6	0	1	1	$-\frac{1}{3}$	$\frac{2}{3}$	0	$\frac{10}{3}$
x_6	0	0	0	0	$\left(-\frac{2}{3}\right)$	$-\frac{2}{3}$	1	$-\frac{1}{3}$
Increased revenues		0	0	1	0	3	0	30

This tableau depicts a basic solution, but one which is not feasible, since x_6 is negative. Intuition suggests then, that we should delete x_6 from the basis and bring another variable into it. This is precisely what is done in practice. How do we determine the incoming variable? We propose the following procedure: Let p_1, p_2, ..., p_5 be the row coefficients for x_6. Thus $p_4 = -\tfrac{2}{3}$ and $p_5 = -\tfrac{2}{3}$. Then the incoming variable corresponds to the column which maximizes

$$\frac{z_j - c_j}{p_j} \qquad \text{for } p_j < 0.$$

Writing this out in detail, we have

$$\max\left\{ \frac{z_4 - c_4}{p_4} = \frac{0}{-\tfrac{2}{3}} = 0;\ \frac{z_5 - c_5}{p_5} = \frac{3}{-\tfrac{2}{3}} = -4.5 \right\} = 0.$$

Thus x_4 should be brought into the basis.

The incoming variable having been determined, we see that the pivot element is in the x_6 row and x_4 column, as indicated in the above simplex tableau. Once the pivot element has been determined, we can use the regular simplex routines to obtain a new simplex tableau.

Thus the new tableau is:

Basis variables	Basis prices	x_1	x_2	x_3	x_4	x_5	x_6	Solution values
x_1	3	1	0	1	0	-1	1	3.0
x_2	6	0	1	1	0	1	-0.5	3.5
x_4	0	0	0	0	1	1	-1.5	0.5
Increased revenues		0	0	1	0	3	0	30

We note that this is an optimum linear-programming solution. Thus we have been able to reoptimize the revised linear-programming problem with just one simplex iteration. The procedure that we have followed is called the *dual simplex method.*

The new optimal linear-programming solution, however, contains noninteger solution values, namely the values of x_2 and x_4. The constraint for x_2 may be expressed as

$$-0.5x_6 \le -0.5.$$

Incorporating this constraint into our previous simplex tableau, we have

Basis variables	Basis prices	x_1	x_2	x_3	x_4	x_5	x_6	x_7	Solution values
x_1	3	1	0	1	0	-1	-1	0	3.0
x_2	6	0	1	1	0	1	-0.5	0	3.5
x_4	0	0	0	0	1	1	-1.5	0	0.5
x_7	0	0	0	0	0	0	⊖0.5	1	-0.5
Increased revenues		0	0	1	0	3	0	0	30

This is again a basic solution, but also not feasible. We can obtain a feasible solution by replacing x_7 by x_6 in the basis. The pivot element is indicated by a circle in the above tableau. The new simplex tableau thus obtained is

Basis variables	Basis prices	x_1	x_2	x_3	x_4	x_5	x_6	x_7	Solution values
x_1	3	1	0	1	0	-1	0	2	2
x_2	6	0	1	1	0	1	0	-1	4
x_4	0	0	0	0	1	1	0	-3	2
x_6	0	0	0	0	0	0	1	-2	1
Increased revenues		0	0	1	0	3	0	0	30

This solution is not only optimal but also integer valued. Therefore, it is an optimal feasible solution for the integer programming problem.

15.5   BRANCH AND BOUND METHOD

Another way of solving integer programming problems is called the *branch and bound* method. The concept is applicable not only to integer programming problems, but to other areas of mathematical programming as well. The branch and bound concept was first used to solve integer programming problems by Land and Doig.

Let us again consider the following integer programming problem, designated as problem 0:

0.
$$\max f_0 = 10x_1 + 7x_2,$$
$$4x_1 + 3x_2 \leq 10,$$
$$x_1, x_2 \text{ be nonnegative integers.}$$

Dropping the integer requirement, we obtain problem 1:

1.
$$\max f_1 = 10x_1 + 7x_2,$$
$$4x_1 + 3x_2 \leq 10,$$
$$x_1, x_2 \geq 0.$$

Problem 1 is easier to solve than problem 0. Therefore, we may ask whether we can obtain the solution for the latter by solving the former. Before answering this question let us examine some relations between the two problems.

One relation is called the *bounding relation*, which may be stated as follows:

Let f_0^* and f_1^* be the values of the objective functions for the optimum feasible solutions of problems 0 and 1, respectively. Then,

$$f_0^* \leq f_1^*.$$

That is, the optimum solution value of the objective function for the integer programming problem (0) cannot exceed that for the linear-programming problem (1). Thus f_1^* is an upper bound for f_0^*.

The second relation between the two problems is called the *optimality relation*:

If an optimal solution for problem 1, is feasible for problem 0, then it is also optimal for problem 0.

That this relation must hold should be evident. If an optimum solution for problem 1 is also feasible for problem 0, then we have in effect found a feasible solution for problem 0 in which f_0^* is equal to f_1^*. But according to the bounding relation, f_0^* cannot be larger than f_1^*. Therefore, the solution must be optimal for problem 0.

In this way, it is possible to solve problem 0 by solving problem 1. That is, if we have a solution to problem 1 which turns out to be also feasible for problem 0, then we have in fact solved problem 0.

Suppose, however, that the optimum solution for problem 1 is not feasible for problem 0. Then we may replace problem 1 with a set of m new problems which satisfies the following requirements:

a. *The optimal solution for problem 1 is infeasible for each of the m new problems.*

b. *At least one optimal solution for problem* 0 *is feasible for at least one of the m new problems.*

The formulation of these m new problems is called *branching*.

There are many different ways of formulating the set of m new problems. One of the most simple and elegant procedures is devised by Dakin. Suppose that one of the variables x_j has a value of t in a solution for problem 1 where t is not an integer. Then let

$$k \text{ be the largest integer smaller than } t.$$

Dakin proposes that we replace problem 1 with two new problems, say 2 and 3, such that problem 2 is equivalent to problem 1 plus the constraint $x_j \leq k$, and problem 3 is equivalent to problem 1 plus the constraint $x_j \geq k + 1$. Then the optimum solution for problem 1 is certainly not feasible for either problem 2 or problem 3. At the same time, an optimum solution for problem 0 must still be in the combined solution space for problems 2 and 3, since no feasible integer solution has been cut out from the solution space.

To illustrate this branching process, let us return to problem 1. The optimal solution is

$$x_1 = 2.5, \qquad x_2 = 0, \qquad f_1^* = 25.$$

This solution is not feasible for problem 0. The new problems that we should formulate are then:

2.
$$\max f_2 = 10x_1 + 7x_2,$$
$$4x_1 + 3x_2 \leq 10,$$
$$x_1 \geq 3,$$
$$x_1, x_2 \geq 0;$$

3.
$$\max f_3 = 10x_1 + 7x_2,$$
$$4x_1 + 3x_2 \leq 10,$$
$$x_1 \leq 2,$$
$$x_1, x_2 \geq 0.$$

The relation between problem 1 and the two new problems is illustrated in Figure 15.7, where the large dots are the feasible solutions for problem 0 and the shaded triangle is the feasible solution space for problem 1.

Problems 2 and 3 divide the solution space for problem 1 into three mutually exclusive regions: those for problems 2 and 3, and the region in between, which we will call the *Dakin cut*. We note that the Dakin cut contains the optimum solution for problem 1 but not any feasible integer solution. Thus problems 2 and 3 together satisfy the requirements a and b.

Let us now solve problem 2. We find that it has no feasible solution. Therefore, there is no point in branching any further from problem 2.

What about problem 3? The optimum solution for it is

$$x_1 = 2, \qquad x_2 = \tfrac{2}{3}, \qquad f_3^* = 24\tfrac{2}{3},$$

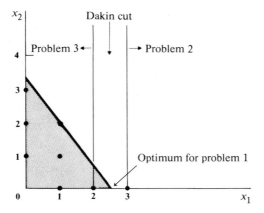

Figure 15.7

which is not feasible for problem 0. We may, therefore, replace problem 3 by the following two problems:

4.
$$\max f_4 = 10x_1 + 7x_2,$$
$$4x_1 + 3x_2 \leq 10,$$
$$x_1 \leq 2,$$
$$x_2 = 0,$$
$$x_1, x_2 \geq 0;$$

5.
$$\max f_5 = 10x_1 + 7x_2,$$
$$4x_1 + 3x_2 \leq 10,$$
$$x_1 \leq 2,$$
$$x_2 \geq 1,$$
$$x_1, x_2 \geq 0.$$

We note that neither problem 4 nor problem 5 will allow $x_2 = \frac{2}{3}$ as a solution.

Before proceeding to the solution of problems 4 and 5, let us recall that $f_3^* = 24\frac{2}{3}$ for problem 3. Thus

$$f_4 \leq f_3^* = 24\frac{2}{3}, \qquad f_5 \leq f_3^* = 24\frac{2}{3}.$$

f_3^* is an upper bound for f_4 and f_5.

Now, an optimum solution for problem 4 is

$$x_1 = 2, \qquad x_2 = 0, \qquad f_4^* = 20.$$

We observe that this solution is feasible for problem 0.

And since $f_4^* = 20$ is a feasible integer solution, we should not be satisfied with another integer solution with a value of f less than 20. Thus $f_4^* = 20$ is a lower bound for any useful integer solution we may obtain subsequently.

Our next task is to solve problem 5. But first, let us ask whether it is worthwhile to solve the problem at all. We already have an integer solution with $f_4^* = 20$. Also we know that the optimum value of f_5 cannot exceed $f_3^* = 24\frac{2}{3}$. Thus the best we can do by solving problem 5 is to increase the value of f by $4\frac{2}{3}$. So if an increase of $4\frac{2}{3}$ in the value of f does not justify further computations, then we should stop at this point.

Assume now that we are not satisfied with $f = 20$. Let us, therefore, solve problem 5. We obtain the optimum solution

$$x_1 = 1\tfrac{3}{4}, \qquad x_2 = 1, \qquad f_5^* = 24.5.$$

Since this solution is not feasible for problem 0, we must replace problem 5

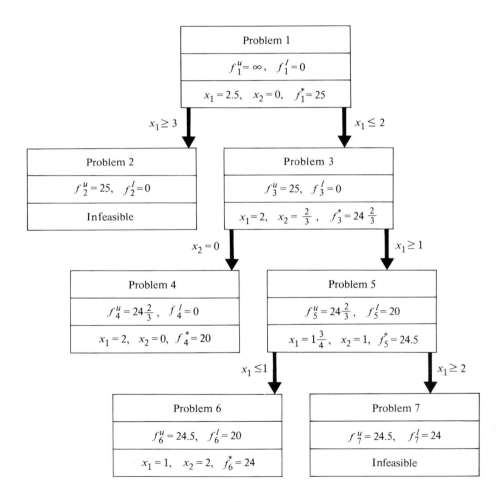

Figure 15.8

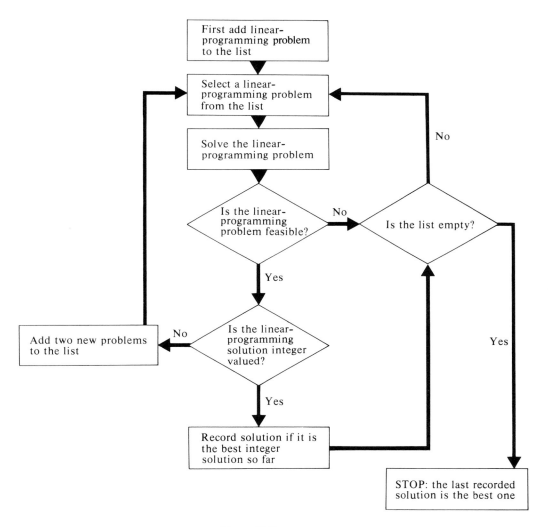

First add linear-programming problem to the list

Select a linear-programming problem from the list

Solve the linear-programming problem

Is the linear-programming problem feasible?

No

Is the list empty?

Yes

Add two new problems to the list

No

Is the linear-programming solution integer valued?

Yes

Record solution if it is the best integer solution so far

Yes

STOP: the last recorded solution is the best one

Figure 15.9

with the following two problems:

6.
$$\max f_6 = 10x_1 + 7x_2,$$
$$4x_1 + 3x_2 \leq 10,$$
$$x_1 \leq 2,$$
$$x_1 \leq 1,$$
$$x_2 \geq 1,$$
$$x_1, x_2 \geq 0,$$

7.
$$\max f_7 = 10x_1 + 7x_2,$$
$$4x_1 + 3x_2 \le 10,$$
$$x_1 \le 2,$$
$$x_1 \ge 2,$$
$$x_2 \ge 1,$$
$$x_1, x_2 \ge 0.$$

An optimum solution of problem 6 is

$$x_1 = 1, \qquad x_2 = 2, \qquad f_6^* = 24.$$

Problem 7 has no feasible solution.

We note that the solution to problem 6 is feasible for problem 0 and has the highest value of f among the integer feasible solutions found. Thus, it is the optimum feasible solution for the given integer programming problem.

Retracing our steps, we find that f_i^u and f_i^l are respectively the upper and lower bounds of f_i, where i is the current linear-programming problem to be solved. We can arbitrarily let $f_i^u = \infty$ and $f_i^l = 0$. Then the steps we have taken to solve the given integer programming problem may be summarized by the diagram in Figure 15.8.

The branch and bound algorithm that we have described thus far, may be summarized by the flow chart in Figure 15.9. Some modification of the algorithm will be needed if it is to be programmed for a computer. However, it will work reasonably well as it is for solving integer programming problems by hand calculation.

The flow chart introduces the term *list*, which may be a piece of paper on which we list the linear-programming problems to be solved. If a computer is used to solve the problem, then the list is some memory locations where we store the linear-programming problems to be solved.

EXERCISES

1. Solve the following integer programming problem by cutting solution space:

$$\max f = 12x_1 + 8x_2 + 6x_3 + 5x_4,$$
$$5x_1 + 4x_2 + 3x_3 + 2x_4 \le 7,$$

where x_1, x_2, x_3, and x_4 are nonnegative integers.

2. Solve the following integer programming problem by cutting solution space:

$$\max f = 10x_1 + 12x_2 + 8x_3 + 11x_4,$$
$$3x_1 + 2x_2 + 2x_3 + 4x_4 \le 11,$$

where x_1, x_2, x_3, x_4 are nonnegative integers.

3. Solve the following integer programming problem by cutting solution space:

$$\max f = 6x_1 + x_2,$$
$$2x_1 + x_2 \le 4,$$
$$4x_1 + x_2 \le 6,$$

where x_1 and x_2 are nonnegative integers.

4. Solve the following integer programming problem by cutting solution space:

$$\max f = 3x_1 + 5x_2 + 2x_3,$$
$$2x_1 + x_2 - x_3 \leq 9,$$
$$x_1 + 3x_2 + x_3 \leq 13,$$

where x_1, x_2, x_3 are nonnegative integers.

5. Solve the following integer programming problem by the branch and bound method:

$$\max f = 12x_1 + 8x_2 + 6x_3 + 5x_4,$$
$$5x_1 + 4x_2 + 3x_3 + 2x_4 \leq 7,$$

where x_1, x_2, x_3, x_4 are nonnegative integers.

6. Solve the following integer programming problem by the branch and bound method:

$$\max f = 10x_1 + 12x_2 + 8x_3 + 11x_4,$$
$$3x_1 + 2x_2 + 2x_3 + 4x_4 \leq 11,$$

where x_1, x_2, x_3, x_4 are nonnegative integers.

7. Solve the following integer programming problem by the branch and bound method:

$$\max f = 6x_1 + x_2,$$
$$2x_1 + x_2 \leq 4,$$
$$4x_1 + x_2 \leq 6,$$

where x_1 and x_2 are nonnegative integers.

8. Solve the following integer programming problem by the branch and bound method:

$$\max f = 3x_1 + 5x_2 + 2x_3,$$
$$2x_1 + x_2 - x_3 \leq 9,$$
$$x_1 + 3x_2 + x_3 \leq 13,$$

where x_1, x_2, x_3 are nonnegative integers.

16

DYNAMIC PROGRAMMING

Let us consider the following problem:

$$\max f = g_1(x_1) + \cdots + g_n(x_n),$$
$$x_1 + \cdots + x_n = d,$$
$$x_1 \geq 0 \cdots + x_n \geq 0,$$

where $g_i(x_i)$ is some function of the decision variable x_i and d is an environmental variable. One typical practical problem which may be formulated in this way is a one-dimensional resource allocation problem, where d units of a resource are to be allocated to n different uses. Then the decision variable x_i represents the amount of the resource allocated for the ith use, and $g_i(x_i)$ represents the amount of revenue generated by such an allocation. The decision concerns the proper allocation that will maximize the total revenue derived from all n uses.

How is the above problem formulation different from a linear-programming formulation? In linear programming we assume that the objective function f is a linear function. In the above formulation we do not make this assumption.

Example 1. Investment Problem 1   There are two different investment options available to us with the following possibilities of return:

Original investment	Amount of return	
	Option 1	Option 2
0	0	0
$1000	$2000	$3000
2000	6000	5000
3000	8000	7000

If we have $3000 to invest, then an examination of the table will reveal that we should invest $2000 in option 1 and $1000 in option 2, thereby reaping a total return of $9000. We note that $9000 is the maximum possible return from investing $3000.

While we were able to solve this particular investment problem without resorting to an explicitly formulated model, we shall nevertheless formulate a model to illustrate the structure of the problem. First, we define the return functions $g_1(x_1)$ and $g_2(x_2)$, where x_1, for example, is the amount invested in option 1 and $g_1(x_1)$ is the amount of return from investing x_1. The return functions are shown in the following table:

x_1 or x_2	$g_1(x_1)$	$g_2(x_2)$
0	0	0
1000	2000	3000
2000	6000	5000
3000	8000	7000

In fact, this is merely the original table with the headings replaced by mathematical symbols.

Now we may write the given investment problem as:

$$\max f = g_1(x_1) + g_2(x_2),$$
$$x_1 + x_2 = 3000,$$
$$x_1 \geq 0, \qquad x_2 \geq 0.$$

16.1   INTUITIVE ANALYSIS

Instead of considering both investment options, let us assume for the moment that only option 1 is available to us. Then, if we have $3000 to invest, the best policy is to invest all of it in option 1, thereby getting $8000 in return.

We let

$x_1(d)$ = optimum investment in option 1 when the amount available for investment is d,

$f_1(d)$ = optimum return from investing d when only option 1 is available

Then we will have:

d	$x_1(d)$	$f_1(d)$
0	0	0
1000	1000	2000
2000	2000	6000
3000	3000	8000

Which indicates that if, for example, we have $2000 to invest and only option 1 is available, then the best policy is to invest all $2000 in option 1 and get $6000 in return.

Now let us assume once again that both option 1 and option 2 are available. Suppose we have arbitrarily decided to invest $2000 in option 2. This investment will return $5000. In notation, we write:

$$g_2(2000) = 5000.$$

If we have $3000 to start with, then the best thing that we can do with the remaining $1000 is to invest it in option 1 for a $2000 return. In notation we may express this as

$$f_1(1000) = 2000.$$

Adding $g_2(2000)$ to $f_1(1000)$, we have that

$$g_2(2000) + f_1(1000) = 5000 + 2000 = 7000;$$

$7000 is the total return from investing $2000 in option 2 and $1000 in the best possible way, in option 1. Thus, if we invest an arbitrary amount x_2 in option 2, then the remainder, $3000 - x_2$, can be invested in option 1. Therefore,

$$g_2(x_2) + f_1(3000 - x_2)$$

is the total return from investing an arbitrary amount x_2 in option 2 and the rest of $3000, $3000 - x_2$, in the best possible way, in option 1.

Assuming that we can invest only in units of thousand dollars, then x_2 must have one of four values: 0, 1000, 2000, or 3000. All the different investment possibilities and their corresponding total returns may then be listed as follows:

$$g_2(\ \ \ 0) + f_1(3000) = \ \ \ \ \ 0 + 8000 = 8000,$$
$$g_2(1000) + f_1(2000) = 3000 + 6000 = 9000,$$
$$g_2(2000) + f_1(1000) = 5000 + 2000 = 7000,$$
$$g_2(3000) + f_1(\ \ \ 0) = 7000 + \ \ \ \ \ \ 0 = 7000.$$

We note that the total return is highest when we invest $1000 in option 2 and the remaining $2000 in option 1. Formally we write:

$$\max \begin{cases} g_2(\ \ \ 0) + f_1(3000) = \ \ \ \ \ 0 + 8000 = 8000 \\ g_2(1000) + f_1(2000) = 3000 + 6000 = 9000 \\ g_2(2000) + f_1(1000) = 5000 + 2000 = 7000 \\ g_2(3000) + f_1(\ \ \ 0) = 7000 + \ \ \ \ \ \ 0 = 7000 \end{cases} = 9000.$$

In abstract notation this is:

$$\max_{x_2=0,1000,2000,3000} \{g_2(x_2) + f_1(3000 - x_2)\} = 9000,$$

So far we have decided that if we have $3000 to invest in the two options, then the best policy is to invest $1000 in option 2 and $2000 in option 1. Suppose we have only $2000 to invest in the two options. Then the optimal investment policy may be obtained by the formula

$$\max_{x_2=0,1000,2000} \{g_2(x_2) + f_1(2000 - x_2)\},$$

Writing out the expressions in the braces, we have

$$\max \begin{cases} g_2(\quad 0) + f_1(2000) = \quad 0 + 6000 = 6000 \\ g_2(1000) + f_1(1000) = 3000 + 2000 = 5000 \\ g_2(2000) + f_1(\quad 0) = 5000 + \quad 0 = 5000 \end{cases} = 6000.$$

The optimal policy in this case is not to invest in option 2 and put $2000 in option 1.

Similarly, if only $1000 is available, then we write:

$$\max_{x_2=0,1000} \{g_2(x_1) + f_1(1000 - x_2)\},$$

Expanding the expressions in the braces, we have

$$\max \begin{cases} g_2(\quad 0) + f_1(1000) = \quad 0 + 2000 = 2000 \\ g_2(1000) + f_1(\quad 0) = 3000 + \quad 0 = 3000 \end{cases} = 3000,$$

which says that the optimal policy is to invest $1000 in option 2 and nothing in option 1.

Finally, if there is nothing to invest in the two options, then obviously we cannot invest any amount in either option.

We may now summarize our calculations in a table.

d	$x_1(d)$	$f_1(d)$	$x_2(d)$	$f_2(d)$
0	0	0	0	0
1000	1000	2000	1000	3000
2000	2000	6000	0	6000
3000	3000	8000	1000	9000

where

$x_2(d) =$ optimal amount of investment in option 2 when d is the amount available for both options,

$f_2(d) =$ optimal return from d when both options are available.

Now suppose that the above table is already available. Then we can determine an optimal investment policy for any given amount of total investment by just referring to the table. For example, if $3000 is available for both options, then the $x_2(d)$ column shows that the optimal amount to be invested in option 2 is $1000, and the $f_2(d)$ column shows that such a policy will return $9000. If $1000 is invested in option 2, then the remaining $2000 must be invested optimally in option 1. The $x_1(d)$ column shows that if $2000 is available for option 1, then all $2000 should be invested in the option. Thus we come to the same conclusion as before.

The procedure we just followed in ascertaining the optimal policy is called the *recursive steps* for the following reason. Suppose that determining how much to invest in option 1 and option 2 is two investment subproblems. Then the fact that we first decided how much to invest in option 2 in a sense means that we really solved the second subproblem first and the first subproblem second.

Example 2. Investment Problem 2 Let us now expand the investment problem of Example 1 as shown below:

x_i	$g_1(x_1)$	$g_2(x_2)$	$g_3(x_3)$
0	0	0	0
1000	2000	3000	4000
2000	6000	5000	7000
3000	8000	7000	9000

Here the $g_1(x_1)$ and $g_2(x_2)$ columns are identical with those in Example 1. We have merely added another investment option whose return function is given by $g_3(x_3)$.

The problem now is to decide how to allocate the investment fund to three options instead of two.

Assume that a total amount of $3000 is available for the three options. The fact that investing $1000 in option 3 will yield $4000 is expressed by the notation

$$g_3(1000) = 4000.$$

If we invest $1000 in option 3, then we will be left with $2000 to be invested in options 1 and 2. The table of $x_2(d)$ and $f_2(d)$ in Example 1, however, shows that the maximum return from investing $2000 in options 1 and 2 is $6000:

$$f_2(2000) = 6000.$$

Thus

$$g_3(1000) + f_2(2000) = 4000 + 6000 = 10,000$$

is the total return from investing $1000 in option 3 and the remaining $2000 optimally in the two remaining options. That is, if x_3 is the amount to be invested in option 3, then

$$g_3(x_3) + f_2(3000 - x_3)$$

is the total return from investing x_3 in option 3 and $3000 - x_3$ optimally in the remaining two options.

Let $f_3(3000)$ be the maximum possible return from investing $3000 in the three options. Then we can see intuitively that

$$f_3(3000) = \max_{x_3 = 0, 1000, 2000, 3000} \{g_3(x_3) + f_2(3000 - x_3)\},$$

Writing out the expressions in the braces, we have

$$f_3(3000) = \max \begin{cases} g_3(\quad 0) + f_2(3000) = \quad\quad 0 + 9000 = \quad 9000 \\ g_3(1000) + f_2(2000) = 4000 + 6000 = 10000 \\ g_3(2000) + f_2(1000) = 7000 + 3000 = 10000 \\ g_3(3000) + f_2(\quad 0) = 9000 + \quad\quad 0 = \quad 9000 \end{cases} = 10,000.$$

The calculations show that the maximum possible return in question is $10,000 and there are two policies which will yield the $10,000 return. The two equivalent policies are:

1. Invest $1000 in option 3 and the remaining $2000 optimally in options 1 and 2.
2. Invest $2000 in option 3 and the remaining $2000 optimally in options 1 and 2.

The next obvious problem is how to determine the optimal division of investments between options 1 and 2. The problem, however, was already solved in Example 1.

Suppose we choose the first of the two policies above and decide to invest $1000 in option 3. Then there is $2000 left to be optimally invested in options 1 and 2. If we now refer to the table of $x_2(d)$ and $f_2(d)$, we will find that if $2000 is to be invested in options 1 and 2, then it is best not to invest anything in option 2, and thus to invest the entire $2000 in option 1.

We have thus determined the optimal investment policy, given three options, by recursive steps. In summary the policy is as follows:

Option	Amount of investment	Return
1	$2000	$6000
2	0	0
3	1000	4000
Total	$3000	$10000

By going through similar recursive steps, we can find that an equally good policy is:

Option	Amount of investment	Return
1	$ 0	$ 0
2	$1000	3000
3	2000	7000
Total	$3000	$10000

The reader should verify this table by means of recursive steps.

16.2 FORMALIZATION OF DYNAMIC PROGRAMMING

The procedure we used to solve the two investment problems in this chapter is one of dynamic programming. Now let us present a more formal description of the procedure.

Consider the investment problem in Example 2. It can be formulated as:

$$\max f = g_1(x_1) + g_2(x_2) + g_3(x_3),$$

$$x_1 + x_2 + x_3 = d,$$

$$x_1, x_2, x_3 \geq 0,$$

where d is the amount available for investment, x_j, for example, is the amount invested in option 1, and $g_1(x_1)$ is the amount of return in investing x_1 in option 1.

To determine the optimal amounts for the three options simultaneously, we may consider the problem as a one-stage three-dimensional problem. Our previous procedure was to first determine the optimal amount for option 3, then for option 2, and finally for option 1. Thus we actually solved the investment problem in three successive stages, in each of which we were concerned only with the optimal amount for one option. Therefore, we transformed a one-stage three dimensional problem into a three-stage one-dimensional problem. That is, we let

$$f_3(d) = \max\{g_1(x_1) + g_2(x_2) + g_3(x_3)\},$$
$$x_1 + x_2 + x_3 = d,$$
$$x_1, x_2, x_3 \geq 0.$$

Then $f_3(d)$ was the maximum return of allocating d to three options. We then let

$$f_2(d - x_3) = \max\{g_1(x_1) + g_2(x_2)\},$$
$$x_1 + x_2 = d - x_3,$$
$$x_1, x_2 \geq 0.$$

The principle which we made use of in the above procedure, known as the Bellman principle of optimality, may be stated as follows:

An optimal policy has the property that whatever the initial environment and initial decisions are, the remaining decisions must constitute an optimal policy with regard to the environment resulting from the initial decision.

In the case of our investment problem, assuming that d is the total amount to be invested in the three options, then the availability of d may be said to constitute the initial environment. Assuming that next we decided to invest x_3 amount in option 3, then x_3 may be said to constitute our *initial decision*. Once x_3 out of d has been allocated for option 3, then the availability of the remaining amount $d - x_3$ is said to be the *environment resulting from the initial decision*. See Figure 16.1.

Suppose we have already decided to invest x_3 in option 3. Then the only sensible thing to do is to allocate the remaining $d - x_3$ to the remaining two options. Such a policy will yield a total return of

$$g_3(x_3) + f_2(d - x_3).$$

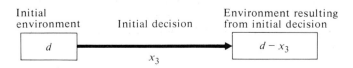

| Initial environment | Initial decision | Environment resulting from initial decision |

$$d \longrightarrow x_3 \longrightarrow d - x_3$$

Figure 16.1

The Bellman principle of optimality has more subtle implications than appears on the surface. The principle seems to say that the initial decision does not matter so long as the remaining decisions are made optimally. But this is not what the principle of optimality is meant to imply. Its actual implication is that, if we know that the remaining decisions will be made optimally with respect to the environment resulting from the initial decision, then we can simplify the problem of making the initial decision.

For example, suppose that we are considering two different allocations of funds to option 3, say $x_3 = 2000$ and $x_3 = 3000$. If we assume further that regardless of whether $2000 or $3000 is invested in option 3, the remaining amount will be optimally invested in options 1 and 2, then

$$g_3(2000) + f_2(d - 2000), \qquad g_3(3000) + f_2(d - 3000)$$

are the total returns from investing $2000 and $3000, respectively, in option 3. The better policy of the two is that which

$$\text{maximizes} \begin{Bmatrix} g_3(2000) + f_2(d - 2000) \\ g_3(3000) + f_2(d - 3000) \end{Bmatrix}.$$

Earlier we showed how the better policy of the two arbitrary investment policies regarding option 3 could be determined. It is now apparent that finding the optimal policy among all possible investment policies regarding option 3 is not any more difficult. This is the policy which

$$\text{maximizes} \{g_3(x_3) + f_2(d - x_3)\}$$

for all possible x_3. If we let $d = 3000$ and $x_3 = 0, 1000, 2000,$ and 3000, then the optimal policy is that which

$$\text{maximizes} \begin{Bmatrix} g_3(\quad 0) + f_2(3000) \\ g_3(1000) + f_2(2000) \\ g_3(2000) + f_2(1000) \\ g_3(3000) + f_2(\quad 0) \end{Bmatrix}$$

which was already shown in Example 3. The policy thus found will then constitute the optimal *initial policy*.

If the values of $f_2(d)$ are available, we can ascertain the optimal initial policy in the manner illustrated above. The question, then, is, How do we ascertain the values of $f_2(d)$?

In applying the principle of optimality, we assumed that the initial decision concerned the amount to be invested in one of three options, namely option 3. Suppose now that the initial decision concerns the amount to be invested in one of two options, namely option 2. Then for each possible value of d we may calculate $f_2(d)$ as

$$f_2(d) = \max \{g_2(x_2) + f_1(d - x_2)\} \qquad \text{for all } x_2.$$

Of course, these calculations require that we know the values of $f_1(d)$. But $f_1(d)$

is

$$f_1(d) = \max\{g_1(x_1) + f_0\} \qquad \text{for all } x_1,$$

where $f_0 = 0$.

This entire procedure, however, is exactly what we followed in Examples 1 and 2. There we first determined the values of $f_1(d)$ for $d = 0$, $d = 1000$, $d = 2000$, and $d = 3000$. Then using the values of $f_1(d)$, we found the values of $f_2(d)$ for $d = 0$, $d = 1000$, $d = 2000$, and $d = 3000$. And using these values of $f_2(d)$, we found the value of $f_3(d)$ for $d = 3000$. We might also have found the values of $f_3(d)$ for $d = 0$, $d = 1000$, and $d = 2000$ in the same way. These results are again summarized in Table 16.1.

Table 16.1

d	$x_1(d)$	$f_1(d)$	$x_2(d)$	$f_2(d)$	$x_3(d)$	$f_3(d)$
0	0	0	0	0	0	0
1000	1000	2000	1000	3000	1000	4000
2000	2000	6000	0	6000	1000 or 2000	7000
3000	3000	8000	1000	9000	1000 or 2000	10000

Having obtained this table, we can recursively ascertain the optimal investment policy for a given d, where d is the total amount of funds available for investment. For example, if $d = 2000$, then $x_3(2000) = 1000$ or $x_3(2000) = 2000$, according to the $x_3(d)$ column, meaning that either \$1000 or \$2000 should be invested in option 3. If we invest \$1000 in option 3, then the remaining \$1000 must be allocated between option 1 and option 2. The $x_2(d)$ column shows that $x_2(1000) = 1000$, which means that all \$1000 should be invested in option 2.

The $f_3(d)$ column shows that $f_3(2000) = 7000$, meaning that the maximum return from investing \$2000 is \$7000. We may also make the following calculation:

Optimal solution	Return
$x_1 = 0$	$g_1(0) = 0$
$x_2 = 1000$	$g_2(1000) = 3000$
$x_3 = 1000$	$g_3(1000) = 4000$
Total	$f_3(2000) = 7000$

which also can be presented as

Option	Optimal amount of investment	Return
1	0	0
2	\$1000	\$3000
3	1000	4000
Total	\$2000	\$7000

16.3   AN ALLOCATION PROBLEM

Let us assume that d is the quantity of a resource to be allocated to three different uses whose return functions are given in Table 16.2.

Table 16.2

x_i	$g_1(x_1)$	$g_2(x_2)$	$g_3(x_3)$
0	0	0	0
1	7	2	8
2	16	8	13
3	16	12	16
4	21	19	16
5	21	23	19

What are the values of x_1, x_2, and x_3 that will

$$\text{maximize } f = g_1(x_1) + g_2(x_2) + g_3(x_3)$$

such that

$$x_1 + x_2 + x_3 = d$$
$$x_1, x_2, x_3 \geq 0?$$

It was shown in the preceding section that if d is the amount of the resource available for all three uses, then

$$f_3(d) = \max\{g_3(x_3) + f_2(d - x_3)\}$$

for $0 \leq x_3 \leq d$; and if d is available only for the first two uses, then

$$f_2(d) = \max\{g_2(x_2) + f_1(d - x_2)\}$$

for $0 \leq x_2 \leq d$; and if d is available only for the first use, then

$$f_1(d) = \max\{g_1(x_1) + f_0\}$$

for $0 \leq x_1 \leq d$, where $f_0 = 0$. Thus we may first find $f_1(d)$, as shown in Table 16.3.

Table 16.3

d	$x_1(d)$	$f_1(d)$
0	0	0
1	1	7
2	2	16
3	2	16
4	4	21
5	4	21

We note that if $d = 3$, the optimal value of x_2 is assumed to be 2, not 3, because both solutions will yield $f_1(d) = 16$.

Using Table 16.3, we can next obtain $x_2(d)$ and $f_2(d)$ as follows. If $d = 5$, for example, then

$$f_2(5) = \max \begin{cases} g_2(0) + f_1(5) = & 0 + 21 = 21 \\ g_2(1) + f_1(4) = & 2 + 21 = 23 \\ g_2(2) + f_1(3) = & 8 + 16 = 24 \\ g_2(3) + f_1(2) = 12 + 16 = 28 \\ g_2(4) + f_1(1) = 19 + 7 = 26 \\ g_2(5) + f_1(0) = 23 + 0 = 23 \end{cases} = 28,$$

which indicates that $x_2(5) = 3$ and $f_2(5) = 28$. Similarly, we can obtain $x_2(d)$ and $f_2(d)$ for $d = 0, 1, 2, 3$, and 4. We now ask the reader to verify Table 16.4 before he proceeds further.

Table 16.4

d	$x_2(d)$	$f_2(d)$
0	0	0
1	0	7
2	0	16
3	1	18
4	2	24
5	3	28

Using Table 16.4, we can ascertain the values of $x_3(d)$ and $f_3(d)$. For example, if $d = 5$, then

$$f_3(5) = \max \begin{cases} g_3(0) + f_2(5) = & 0 + 28 = 28 \\ g_3(1) + f_2(4) = & 8 + 24 = 32 \\ g_3(2) + f_2(3) = 13 + 18 = 31 \\ g_3(3) + f_2(2) = 16 + 16 = 32 \\ g_3(4) + f_2(1) = 16 + 7 = 23 \\ g_3(5) + f_2(0) = 19 + 0 = 19 \end{cases} = 32$$

shows that there are two optimal values of x_3: 1 and 3, both yielding $f_3(5) = 32$.

The remaining values of $x_3(d)$ and $f_3(d)$ are shown in Table 16.5 along with $x_1(d)$, $f_1(d)$, $x_2(d)$, and $f_2(d)$.

Again we ask the reader to verify the last two columns of the table before proceeding further.

Having obtained Table 16.5, we can proceed to solve the three-dimensional allocation problem in three stages.

Assuming that the total quantity of the available resource is 5 units, that is $d = 5$, then the $x_3(d)$ and $f_2(d)$ columns show that both $x_3(5) = 1$ and $x_3(5) = 3$ are optimal with $f_3(5) = 32$.

Then if we allocate 1 unit of the resource to the third use, that is $x_3(5) = 1$,

Table 16.5

d	$x_1(d)$	$f_1(d)$	$x_2(d)$	$f_2(d)$	$x_3(d)$	$f_3(d)$
0	0	0	0	0	0	0
1	1	7	0	7	1	8
2	2	16	0	16	0	16
3	2	16	1	18	1	24
4	4	21	2	24	2	29
5	4	21	3	28	1, 3	32

leaving 4 units to be allocated to the remaining two uses, columns $x_2(d)$ and $f_2(d)$ indicate that $x_2(4) = 2$ and $f_2(4) = 24$, with $d = 4$.

Allocating 2 units to the second use leaves only 2 units for the first use, and the $x_1(d)$ column indicates that if $d = 2$, then $x_1(2) = 2$. In summary we have:

Optimal solution	Return
$x_1 = 2$	$g_1(2) = 16$
$x_2 = 2$	$g_2(2) = 8$
$x_3 = 1$	$g_3(1) = 8$
Total $d = 5$	$f_3(5) = 32$

As was pointed out, another optimal value of x_3 is 3; that is, $x_3(5) = 3$. The reader should verify that the corresponding optimal solution for this value of x_3 is:

Optimal solution	Return
$x_1 = 2$	$g_1(2) = 16$
$x_2 = 0$	$g_2(0) = 0$
$x_3 = 3$	$g_3(3) = 16$
Total $d = 5$	$f_3(5) = 32$

16.4 SENSITIVITY ANALYSIS

Once we have a table for $x_i(d)$ and $f_i(d)$, we can evaluate the *sensitivity* of $f_i(d)$ to any change in d. For the three-dimensional allocation problem in the preceding section we observe that

$$f_3(4) = 29, \qquad f_3(5) = 32.$$

Thus by increasing the resource level of d from 4 to 5 units, we can increase the maximum return by 3 units.

16.5 SOME APPLICATION MODELS

In this section we shall describe a number of problems which can be formulated with dynamic-programming models.

Example 4. Cargo-Loading Problem Huckleberry Finn is a barge line on the Mississippi River. A 10-ton barge is scheduled to sail from a point on the river to another point. Four different types of commodities are acceptable for shipment. The unit weights in tons and freight charge for the different types of commodities are summarized below:

Commodity	Unit weight (tons)	Freight charge/ton
1	3	$40
2	1	10
3	2	25
4	4	60

The management problem is to accept the shipment of these commodities in such proportions as to maximize the total freight bill.

This problem may be formulated in a dynamic-programming framework as follows. Let $g_i(x_i)$ be the freight charge deriving from allocating x_i units of the barge's capacity to the ith commodity. Then $g_i(x_i)$ takes on the values as shown in Table 16.6, where the $g_1(x_1)$ column, for example, is obtained as follows. So long as we allocate 2 tons or less of the barge's capacity to this commodity, none of this commodity can be loaded since its unit weight is 3 tons. Therefore,

$$g_1(0) = 0, \qquad g_1(1) = 0, \qquad g_1(2) = 0.$$

Table 16.6

x_i	$g_1(x_1)$	$g_2(x_2)$	$g_3(x_3)$	$g_4(x_4)$
0	0	0	0	0
1	0	10	0	0
2	0	20	25	0
3	40	30	25	0
4	40	40	50	60
5	40	50	50	60
6	80	60	75	60
7	80	70	75	60
8	80	80	100	120
9	120	90	100	120
10	120	100	125	120

If we allocate between 3 and 5 tons, only one unit of this commodity can be loaded. Therefore,

$$g_1(3) = 40, \qquad g_1(4) = 40, \qquad g_1(5) = 40.$$

Similarly,

$$g_1(6) = 80, \qquad g_1(7) = 80, \qquad g_1(8) = 80, \qquad g_1(9) = 120, \qquad g_1(10) = 120.$$

The $g_2(x_2)$, $g_3(x_3)$, and $g_4(x_4)$ columns are generated in a similar manner.

Once we have Table 16.6, we can apply the dynamic-programming algorithm described in Section 16.2 to solve the problem.

Example 5. Product Mix Problem   Alpha Beta Manufacturing uses one raw material to manufacture three different products, named product 1, product 2, and product 3. One unit of product 1 uses three units of the raw material; one unit of product 2 uses two units of the raw material; and one unit of product 3 uses four units of the raw material. The selling prices of these products are \$8, \$6, and \$10, respectively. Given d units of the raw material, the manufacturer wants to allocate this material to the manufacturing of the three products so as to maximize the total revenue.

To simplify our calculations, let us assume that the quantity of any product produced is an integer value. Then we have the following integer programming problem:

$$\max f = 8x_1 + 6x_2 + 10x_3,$$
$$3x_1 + 2x_2 + 4x_3 \leq d,$$

where x_1, for example, is the quantity of product 1 manufactured. We can solve the problem by means of the dynamic-programming algorithm. To do so, we need to calculate the revenue functions $g_1(x_1)$, $g_2(x_2)$, and $g_3(x_3)$.

Let us find the values of $g_1(x_1)$. We observe that if we allocate less than 3 units of the raw material to product 1, we cannot manufacture any unit of this product. Thus

$$g_1(0) = 0, \qquad g_1(1) = 0, \qquad g_1(2) = 0.$$

Table 16.7

x_i	$g_1(x_1)$	$g_2(x_2)$	$g_3(x_3)$
0	0	0	0
1	0	0	0
2	0	6	0
3	8	6	0
4	8	12	10
5	8	12	10
6	16	18	10
7	16	18	10
8	16	24	20

If we allocate between 3 and 5 units of the raw material, then we can produce only 1 unit of this product. Thus

$$g_1(3) = 8, \qquad g_1(4) = 8, \qquad g_1(5) = 8.$$

Similarly, we find that

$$g_1(6) = 16, \qquad g_1(7) = 16, \qquad g_1(8) = 16.$$

We can also find the values of $g_2(x_2)$ and $g_3(x_3)$ in the same way. Table 16.7 is a sample table of $g_1(x_1)$, $g_2(x_2)$, and $g_3(x_3)$.

In any case, once we have the values of $g_i(x_i)$, we can again apply the dynamic-programming algorithm described in Section 16.2 to solve this problem.

EXERCISES

1. Three investment options are available to Sam Smith with returns on investment as shown in Table 16.8.

Table 16.8

Original investment	Amount of return		
	Option 1	Option 2	Option 3
0	0	0	0
$1,000	$ 2,000	$ 3,000	$ 4,000
2,000	5,000	4,000	5,000
3,000	8,000	6,000	7,000
4,000	10,000	9,000	10,000
5,000	11,000	10,000	12,000

a. Obtain a three-stage optimal policy table for Sam Smith.
b. Suppose that Sam Smith has $5,000 to invest and he wants to invest it optimally in options 1 and 2. How should he invest the money?
c. Suppose that Sam Smith wants to invest the $5000 in all three options. What is his optimal investment policy?
d. Suppose Sam Smith wants to invest only $4000 in the three options. What is his optimal investment policy?

2. Swanson Company is a small publisher of college textbooks. The company has divided the United States into three marketing territories and hired five new sales representatives. The expected relation between the number of new representatives and the additional sales revenue from the three territories is shown in Table 16.9.

a. Assuming that the company wants to maximize the additional sales revenue, how many representatives should be assigned to each territory?
b. Suppose the company is having second thoughts about adding five new sales representatives and is considering dropping one of the five. How much can the company lose in revenue by letting the fifth man go?

Table 16.9

Number of new representatives	Additional sales revenue		
	Territory 1	Territory 2	Territory 3
0	0	0	0
1	$100,000	$120,000	$180,000
2	220,000	250,000	260,000
3	300,000	320,000	340,000
4	360,000	380,000	350,000
5	400,000	420,000	380,000

3. Jack Gould is a management consultant. Three different companies have asked for his services. The schedule of weekly consulting fees proposed by the three companies is shown in Table 16.10.

Table 16.10

Number of consulting days	Company A	Company B	Company C
0	0	0	0
1	$ 200	$350	$300
2	400	550	500
3	600	650	600
4	800	700	700
5	1000	850	800

How can Jack Gould maximize his total weekly income? Solve the problem by dynamic programming.

4. Hand Tooled Machine Company produces three different types of machines. At the moment the company has on hand only ten units of a certain critical part required for these machines. The number of this part required for each machine, as well as the amount of profit from each machine, is as follows:

Type of machine	Number of parts required	Profit per unit
A	2	$5000
B	4	8000
C	3	7000

The company wants to schedule its production so as to maximize its total profit. Solve the problem by dynamic programming.

5. Pacific Air Transport Company has scheduled a flight of a cargo plane from Oakland to a Far Eastern city. The plane assigned for the flight has a weight capacity of 10 tons.

Three different types of commodities may be accepted for transport. The unit weight and unit freight charge for each commodity is listed below:

Commodity	Unit weight	Unit revenue
1	4 tons	$ 8,000
2	3 tons	7,000
3	7 tons	16,000

The company wants to allocate its transport capacity to these commodities in such a way as to maximize the total revenue. Solve the problem by dynamic programming.

MARKOV CHAIN

In recent years many important applications have been found for the concept of Markov chain in managerial decision-making. The fundamental notion of a Markov chain is best introduced by means of examples.

Example 1. Marble-Drawing Game   Two urns A and B each contain 10 marbles. Urn A contains 4 red and 6 green marbles; urn B contains 9 red and 1 green marbles. Suppose that we play the following game drawing marbles from the urns. If we draw one marble from one of these urns and it turns out to be red, then we win \$40; if it turns out to be green, then we lose \$50. The urn from which a marble is to be drawn is selected as follows. If we have just won \$40, then the next time we will draw from urn A. If we have just lost \$50, then we will draw from urn B. The drawing is to be repeated a large number of times where a marble drawn is replaced into the urn before the next game.

Let x_t be the amount of win or loss this time and x_{t+1} the amount of win or loss the next time. Suppose that the current draw has just resulted in a win; that is, $x_t = 40$. Then since the next draw will be from urn A, there is a 0.4 probability that we will win \$40 and 0.6 probability that we will lose \$50 next time. We write:

$$p(x_{t+1} = 40 \mid x_t = 40) = 0.4,$$
$$p(x_{t+1} = -50 \mid x_t = 40) = 0.6.$$

If our current draw has just resulted in a loss, that is $x_t = -50$, then the next draw will be from urn B, which contains 9 red and 1 green marbles. Consequently,

$$p(x_{t+1} = 40 \mid x_t = -50) = 0.9,$$
$$p(x_{t+1} = -50 \mid x_t = -50) = 0.1.$$

Note that $t = 1$ refers to the first draw, $t = 2$ to the second draw, and so on. At $t = 2$ we say that the game is in *stage* 2. Thus if t is the current stage, then $t + 1$ is the next stage.

In any stage t the game results in one of two possible outcomes, namely $x_t = 40$ and $x_t = -50$. Whichever outcome occurs, it will then constitute the *environmental setting* for the next draw. Thus $x_t = 40$ is one possible environment and $x_t = -50$ is the other possible environment. In Markov chain analysis the environmental settings are called *states*. Therefore, here $x_t = 40$ is one possible state and $x_t = -50$ is the other possible state. We shall stay with this terminology in the remainder of this chapter.

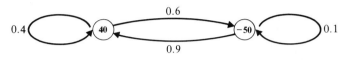

Figure 17.1

Consider, for example,

$$p(x_{t+1} = 40 \,|\, x_t = -50) = 0.9.$$

It is the probability that the next stage will result in $x_{t+1} = 40$, given that the current stage has just resulted in $x_t = -50$. This probability is called a *transition probability* from one state of the current stage to a state of the next stage. The transition probabilities for the marble drawing game are illustrated in Figure 17.1. They may also be given by an array of numbers as shown in the brackets below:

$$
\begin{array}{cc}
 & x_{t+1} \\
 & \begin{array}{cc} 40 & -50 \end{array} \\
x_t \;\; \begin{array}{c} 40 \\ -50 \end{array} & \begin{bmatrix} 0.4 & 0.6 \\ 0.9 & 0.1 \end{bmatrix}
\end{array}
$$

This array is called the *transition probability matrix*. We will further call any row of a transition probability matrix a *transition probability vector*.

By continually drawing the marbles according to the given rules we can generate a sequence of numbers corresponding to $x_1, x_2, \ldots, x_t, \ldots, x_n$. At any stage t of the process, however, the probability function of x_t depends on the state of the preceding stage. Such a process is said to be a *Markov process*.

Example 2. Brand-Switching   A consumer survey by Clean Soap Company indicates that 80 percent of the people who bought the company's soap this time will buy it again next time, but the remaining 20 percent will buy some other brand next time. The survey also shows that 10 percent of those who bought other brands this time will buy Clean Soap's brand next time, but 90 percent of them will continue to buy other brands.

The transition probability matrix for brand-switching is:

	Next time	
This time	**Clean Soap**	**Other brands**
Clean Soap	0.8	0.2
Other brands	0.1	0.9

If we let

$$x_t = \begin{cases} 1 & \text{if customer buys a Clean Soap brand at } t, \\ 0 & \text{if customer buys other brands at } t, \end{cases}$$

then the transition probability matrix becomes:

	x_{t+1}	
x_t	1	0
1	0.8	0.2
0	0.1	0.9

We may now consider the process of generating a series of ones and zeros for $x_1, x_2, \ldots$ to be a Markov process. That is, the consumer behavior with respect to the buying of soap may be characterized as a Markov chain.

Example 3. Production Inventory Control Alpha Beta Manufacturing faces the following demand probability function for one of its products:

Size of demand	Probability
1	0.8
3	0.2
	1.0

But the company's storage capacity is only 3 units. A production and inventory control policy must be devised so that the demand is always satisfied.

One such policy may be specified as follows:

If the beginning inventory is	Produce
0	3
1	3
2	2
3	0

We can let x_t be the beginning inventory at period t and x_{t+1} be the beginning inventory at period $t + 1$. Then the transition probability matrix may be given as:

	x_{t+1}			
x_t	0	1	2	3
0	0.2	0.0	0.8	0
1	0.0	0.2	0	0.8
2	0.0	0.2	0	0.8
3	0.2	0.0	0.8	0

This matrix is obtained as follows. Suppose the beginning inventory at t is one. Since the production policy specifies that three units be produced when the beginning inventory is one, there will be altogether four units available to satisfy the demand for the period. Since there is a 0.2 probability that the demand will be three, the probability of end inventory for the period being one is also 0.2. Similarly, the probability of end inventory being three is 0.8, since there is a 0.8 probability that the demand will be one unit. But since the end inventory for this period is the beginning inventory for the next period, we have

$$p(x_{t+1} = 1 \mid x_t = 1) = 0.2,$$
$$p(x_{t+1} = 3 \mid x_t = 1) = 0.8.$$

Other elements of the above transition probability matrix may be found in the same way.

If the manufacturer follows the same policy period after period, then the sequence of the beginning inventories $x_1, x_2, \ldots, x_n$ may be said to have been generated by a Markov process. That is, this inventory production process may be understood as a Markov chain.

17.2 STATE PROBABILITIES

Let us return to the marble-drawing game of Example 1. We present the transition probability matrix again for easy reference:

	x_{t+1} 40	-50
40	0.4	0.6
-50	0.9	0.1

This time assume that we will start the game by paying \$50 and drawing from urn B. Let $p(x_t = 40)$ and $p(x_t = -50)$ be the state probabilities for the first draw, that is for $t = 1$. Then according to the transition probability matrix,

x_1	$f(x_1)$
40	0.9
-50	0.1
	1.0

This probability distribution is called the *state probability distribution*, since it gives the probabilities of the two states at $t = 1$. We note that this state probability distribution is identical to the conditional probability distribution for x_{t+1} given $x_t = -50$, which is not surprising since the initial state $t = 0$ is assumed to be $x_0 = -50$.

The process of obtaining the state probability distribution for $t = 2$, is

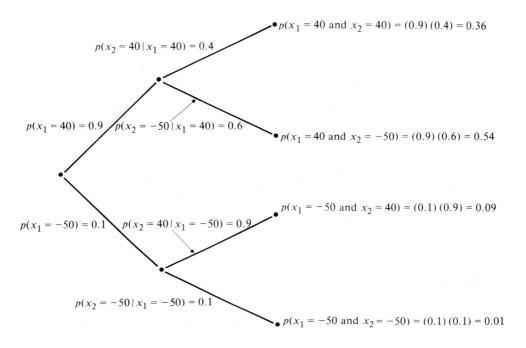

$p(x_1 = 40$ and $x_2 = 40) = (0.9)(0.4) = 0.36$

$p(x_2 = 40 \mid x_1 = 40) = 0.4$

$p(x_1 = 40) = 0.9$ $p(x_2 = -50 \mid x_1 = 40) = 0.6$

$p(x_1 = 40$ and $x_2 = -50) = (0.9)(0.6) = 0.54$

$p(x_1 = -50$ and $x_2 = 40) = (0.1)(0.9) = 0.09$

$p(x_1 = -50) = 0.1$ $p(x_2 = 40 \mid x_1 = -50) = 0.9$

$p(x_2 = -50 \mid x_1 = -50) = 0.1$

$p(x_1 = -50$ and $x_2 = -50) = (0.1)(0.1) = 0.01$

Figure 17.2

illustrated by the diagram in Figure 17.2. From this diagram we can find:

x_2	$f(x_2)$
40	0.45
-50	0.55
	1.00

An examination of Figure 17.2 will show that the state probabilities for $t + 1$ may be obtained as follows:

$$p(x_{t+1} = 40) = p(x_t = 40)p(x_{t+1} = 40 \mid x_t = 40)$$
$$+ p(x_t = -50)p(x_{t+1} = 40 \mid x_t = -50)$$
$$= (0.9)(0.4) + (0.1)(0.9) = 0.45,$$
$$p(x_{t+1} = -50) = p(x_t = 40)p(x_{t+1} = -50 \mid x_t = 40)$$
$$+ p(x_t = -50)p(x_{t+1} = -50 \mid x_t = -50)$$
$$= (0.9)(0.6) + (0.1)(0.1) = 0.55.$$

To simplify our notations, we can write

$$[\pi_1(t), \pi_2(t)] = [p(x_t = 40), p(x_t = -50)],$$
$$[\pi_1(t + 1), \pi_2(t + 1)] = [p(x_{t+1} = 40), p(x_{t+1} = -50)],$$

respectively, for the state probability distributions for t and $t + 1$, and

$$\begin{bmatrix} p_{11} & p_{12} \\ p_{21} & p_{22} \end{bmatrix} = \begin{bmatrix} 0.4 & 0.6 \\ 0.9 & 0.1 \end{bmatrix}$$

for the transition probability matrix. Then

$$\pi_1(t + 1) = \pi_1(t)p_{11} + \pi_2(t)p_{21} = \pi_1(t)(0.4) + \pi_2(t)(0.9),$$
$$\pi_2(t + 1) = \pi_1(t)p_{12} + \pi_2(t)p_{22} = \pi_1(t)(0.6) + \pi_2(t)(0.1).$$

Note that the coefficients p_{11} and p_{21} in the equation for $\pi_1(t + 1)$ make up the first column of the transition probability matrix and the coefficients p_{12} and p_{22} in the equation for $\pi_2(t + 1)$ make up the second column of this matrix.

Using these two equations, then, we can obtain the state probabilities for different values of t. For example, if $\pi_1(1) = 0.9$ and $\pi_2(1) = 0.1$, then

$$\pi_1(2) = \pi_1(1)(0.4) + \pi_2(1)(0.9) = (0.9)(0.4) + (0.1)(0.9) = 0.45,$$
$$\pi_2(2) = \pi_1(1)(0.6) + \pi_2(1)(0.1) = (0.9)(0.6) + (0.1)(0.1) = 0.55.$$

In turn,

$$\pi_1(3) = \pi_1(2)(0.4) + \pi_2(2)(0.9) = (0.45)(0.4) + (0.55)(0.9) = 0.675,$$
$$\pi_2(3) = \pi_1(2)(0.6) + \pi_2(2)(0.1) = (0.45)(0.6) + (0.55)(0.1) = 0.325.$$

17.3   STEADY-STATE PROBABILITIES

The state probabilities for the marble-drawing game are listed for different values of t in Table 17.1. They can also be shown graphically, as in Figure 17.3.

Table 17.1

x_t \ t	0	1	2	3	4	5	6	7
40	0	0.9	0.45	0.675	0.5625	0.61875	0.590625	0.6048875
−50	1	0.1	0.55	0.325	0.4375	0.38125	0.409375	0.3951125

Both the table and the graph indicate that these state probabilities approach limiting values as t becomes larger and larger. These limiting values are called the *steady-state* probabilities. When a Markov process has reached the steady state, sometimes we say that the process is in an *equilibrium state*.

One intriguing property of the Markov process as applied to the marble-drawing game is that its steady-state probabilities are independent of the initial-state probabilities. That is, the steady-state probabilities are the same regardless of what the initial-state probabilities are.

There are many Markov processes whose steady-state probability distribution is independent of the initial-state probability distribution. They are said to be *ergodic*.

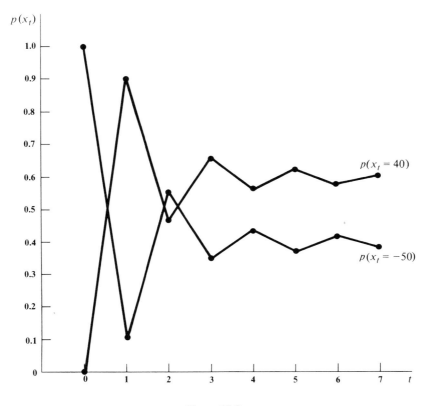

Figure 17.3

Let us now describe the manner in which we can obtain the steady-state probability distribution for our marble-drawing game. We have the equations

$$\pi_1(t + 1) = \pi_1(t)(0.4) + \pi_2(t)(0.9),$$
$$\pi_2(t + 1) = \pi_1(t)(0.6) + \pi_2(t)(0.1).$$

But when a Markov process has reached its steady state, the state probabilities are by definition the same from one stage to the next. Thus $\pi_1(t + 1) = \pi_1(t)$ and $\pi_2(t + 1) = \pi_2(t)$. If we let π_1^* and π_2^*, respectively, be the steady-state probabilities, then

$$\pi_1^* = 0.4\pi_1^* + 0.9\pi_2^*,$$
$$\pi_2^* = 0.6\pi_1^* + 0.1\pi_2^*.$$

Transposing the terms, we get

$$0.6\pi_1^* - 0.9\pi_2^* = 0,$$
$$0.6\pi_1^* - 0.9\pi_2^* = 0,$$

one of which is obviously redundant. Since $\pi_1^* + \pi_2^* = 1$, the steady-state probabilities may be obtained by solving the system of equations

$$0.6\pi_1^* - 0.9\pi_2^* = 0,$$
$$\pi_1^* + \pi_2^* = 1.$$

We get $\pi_1^* = 0.6$ and $\pi_2^* = 0.4$. If we now reexamine the diagram in Figure 17.3, we will see that as t becomes larger, $p(x_t = 40)$ approaches 0.6 and $p(x_t = -50)$ approaches 0.4.

17.4   EXPECTED RETURN

In the marble-drawing game if we let $E(x_t)$ be the expected return for stage t, then for $t = 1$

$$E(x_1) = (0.9)(40) + (0.1)(-50) = 31.00.$$

The values of $E(x_t)$ for different values of t are shown in Table 17.2 and Figure 17.4.

Table 17.2

t	$E(x_t)$
0	−50.0
1	31.0
2	−9.50
3	10.75
4	0.625
5	5.6875
6	3.15625
7	4.439875

We note that $E(x_t)$ is apparently approaching a limit as t becomes larger, which is not very surprising since the state probabilities also approach limiting values. Therefore, the limiting value of $E(x_t)$ must be the expected return associated with the steady state. If we let $E(x^*)$ be this expected return, then since $\pi_1^* = 0.6$ and $\pi_2^* = 0.4$, we have

$$E(x^*) = (0.6)(40) + (0.4)(-50) = 4.$$

Thus the expected return is $4 in the steady state.

17.5   CRITERIA FOR EVALUATING RETURNS

Let Figure 17.5 depict the process of drawing the marbles. Subscript 1 attached to the letter "W" indicates winning $40, and subscript 2 indicates losing $50. The numbers in parentheses next to the arrow from W_i to W_j are, respectively, the probability of moving to the state corresponding to subscript j from the state corresponding to subscript i, and the amount of gain or loss in moving from i to j.

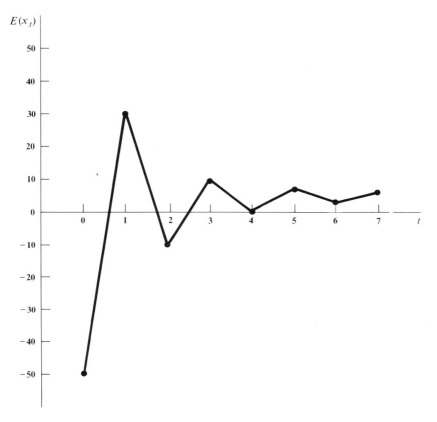

Figure 17.4

Now, if $W_i(n)$ is the expected total return of drawing n times, starting from state i of stage 1, then $W_i(n)$ must be the sum of the following two elements:

1. expected immediate return for the first draw starting from state i;
2. expected total return from the $n - 1$ subsequent draws.

For example, if the initial draw starts from state 1, then, as illustrated in

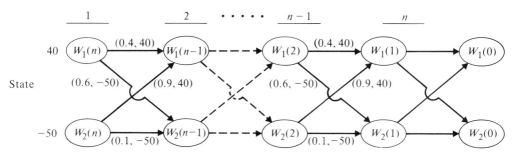

Figure 17.5

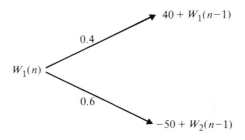

Figure 17.6

Figure 17.6, $W_1(n)$ can be calculated as follows:

$$W_1(n) = \{0.4 \times [40 + W_1(n - 1)]\} + \{0.6 \times [-50 + W_2(n - 1)]\}.$$

If c_i is the expected immediate return for the first game, starting from state i, then

$$c_1 = (0.4 \times 40) + [0.6 \times (-50)] = -14,$$
$$c_2 = (0.9 \times 40) + [0.1 \times (-50)] = 31,$$

and we have

$$W_1(n) = -14 + \{0.4[W_1(n - 1)] + 0.6[W_2(n - 1)]\},$$
$$W_2(n) = 31 + \{0.9[W_1(n - 1)] + 0.1[W_2(n - 1)]\}.$$

Table 17.3 gives the values of $W_i(n)$ for different values of n.

Table 17.3

n	0	1	2	3	4	5	6
$W_1(n)$	0	−14	−1	−1.5	2.75	6.83	10.79
$W_2(n)$	0	31	21.5	32.25	32.88	36.76	40.82
$W_2(n) - W_1(n)$	0	45	22.5	33.75	30.13	29.93	30.03

We note that both $W_1(n)$ and $W_2(n)$ become larger and larger as we increase the value of n. If n is infinitely large, then both $W_1(n)$ and $W_2(n)$ also become infinitely large. Does this mean that we should be indifferent to the initial state of the game? The answer is, No.

We note that $W_1(n)$ is always larger than $W_2(n)$. Also the difference between $W_2(n)$ and $W_1(n)$ approaches $30 as n becomes larger. In fact, it can be shown that the limiting value of the difference between $W_2(n)$ and $W_1(n)$ is $30 as we increase n. This means that for large n the expected total return of starting the draw from state 2 is $30 more than starting from state 1. We say that $30 is the *comparative advantage* of starting from state 2 when n draws are made.

The comparative advantage of starting from state 2 over starting from state

1 can be determined in another way. From Table 17.3 we find that

$$W_1(5) - W_1(4) = 6.83 - 2.75 = 4.08,$$
$$W_1(6) - W_1(5) = 10.79 - 6.83 = 3.96.$$

The values of $W_1(n) - W_1(n - 1)$ seem to fluctuate around 4, which is exactly what was obtained earlier as the expected return in the steady state. We can show that $W_1(n) - W_1(n - 1)$ will approach 4 for a larger n, indeed, as n becomes larger and larger.

Let us now reexamine the system of equations

$$W_1(n) = -14 + [0.4W_1(n - 1) + 0.6W_2(n - 1)],$$
$$W_2(n) = 31 + [0.9W_1(n - 1) + 0.1W_2(n - 1)].$$

We let g be the expected return in the steady state and assume that the value of g is not known. Nevertheless, for large n, we must have $W_1(n - 1) = W_1(n) - g$ and $W_2(n - 1) = W_2(n) - g$. Substituting these expressions into the above equations, we have

$$W_1(n) = -14 + [0.4W_1(n) + 0.6W_2(n) - g],$$
$$W_2(n) = 31 + [0.9W_1(n) + 0.1W_2(n) - g],$$

or

$$0.6W_1(n) - 0.6W_2(n) + g = -14,$$
$$-0.9W_1(n) + 0.9W_2(n) + g = 31.$$

Since these are two equations with three variables, they have infinitely many solutions. But if an arbitrary value is assigned to one of the variables, then the remaining variables will have unique solution values. Since we are interested only in the comparative advantage, we do not lose any useful information by assigning an arbitrary value to one of the $W_i(n)$. We can let $W_1(n) = 0$, for example. Then the resulting equations are

$$-0.6W_2(n) + g = -16,$$
$$0.9W_2(n) + g = 31,$$

which have the solution $W_2(n) = 30$ and $g = 4$, so that $W_2(n) - W_1(n) = 30$.

In this way we can determine the comparative advantage for state 2 and the expected return in the steady state in one shot. It is interesting to note that the last calculation of the expected return in the steady state did not require that we first obtain the steady-state probabilities. Systems of equations of the kind given above play a crucial role in our subsequent analysis of managerial decision problems.

17.6 ALTERNATIVE TRANSITION PROBABILITY VECTORS

In our discussions so far we have assumed that there is only one transition probability vector associated with each state. In practice, however, a decision-maker may be confronted with more than one transition probability vector for some states. The problem, then, is to select the optimal transition probability vector from several alternatives for that state. In the remaining portions of this chapter we shall be concerned with the methods of selecting such transition probability vectors.

Let us consider some practical situations where such problems may arise.

Example 4. Marble-Drawing Game   In the marble-drawing game of Example 1, suppose we are allowed to choose either urn A or B regardless of the current state. Then the selection of an urn amounts to selecting a transition probability vector. The transition probability vectors available for each of the two states are listed in Table 17.4.

Table 17.4

x_t \ x_{t+1}	40	−50	Choice of urn
40	0.4	0.6	A
	0.9	0.1	B
−50	0.4	0.6	A
	0.9	0.1	B

A little reflection will reveal that we should choose urn B in both states. If we do so, the transition probability matrix will become:

x_t	x_{t+1} 40	−50
40	0.9	0.1
−50	0.9	0.1

Example 5. Preventive Maintenance   During one week a machine in Reliable Machine Shop is in one of two possible states: it is in working order all week, which we call state 1; it is broken sometime during the week, which we call state 2. If the machine works all through the week, it will bring in $1000 of profit. If it breaks down during the week, there will be no profit at all. If at the beginning of the week the company does preventive maintenance on the machine, then the probability that the machine will break down during the week is only 0.1. In the absence of such maintenance the probability of breakdown is 0.3. Preventive maintenance, however, costs $100 every time is is done.

If the machine breaks down, it can be repaired before the beginning of the next week for $500. The probability of the repaired machine breaking down again during the week is 0.3. A new machine can be purchased for only $800. The probability of the new machine breaking down during the first week is 0.2.

The problem of the machine shop may first be depicted by the probability tree in Figure 17.7. The information contained in this probability tree is also summarized in Table 17.5.

The expected immediate return with repair, in state 2, for example, is:

$$(0.7 \times 500) + [0.3 \times (-500)] = 200.$$

The problem for the machine shop is to decide whether to do maintenance

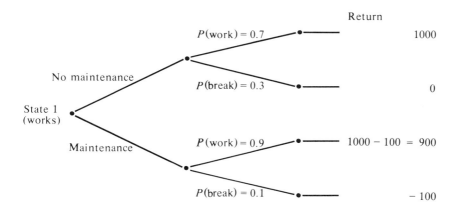

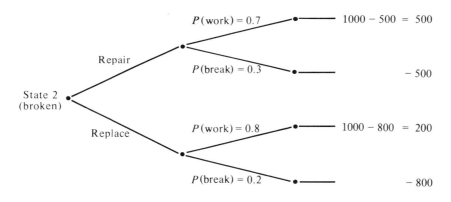

Figure 17.7

work when the machine is in working order and whether to repair or replace a machine when it is broken. With a Markov chain the problem becomes one of selecting an optimal transition probability vector for each state. The method of making such a selection is the subject of the next section.

Table 17.5

State at t	Decision	Transition probability of state 1	of state 2	Return 1	2	Expected immediate return
1 (Working)	no maintenance	0.7	0.3	1000	0	700
	maintenance	0.9	0.1	900	-100	800
2 (Broken)	repair	0.7	0.3	500	-500	200
	replace	0.8	0.2	200	-800	0

17.7 EVALUATION OF ALTERNATIVES

Let us assume that the machine shop of Example 5 will pursue the following policy with respect to its machine:

State	Policy
1	no maintenance
2	repair

The transition probability matrix for this policy is:

State at t	State at $t + 1$	
	1	2
1	0.7	0.3
2	0.7	0.3

Let W_1 be the expected total return for n subsequent weeks, given that the machine is now in state 1, and W_2 be the expected total returns for the n subsequent weeks, given that machine is now in state 2. It was shown in Section 17.5 that, if n is very large, we may obtain the values of W_1 and W_2 by solving the system of equations

$$W_1 + g = 700 + 0.7W_1 + 0.3W_2,$$
$$W_2 + g = 200 + 0.7W_1 + 0.3W_2,$$

which reduce to:

$$0.3W_1 - 0.3W_2 + g = 700,$$
$$-0.7W_1 + 0.7W_2 + g = 200.$$

If we let $W_2 = 0$, then the solution of these equations is

$$W_1 = 500, \qquad g = 550.$$

Thus, if the given policy is to be pursued for many weeks, an average weekly return of $550 can be expected, and the expected total return for n weeks will be $500 higher if the machine is now in state 1 than if it is now in state 2.

The next obvious question is whether there is a better policy, and if so, how do we go about finding it. There is, indeed, a method for finding a better policy, if it exists, but the formal proof for the validity of the method we shall describe is quite involved. Therefore, we shall justify the method on heuristic ground.

Assume now that the machine is in state 1. If the above policy is pursued, then during the next n weeks the machine shop will not do any preventive maintenance. But taking into consideration $n + 1$ weeks, we see that this policy has two variations:

Policy	First week	Remaining n weeks
a	no maintenance	no maintenance
b	maintenance	no maintenance

We can let W_1^* be the expected total returns for the next $n + 1$ weeks, starting from state 1, and W_1 and W_2 be the expected total returns for the subsequent n weeks. We have already ascertained that $W_1 = 500$ and $W_2 = 0$. The value of W_1^*, however, will depend on whether policy a or b is followed. If policy a is followed, then

$$W_1^* = 700 + 0.7W_1 + 0.3W_2$$
$$= 700 + (0.7)(500) + (0.3)(0) = 1050.$$

If policy b is followed, then

$$W_1^* = 800 + 0.9W_1 + 0.1W_2$$
$$= 800 + (0.9)(500) + (0.1)(0) = 1250.$$

Clearly doing preventive maintenance for one week and no more preventive maintenance for the remaining n weeks is a superior policy to doing no preventive maintenance at all.

But if doing preventive maintenance for one week followed by n weeks of no maintenance is superior to $n + 1$ weeks of no maintenance, then doing preventive maintenance for $n + 1$ weeks must be even better than either of the two policies we have just examined. Consequently, we may conclude for state 1 that the no preventive maintenance policy should be discarded in favor of the policy of doing preventive maintenance.

In a similar way we can evaluate for state 2 whether the policy of repair is superior to the policy of replacement. To do so, we first calculate for the policy of repair

$$W_1^* = 200 + 0.7W_1 + 0.3W_2$$
$$= 200 + (0.7)(500) + (0.3)(0) = 550,$$

and for the policy of replacement

$$W_2^* = 0 + 0.9W_1 + 0.1W_2$$
$$= 0 + (0.9)(500) + (0.2)(0) = 450.$$

Evidently repair is superior to replacement.

Thus we can now propose the policy:

State	Policy
1	maintenance
2	repair

The transition probability matrix for this policy is:

State for t	State for $t + 1$	
	1	2
1	0.9	0.1
2	0.7	0.3

With this matrix we can determine the values of W_1 and W_2 by solving the equations:

$$W_1 + g = 800 + 0.9W_1 + 0.1W_2,$$
$$W_2 + g = 200 + 0.7W_1 + 0.3W_2.$$

Letting $W_2 = 0$ and rearranging the terms, we have

$$0.1W_1 + g = 800,$$
$$-0.7W_1 + g = 200,$$

which have the solution:

$$W_1 = 750, \qquad g = 725.$$

Thus the expected average weekly return is $725 for the new policy, which is $175 more than the expected average return for the initial policy.

We can next evaluate the optimality of this policy in the following manner. Let

$$W_1^* = \max \begin{Bmatrix} 700 + (0.7)(750) + (0.3)(0) = 1225 \\ 800 + (0.9)(750) + (0.1)(0) = 1475 \end{Bmatrix} = 1475,$$

$$W_2^* = \max \begin{Bmatrix} 200 + (0.7)(750) + (0.3)(0) = 725 \\ 0 + (0.8)(750) + (0.2)(0) = 675 \end{Bmatrix} = 725.$$

We note that $W_1^* = 1475$ corresponds to the policy of doing preventive maintenance in state 1, meaning that if the machine is in state 1, then doing preventive maintenance for the next $n + 1$ weeks is superior to doing no maintenance for the first week and maintenance for the remaining n weeks. Obviously it also means that doing preventive maintenance for the next $n + 1$ weeks is superior to no maintenance at all for the next $n + 1$ weeks. Similarly, we can conclude that $W_2^* = 725$ corresponds to the policy of repair and that it is better to repair than to replace a broken machine.

Thus by calculating the values of W_1^* and W_2^* we have verified that our proposed policy is in fact optimal.

17.8 POLICY ITERATION

The procedure described in the preceding section for evaluating alternative transition probability vectors in essence consists of two basic steps:

1. Decide on a policy and then determine the corresponding values of W_i and g.

2. Evaluate the optimality of the policy by calculating the values of W_i^*.

The procedure was originated by Howard and is illustrated by the flow chart shown in Figure 17.8. The first step is sometimes called the *value determination operation*, and the second step the *policy improvement routine*.

Earlier we showed how the policy iteration technique could work for a particular example. Now we shall demonstrate that the technique works for any Markov chain problem having alternative transition probability vectors for various states.

Let us assume that there are m possible p_i in a Markov process and for

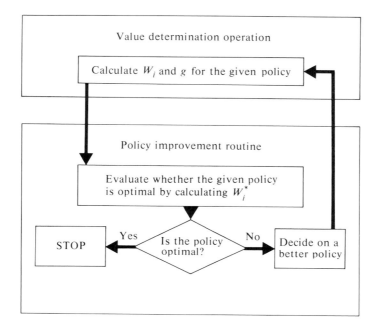

Figure 17.8

state i in the process we can select one of the transition probability vectors p_i. Let

$$p_i^k = [p_{i1}^k, \ldots, p_{im}^k]$$

be the kth transition probability vector and

$$r_i^k = [r_{i1}^k, \ldots, r_{im}^k]$$

be the return vector associated with p_i^k. Now let

$$c_i^k = p_{i1}^k r_{i1}^k + \cdots + p_{im}^k r_{im}^k.$$

Then c_i^k is the expected immediate return for choosing the transition probability vector p_i^k when the process is in state i. For the sake of clarity we shall list in Table 17.6 the notations for the preventive maintenance problem of Example 4.

Table 17.6

State at t	State at $t+1$ Decision	Transition probability		Return		Expected immediate return
		1	2	1	2	
1 (work)	no maintenance maintenance	p_{11}^1 p_{11}^2	p_{12}^1 p_{12}^2	r_{11}^1 r_{11}^2	r_{12}^1 r_{12}^2	c_1^1 c_1^2
2 (broken)	repair replace	p_{21}^1 p_{21}^2	p_{22}^1 p_{22}^2	r_{21}^1 r_{21}^2	r_{22}^1 r_{22}^2	c_2^1 c_2^2

Let $p_i = [p_{i1}, \ldots, p_{im}]$ be the transition probability vector chosen for a given policy in state i and $r_i = [r_{i1}, \ldots, r_{im}]$ be the corresponding return vector. Then

$$c_i = p_{i1}r_{i1} + \cdots + p_{im}r_{im}$$

is the expected immediate return of being in state i with the given policy. Now let W_i be the expected total return for the n remaining stages, where the Markov process is now in state i. Then the values of W_i may be obtained by solving the following system of equations:

$$W_1 + g = c_1 + p_{11}W_1 + \cdots + p_{1m}W_m,$$
$$W_2 + g = c_2 + p_{22}W_1 + \cdots + p_{2m}W_m,$$
$$\cdot$$
$$\cdot$$
$$\cdot$$
$$W_m + g = c_m + p_{m1}W_1 + \cdots + p_{mm}W_m.$$

To evaluate the optimality of this policy, we next calculate

$$W_1^* = \max_{\text{all } k} \{c_1^k + p_{11}^k W_1 + \cdots + p_{1m}^k W_m\},$$
$$W_2^* = \max_{\text{all } k} \{c_2^k + p_{21}^k W_1 + \cdots + p_{2m}^k W_m\},$$
$$\cdot$$
$$\cdot$$
$$\cdot$$
$$W_m^* = \max_{\text{all } k} \{c_m^k + p_{m1}^k W_1 + \cdots + p_{mm}^k W_m\}.$$

If p_i, the current transition probability vector for state i, yields W_i^*, then p_i should be retained in a new policy. However, if some other transition probability vector besides p_i yields W_i^*, then that vector instead of p_i should be incorporated in a new policy.

If the above policy improvement routine results in discarding one or more p_i in the current policy, then obviously the current policy is not optimal and the whole procedure must be repeated again.

Example 6. Production Inventory Control   Let d be the demand for a certain product of Alpha Beta Manufacturing whose probability distribution is given by:

d	$f(d)$
1	0.6
2	0.4
	1.0

Let x be the quantity of this commodity produced with the following cost function $c(x)$:

x	$c(x)$
0	0
1	1000
2	1200
3	1300

The maximum production capacity for this product is three units per period, and the maximum storage capacity is two units. The storage cost function is $h(s) = 100s$, where s is the end inventory for a period.

The company wants to follow a production policy so that the demand is always satisfied. Suppose that the beginning inventory is zero. Then the company must produce at least two units, since if it produces less than two units, there is some probability that the demand will not be satisfied. On the other hand, suppose that the beginning inventory is two units. Then no more than one unit should be produced, because if more than one unit is produced, the end inventory may be larger than the storage capacity.

Using a Markov chain, we may let the states correspond to the beginning inventories as follows: state 0 corresponding to zero beginning inventory, state 1 to one unit of beginning inventory, and so on. If i refers to a state, then the feasible production policies together with other information pertaining to these policies are given in Table 17.7.

Table 17.7

i	x	Transition probability			Return			Expected immediate return c_i^k
		p_{i0}	p_{i1}	p_{i2}	r_{i0}	r_{i1}	r_{i2}	
0	2	0.4	0.6		1200	1300	1400	1260
	3		0.4	0.6	1300	1400	1500	1460
1	1	0.4	0.6		1000	1100	1200	1060
	2		0.4	0.6	1200	1300	1400	1360
2	0	0.4	0.6		0	100	200	60
	1		0.4	0.6	1000	1100	1200	1160

Assume now that the company wants to find the production policy that will minimize the long-run expected average cost. Table 17.7 suggests that it may be sensible to adopt the following policy:

If beginning inventory is	Produce
0	2
1	1
2	0

Then the value determination operation consists in solving

$$W_0 + g = 1260 + 0.4W_0 + 0.6W_1,$$
$$W_1 + g = 1060 + 0.4W_0 + 0.6W_1,$$
$$W_2 + g = 60 + 0.4W_0 + 0.6W_1.$$

Letting $W_2 = 0$ and rearranging the terms, we have

$$0.6W_0 - 0.6W_1 + g = 1260,$$
$$-0.4W_0 + 0.4W_1 + g = 1060,$$
$$-0.4W_0 - 0.6W_1 + g = 60,$$

which have the solution $W_0 = 1200$, $W_1 = 1000$, and $g = 1140$. Thus the expected average cost of pursuing this policy is \$1140.

Next we evaluate the optimality of this policy by first calculating

$$W_0^* = \min \left\{ \begin{array}{l} 1260 + (0.4 \times 1200) + (0.6 \times 1000) = 2340 \\ 1460 + (0.4 \times 1000) + (0.6 \times \quad 0) = 1860 \end{array} \right\} = 1860,$$

$$W_1^* = \min \left\{ \begin{array}{l} 1060 + (0.4 \times 1200) + (0.6 \times 1000) = 2140 \\ 1360 + (0.4 \times 1000) + (0.6 \times \quad 0) = 1760 \end{array} \right\} = 1760,$$

$$W_2^* = \min \left\{ \begin{array}{l} \quad 60 + (0.4 \times 1200) + (0.6 \times 1000) = 1140 \\ 1160 + (0.4 \times 1000) + (0.6 \times \quad 0) = 1560 \end{array} \right\} = 1140.$$

Note that here we are doing a minimizing calculation because the objective is to minimize the expected average cost. These calculations show that the suggested policy is not optimal; it should be revised to read:

If beginning inventory is	Produce
0	3
1	2
2	0

We have now completed a policy improvement.

Next, going back to the value determination operation and solving the system of equations

$$W_0 + g = 1460 + 0.4 W_1 + 0.6 W_2,$$

$$W_1 + g = 1360 + 0.4 W_1 + 0.6 W_2,$$

$$W_2 + g = \quad 60 + 0.4 W_0 + 0.6 W_1,$$

by letting $W_2 = 0$, we obtain $W_0 = 887.50$, $W_1 = 787.50$, and $g = 887.50$.

We can see that the revised policy is superior to the initial policy, the expected average cost now being \$252.50 less than in the initial policy.

To see whether this new policy is optimal, we calculate

$$W_0^* = \min \left\{ \begin{array}{ll} 1260 + (0.4 \times 887.5) + (0.6 \times 787.50) = 2087.50 \\ 1460 + (0.4 \times 787.5) + (0.6 \times 0) \quad\quad = 1775.00 \end{array} \right\} = 1775.0,$$

$$W_1^* = \min \left\{ \begin{array}{ll} 1060 + (0.4 \times 887.5) + (0.6 \times 787.5) = 1887.5 \\ 1360 + (0.4 \times 785.5) + (0.6 \times 0) \quad\quad = 1675.0 \end{array} \right\} = 1675.0,$$

$$W_2^* = \min \left\{ \begin{array}{ll} \quad 60 + (0.4 \times 887.5) + (0.6 \times 787.5) = 887.5 \\ 1160 + (0.4 \times 787.5) + (0.6 \times 0) \quad\quad = 1475.0 \end{array} \right\} = 887.5.$$

Evidently it is optimal.

17.9 DISCOUNTING OF RETURNS

We have thus far assumed that a dollar which we receive in the future will be worth as much as a dollar is now. It is universally agreed, however, that this assumption is not true. A dollar to be received in the future is worth less than a dollar that we can have now since the dollar that we have now can be invested to earn a return.

How much a future dollar is worth in terms of a current dollar is called the *present value* of the future dollar. The process of assessing the present value of a future dollar is called the *discounting process*.

Assume that a dollar invested at the beginning of a period will earn i amount of return at the end of that period. Then a dollar to be received at the end of the period is worth only $1/(1 + i)$ of a dollar at the beginning of the period for the following reason. Now suppose we have the amount $[1/(1 + i)]$ at the beginning of the period. It will then earn $[1/(1 + i)]i$ amount of return during the period. The initial amount and the amount earned during the period has a sum of

$$[1/(1 + i)] + [1/(1 + i)]i = 1.$$

Thus we will wind up having a dollar at the end of the period. We will call i the *discount rate* and α the *discount factor*, where $\alpha = 1/(1 + i)$.

One significance of the discount factor α is that it gives us a formula for calculating the present value of any amount of return to be received in any future period. Let R_t be the amount to be received at the end of the period t. Then if $t = 1$,

$$P = \alpha R_t,$$

where P is the present value. If $t = 2$, the present value of R_2 at the beginning of the second period is αR_2, which in turn is worth only $\alpha(\alpha R_2)$ at the beginning of the first period. Thus for $t = 2$, we have $P = \alpha^2 R_2$. In general, for any arbitrary t

$$P = \alpha^t R_t.$$

Suppose now that we are to receive R_0 at the beginning of the first period, R_1 at the end of the first period, R_2 at the end of the second period, and so on, for $R_0, R_1, \ldots, R_n$. Then the present value of this stream of returns is

$$P = \alpha^0 R_0 + \alpha^1 R_1 + \cdots + \alpha^n R_n.$$

If $n = \infty$ and $R_0 = R_1 = \cdots = R_n = R$, then P is the present value of an infinitely long stream of returns and

$$P = R(1 + \alpha^1 + \cdots + \alpha^n).$$

It can be shown that, if $|\alpha| < 1$, then

$$P = R/(1 - \alpha).$$

We will first show the intuitive validity of this formula. Suppose that we are to receive a dollar now, a dollar at the end of the first period, and so on until infinity. Assume also that the discount rate is 10%. Then $\alpha = 1/(1 + i) = 1/1.1$, so that

$$P = \frac{1}{1 - (1/1.1)} = 11.$$

Thus the present value of the stream of returns is $11. A present value of $11 may seem awfully little for an infinite stream of returns. But a careful reflection will reveal the reasonableness of this value. Suppose we are given $11 of which we keep $1 and invest the rest ($10) for 10% returns. Then our investment will yield a $1 return for each period forever. Thus the present value of the stream of returns in question is only $11 if the discount rate is 10%.

Consider another situation. Assume that we are to receive one dollar now, one dollar at the end of the first period, and so on, until at the end of the nth period, where n is an infinitely large number. Let $P(n)$ be the present value of this stream of returns at the beginning of period 1, $P(n - 1)$ be the present value of the returns at the beginning of period 2. Then

$$P(n) = R + \alpha P(n - 1).$$

We note, however, that by definition

$$P(n) = R(1 + \alpha^0 + \cdots + \alpha^n)$$

and

$$P(n - 1) = R(1^0 + \alpha + \cdots + \alpha^{n-1}),$$

where $0 \le \alpha < 1$ by assumption. Consequently, the limiting value of α^n is zero as n approaches infinity. Therefore, if $n = \infty$, then $P(n) = P(n - 1)$, so that

$$P(n) = R + \alpha P(n).$$

Substituting $\alpha = 1/(1 + i) = 1/1.1$ and $R = 1$ into the equation, we obtain

$$P(n) = 1 - (1/1.1)P(n),$$

which yields $P(n) = \$11$, as before.

17.10 MARKOV CHAIN WITH DISCOUNTING

Let us now return to our Markov chain models and introduce the concept of discounting future returns. To simplify our notations, let us assume that a Markov chain consists of two states and a given policy yields the transition probability and return matrices as given in Table 17.8.

Table 17.8

State at t	Transition probability 1	2	Return 1	2	Expected immediate return
1	p_{11}	p_{12}	r_{11}	r_{12}	c_1
2	p_{21}	p_{22}	r_{21}	r_{22}	c_2

Let $Y_i(n)$ be the expected present value of the stream of returns for the remaining n stages, given that the current state is i. Then $Y_i(n)$ must be the sum of the following elements:

1. the expected immediate return of going from the current stage to the next stage, given that the current state is i;

2. the expected present value of the stream of returns from the next stage through the remaining $n - 1$ stages, given that the current state is i.

Let $Y_i(n - 1)$ be the expected value, at the end of the first stage, of the stream of returns for the remaining $n - 1$ stages, given that the Markov process is in state i at the end of the first stage. But $Y_i(n - 1)$ is worth only $\alpha Y_i(n - 1)$ at the beginning of the first stage. Thus

$$Y_1(n) = c_1 + p_{11}\alpha Y_1(n - 1) + p_{12}\alpha Y_2(n - 1),$$

$$Y_2(n) = c_2 + p_{21}\alpha Y_1(n - 1) + p_{22}\alpha Y_2(n -).$$

On the basis of our discussion in the preceding section we may conclude that $Y_i(n) = Y_i(n - 1)$ if $n = \infty$. Consequently,

$$Y_1(n) = c_1 + p_{11}\alpha Y_1(n) + p_{12}\alpha Y_2(n),$$

$$Y_2(n) = c_2 + p_{21}\alpha Y_1(n) + p_{22}\alpha Y_2(n).$$

By letting $Y_i(n) = Y_i$ and rearranging the terms, we can transform the above equations into:

$$(1 - p_{11}\alpha)Y_1 - p_{12}\alpha Y_2 = c_1,$$

$$-p_{21}\alpha Y_1 + (1 - p_{22}\alpha)Y_2 = c_2.$$

We note that these are two equations with two variables. Therefore, their solution will yield unique values of Y_i.

In a Markov chain model with discounting, the values of Y_i serve the same purpose as the values of W_i in a Markov chain model without discounting. The process of determining the values of Y_i is then the equivalent value determination operation for a Markov chain with discounting.

While the value determination operation for a Markov chain with discounting is different from that for a chain without discounting, the policy improvement routines for the two types of Markov chain models are essentially the same. Therefore, without getting into any detailed explanation, we present the policy iteration technique with discounting in the flow chart in Fig. 17.9.

Example 7. Production Inventory Control with Discounting Let us return to the production inventory control problem of Example 6 and assume that the discount factor is $\alpha = 0.5$. Even though such a discount factor is too small to be realistic, we will nevertheless use this figure in order to simplify our calculations.

In Example 6 our objective was to find a policy to minimize the expected average cost. Here our objective is to find a policy which will minimize the expected present value of the total production and inventory holding cost.

Assume that the initial policy is given by:

If beginning inventory is	Produce
0	2
1	1
2	0

Then the value determination operation consists in solving

$$Y_0 = 1260 + (0.4)(0.5)Y_0 + (0.6)(0.5)Y_1,$$

$$Y_1 = 1060 + (0.4)(0.5)Y_0 + (0.6)(0.5)Y_1,$$

$$Y_2 = 60 + (0.4)(0.5)Y_0 + (0.6)(0.5)Y_1,$$

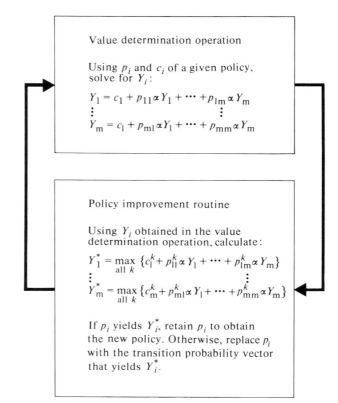

Figure 17.9

or

$$0.8 Y_0 - 0.3 Y_1 = 1260,$$
$$-0.2 Y_0 + 0.7 Y_1 = 1060,$$
$$-0.2 Y_0 - 0.3 Y_1 + Y_2 = 60.$$

The solution is $Y_0 = 2400$, $Y_1 = 2200$, and $Y_2 = 1260$.

To evaluate the optimality of this policy, we calculate

$$Y_0^* = \min \begin{Bmatrix} 1260 + (0.4)(0.5)(2400) + (0.6)(0.5)(2200) = 2400 \\ 1460 + (0.4)(0.5)(2200) + (0.6)(0.5)(1200) = 2260 \end{Bmatrix} = 2260,$$

$$Y_1^* = \min \begin{Bmatrix} 1060 + (0.4)(0.5)(2400) + (0.6)(0.5)(2200) = 2200 \\ 1360 + (0.4)(0.5)(2200) + (0.6)(0.5)(1200) = 2160 \end{Bmatrix} = 2160,$$

$$Y_2^* = \min \begin{Bmatrix} 60 + (0.4)(0.5)(2400) + (0.6)(0.5)(2200) = 1200 \\ 1160 + (0.4)(0.5)(2200) + (0.6)(0.5)(1200) = 1960 \end{Bmatrix} = 1200,$$

which indicate that the policy should be revised as follows:

If beginning inventory is	Produce
0	3
1	2
2	0

Again determining the values of Y_i, we solve:

$$Y_0 = 1460 + (0.4)(0.5)Y_1 + (0.6)(0.5)Y_2,$$
$$Y_1 = 1360 + (0.4)(0.5)Y_1 + (0.6)(0.5)Y_2,$$
$$Y_2 = 60 + (0.4)(0.5)Y_0 + (0.6)(0.5)Y_1,$$

or

$$Y_0 - 0.2Y_1 - 0.3Y_2 = 1460,$$
$$0.8Y_1 - 0.3Y_2 = 1360,$$
$$-0.2Y_0 - 0.3Y_1 + Y_2 = 60.$$

The solution is $Y_0 \cong 2229$, $Y_1 \cong 2129$, and $Y_2 \cong 1144$. We note that the values of Y_i here are lower than for the initial policy. Clearly the revised policy is superior.

To evaluate whether the new policy is optimal, we calculate

$$Y_0^* = \min \begin{Bmatrix} 1260 + (0.4)(0.5)(2229) + (0.6)(0.5)(2129) = 2344 \\ 1960 + (0.4)(0.5)(2129) + (0.6)(0.5)(1144) = 2229 \end{Bmatrix} = 2229,$$

$$Y_1^* = \min \begin{Bmatrix} 1060 + (0.4)(0.5)(2229) + (0.6)(0.5)(2129) = 2144 \\ 1360 + (0.4)(0.5)(2129) + (0.6)(0.5)(1144) = 2129 \end{Bmatrix} = 2129,$$

$$Y_2^* = \min \begin{Bmatrix} 60 + (0.4)(0.5)(2229) + (0.6)(0.5)(2129) = 1144 \\ 1160 + (0.4)(0.5)(2129) + (0.6)(0.5)(1144) = 1929 \end{Bmatrix} = 1144.$$

The policy is indeed optimal.

EXERCISES

1. In the following diagrams the nodes represent the states in Markov processes, and the arcs are the transition probabilities. Obtain the transition probability matrices for the two Markov processes.

a.

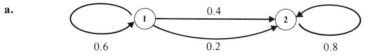

b.

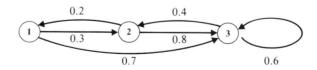

2. Find the steady-state probabilities for the Markov chains given by the following transition probability matrices:

a.

		States at $t + 1$	
		1	**2**
States	**1**	0.2	0.8
at t	**2**	0.6	0.4

b.

		States at $t + 1$		
		1	**2**	**3**
States	**1**	0.0	0.3	0.7
at t	**2**	0.4	0	0.6
	3	0.8	0.2	0

3. Eastgate Department Store classifies its weekly sales according to three grades: good, fair, and bad. Each week's sales are dependent on those of the immediately preceding week. The transition probability matrix for the weekly sales is:

		Next week's sales		
		good	**fair**	**bad**
This week's	**good**	0.2	0.3	0.5
sales	**fair**	0.3	0.4	0.3
	bad	0.5	0.3	0.2

What are the steady-state probabilities?

Suppose the average profits $8,000 during the good weeks, $3,000 during the fair weeks, and store loses $2,000 during the bad weeks. What is the average profit in the steady state?

4. In Exercise 3 assume that the store can change the transition probabilities by weekend advertising. The effects of such advertising are reflected in the following transition probability matrix:

		Next week's sales		
		good	**fair**	**bad**
This week's	**good**	0.4	0.3	0.3
sales	**fair**	0.6	0.3	0.1
	bad	0.7	0.2	0.1

The matrix shows that advertising after a good week, for example, will improve the transition probability vector from $[0.2, 0.3, 0.5]$ to $[0.4, 0.3, 0.3]$.

The cost of weekend advertising is $3,000.

What kind of advertising policy should the store follow if it wants to maximize the average weekly profit in the steady state?

5. The probability distribution of the monthly demand for a certain machine produced by Precision Machines is:

Demand	Probability
0	0.3
1	0.5
2	0.2
	1.0

The company now has the following production policy. If there is any inventory of this machine at the beginning of a month, there will be no production of this machine during that month. If there is no beginning inventory, then two units of this machine will be produced during the month.

Portray the situation described above as a Markov process. Identify the states in the process and then obtain the transition probability matrix. What are the steady-state probabilities?

6. In Exercise 5 assume that the machine sells for $70,000 per unit. The production costs are:

Quantity produced	Cost
0	0
1	$50,000
2	80,000

It costs $10,000 per month to carry one unit of unsold machine.

a. What is the average monthly profit of the proposed policy when the steady state is attained?

b. Assume that the company does not want to have more than two units of the machine at the beginning of any month. Will the proposed production policy given in Exercise 5 maximize the average monthly profit in the steady state? If not, what is the policy that will maximize the average return in the steady state?

7. A machine in Reliable Machine Shop is in one of two possible states during the week: (1) it is in working order all through the week and (2) it is broken sometime during the week. In the absence of preventative maintenance at the beginning of the week, the probability of the machine's breaking down during the week is 0.4. With preventative maintenance work at the beginning of the week the probability of breakdown during the week is reduced to 0.2.

If the machine breaks down during a week, it may be simply repaired or over-hauled. If it is repaired, the probability of breakdown during the next week is 0.5. But if it is overhauled, the probability of a breakdown during the following week is 0.1.

Suppose the machine shop does not do any preventative maintenance so long as the machine is working, and in the event of a breakdown, it is simply repaired. What is the probability of a machine breakdown during a week when the steady state has been reached?

8. In Exercise 7 the machine shop nets $400 per day or $2000 during a 5-day week if the machine works all week. However, the average profit during a week that the machine breaks down is only $1000. Preventative maintenance takes about half a day. The lost revenue for this duration is $200. An additional $100 must be expended for the labor and materials required for the maintenance. The labor and material cost of repairing a broken-down machine is $400 and that of overhauling a broken-down machine is $800.

a. What is the average weekly profit in the steady state if the machine shop pursues the maintenance and repair policy proposed in Exercise 7?

b. Will the policy proposed in Exercise 7 maximize the average weekly profit in the steady state? If not, find one that will.

9. Friendly City Sunday Gazette has an advertiser who tends to alternate the placing of his advertisement between the Sunday Gazette and a competing magazine. If he runs an advertisement this week in the Sunday Gazette, then the probability is 0.2 that he will place one again in the Gazette next week. However, if he does not run an advertisement in the Gazette this week, then the probability is 0.6 that he will place one in the Gazette next week.

When the steady state has been reached, what percentage of the time will this advertiser have an advertisement in the Gazette?

10. In Exercise 9 assume that the advertiser's advertising decision is subject to influence. If he runs an advertisement in the Gazette this week, then the probability of his running one again in the Gazette can be increased from 0.2 to 0.6 by entertaining him at a fashionable night spot. Such entertainment will also increase the probability of his running an advertisement in the Gazette next week from 0.6 to 0.8 when he has none in the Gazette this week. On the other hand, the advertiser has a short memory. If he is not entertained in any week, he returns to the transition probability given in Exercise 9.

The weekly cost of entertainment is $200, and the amount of billing for one Sunday advertisement is $1000.

What kind of policy with regard to entertaining this advertiser will maximize the average weekly profit of the Gazette in the steady state?

11. Once a year Sayer Mail Order Company mails either its regular or comprehensive catalog to each of its customers on the mailing list. Before sending out the catalog, the company classifies the customers into groups of high, intermediate, and low according to the volume of each one's purchases during the preceding twelve months. A statistical analysis of customer behavior in the past yielded the following transition probabilities:

Customer class	Catalog sent	Transition probabilities		
		High	Intermediate	Low
high	regular	0.5	0.3	0.2
	comprehensive	0.7	0.2	0.1
middle	regular	0.4	0.5	0.1
	comprehensive	0.5	0.4	0.1
low	regular	0.2	0.3	0.5
	comprehensive	0.4	0.3	0.3

a. Suppose the company sends the regular catalogs to all its customers every year. When the steady state has been reached, what are the percentages of its customers who will belong to each of the three categories?

b. Suppose the company sends the comprehensive catalog to all its customers every year. What are the steady-state probabilities for the three categories?

12. In Exercise 11 assume that the regular catalog costs $2 per copy and the comprehensive catalog costs $6 per copy. The average amounts of profit are $20 from each high purchaser, $10 from each intermediate purchaser, and zero from the low purchaser. The company considers the cost of its investment capital to be 25 percent per year. There are 500,000 customers on the company's mailing list.

a. What is the expected present value of profit if the company sends the regular catalog to all its customers every year?

b. What is the expected present value of profit if the company sends the comprehensive catalog to all its customers every year?

c. Will either one of the policies in part (a) or (b) maximize the present value of profit for the company? If not, what is a policy that will maximize it?

CHAPTER

18

WAITING LINES

18.1 INTRODUCTION

Waiting lines, otherwise known as queues, are common occurrences. They come up in many business situations and a manager must deal with them quite often.

In this chapter we shall examine the nature of waiting lines and describe some of the ways of resolving problems involving them. First, let us consider some concrete examples.

Example 1. Machine Repair Problem Alpha Beta Manufacturing uses a large number of machines in its production operations. There is at present one repair crew to handle broken-down machines. As a result, there is a long waiting line of machines to be repaired. Idle machines mean substantial costs in lost production.

Example 2. Bank Tellers Problem Small Town Bank has five regular tellers. Between Monday and Thursday there is seldom a long waiting line, but Friday is pay day for the workers in a nearby factory and usually there are long waiting lines.

The bank management has discovered that some of the depositors have been transferring their accounts to another bank in town. A survey revealed that the most frequently given reason for transferring accounts was the inconvenience of having to wait too long in the lines.

Example 3. Weigh Bridge Problem Jamestown Steel Company uses a large number of trucks to collect scrap iron from various scrap yards. The trucks deposit their loads at the open hearth shop when they arrive at the steel plant.

327

Before depositing their loads, however, they must go across a weigh bridge for weighing the loads. There is always a long line of waiting trucks at the weigh bridge. Consequently, each truck wastes a considerable amount of time standing idle.

18.2 WAITING-LINE SYSTEM

The above examples of waiting line differ one from another, but they all have some common features.

Customers Consider the broken machines, the bank depositors, and the trucks to be weighed. They all need service and are therefore called *customers*.

Server Consider the repairman, the bank tellers, and the weigh bridge in the preceding examples. They each perform the services required by their respective customers and are therefore called *servers*.

Service Mechanism There may be one or more servers performing the services required by a customer. If more than one, then they must be organized in some manner in order to meet collectively the service requirement of their customers. The group of servers and the manner in which they are organized to perform the services will be called the *service mechanism*.

To illustrate the service mechanism, consider the bank in Example 2. Assume that each teller can perform all the services required by a depositor. Then the service mechanism may be characterized by the diagram in Figure 18.1.

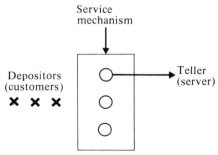

Figure 18.1

In some situations, however, more than one server may be needed to meet the service requirements of a customer. For example, one server may perform a part of the service requirement, and another server the remaining service requirement. We encounter such situations, for example, in cafeterias.

A group of servers that can collectively perform all the service requirements of a customer will be called a *channel*. The terms *channel*, *server*, and *service mechanism* are illustrated in Figure 18.2.

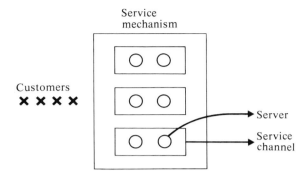

Figure 18.2

If a service channel contains only one server, then that server constitutes the entire channel and the distinction between the two terms is immaterial. In such a situation, we shall use the two terms interchangeably.

Waiting Line At any given time a customer is in one of two states: being served or waiting to be served. The totality of customers waiting to be served are said to constitute a *waiting line.*

Waiting Line System The components of a waiting line system are depicted in Figure 18.3.

Service Discipline The manner in which customers are selected from the waiting line for service is called the *service discipline.* One possible service discipline is to serve the customers in order of their arrival; it is called the FIFO (first-in-first-out) discipline. Instead of being served in the order of their arrival, customers may be selected from the waiting line for service in some other manner. For example, they may be given different priorities, with those

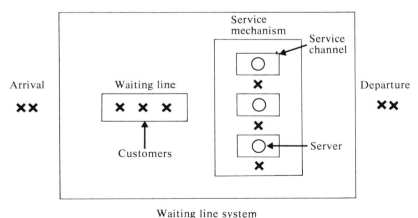

Waiting line system

Figure 18.3

having higher priorities selected over others having lower priorities even when the latter may have arrived first at the waiting line.

18.3   MODIFYING THE WAITING-LINE SYSTEM

When a given waiting line system is not performing well, there may be various ways of modifying the system.

Modify Arrival   We may try to modify either the pattern or the rate of customer arrival at the waiting line. For example, the bank confronted with Friday depositors may try to induce some local companies to pay their workers on some other day in the week. In the case of a toll bridge with serious traffic congestions during rush hours, the governing authority may try to reduce the arrival rate by inducing commuters to use car pools.

Modify Service Discipline   We may also try to improve a waiting-line system by modifying the service discipline, for example introducing a new priority system. Thus if the priority system now in use is the FIFO, then the following are alternative priority systems:

a. More important customers have priority over less important customers. In the case of the manufacturing company, for example, if the idle costs are different for the different types of incapacitated machines, then the machines having the higher idle costs might have higher priority over others with lower idle costs.

b. Give higher priority to those customers whose expected service time is short. Again in the case of the manufacturer with the machine breakdowns, this priority system would have the machines requiring only minor repairs given priority over those requiring major overhauls, if the idle costs are the same.

c. Certain types of customers are assigned to certain specific servers. For example, there are frequently express checkout counters in grocery stores for customers purchasing only a few items.

Modify Service Mechanism   We may also try to improve a waiting-line system by modifying the service mechanism:

a. Improve the efficiency of the servers. For example, the manager of a secretarial pool who is beset by slow work may try to improve the efficiency of his work force by replacing the slow workers with more efficient ones.

b. Increase the number of servers. For example, the secretarial pool manager may decide to hire additional secretaries instead.

18.4   ANALYSIS OF ARRIVAL PATTERN

One factor responsible for the congestion in a waiting-line system is the irregularity of customer arrival. Sometimes several customers may arrive almost simultaneously, and at other times no customer may arrive for extended periods.

The first step in evaluating a waiting-line system, therefore, is to make a careful study of the pattern of customer arrival.

Example 4. Machine Repair Problem   In the case of Alpha Beta Manufacturing of Example 1, suppose that we have the 100-day statistics as shown in Table 18.1.

Table 18.1

Number of breakdowns in a day	Number of days	Empirical probability
0	14	0.14
1	28	0.28
2	26	0.26
3	18	0.18
4	8	0.08
5	4	0.04
6	2	0.02
	100	1.0

Then on the average 1.98 machines break down in a day. Suppose on any day we ask, What is the probability that exactly two machines will break down today? According to Table 18.1, this probability is 0.26.

A probability distribution like the one in the right-hand column of Table 18.1, which reflects past history, will be called an *empirical probability distribution*. This probability distribution is much like a theoretical probability distribution. Using an arbitrarily conceived Poisson distribution for the theoretical model, we show in Figure 18.4 a possible relation between the empirical and the theoretical probability distributions. In fact the arrival patterns of the customers in many waiting lines seem to approximate a Poisson probability distribution.

Assumptions of Poisson Distributions

A Poisson probability distribution can be used as a valid model for the patterns of customer arrival if the following assumptions hold:

1. The arrival pattern is random.
2. The probability of an arrival in any small interval is not influenced by the history of the previous arrivals.
3. For very small time intervals the probability of an arrival is proportional to the length of the interval.

Let us now examine how valid these assumptions are, for example, in the case of machine breakdowns. Given the situation in Example 4, it is quite

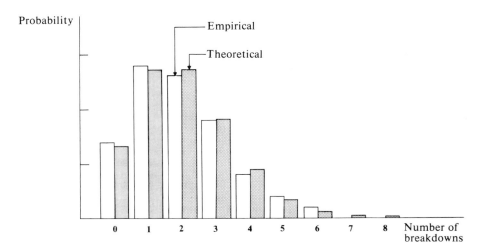

Figure 18.4

unlikely that we can predict exactly when the next breakdown will occur. It would be reasonable to say that the exact time of breakdown is a matter of chance, that is, the arrival pattern is random.

Now suppose that there were a relatively large number of machine breakdowns on the day before. If many of these machines still await repair, then relatively few machines will be in operation today. This in turn will influence the number of machine breakdowns today. That is, if there are only a finite number of machines in the manufacturing outfit, the probability of a machine breakdown in any given time interval is not independent of the past history of machine breakdown. Thus the second assumption of Poisson distribution is not satisfied. However, if the average number of breakdowns is very small compared to the total number of machines, then we can assume for all practical purposes that the probability of breakdown in any time interval is independent of the past history.

Our 100-day statistics show that on the average two machine breakdowns occur daily. Assuming that the manufacturing plant operates 8 hours a day or 480 minutes, then the probability of two machine breakdowns per day is equivalent to a probability of

$$\tfrac{2}{480} \cong 0.004$$

breakdown per minute. Then it is reasonable to assume that the probability of a breakdown in any two-minute interval is 0.008. This is the third assumption of Poisson distribution.

Parameter of Poisson Distribution

One convenient feature of making the Poisson assumption on customer arrival is that the complete probability distribution of the pattern of customer arrival is automatically specified once we have ascertained the average number of arrivals for a given time interval. For example, if λ is the average number of arrivals and $f(k)$ is the probability of k number of customers arriving in a given time interval, then

$$f(k) = \frac{\lambda^k e^{-\lambda}}{k!}.$$

A table of Poisson probabilities is provided in Appendix 2 for various values of λ.

Suppose that on the average two customers arrive per unit of time. Then from Appendix 2 we can obtain the following probability distribution of the customers' arrival:

Number of arrivals	Probability
0	0.1353
1	0.2707
2	0.2707
3	0.1804
4	0.0902
5	0.0361
6	0.0120
7	0.0009
8	0.0002

The theoretical probability distribution shown in Figure 18.4 is based on just this probability distribution.

Once the empirical and theoretical probability distributions of customer arrivals have been obtained, there are elegant statistical procedures for testing the reasonableness of the Poisson assumptions. However, we suggest that these assumptions be evaluated by comparing the graphs of the two probability distributions as was illustrated in Figure 18.4.

18.5 ANALYSIS OF SERVICE TIME

The actual length of time required to service each customer may be fairly constant in some service mechanisms and vary considerably from one customer to another in other service mechanisms. The second step in evaluating a waiting-line system, therefore, is to make a careful study of the service time distribution.

Example 5. Machine Repair Suppose that the records of 200 repairs done in the machine shop of Example 4 are as shown in Table 18.2. Assuming that those machines requiring 0 to 1 hour repair times had an average repair time of 0.5 hour, those requiring 1 to 2 hours had an average repair time of 1.5 hour, and so on, then, the total number of hours required to repair all 200 machines

Table 18.2

Repair hours required	Number of machines	Percentage of of machines
0–1	50	0.25
1–2	80	0.40
2–3	30	0.15
3–4	20	0.10
4–5	12	0.06
5–6	4	0.02
6–7	2	0.01
7–8	2	0.01
	200	1.00

may be calculated as follows:

Assumed average repair time	Number of machines	Product of two columns
0.5	50	25
1.5	80	120
2.5	30	75
3.5	20	70
4.5	12	54
5.5	4	22
6.5	2	13
7.5	2	15
Total	200	394

Thus 394 hours were required to repair the 200 machines: an average of 1.97 hours or approximately 2 hours per machine.

An interesting feature of this empirical probability distribution of service time is that it bears a striking resemblance to a theoretical probability distribution known as *exponential probability distribution*.

In Figure 18.5 the empirical probability distribution is indicated by the vertical bars and the smooth curve represents a theoretical exponential distribution.

Assumptions of Exponential Distributions

In evaluating waiting-line systems one very common assumption is that the service time has an exponential probability distribution. This assumption is likely to be quite appropriate if a large number of customers require very short service time and a small number of customers require relatively long service time.

In the actual world we will probably find exactly exponentially distributed service times to be uncommon. On the other hand, it has frequently been observed that actual service time distributions do not differ significantly from exponential distributions.

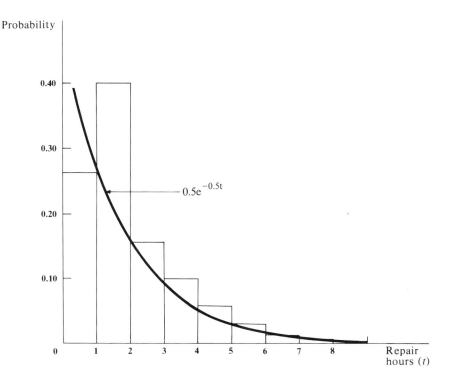

Figure 18.5

Parameter of Exponential Probability

As we pointed out earlier, if customer arrivals are Poisson distributed, the complete probability distribution can be specified by simply ascertaining the average number of customer arrivals per unit time. It can also be shown that if service times are exponentially distributed, then the complete probability distribution of service times can be specified by the average number of customers served per unit of time. For example, if μ is the average number of customers served per unit of time and t is the time at which the service is completed, then the probability distribution $f(t)$ is given by:

$$f(t) = \begin{cases} \mu e^{-\mu t} & \text{for } 0 \le t < \infty, \\ 0 & \text{otherwise.} \end{cases}$$

In the machine repair example we recall that the average service time is approximately two hours. Therefore, on the average, 0.5 machine is repaired per hour. Thus if we let $\mu = 0.5$, then

$$f(t) = \begin{cases} 0.5 e^{-0.5t} & \text{for } 0 \le t < \infty, \\ 0 & \text{otherwise.} \end{cases}$$

This $f(t)$ is in fact the distribution depicted by the smooth curve in Figure 18.5.

Another convenient feature of assuming that the service time has an exponential distribution is that if $p(t_1 \leq t \leq t_2)$ is the probability of the service being completed between the times t_1 and t_2, then

$$p(t_1 \leq t \leq t_2) = e^{-\mu t_1} - e^{-\mu t_2}.$$

In the machine repair problem the probability of the service being completed between one and two hours, for example, is

$$p(1 \leq t \leq 2) = e^{-(0.5)(1)} - e^{-0.5(2)} = 0.239.$$

Using this formula, therefore, we can obtain a theoretical probability distribution of the service time, as shown in Table 18.3 for the machine repair problem.

Table 18.3

Repair hours required	Empirical probability	Theoretical probability
0–1	0.25	0.397
1–2	0.40	0.239
2–3	0.15	0.145
3–4	0.10	0.088
4–5	0.06	0.053
5–6	0.02	0.033
6–7	0.01	0.019
7–8	0.01	0.012
8+	0.00	0.018
	1.00	1.000

Once these two probability distributions have been obtained, we can use elegant statistical procedures to test the assumption that the service time is in fact exponentially distributed. Again, however, we suggest, that this assumption can be evaluated by comparing the graphs of the two probability distributions.

18.6   ANALYSIS OF SINGLE-CHANNEL SYSTEM

In practice most waiting-line systems are likely to have more than one channel. Nevertheless, we shall describe in this section some of the characteristics of the single-channel system. Our study of these characteristics will certainly help us understand the characteristics of multi-channel waiting line systems.

The mathematical theories of waiting-line systems are quite complicated. Fortunately it is not necessary for us to understand these theories in full in order to intelligently evaluate the decision problems pertaining to waiting lines. Therefore, we shall not concern ourselves with rigorous mathematical justifications in the subsequent discussion.

One factor which influences the operating characteristics of a waiting-line system is the length of time over which the system has been in operation. However, describing the operating characteristics of a waiting-line system as a function of this time span is very difficult, even with the use of rigorous mathematics. On the other hand, usually as the elapsed time in question becomes longer and longer, the operating characteristics will tend to stabilize. Therefore, if we assume that a waiting line system has been in operation for quite a long time, we do not need to be concerned with this time factor in evaluating the operating characteristics.

In our subsequent discussion we shall assume either that the waiting system under discussion has been in operation for a long time or, if it has not already been in operation for a long time, we are nevertheless interested only in the stabilized operating characteristics after it has been in operation for a long time. A waiting-line system is said to be in a *steady state* or *statistical equilibrium* if it has been in operation for a long time such that its operating characteristics are not dependent on the elapsed time factor.

In discussing single-channel waiting-line systems we shall make the following assumptions.

Assumptions   **1.** The customer arrivals are Poisson distributed with an average arrival rate of λ.
2. The service time is exponentially distributed with an average service rate of μ.
3. Customers are not repelled by a long waiting line and do not leave a waiting line once they have entered it.
4. Customers are served in the order of their arrival; that is, the service discipline is FIFO.

Then we propose that the systems have the following characteristics.

Traffic Intensity

Let us define $\rho = \lambda/\mu$. Then ρ is called the *ratio of traffic intensity*; it is the ratio between the arrival rate and the service rate.

Obviously the higher the traffic intensity, the more likely will there be a long waiting line, and conversely. In fact, as we will later show, the traffic intensity ratio plays a very important role in defining various operating characteristics of a waiting line.

Busy Period

When a customer arrives in a waiting-line system, either the service mechanism is busy and he has to wait or the service mechanism is not busy and he can receive immediate service. If the service mechanism is busy, we will say that the waiting-line system is in a *busy period*.

The probability that a waiting-line system will be in a busy period at any randomly selected time is called the *busy-period probability*. One convenient feature of the single-channel waiting-line system under consideration is that the busy-period probability is equal to the traffic intensity ratio. Thus if we let $f(b)$ be the busy-period probability, then

$$f(b) = \rho = \lambda/\mu.$$

Probability Distribution of Customers in the System

If ρ is the probability that the waiting-line system will be busy, then $1 - \rho$ must be the probability that it will not be busy at any randomly selected time. That is, $1 - \rho$ is the probability that the waiting-line system will have no customers.

Let p_n be the probability that the waiting-line system will have n customers. Then for $n = 0$,

$$p_0 = 1 - \rho.$$

Suppose we want to determine the probability that the waiting-line system will have more than n customers. Then we need to know the value of p_n for all n greater than k. The numerical calculations of p_n are quite simple. The formula is:

$$p_n = \rho^n p_0.$$

Note that $p_0 = 1 - \rho$. Therefore, the formula is also

$$p_n = \rho^n (1 - \rho).$$

Example 6   For any single-channel waiting-system satisfying the assumption listed above let us assume that $\lambda = 2$ and $\mu = 5$; that is, on the average two customers arrive and five customers can be serviced per unit of time. Then the traffic intensity ratio is

$$\rho = \tfrac{2}{5} = 0.4,$$

and the busy-period probability is also 0.4.

Therefore,

$$
\begin{aligned}
p_0 &= 1 - \rho & &= 1 - 0.4 & &= 0.6000 \\
p_1 &= \rho(1 - \rho) & &= (0.4)(0.6) & &= 0.2400 \\
p_2 &= \rho^2(1 - \rho) & &= (0.4)^2(0.6) & &= 0.0960 \\
p_3 &= \rho^3(1 - \rho) & &= (0.4)^3(0.6) & &= 0.0384 \\
p_4 &= \rho^4(1 - \rho) & &= (0.4)^4(0.6) & &= 0.0154 \\
\end{aligned}
$$

$$\text{Sum} = 0.9898$$

which means that the probability of the waiting-line system having four or fewer customers is 0.9898. Suppose we do not want the waiting-line system to have more than four customers at any given time. Then we have $1 - 0.9898 = 0.0102$ as the probability that the system may be in such an undesirable state.

18.7   OPERATING CHARACTERISTICS

Among the characteristics of a waiting-line system some are important to know for analytical purposes, for example:

1. The expected (or average) number of customers in the system,
2. The expected (or average) number of customers in the waiting line,
3. The expected (or average) time required for a customer to enter and leave the system after receiving the service.
4. The expected (or average) length of time that a customer will spend in a waiting line.

We called these the *operating characteristics* of the system. They are evaluated as follows.

Expected Number in the System   Let $E(N_t)$ be the expected number of customers in the waiting-line system, include both the waiting customers and those now being served. Then

$$E(N_t) = \frac{\lambda}{\lambda - \mu}.$$

This formula indicates that as the arrival rate λ approaches the service rate μ, the expected number $E(N_t)$ becomes larger and larger. When $\lambda = \mu$, we will have $E(N_t) = \infty$. Thus, the expected number of customers in the system will increase as the traffic intensity ratio increases, and if the traffic intensity ratio is one, the expected number of customers will be infinitely large.

Expected Number in the Waiting Line   Let $E(N_w)$ be the expected number of customers in the waiting line. Then

$$E(N_w) = \frac{\lambda}{\mu}\left(\frac{\lambda}{\mu - \lambda}\right).$$

Expected Number Receiving Service   Suppose we define $E(N_s) = E(N_t) - E(N_w)$. Then $E(N_s)$ is the expected number of customers receiving services and

$$E(N_s) = E(N_t) - E(N_w)$$
$$= \frac{\lambda}{\mu - \lambda} - \frac{\lambda}{\mu}\frac{\lambda}{\mu - \lambda} = \frac{\lambda}{\mu}.$$

Relation Between Number and Time   It is intuitively true that the average waiting time must be related to the average number of customers in the waiting line.

Let N be the number of customers in a certain phase of a waiting-line system, and let T be the time required of a customer to complete that phase. Then

$$E(T) = \frac{E(N)}{\lambda},$$

where $E(T)$ and $E(N)$ are respectively the expected values of T and N. This relation can be used to find the remaining operating characteristics of the single-channel waiting-line system.

Expected Time in System   Let $E(T_t)$ be the expected time that a customer will spend in the system. Then

$$E(T_t) = \frac{E(N_t)}{\lambda} = \frac{\lambda/(\mu - \lambda)}{\lambda} = \frac{1}{\mu - \lambda}.$$

Expected Time in Waiting Line   Let $E(T_w)$ be the expected length of time that a customer will spend in the waiting line. Then

$$E(T_w) = \frac{E(N_w)}{\lambda} = \frac{\lambda}{\mu}\left[\frac{\lambda/(\mu - \lambda)}{\lambda}\right] = \frac{\lambda}{\mu}\left(\frac{1}{\mu - \lambda}\right).$$

Expected Service Time   Let $E(T_s)$ be the expected length of time required for a customer to receive the actual service. Then

$$E(T_s) = \frac{E(N_s)}{\lambda} = \frac{\lambda/\mu}{\lambda} = \frac{1}{\mu}.$$

We also note that by definition

$$E(T_s) = E(T_t) - E(T_w),$$

so that

$$E(T_s) = E(T_t) - E(T_w)$$

$$= \frac{1}{\mu - \lambda} - \frac{\lambda}{\mu}\left(\frac{1}{\mu - \lambda}\right) = \frac{1}{\mu}.$$

18.8 APPLICATIONS

Example 7. Tool Crib Problem   Mechanics come to the tool crib of Smooth Flying Aircraft Company, for the tools they need. There is now one clerk who hands out the tools. A study of past records indicates that on the average two mechanics per minute arrive at the tool crib. The average service time is 25 seconds. We want to evaluate the operating characteristics of this waiting-line system.

Since on the average two mechanics arrive every minute, we have $\lambda = 2$. The average service time is 25 seconds. Therefore, the clerk can serve 2.4 mechanics per minute on the average: $\mu = 2.4$. Thus

$$E(N_t) = \frac{\lambda}{\mu - \lambda} = \frac{2}{2.4 - 2} = 5;$$

that is, on the average five mechanics will be in the waiting-line system at a given time. The average waiting line is:

$$E(N_w) = \frac{\lambda}{\mu}\left(\frac{\lambda}{\mu - \lambda}\right) = \frac{2}{2.4}\left(\frac{2}{2.4 - 2}\right) = 4.41.$$

The average time in minutes for a mechanic to get his tools and leave the crib, including waiting time, is

$$E(T_t) = \frac{1}{\mu - \lambda} = \frac{1}{2.4 - 2} = 2.5,$$

and his average waiting time is

$$E(T_w) = \frac{\lambda}{\mu(\mu - \lambda)} = \frac{2}{2.4(2.4 - 2)} = 2.205.$$

Example 8. Machine Repair   A manufacturer with a large number of production machines has been experiencing on the average one machine breakdown every four hours. The average repair time is two hours. The hourly cost of maintaining the repair crew is $150, and one idle machine hour means $300 in lost production revenue. The company is contemplating whether to double the size of the repair crew. By doubling the repair crew, the company expects that the average repair time will be reduced to one hour but the repair crew cost will double to become $300.

On the surface it seems that the contemplated advantage will be canceled out by the expected disadvantage so that the new policy will be equivalent to the old, but this is not true.

First Option.   If the company keeps the present small repair crew, then $\lambda = 0.25$ and $\mu = 0.5$, so that

$$E(N_t) = \frac{\lambda}{\mu - \lambda} = \frac{0.25}{0.50 - 0.25} = 1,$$

$$E(N_w) = \frac{\lambda}{\mu}\left(\frac{\lambda}{\mu - \lambda}\right) = \frac{0.25}{0.50}\left(\frac{0.25}{0.50 - 0.25}\right) = 0.5,$$

$$E(T_t) = \frac{E(N_t)}{\lambda} = \frac{1}{\mu - \lambda} = \frac{1}{0.50 - 0.25} = 4,$$

$$E(T_w) = \frac{E(N_\mu)}{\lambda} = \frac{\lambda}{\mu(\mu - \lambda)} = \frac{0.25}{0.50(0.50 - 0.25)} = 2.$$

We see that one machine, on the average, is either being repaired or waiting to be repaired. If we define the total cost associated with a given repair crew policy as the sum of repair crew cost and idle machine hour cost, then for the first option:

$$\text{total cost} = \text{repair crew cost} + \text{idle machine hour cost}$$
$$= 150 + (300 \times 1) = 450.$$

Option 2.   If the size of the repair crew is doubled, then $\lambda = 0.25$ and $\mu = 1$, so that

$$E(N_t) = \frac{\lambda}{\mu - \lambda} = \frac{0.25}{1.0 - 0.25} = \frac{1}{3},$$

$$E(N_w) = \frac{\lambda}{\mu}\left(\frac{\lambda}{\mu - \lambda}\right) = \frac{0.25}{1.0}\left(\frac{0.25}{1.0 - 0.25}\right) = \frac{1}{12},$$

$$E(T_t) = \frac{1}{\mu - \lambda} = \frac{1}{1.0 - 0.25} = 1\tfrac{1}{3},$$

$$E(T_w) = \frac{\lambda}{\mu(\mu - \lambda)} = \frac{0.25}{1.0(1.0 - 0.25)} = \frac{1}{3}.$$

Thus the average number of machines either in repair or waiting to be repaired is now reduced to $\frac{1}{3}$ machine. The total cost for the second option is then

$$\text{total cost} = \text{repair crew cost} + \text{idle machine hour cost}$$
$$= 300 + (300 \times \tfrac{1}{3}) = 400.$$

The second option is obviously superior to the first option by saving \$50 in total cost.

18.9 ANALYSIS OF MULTICHANNEL SYSTEM

We have shown that one way to reduce the average waiting line is to make the service channel more effective. Another way is obviously to increase the number of service channels. When a waiting-line system has more than one service channel, it is called a *multichannel waiting-line system.*

In evaluating the various characteristics of such a system, we shall assume that:

1. the customer arrivals are Poisson distributed, with a mean arrival rate of λ;

2. the service time at each channel is exponentially distributed with a mean service rate of μ;

3. only one waiting line is formed for all service channels;

4. the service discipline is FIFO;

5. customers are not repelled by a long waiting line.

Busy Period

Assuming that there are m service channels in the service mechanism, then the service mechanism is busy whenever the waiting-line system has m or more customers. The formula for finding a busy-period probability is quite difficult to derive. The result of the derivation is given in Appendix 3. The table in this appendix gives the busy-period probabilities for various combinations of $\rho = \lambda/\mu$ and m.

We shall illustrate how this table of busy-period probabilities can be used.

Example 9 Customers arrive at the average rate of four per hour. The service rate is eight per hour. Thus $\lambda = 4$ and $\mu = 8$.

Suppose the system has only one service channel. Then the busy-period probability is $\rho = \lambda/\mu = 0.5$; that is, the system is busy 50 percent of the time.

We can determine this busy period by means of the table as well. In the table we find that the busy-period probability corresponding to $\rho = 0.5$ and $m = 1$ is 0.5. The row for $\rho = 0.5$ is reproduced below:

	$m = 1$	$m = 2$	$m = 3$	$m = 4$
$\rho = 0.5$	0.5000	0.1000	0.0151	

The table can be used as follows. Suppose the service mechanism has two service channels. Then the busy-period probability is 0.1000; that is, only 10 percent of the time will the system be busy. And if the service mechanism has three service channels, then the busy-period probability is 0.0151.

Example 10 Suppose that on the average four customers arrive per hour but the service rate is two per hour. If there are two or fewer servers, the waiting line will become infinitely large. Therefore, the service mechanism should have at least 3 service channels.

The relevant portion of the busy-period probability table is again reproduced below:

	$m = 3$	$m = 4$	$m = 5$	$m = 6$
$\rho = 2$	0.4444	0.1739	0.0597	0.0180

According to the table, the system will be busy 44.44 percent of the time if it has three channels and 17.39 percent of the time if it has four channels.

Operating Characteristics

The rules for evaluating the operating characteristics of multichannel waiting-line systems are similar to those for the single-channel waiting-line systems.

Expected Number in the Waiting Line For the single-channel waiting-line system this number, we recall, is

$$E(N_w) = \frac{\lambda}{\mu}\left(\frac{\lambda}{\mu - \lambda}\right).$$

Since λ/μ is also the busy-period probability, we can also write:

$$E(N_w) = \left(\frac{\text{busy-period}}{\text{probability}}\right)\left(\frac{\text{arrival rate}}{\text{service rate} - \text{arrival rate}}\right).$$

We can use this formula for the multichannel waiting-line system with a minor change in the definitions of the terms. When the waiting line has only one channel, the mean service rate of a channel is equivalent to the mean service rate of the entire service mechanism. Therefore, it is not material whether the "service rate" in the formula refers to that of a channel or of the whole service mechanism.

However, if the service mechanism contains more than one service channel where each channel has the service rate of μ, then the service rate of the entire service mechanism is μ times the number of channels, that is $m\mu$. We say $m\mu$ is the *mechanism service rate* and μ is the *channel service rate*. Then for a multichannel waiting-line we can write:

$$E(N_w) = \left(\frac{\text{busy-period}}{\text{probability}}\right)\left(\frac{\text{arrival rate}}{\dfrac{\text{mechanism}}{\text{service rate}} - \dfrac{\text{arrival}}{\text{rate}}}\right)$$

$$= f(b)\left(\frac{\lambda}{m\mu - \lambda}\right).$$

Expected Number in the System In the case of a single-channel waiting system we have

$$E(N_t) = \frac{\lambda}{\mu - \lambda} = \frac{\lambda}{\mu}\left(\frac{\lambda}{\mu - \lambda}\right) + \frac{\lambda}{\mu}.$$

Let the first λ/μ be the busy-period probability. Then it can be shown that for a multichannel waiting system:

$$E(N_t) = \left(\begin{array}{c}\text{busy-period}\\\text{probability}\end{array}\right)\left(\dfrac{\text{arrival rate}}{\begin{array}{c}\text{mechanism}\\\text{service rate}\end{array} - \begin{array}{c}\text{arrival}\\\text{rate}\end{array}}\right) + \dfrac{\text{arrival rate}}{\begin{array}{c}\text{channel}\\\text{service rate}\end{array}}$$

$$= f(b)\left(\dfrac{\lambda}{m\mu - \lambda}\right) + \dfrac{\lambda}{\mu}.$$

Here the last term λ/μ is the expected number of customers in the service mechanism. It can be shown that for both single-channel and multichannel systems the expected number of customers in the service mechanism is λ/μ.

Expected Time in System   For single-channel waiting systems we have

$$E(T_t) = \dfrac{1}{\mu - \lambda} = \dfrac{\lambda}{\mu}\left(\dfrac{1}{\mu - \lambda}\right) + \dfrac{1}{\mu}.$$

By letting λ/μ be the busy-period probability, we can write for the multichannel system:

$$E(T_t) = \left(\begin{array}{c}\text{busy-period}\\\text{probability}\end{array}\right)\left(\dfrac{\text{arrival rate}}{\begin{array}{c}\text{mechanism}\\\text{service rate}\end{array} - \begin{array}{c}\text{arrival}\\\text{rate}\end{array}}\right)\dfrac{1}{\begin{array}{c}\text{channel}\\\text{service rate}\end{array}}$$

$$= f(b)\left(\dfrac{\lambda}{m\mu - \lambda}\right) + \dfrac{1}{\mu}.$$

Expected Waiting Time   For single-channel systems we have

$$E(T_w) = \dfrac{\lambda}{\mu}\dfrac{1}{\mu - \lambda}.$$

Again by letting λ/μ be the busy-period probability, we can write for the multichannel system:

$$E(T_w) = \left(\begin{array}{c}\text{busy-period}\\\text{probability}\end{array}\right)\left(\dfrac{\text{arrival rate}}{\begin{array}{c}\text{mechanism}\\\text{service rate}\end{array} - \begin{array}{c}\text{arrival}\\\text{rate}\end{array}}\right).$$

The operating characteristics of both single-channel and multichannel systems are summarized in Table 18.4 for easy reference.

18.10   APPLICATIONS: MULTICHANNEL

Example 11. Bank Teller Problem   During the afternoon hours of every Friday on the average 9.6 customers per minute come to Large City Bank for deposit transactions. There are five tellers serving these depositors now. It takes, on the average, 30 seconds for a teller to serve a depositor. Thus each teller serves two depositors per minute.

Quite frequently a long waiting line has formed in front of the tellers on Friday afternoons, and sometimes the waiting line extends to the outside of the

Table 18.4

Operating characteristics	General rule	Single-channel system	Multichannel system
Expected number in system: $E(N_t)$	B.P.P.* $\left(\dfrac{\text{arrival rate}}{\text{mechanism service rate} - \text{arrival rate}} \right) + \dfrac{\text{arrival rate}}{\text{channel service rate}}$	$f(b)\left(\dfrac{\lambda}{\mu - \lambda}\right) + \dfrac{\lambda}{\mu} = \dfrac{\lambda}{\mu - \lambda}$	$f(b)\left(\dfrac{\lambda}{m\mu - \lambda}\right) + \dfrac{\lambda}{\mu}$
Expected number in waiting line: $E(N_w)$	B.P.P. $\left(\dfrac{\text{arrival rate}}{\text{mechanism service rate} - \text{arrival rate}} \right)$	$f(b)\left(\dfrac{\lambda}{\mu - \lambda}\right) = \dfrac{\lambda^2}{\mu(\mu - \lambda)}$	$f(b)\left(\dfrac{\lambda}{m\mu - \lambda}\right)$
Expected time in system: $E(T_t)$	B.P.P. $\left(\dfrac{1}{\text{mechanism service rate} - \text{arrival rate}} \right) + \dfrac{1}{\text{channel service rate}}$	$f(b)\left(\dfrac{1}{\mu - \lambda}\right) + \dfrac{1}{\mu} = \dfrac{1}{\mu - \lambda}$	$f(b)\left(\dfrac{1}{m\mu - \lambda}\right) + \dfrac{1}{\mu}$
Expected time in waiting line: $E(T_w)$	B.P.P. $\left(\dfrac{1}{\text{mechanism service rate} - \text{arrival rate}} \right)$	$f(b)\left(\dfrac{1}{\mu - \lambda}\right) = \dfrac{\lambda}{\mu(\mu - \lambda)}$	$f(b)\left(\dfrac{1}{m\mu - \lambda}\right)$

* B.P.P. is the abbreviation for busy-period probability.

bank. The bank management is now evaluating the feasibility of hiring some additional tellers during these hours.

By definition, if no teller is added, then

$$\lambda = 9.6, \qquad \mu = 2.0,$$

and $\lambda/\mu = 4.8$. Since $m = 5$, from the table in Appendix 3 we find that the busy-period probability is 0.9016. The expected number of customers in the waiting line is then

$$E(N_w) = f(b)\left(\frac{\lambda}{m\mu - \lambda}\right) = (0.9016)\left[\frac{9.6}{(5 \times 2) - 9.6}\right] \cong 21.2.$$

If the bank hires one additional teller, then the busy-period probability will be 0.5177, with the following expected number of customers in the waiting line:

$$E(N_w) = f(b)\left(\frac{\lambda}{m\mu - \lambda}\right) = 0.5177\left[\frac{9.4}{(6 \times 2) - 9.4}\right] \cong 2.06.$$

Thus having one additional teller will reduce the average waiting line from 21 persons to 2 persons.

Example 12. Machine Repair Problem   At Alpha Beta Manufacturing, which uses a large number of production machines, on the average six machines break down every day. One service mechanic can repair 2.5 machines per day on the average. There are now three mechanics in the repair shop.

Some of the operating characteristics of the waiting-line system here may be obtained as follows. Since an average of six machines break down every day, $\lambda = 6$. The fact that each mechanic can repair 2.5 machines per day means that $\mu = 2.5$. Since there are three mechanics, we have $m = 3$. From the table in Appendix 3 we find that the busy-period probability is 0.6471, so that

$$E(N_t) = f(b)\left(\frac{\lambda}{m\mu - \lambda}\right) + \frac{\lambda}{\mu}$$

$$= (0.6471)\left[\frac{6}{(3 \times 2.5) - 6}\right] + \frac{6}{2.5} = 4.99,$$

$$E(N_w) = f(b)\left(\frac{\lambda}{m\mu - \lambda}\right)$$

$$= (0.6471)\left[\frac{6}{(3 \times 2.5) - 6}\right] = 2.59,$$

$$E(T_t) = f(b)\left(\frac{1}{m\mu - \lambda}\right) + \frac{1}{\mu}$$

$$= (0.6471)\left[\frac{1}{(3 \times 2.5) - 6}\right] + \frac{1}{2.5} = 0.83,$$

$$E(T_w) = f(b)\left(\frac{1}{m\mu - \lambda}\right)$$

$$= (0.6471)\left[\frac{1}{(3 \times 2.5) - 6}\right] = 0.43.$$

Thus the average number of machines either in repair or waiting to be repaired is approximately five, and it will take on the average 0.83 days, including waiting time, for a machine to be repaired.

Now assume that an idle machine will cost $500 per day in lost production revenue, and the cost per mechanic is $100 per day. Then the total cost associated with having three is:

$$\text{total cost} = \text{repair crew cost} + \text{idle machine hour cost}$$
$$= (100 \times 3) + (500 \times 4.99) = 2795.$$

If there are four mechanics, then busy-period probability will be 0.2870, so that

$$E(N_t) = (0.2870)\left[\frac{6}{(4 \times 2.5) - 6}\right] + \frac{6}{2.5} = 2.81.$$

The total cost will then be:

$$\text{total cost} = (100 \times 4) + (500 \times 2.81) = 1805.$$

Similarly, we can find the total costs of having five, six, and seven mechanics. The results are summarized in Table 18.5. We see that the total cost will initially decrease with increasing number of mechanics, but after adding the fifth mechanic, any additional mechanic will increase the total cost. The optimal repair crew size is obviously five mechanics.

Table 18.5

Number of mechanics	Busy-period probability	$E(N_t)$	Repair crew cost	Idle machine cost	Total cost
3	0.6471	4.99	300	2495	2795
4	0.2870	2.81	400	1405	1805
5	0.1135	2.50	500	1250	1750
6	0.0399	2.43	600	1215	1815
7	0.0125	2.41	700	1205	1905

EXERCISES

1. Groovy Textile Company has a large number of looms for its weaving operations. The records for the last 200 days yield the following statistics on the breakdown of the looms as shown in Table 18.6.

a. What is the average number of loom breakdowns per day?

b. What is the empirical probability distribution of the daily loom breakdowns?

c. On the basis of the empirical probability distribution obtained in part (b) determine the probability that more than two looms will break down on any given day.

d. Obtain the Poisson probability distribution with the same average number of loom breakdowns as your answer to part (a).

Table 18.6

Number of looms which broke down on a day	Number of days
0	44
1	60
2	50
3	30
4	10
5	6

e. Compare the empirical probability distribution obtained in part (b) with the Poisson distribution obtained in part (d). In light of this comparison, would you say that the daily breakdowns of the looms may reasonably be approximated by a Poisson probability distribution?

2. The customer service department of Eastgate Department Store handles customer complaints. A random sample of 400 one-hour blocks have been selected, and the number of customers arriving at the department during each of the selected hour blocks has been observed. The result of the observations is summarized in Table 18.7.

Table 18.7

Number of customers arriving	Number of hours
0	50
1	100
2	110
3	80
4	40
5	20
6	10

a. What is the average number of hourly customer arrivals at the customer service department?
b. Obtain the empirical probability distribution of the hourly customer arrivals at the department.
c. Obtain the Poisson probability distribution which has the same average number of customer arrivals as your answer to part (a).
d. Compare the empirical probability distribution obtained in part (b) and the Poisson distribution obtained in part (d). In light of this comparison, would you say that the hourly customer arrivals at the customer service department may reasonably be approximated by a Poisson distribution?

3. The repair records of 200 looms used by Groovy Textile Company of Exercise 1 yield the statistics contained in Table 18.8. Assume that the average repair time of those looms requiring 0 to 1 hour is 0.5 hour, and that for those requiring 1 to 2 hours is 1.5 hours, and so on.

Table 18.8

Repair hours required	Number of looms
0–1	68
1–2	46
2–3	32
3–4	20
4–5	12
5–6	8
6–7	6
7–8	4
8–9	2
9–10	2

a. Calculate the average repair hours for all 200 looms.
b. Obtain the empirical probability distribution of the required repair hours.
c. Obtain the theoretical probability distribution for the repair hours, assuming that the distribution is exponential.
d. Comparing the graphs of the two probability distributions you have found, would you say that the repair hours of the looms may reasonably be approximated by an exponential distribution?

4. The records of services to 1000 complaining customers kept by the customer service department of Eastgate Department Store of Exercise 2 yield the statistics given in

Table 18.9

Service time in minutes	Number of customers
0–20	640
20–40	240
40–60	100
60–80	20
	1000

Table 18.9. Assume that the average service time for those customers requiring 0 to 20 minutes is 10 minutes, and that for those requiring 20 to 40 minutes is 30 minutes, and so on.

a. What is the average service time for all customers?
b. Obtain the empirical probability distribution of the service times.
c. Obtain the theoretical probability distribution of the service times, assuming that they are exponentially distributed.

d. Comparing the graphs of the two probability distributions, would you say that the service times for the complaining customers may be reasonably approximated by an exponential distribution?

5. Consider again Groovy Textile Company of Exercises 1 and 3. Assume that the loom breakdowns are Poisson distributed and the loom repair times are exponentially distributed. Further assume that the repair crew works only eight hours a day and the broken looms are repaired in the order in which they broke down.

a. What is the traffic intensity ratio?
b. On the average how many hours will the repair crew be busy on a given day?
c. Obtain the probability distribution of the looms in the waiting-line system.
d. Calculate the various operating characteristics of the waiting line system.
e. What is the probability that a broken loom will stay idle for a while before the repair crew gets to it?
f. What is the probability that three or more broken looms may be in the waiting-line system at any given time?
g. What is the average length of unproductive time for each broken loom?
h. Suppose the cost in lost production of a broken loom is $100 per hour. What, then, is the average daily cost in lost production due to loom breakdowns?

6. Again consider Eastgate Department Store of Exercises 2 and 4. Assume that customer arrivals are Poisson distributed and the service times for the complaining customers are exponentially distributed. Assume further that the customers are served in the order of their arrival.

a. What is the traffic intensity ratio?
b. Obtain the probability distribution of the customers in the waiting-line system at the customer service department.
c. Calculate various operating characteristics of this waiting-line system.
d. What is the probability that a customer arriving at the customer service department will be served immediately without having to wait?
e. What is the probability of there being four or more customers at the customer service department at any given time?
f. What is the average length of the waiting line at the customer service department?
g. Joe Brown has just arrived at the department with a complaint. How long will he probably have to stay to complete his business?

7. Friendly Medical Clinic has one appointment clerk who handles all the appointments for the several doctors in the clinic. Incoming calls are answered by the switchboard operator. If the caller wants a doctor's appointment, then the call is transferred to the appointment clerk. If the clerk is busy, the operator asks the caller to wait. When the clerk becomes free, the operator transfers the caller who has been waiting the longest to the appointment clerk. The calls for appointments come in at a rate of nine per hour, and the average length of time it takes for the clerk to complete an appointment is 6 minutes. Assume that the incoming calls are Poisson distributed and the lengths of time taken by the clerk to complete the appointments are exponentially distributed.

a. What is the probability that a person calling for an appointment will have to wait before reaching the appointment clerk?
b. What is the average length of time the callers must be on the phone to receive their medical appointments?

c. At any given time what is the average number of callers who are waiting to have their calls transferred to the appointment clerk?

8. On the average the computer system of Knowledgeable Consultants, Inc. gets two batches of processing jobs per hour. The average length of time required to process each job is 20 minutes. The incoming jobs resemble a Poisson process, and the processing times are exponentially distributed. The jobs are processed in the order in which they are received.

    a. What is the probability that an incoming job will be processed immediately without having to wait?
    b. What is the average length of time between a job's coming into the computer system and its leaving the system?
    c. On the average how many jobs will be waiting for processing at any time?
    d. The company is thinking of leasing some of its computer's idle time. The computer system now operates 16 hours a day. On the average how many of these 16 hours will the system be idle?

9. Drive-in customers arrive at an average rate of 20 cars per hour at the Drive-N-Carry hamburger stand. The arrivals are Poisson distributed. It takes on the average $2\frac{1}{2}$ minutes to serve a customer. The service times are exponentially distributed. One waiting line of cars is allowed before the service window.

    a. What is the probability that an arriving customer can drive directly to the service window?
    b. On the average how many customers will be waiting at any time to receive service?
    c. On the average how long will a customer have to wait before starting to receive his service?
    d. A customer who finds no waiting space will leave. How many waiting spaces must there be if Drive-N-Carry wants to ensure that at least 90 percent of the time an arriving customer will have a waiting space?

10. On the average two buses come into the repair shop of Inter-City Transit Company every five days. It takes on the average one day to repair a bus. The pattern of bus arrivals in the repair shop is Poisson distributed, and the repair times are exponentially distributed. The buses are repaired in the order of their arrivals.

    a. What is the probability that a bus that comes into the repair shop will have to wait before the repair crew can get to it?
    b. What is the probability of there being two or more buses in the repair shop at any given moment?
    c. How long should a bus arriving at the repair shop be expected to stay?
    d. The cost in lost revenue of an idle bus is $600 per day. What is the average daily cost in lost revenue due to idle buses?
    e. The repair shop can reduce the average repair time to half a day by hiring additional mechanics. The cost of these additional mechanics is $200 per day. Will it benefit the company to hire the additional mechanics?

11. On the average 18 cars per hour come to Convenient Service Station during the morning hours on a weekday. It takes on the average 6 minutes to serve a customer. The arrivals of the cars are Poisson distributed, and the service times are exponentially distributed. There are two attendants during the morning hours on weekdays. Customers are served in the order of their arrivals.

a. What percentage of the time during these hours will both attendants be busy serving the customers?

b. On the average how many cars at any time will be waiting to be served during the morning hours?

c. What is the average length of time that a customer must spend at the service station before departing the service station?

d. Suppose that the service station adds one more attendant. How will your answers for parts (a), (b), and (c) be affected?

12. On the average 60 customers arrive at Betty's Bakery per hour. There are seven attendants who wait on customers. Each can serve an average of ten customers per hour. The customer arrivals are Poisson distributed, and the service times are exponentially distributed. The customers are served in the order of their arrivals.

a. What is the probability that a customer will have to wait before being served by an attendant?

b. On the average how many customers will be waiting to be served at any time?

c. What is the average length of time that a customer must spend in the bakery in order to make his purchases?

d. Suppose that the bakery adds one more attendant. How will your answers for parts (a), (b), and (c) be affected?

e. If the bakery has ten attendants, how different will your answers for parts (a), (b), and (c) be?

13. On the average 18 requests for typewriter service come to the office manager of Oriental Life and Casualty Company in a day. The services requested range from changing a ribbon to replacing a typewriter. A repairman can service an average of ten requests a day. The incoming requests are Poisson distributed, and the service times are exponentially distributed. There are at present two typewriter repairmen in the company. The service requests are filled by the two repairmen in the order in which they are received.

a. On the average how many typewriters will be standing idle at any time because they are either waiting to be serviced or actually being serviced?

b. What is the average length of the idle time of each typewriter, where the idle time is defined as the length of time between the making of a service request and completion of requested service?

c. Suppose the idle-time cost of a typewriter is $6.00 per hour. What is the average daily typewriter idle-time cost (assume an eight-hour work day)?

d. A repairman is paid $10 per hour. Is it a sound policy to have only two repairmen? If not, what is the optimal number of repairmen the company should have?

14. Worldwide Shipping Company has two unloading berths at a West Coast port. On the average nine ships arrive at the port per week. Each berth can handle six ships per week on the average. The ship arrivals at the port are Poisson distributed, and the unloading times are exponentially distributed. The ships are unloaded in the order of their arrivals.

a. What is the probability that an arriving ship will have to wait before docking at a berth?

b. What is the average number of ships which will be waiting to dock at one of the company's berths?

c. On the average, how long will a ship have to wait at the port before docking at one of the berths?

d. Suppose the revenue lost by a ship while either waiting or unloading is $30,000 per week. What is the company's average revenue loss per week due to its ships waiting and unloading at the port?

e. The cost of operating a berth is $10,000 per week. Is the policy of operating just two berths optimal? If not, how many berths should the company operate?

19

GAMES AND STRATEGIES

Managerial decisions are quite frequently made in situations where the decisions of others with conflicting interests must be taken into account. Those with conflicting interests may, for example, be a competing business enterprise, a labor union, or government regulatory agencies.

Such situations are in a sense analogous to gaming situations. In a game between two players, say A and B, the strategy chosen by player A will depend on his evaluation of the strategy which will be chosen by his opponent, player B. On the other hand, the strategy to be chosen by the player B will be influenced by his assessment of the strategy to be chosen by the player A. Similarly, managerial decision-making in business enterprises also has this kind of wary mutual dependences.

The mathematical theory of games is meant to explain how the players in a game might select their strategies. The theory was originated in 1928 by the great mathematician John von Neumann to describe the rationale of economic competition. Subsequently, the theory and its applications were greatly expanded in the book *Theory of Games and Economic Behavior* by von Neumann and Oskar Morgenstern.*

In this chapter we shall illustrate some applications of the game theory to some managerial decision-making in competitive situations.

19.1 TWO-PERSON GAME

Two players, We and They, are playing the following game. We have m different ways of playing the game, each of which will be called a *strategy*. They

---

* John von Neumann and Oskar Morgenstern, *Theory of Games and Economic Behavior*, Princeton University Press, Princeton, N.J., 1947.

have n different ways of playing the game, or n different strategies. If we choose the strategy x and they choose the strategy y, then the amount that we lose to them, say C, is given by the payoff function

$$C = f(x, y).$$

The set of our m strategies and the set of their n strategies, together with the payoff function $C = f(x, y)$, are said to constitute a *two-person zero-sum game*.

The reason for calling it a two-person game is obvious. "Zero sum" means that one player will gain all that the other player loses; the sum of their payoffs will therefore be zero.

Example 1. Guessing Game   Assume that "they" have two bills: $1 and $10. They will pick out one of the bills and let us guess which bill is chosen: $1 or $10. If "we" guess correctly, they will give us the bill thus chosen. But if we guess incorrectly, then we must pay them an amount equal to the bill that they picked out.

Their strategies are:

Their strategies	Description
1	choose $1
2	choose $10

Our strategies are:

Our strategies	Description
1	guess that the bill chosen is $1
2	guess that the bill chosen is $10

Suppose they choose strategy 1 and we choose our strategy 1. Then according to the rules of the game, they must pay us $1. This payoff may be expressed as:

$$C = f(1, 1) = -1.$$

The minus sign means that we will receive $1 from them. But suppose we choose, instead, our strategy 2. Then we will have to pay $1 to them. This transaction can be described as:

$$C = f(2, 1) = 1.$$

Similarly, $C = f(1, 2) = 10$ indicates that when they choose their strategy 2 and we choose our strategy 1, then we must pay them $10. On the other hand, $C = f(2, 2) = -10$ means that if both choose our respective strategies 2, then they will have to pay $10 to us.

This complete description of the guessing game can be given in a more compact form, as in the following table, where the payoff scheme is by the array of numbers:

	Opponent's strategies		
Our strategies		1	2
1		$-1	$10
2		1	-10

Such a table is sometimes called a *payoff matrix table*. It provides a complete description of the game to be played.

19.2 SITUATIONS OF BUSINESS CONFLICTS

Conflicts in the business world frequently involve more than two interested parties, in which case they cannot be modeled on two-person games. However, there are some conflicts which may essentially involve only two parties and therefore can be formulated as two-person games.

Example 2. Two Whiskey Distillers Conflict Able Whiskey Company has used up a substantial portion of its whiskey inventory in gaining record sales. Confronted with an inventory shortage, it is considering the following two strategies:

1. buy the bulk whiskey from its competitor, Baker Whiskey Company, at a premium bulk price and maintain the brand sales;

2. do not buy the bulk whiskey from Baker Whiskey Company.

Strategy 1 means that in the short run the company will incur some loss, since it will have to pay a very high price for the bulk whiskey. But the company believes that it can maximize long-term profit by maintaining its position in the market. The strategy 2, on the other hand, will enable the company to maintain its short-term profit at the expense of the long-term profit.

In contrast to the situation of Able Whiskey Company, Baker Whiskey Company is having very poor brand sales and therefore has a large bulk whiskey inventory. The following strategies are being evaluated by Baker Whiskey Company:

1. sell the bulk whiskey to Able Whiskey Company at a premium bulk price;

2. do not sell the bulk whiskey to Able Whiskey Company.

Strategy 1 will bring about a high short-term profit, but the company believes that this strategy will allow Able Whiskey to maintain its current market position for a long time. Strategy 2, on the other hand, will force the company to incur a short-term loss but might enable it to gain greater market share in the long run.

The consequences of each company's choice of strategies are summarized in Table 19.1. This table shows that it is impossible for both distillers to have long-term gain. Consequently, insofar as they may both prefer long-term gain to short-term gain, the two distillers have conflicting interests in the given situation.

Table 19.1

Able \ Baker	Sell bulk whiskey	Do not sell bulk whiskey
Buy bulk whiskey	Able: short-term loss, long-term gain Baker: short-term gain, long-term loss	Able: short-term gain, long-term loss Baker: short-term loss, long-term gain
Not to buy bulk whiskey	Able: short-term gain, long-term loss Baker: short-term loss, long-term gain	Able: short-term gain, long-term loss Baker: short-term loss, long-term gain

Example 3. Automobile Model Changes   Charles Motor and Delta Motor Company together command the major share of the automobile sales in a country. In making decisions regarding new models for the coming year, each company always tries to take into account what the other company might do. However, the policy regarding model change is such a tightly kept secret that each company must make its own decisions without knowing exactly what the other company will do.

A particular decision confronting the two companies is what to do about the introduction of a new safety device. The consequences of the two companies' decisions on their sales and profits are believed to be as shown in Table 19.2. The table reveals that neither company will benefit if both introduce the new safety device at the same time. However, neither one wants to wind up not having the new safety device if its competitor has it in its new model. In this respect, then, the interests of the two companies are in conflict.

19.3   CONVERTING CONFLICT SITUATIONS INTO GAMES

The conflict situations described above may be transformed into two-person games by converting the various consequences of the parties' choice of strategies into payoff matrices.

In the case of the two whiskey distillers, suppose we assume that Able Whiskey Company believes that it will incur a short-term loss of $5 million but attain a long-term gain of $30 million by buying the bulk whiskey and maintaining its brand sales. Then the net gain of $25 million may be considered

Table 19.2

Charles \ Delta	No new safety device	New safety device
No new safety device	Both Charles and Delta will have about the same market shares and therefore same profits as this year	Delta will gain market share and therefore profit at the expense of Charles
New safety device	Charles will gain market share and therefore profit at the expense of Delta.	Both Charles and Delta will have about the same market shares as this year, but their profits will decline a little due to added cost of the safety device

an element of the payoff matrix from Able to Baker, as shown below:

Able \ Baker	Sell	Not to sell
Buy	25	
Not to buy		

A positive number is used to indicate that Baker will be paying Able the sum in question. Of course, in reality Baker may not pay any money at all directly to Able. The amount of $25 million is one which Able believes it will gain at the expense of Baker's profitability, but not as a direct payment from Baker.

The remaining elements of the payoff matrix may be obtained in a similar way. We will assume that the complete payoff matrix as conceived by Able Whiskey Company is as shown below:

Able \ Baker	Sell	Not to sell
Buy	25	−20
Not to buy	−20	−20

Assuming that the amount of gain for Able Whiskey Company will be the amount of loss to Baker Whiskey, and vice versa. Therefore, the payoff matrix as conceived by Baker may be given as follows:

Able \ Baker	Sell	Not to sell
Buy	−25	20
Not to buy	20	20

The last two tables are identical except that the signs are reversed. Thus if a payoff in one of these two tables is added to the corresponding payoff in the other table, the sum will be zero. The game is thus a zero-sum game.

When we are dealing with a zero-sum game, we do not need both the above tables. We will adhere to the practice of using only the second table to depict the payoff matrices for both players. There should not be any confusion so long as we keep in mind that a positive number implies a payoff from Able to Baker and a negative number implies a payoff from Baker to Able.

Nonzero-Sum Game

In the preceding illustration we assumed that the amount of gain for Able will exactly equal the amount of loss for Baker, and vice versa. In practice, however, this may not be the case. In the first place, the two distillers are likely to have different costs of operation. Therefore, even if one distiller gains exactly the sales lost by the other distiller, the profit gained by the former will not likely be equal to the profit lost by the latter. Consequently, while Able Whiskey Company might assess its payoff matrix as

Able \ Baker	Sell	Not to sell
Buy	25	−20
Not to buy	−20	−20

Baker Whiskey Company might very well assess its payoff matrix as

Able \ Baker	Sell	Not to sell
Buy	−20	15
Not to buy	15	15

Thus the corresponding elements of the matrices would not add up to zero, and we say the game is a *nonzero-sum game*.

Nonzero-sum games are much more difficult to solve than zero-sum games, although in recent years a good deal of research effort has been directed towards solving nonzero-sum games. So while we now know much more about how such games should be solved than before, in our subsequent discussions we shall nevertheless confine our analyses to zero-sum games.

19.4   STRUCTURE OF A GAME MODEL

Let us assume that "we" are to play a two-person zero-sum game with "them." Let y be a variable such that:

$$y = \begin{cases} 1 & \text{if they select their strategy 1,} \\ 2 & \text{if they select their strategy 2, etc.,} \end{cases}$$

and let x be a variable such that:

$$x = \begin{cases} 1 & \text{if we choose our strategy 1,} \\ 2 & \text{if we choose our strategy 2, etc.} \end{cases}$$

From our point of view, then we can consider x to be our decision variable and y to be our environmental variable. The resulting structure of the game model may then be depicted as shown in Figure 19.1.

In the preceding chapters the decision situations were such that the environmental variables were understood as either deterministic variables whose values were known with certainty or random variables having probability distributions. Accordingly the manner in which we obtained optimal decisions was influenced by our assumption regarding the environmental variables.

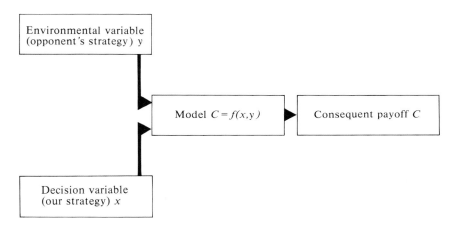

Figure 19.1

In the gaming situation here, what shall we assume about the environmental variable? Certainly it is not a deterministic variable. It is not even likely to be a random variable, since "we" are not in a position to know the probabilities of "their" choosing the various strategies. A more realistic assumption is that we are completely ignorant of what our opponent might select for strategy. Thus the environmental setting is completely uncertain.

In Chapter 2 we proposed two decision criteria for just such a situation: maximin gain and minimax loss.

We shall now illustrate how we can utilize these criteria in arriving at an optimal strategy for our game.

19.5 OPTIMAL PURE STRATEGY

Let us assume that the following table describes a game to be played by us and our opponent (them).

	Their strategy		
Our strategy		1	2
1		3	4
2		2	6

The number 3, for example, means that we will lose 3 if we choose our strategy 1 and they choose their strategy 1.

How can we arrive at our optimal strategy? We might be tempted to choose our strategy 2, since in this case if they choose their strategy 1, then we will lose only 2 to them. On the other hand, if they choose their strategy 2, then we will lose 6.

Von Neumann, the originator of game theory, proposed that one rational way to resolve the problem was to select the strategy in such a way that the worst possible consequence associated with the strategy chosen would not be any worse than the worst possible consequence associated with any other possible strategy. This is the principle of choosing our strategy so as to minimize the maximum possible loss; the strategy is called the *minimax strategy*.

In the present case we find that:

1. If we choose our strategy 1, then the maximum possible loss is 4; that is,

$$\max\{3, 4\} = 4.$$

2. If we choose our strategy 2, then the maximum possible loss is 6; that is,

$$\max\{2, 6\} = 6.$$

Thus the maximum possible losses are 4 and 6, respectively, for strategies 1 and 2. The strategy that minimizes the maximum possible loss is then strategy 1, because

$$\min\{4, 6\} = 4.$$

Let us call 4 the minimax loss for us for obvious reasons. Indeed, another way of describing the process by which we obtained that value is:

$$\min\{\max[3, 4] = 4, \max[2, 6] = 6\} = \min\{4, 6\} = 4.$$

They (our opponent), however, have a somewhat different problem. It is to select the strategy in such a way as to maximize their gains. Suppose they adhered to the Von Neumann principle. Then they would choose their strategy so as to maximize the minimum possible gains associated with the two strategies. We will call this the *maximin strategy*.

The maximin strategy of our opponent may be described as follows:

1. If strategy 1 is chosen, then the minimum possible gain is 2; that is,

$$\min\{3, 2\} = 2.$$

2. If strategy 2 is chosen, then their minimum possible gain is 4; that is,

$$\min\{4, 6\} = 4.$$

The minimum possible gains being 2 and 4, respectively for their strategies 1 and 2, the strategy that will maximize the minimum possible gain for them is strategy 2:

$$\max\{2, 4\} = 4.$$

Let us call 4 the *maximin gain* for them; then the process by which this value is obtained may be summarized as:

$$\max\{\min[3, 2] = 2, \min[4, 6] = 4\} = \max\{2, 4\} = 4.$$

In the above example each player had two possible strategies. Moreover, they are *pure strategies* as distinguished from *randomized strategies* in the sense we shall soon describe.

19.6 STABILITY OF GAME

In the example just discussed the minimax loss for us is 4, as is the maximin gain for them; that is,

$$\text{minimax loss for us} = \text{maximin gain for them.}$$

When this equation obtains the game is said to be *stable* and the quantity 4 is said to be the *value of the game.*

In a stable game we do not have to lose any more than the value of the game, that is if we choose not to lose any more. Similarly, our opponent can gain at least the value of the game. Thus if we choose our strategy 1, which is our minimax strategy, then it will be impossible for our opponent to make us lose more than 4, which is the value of the game, even if we announce in advance that we will choose our strategy 1. Conversely, if they choose their strategy 2, which is their maximin strategy, then it will be impossible for us to make them gain less than 4, even if they announce in advance the choice of strategy 2.

19.7 FINDING THE SADDLE POINT STRATEGY

Let us now consider the following game, where the participants in the game will simply be called player 1 and player 2. The payoff table from player 1 to player 2 is given below:

Player 1 \ Player 2	1	2	3	4
1	5	9	8	7
2	5	6	7	1
3	1	2	4	3
4	4	3	5	6

To find the minimax strategy of player 1, we note that the maximum possible loss in adopting his strategy 1 is 9 (the circled element in the first row of the payoff matrix below):

Player 1 \ Player 2	1	2	3	4	Maximum loss
1	5	⑨	8	7	9
2	5	6	⑦	1	7
3	1	3	④	3	④ ← minimax
4	4	2	5	⑥	6

The maximum losses associated with the available strategies are also listed in the right-hand column: 9, 7, 4, and 6. The smallest among these is 4, as indicated. The minimax strategy of player 1 is therefore his strategy 3.

To find the maximin strategy of player 2, we note that the minimum possible gains associated with his strategies are as circled in the matrix below and also listed in the bottom row of Table 19.3.

Table 19.3

Player 1 \ Player 2	1	2	3	4
1	5	9	8	7
2	5	6	7	①
3	①	3	④	3
4	4	②	5	6
Minimum gain	1	2	④	1

↑
maximin

The minimum possible gains are: 1, 2, 4, and 1. The maximum among these is 4. Thus the maximin strategy of player 2 is his strategy 3.

If we reexamine the preceding two tables, we will see that 4 is the only number in the payoff matrix that is circled in both tables. Moreover, it is the smallest among the four numbers circled in the first table and it is the largest among the four numbers circled in the second table. The position in the payoff matrix occupied by 4, which is the value of a stable game, is sometimes called the *saddle point* of the payoff matrix.

19.8   UNSTABLE GAME

Let us now consider the game described by Table 19.4, where the payoff is from player 1 to player 2.

Table 19.4

Player 1 \ Player 2	Strategy 1	Strategy 2
Strategy 1	3	6
Strategy 2	4	2

The minimax strategy of player 1 is obtained by means of Table 19.5

Table 19.5

Player 2 / Player 1	Strategy 1	Strategy 2	Maximum loss
Strategy 1	3	⑥	6
Strategy 2	④	2	④ ← minimax

The maximin strategy of the player 2 is obtained by means of Table 19.6.

Table 19.6

Player 2 / Player 1	Strategy 1	Strategy 2
Strategy 1	③	6
Strategy 2	4	②
Minimum gain	③	2

↑
maximin

We note that, while the minimax loss for player 1 is 4, the maximin gain of player 2 is only 3. Such a game where the minimax loss value for player 1 and the maximin gain value for player 2 are not equal, is said to be an *unstable game.* We pointed out earlier that, if a game is stable, then players 1 and 2 will always adhere respectively to the minimax and maximin strategies, even if they each know what their opponent's strategy will be. But this is no longer true when the game is unstable.

Consider the game above. Suppose player 1 believes that player 2 will choose his maximin strategy, that is strategy 1. Then player 1 will choose his own strategy 1, which is not his minimax strategy, hoping to lose only 3. Here 3 is less than his minimax loss.

Player 1, however, cannot choose his strategy 1 repeatedly. If he did, player 2 would catch on and choose his strategy 2, thereby forcing player 1 to lose 6 instead of 3.

19.9   RANDOMIZED STRATEGY

Let us return to the unstable game of the preceding section. Suppose player 1 decides to pursue the following course of action: toss a coin and choose strategy 1 if he gets heads and strategy 2 if he gets tails. This is called a *randomized strategy.* A randomized strategy is one in which a player chooses a certain chance mechanism to determine his game strategy.

If we assume that the coin used is fair, then the following probability distribution may be assigned to player 1's two game strategies:

Strategy	Probability
1	0.5
2	0.5
	1.0

Let us assume now that player 1 will pursue this randomized strategy, and player 2 will choose his strategy 1. Then the expected loss of player 1, written $L(1)$, may be ascertained:

$$L(1) = 0.5(3) + 0.5(4) = 3.5,$$

whic is 0.5 less than 4, the minimax loss value for player 1.

This result, however, is based on the assumption that player 2 will choose his strategy 1. But player 2 may, instead, choose his strategy 2. Let $L(2)$ be the expected loss for the player 1 associated with player 2's choosing his strategy 2. Then,

$$L(2) = 0.5(6) + 0.5(2) = 4,$$

which is the same as the minimax value for player 1.

Thus for player 1 the randomized strategy is as good as his minimax strategy. Is there some other even better randomized strategy for player 1? Yes, there is for the given game.

Let us assume that player 1 selects his chance mechanism so that the probabilities of choosing his available strategies are:

Strategy	Probability
1	0.45
2	0.55
	1.00

Then the expected loss for player 1 will be

$$L(1) = 0.45(3) + 0.55(4) = 3.55$$

if player 2 chooses his strategy 1, and

$$L(2) = 0.45(6) + 0.55(2) = 3.80$$

if player 2 chooses his strategy 2.

Here even the larger of $L(1)$ and $L(2)$ is less than the minimax loss value for player 1. Therefore, the randomized strategy is clearly superior to the nonrandomized minimax strategy for player 1.

It is conceivable that there are even better ways to randomize strategies than the one just described. In the following section we will describe a procedure for finding an optimal randomized strategy.

19.10 OPTIMAL RANDOMIZED STRATEGY

When player 1 has only two pure strategies, his optimal randomized strategy may be ascertained graphically. Let

p_1 = probability that player 1 will select strategy 1,

p_2 = probability that player 1 will select strategy 2.

Then the expected loss for player 1 when player 2 selects his strategy 1 is

$$L(1) = 3p_1 + 4p_2 = 3p_1 + 4(1 - p_1) = 4 - p_1$$

and when the player 2 chooses his strategy 2, it is

$$L(2) = 6p_1 + 2p_2 = 6p_1 + 2(1 - p_1) = 2 + 4p_1.$$

Table 19.7 lists the values of $L(1)$ and $L(2)$ for some arbitrary values of p_1. These values of $L(1)$ and $L(2)$ are also shown in the graph in Figure 19.2.

Table 19.7

	0	0.2	0.4	0.45	0.5	0.6	0.8	1.0
$L(1)$	4	3.8	3.6	3.55	3.5	3.4	3.2	3.0
$L(2)$	2	2.6	3.6	3.8	4.0	4.4	5.2	6.0
$\max\{L(1), L(2)\}$	4	3.8	3.6	3.8	4.0	4.4	5.2	6.0

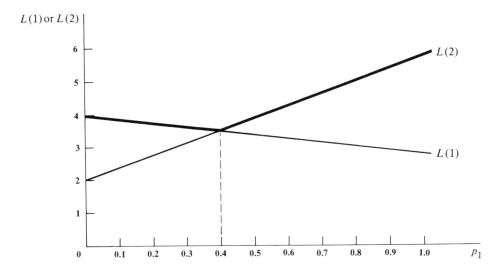

Figure 19.2

If player 1 adheres to the Von Neumann principle that the worst possible consequence associated with the strategy chosen should not be any worse than the worst consequence associated with any other strategy that he could have chosen, then he should choose the value of p_1 such that the largest number between $L(1)$ and $L(2)$ is as small as possible. That is, he should choose his p_1 so as to

$$\text{Minimize } \{\max [L(1), L(2)]\}.$$

The maximum between $L(1)$ and $L(2)$ is indicated by the bold line in Figure 19.2; it has the smallest value when p_1 is 0.4. Thus the optimal randomized strategy of player 1 is to devise a chance mechanism so that the probability of selecting his strategy 1 is 0.4 and that of choosing his strategy 2 is 0.6. If such a randomized strategy is pursued, the worst possible expected loss for player 1 is 3.6, which is 0.4 less than the minimax loss with the nonrandomized pure strategy.

We note that in Figure 19.2 when p_1 is 0.4 the values of $L(1)$ and $L(2)$ are the same, meaning that regardless whether player 2 chooses his strategy 1 or his strategy 2, the expected loss for player 1 will be the same. What if player 2 himself utilizes a randomized strategy? It can be shown that the expected loss for player 1 will still be the same so long as player 1 utilizes his optimal randomized strategy.

19.11 ALGEBRAIC SOLUTION FOR OPTIMAL RANDOMIZED SOLUTION

According to our preceding analysis, the values of $L(1)$ and $L(2)$ are the same when p_1 is at its optimal value. This suggests that the optimal value of p_1 might also be obtained algebraically.

The fact that $L(1) = L(2)$ implies that, for the optimal value of p_1 we must have

$$3p_1 + 4(1 - p_1) = 6p_1 + 2(1 - p_1).$$

Rearranging the terms, we have

$$3p_1 + 4 - 4p_1 = 6p_1 + 2 - 2p_1$$

or

$$5p_1 = 2.$$

Consequently, $p_1 = 0.4$. Since $p_1 + p_2 = 1$, we must also have $p_2 = 0.6$. Thus the optimal randomized strategy that we obtained algebraically is identical to the strategy obtained graphically.

So far we have been concerned only with player 1. But finding the optimal randomized strategy for player 2 is quite similar to finding it for player 1. We let

q_1 = probability that player 2 will choose his strategy 1,

q_2 = probability that player 2 will choose his strategy 2.

Let $G(1)$ be the expected gain for player 2 when player 1 chooses his strategy 1, and $G(2)$ the expected gain for player 2 when player 1 chooses his strategy 2. We can again show that $G(1)$ is equal to $G(2)$ if player 2 adopts his optimal randomized strategy. This in turn implies that for the optimal value of q_1 we must have

$$3q_1 + 6(1 - q_1) = 4q_1 + 2(1 - q_1),$$

which may be rearranged to read:

$$3q_1 + 6 - 6q_1 = 4q_1 + 2 - 2q_1.$$

Further rearranging the terms, we have

$$5q_1 = 4.$$

Thus $q_1 = 0.8$, which means $q_2 = 0.2$. Player 2, then, should devise his chance mechanism so that the probability of choosing strategy 1 is 0.8 and that of choosing strategy 2 is 0.2.

The expected gain for player 2 is then

$$G(1) = 0.8(3) + 0.2(6) = 3.6$$

or

$$G(2) = 0.8(4) + 0.2(2) = 3.6.$$

We note that now the expected gain with the optimal randomized strategy for player 2 is exactly the same as the expected loss with the optimal randomized strategy for player 1.

EXERCISES

1. The following table describes a game to be played between us and our opponent (them). The numbers in the lower right-hand box represent the amounts to be paid by us to our opponent.

Our strategies / Their strategies	1	2
1	5	10
2	4	6

  a. What is our optimal strategy?
  b. What is their optimal strategy?
  c. Is the game stable? Explain your answer.
  d. What is the value of the game?

2. The following table describes a game to be played between us and our opponent (them). The positive number in the lower right-hand box represents the amount to be paid to them by us, and the negative numbers represent the amounts to be paid by them to us.

Our strategies / Their strategies	1	2
1	−1	10
2	−4	−5

   a. What is our optimal strategy?
   b. What is their optimal strategy?
   c. Is the game stable? Explain your answer.
   d. What is the value of the game?

3. The following table describes a game to be played by two players. The numbers in the lower right-hand box represent the amounts to be paid by player 1 to player 2.

Player 1 \ Player 2	1	2	3
1	6	8	7
2	5	6	8
3	4	3	1
4	7	8	9

   a. What are the respective optimal strategies of players 1 and 2?
   b. Is the game stable? Explain your answer.
   c. What is the value of the game?

4. The following table describes a game to be played by two players. The positive numbers in the lower right-hand box represent the amounts to be paid by player 1 to player 2, and the negative numbers represent the amounts to be paid by player 2 to player 1.

Player 1 \ Player 2	1	2	3	4
1	−2	3	−2	5
2	−1	1	0	−2
3	0	2	−1	4

   a. What are the respective strategies of players 1 and 2?
   b. Is the game stable? Explain your answer.
   c. What is the value of the game?

5. The following table describes a game to be played between us and our opponent (them). The numbers in the lower right-hand box represent the amount to be paid by us to them.

Our strategies \ Their strategies	1	2
1	2	8
2	6	4

   a. Show that the game is not stable.
   b. Find the optimum randomized strategy for us.
   c. Find the optimum randomized strategy for them.
   d. Find the expected value of the game.

6. The following table describes a game to be played by two players. The payoffs are to be made by player 1 to player 2.

Player 1 \ Player 2	1	2
1	10	4
2	2	8

a. Show that the game is not stable.
b. Find the optimal randomized strategies for players 1 and 2.
c. Find the expected value of the game.

7. Charles Motor Company is debating whether to increase the prices of its cars starting with next year's models. If Charles Motors and its principal competitor, Delta Motors, do not raise prices in the next year, then Charles Motors will have about the same amount of profit next year as this year. But if Delta Motors raises its prices while Charles Motors does not, then Charles Motors is expected to increase its profits by $100 million due to added sales. On the other hand, if both Charles Motors and Delta Motors raise their prices, then both companies are expected to maintain their present market shares. Nevertheless, Charles Motors is expected to increase its profits by $50 million due to larger profit margin per car. If Charles Motors raises its prices and Delta Motors does not, then Charles Motors will lose some of its market share, and in turn its profit is expected to decrease by $80 million.

a. Suppose Charles Motors has absolutely no idea as to what Delta Motors will do regarding the pricing of the new models. Can the problem confronting Charles Motors be formulated as a game? If so, what is the company's optimal strategy?
b. Suppose Charles Motors is reasonably sure that Delta Motors will raise its prices. Should the problem of Charles Motors still be formulated as a game? Explain your answer.

8. De Paris and De Lyon are the two principal producers of perfumes. The market shares of the two companies are highly sensitive to their advertising efforts. At present both have about the same share of the American market. The net effects of advertising efforts on the market shares are provided by the following table.

De Paris \ De Lyon	No advertising	Some advertising	Extensive advertising
No advertising	0%	5%	15%
Some advertising	−5%	0%	10%
Extensive advertising	−15%	−10%	0%

Thus if De Paris advertises extensively, for example, and De Lyon does not advertise at all, then De Paris will gain 15% of the market from De Lyon. The cost of advertising is not very significant in comparison with the profit loss due to a decrease in market share.

a. Suppose De Paris is completely ignorant of the advertising strategy of De Lyon. What is the optimal advertising strategy of De Paris according to the Von Neumann principle?

b. Suppose De Lyon is completely ignorant of the advertising strategy of De Paris. What is the optimal advertising strategy of De Lyon according to the Von Neumann principle?

c. Suppose De Paris is absolutely certain that De Lyon will advertise extensively. Should the advertising strategy of De Paris as obtained in part (a) be modified? Explain your answer.

d. Suppose De Lyon is absolutely certain that De Paris will advertise extensively. Should the advertising strategy of De Lyon as obtained in part (b) be modified? Explain your answer.

9. Two Far Eastern countries, say countries K and T, have just passed laws allowing American manufacturers of widgets to establish production plants. However, the widgets manufactured in either of the two countries cannot be exported to the other country. The anticipated sales of widgets are $100 million in country K and $120 million in country T.

Abot Widget Company and Babot Widget Company are currently considering the establishment of manufacturing facilities in one or both countries. Each of the two companies is aware that the other might also establish manufacturing facilities in one or both countries.

If only one of the two companies establishes a manufacturing plant in a country, then that company will have all the market in that country to itself. However, if both companies establish manufacturing plants in a country, then each company is expected to get exactly 50% of the market in that country.

The problem for Abot Widget, for example, is to decide whether to establish a manufacturing plant in country K, country T, or both of these countries. Abot Widget, however, is completely unsure of what Babot Widget might do.

a. Formulate the problem for Abot Widget as a game. Construct a payoff table in terms of sales revenues.

b. On the basis of the payoff table obtained for part (a), what is the optimal strategy for Abot Widget?

c. Would this optimal strategy have to be modified if the company knew in advance what Babot Widget would do? Explain your answer.

10. In Exercise 9, assume that the total investment and operating costs are $60 million in country K and $50 million in country T.

a. Now construct the payoff table for Abot Widget in terms of profit.

b. On the basis of the table obtained for part (a), what is the optimal strategy for Abot Widget?

c. Would this optimal strategy have to be modified if the company knew in advance what Babot Widget would do? Explain your answer.

CHAPTER

20

SIMULATION

In the preceding chapters we were able to solve the decision problems by following a set of well-established mathematical procedures. When a decision problem has been solved in this manner, we say that it has been solved *analytically*. Some decision problems, however, cannot be easily solved in this manner. They may be so complex as to require very complicated mathematical procedures for their solution; or even when appearing very simple, they may have so far defied mathematical solution.

When a decision problem cannot be solved analytically, we may nevertheless be able to evaluate the model for the problem by simulating the decisions and environments. The techniques are called *simulation techniques*, which have been found to be very powerful tools for tackling many important managerial decision problems.

The application of the simulation techniques to managerial decision problems usually requires a large amount of numerical calculations. Therefore, they often require the use of computers, in which case the simulation is called *computer simulation*.

There are several techniques of computer simulation. One very useful technique is the so-called *Monte Carlo method*. In this chapter we shall be concerned solely with the Monte Carlo method.

20.1 ANALYTIC METHOD VERSUS MONTE CARLO METHOD

Before describing the various applications of the Monte Carlo method, perhaps we should illustrate the difference between the ways in which a problem may be handled analytically and by the Monte Carlo method.

Consider the system shown in Figure 20.1. It must take an input and let it pass through the system. The system works if the input successfully passes

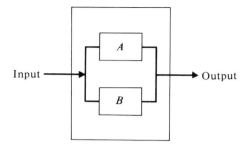

Figure 20.1

through the system; otherwise, it does not work. The system will work if either of the two components A and B works. Of course, the system will work if both components A and B work. The only time that the system will fail to work is when both A and B fail to work.

Assuming the following probability distributions for the components of the system:

	A	B
Probability of working	$\frac{1}{2}$	$\frac{2}{3}$
Probability of not working	$\frac{1}{2}$	$\frac{1}{3}$
	1.0	1.0

and that the components A and B work independently of each other, then we can have the following probability for the system as a whole:

$$\begin{pmatrix} \text{Probability} \\ \text{of system} \\ \text{working} \end{pmatrix} = \begin{pmatrix} \text{Probability} \\ \text{of } A \\ \text{working} \end{pmatrix} + \begin{pmatrix} \text{Probability} \\ \text{of } B \\ \text{working} \end{pmatrix} - \begin{pmatrix} \text{Probability} \\ \text{of both } A \\ \text{and } B \text{ working} \end{pmatrix}$$

$$= \frac{1}{2} + \frac{2}{3} - \frac{2}{6} \doteq \frac{5}{6}.$$

We will say $\frac{5}{6}$ is the *reliability coefficient* of the system.

Note that this reliability coefficient was obtained by utilizing the laws of mathematical probability. Thus we can say that it was obtained by an analytical method.

But we may not know the laws of mathematical probability, in which case can we nevertheless find the reliability coefficient for the given system? The answer is that we may not be able to find the exact value of the reliability coefficient, but we can obtain a reasonably good approximation of this coefficient by means of the Monte Carlo method.

We note that the probability of A working is $\frac{1}{2}$. The probability of getting heads in a fair coin toss is also $\frac{1}{2}$. We can therefore simulate the workings of component A by tossing a coin and without physically activating the component. The rule of association between the outcomes of coin tosses and the workings of component A may be as follows:

Coin lands on	Associated outcome for component A
heads	it works
tails	it does not work

Similarly, we can simulate the working of component B by throwing a die, for example. The rule of association between the outcomes of die throws and the workings of component B may be as follows:

Outcome of die throw	Outcome for component B
1, 2, 3, or 4	it works
5 or 6	it does not work

Note that this rule of association will yield $\frac{2}{3}$ as the probability of B working.

We can now simulate the workings of the entire system by tossing a coin and a die. Suppose, for example, that one toss yields:

$$\text{heads,   5.}$$

Then according to the previously described rule of association, component A works but B does not, which in turn means that the system as a whole works. Suppose on the other hand, the outcome is:

$$\text{tail,   5.}$$

Then both components A and B do not work and therefore the system does not work.

The coin and die have been tossed 12 times with the results as given in Table 20.1. The right-hand column of the table says the system worked 9 times out of 12 simulated trials. Then the estimated value of the reliability coefficient is $\frac{9}{12}$ or 4.5/6. This is not quite the same value we got by means of the analytical method, which is $\frac{5}{6}$. Nevertheless, the estimated value is a very good approximation of the correct value of the reliability coefficient.

20.2   THE MONTE CARLO METHOD

The Monte Carlo method is a mathematical technique originally designed to solve a difficult nonprobabilistic problem by selecting a random sample from a probability distribution. It was initially developed by Von Neumann and Ulam during World War II for a group of nuclear shielding problems which were too difficult to solve analytically but too expensive to evaluate experimentally. Von Neumann and Ulam invented a stochastic process satisfying the relations of their problems and then selected random samples from these stochastic processes. They gave the code name "Monte Carlo" to their technique.

Table 20.1

	Outcome of coin and die toss*		Simulated outcome for†		
Trial	Coin	Die	A	B	System
1	T	4	N	W	W
2	H	6	W	N	W
3	T	1	N	W	W
4	T	5	N	N	N
5	T	3	N	W	W
6	H	2	W	W	W
7	H	4	W	W	W
8	T	5	N	N	N
9	H	3	W	W	W
10	T	6	N	N	N
11	H	2	W	W	W
12	H	4	W	W	W

* *H* means "heads" and *T* means "tail."
† *W* means "works" and *N* means "does not work."

Today, however, the Monte Carlo method has a somewhat broader meaning. We may define it as a technique designed to solve either a nonprobabilistic or probabilistic problem by selecting a random sample from a probability distribution.

First, let us explain what we mean by "selecting a random sample from a probability distribution." Let us consider the following probability distribution.

Integer	Probability
1	1/6
2	1/6
3	1/6
4	1/6
5	1/6
6	1/6
	1.0

Each integer between 1 and 6 has a $\frac{1}{6}$ probability of being selected. How can we select a random sample from this probability distribution? We can do so by devising a physical process which generates the integers according to the given probability distribution. Such a process is called a *stochastic process*.

If we toss a fair die, then each integer between 1 and 6 is equally likely to appear on top. Therefore, given one of these integers, there is a probability of $\frac{1}{6}$ that we will obtain that integer in one toss. Therefore, the integers we obtain by tossing a fair die repeatedly may be said to be generated by a stochastic process that behaves according to the given probability distribution.

Once this stochastic process has been devised, each number generated by the process constitutes a random sample observation of the underlying probability distribution. That is, whenever we toss a die and observe the number on top, that number constitutes a sample observation. A set of *n* numbers generated in this way, then, will constitute a random sample of size n of the probability distribution.

In the case of the reliability coefficient in the preceding section the problem which confronted us was a probabilistic one as we were able to solve it by utilizing the laws of probability. Also a reasonably good approximation to this solution was obtained by tossing a coin and a die. But it is clear that tossing a coin and a die really amounted to selecting random samples from two different probability distributions. Thus the approximation was in fact obtained by means of the Monte Carlo method.

20.3 RANDOM NUMBERS

Even though a simulation experiment can be carried out by tossing coins and dice or spinning roulette wheels, it is obviously not very practical to employ such devices, especially when the simulation is to be done with a computer. Therefore, random numbers are often used instead.

Suppose we write $0, 1, \ldots, 9$ separately on ten different chips, put these chips in a box, then select a chip and record the number written on the chip, replace the chip in the box, select another chip and record its number, and so on, repeating the process. Then in each selection, the probability of getting any integer between 0 and 9 is the same as that of getting any other. Furthermore, since the chip selected is replaced, the numbers successively obtained will be independent of the numbers previously selected. The numbers generated in this manner are called the *random numbers.*

Of course, the actual generation of random numbers by such a device is no more convenient than tossing coins or dice. However, there are tables of random numbers which have already been generated, one of which is the table of one million random digits produced by the Rand Corporation. An excerpt from this table is shown in Table 20.2.

Table 20.2

98 52 01 77 67	14 90 56 86 07	22 10 94 05 58	60 97 09 34 33	50 50 07 39 98
11 80 50 54 31	39 80 82 77 32	50 72 56 82 48	29 40. 52 42 01	52 77 56 78 51
83 45 29 96 34	06 28 89 80 83	13 74 67 00 78	18 47 54 06 10	68 71 17 78 17
88 68 54 02 00	86 50 75 84 01	36 76 66 79 51	90 36 47 64 93	29 60 91 10 62
99 59 46 73 48	87 51 76 49 69	91 82 60 89 28	93 78 56 13 68	23 47 83 41 13
65 48 11 76 74	17 46 85 09 50	58 04 77 69 74	73 03 95 71 86	40 21 81 65 44
80 12 43 56 35	17 72 70 80 15	45 31 82 23 74	21 11 57 82 53	14 38 55 37 63
74 35 09 98 17	77 40 27 72 14	43 23 60 02 10	45 52 16 42 37	96 28 60 26 55
69 91 62 68 03	66 25 22 91 48	36 93 68 72 03	76 62 11 39 90	94 40 05 64 18
09 89 32 05 05	14 22 56 85 14	46 42 75 67 88	96 29 77 88 22	54 38 21 45 98

If a digital computer is used, there are two different ways of generating random numbers. First, we may feed into the computer memory a table of random numbers so that the computer can generate the random numbers by reference to the table in its memory. Second, the computer may generate random numbers by calling a subroutine that generates so-called *pseudorandom numbers.*

Since the methods of generating random numbers is a rather technical issue in simulation, we shall not elaborate on it here. Our concern will be with the way in which random numbers are actually used in simulation experiments.

Example 1. Reliability Problem   Consider the system shown in Figure 20.2. It will work if both components A and B work. The probability of A working is 0.8, and that of B working is 0.9. The probability that both A and B will work at the same time is $(0.8)(0.9) = 0.72$.

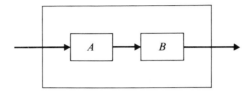

Figure 20.2

If we want to determine this coefficient by simulation, we may do so as follows. Draw two-digit random numbers. If the first digit is 0, 1, 2, 3, 4, 5, 6, or 7, then assume that A works. If the digit is 8 or 9, then assume that A does not work. With this simulation, the probability of A working is 0.8. Similarly, if the second digit is between 0 and 8, then we assume that B works. But if the digit is 9, then we assume that B does not work.

Table 20.3 lists the result of ten simulation trials. We observe that out of ten trials, the system worked seven times. Thus the estimated reliability coefficient for the system is 0.7, which is strikingly close to the correct value of 0.72.

Table 20.3

Trial number	Random number	Simulated outcome for		
		A	B	System
1	76	work	work	work
2	64	work	work	work
3	19	work	not work	not work
4	09	work	not work	not work
5	80	not work	work	not work
6	34	work	work	work
7	45	work	work	work
8	02	work	work	work
9	05	work	work	work
10	03	work	work	work

Example 2. Demand Simulation To evaluate inventory control policies by simulation, we must usually generate simulated demands, for which we can also use random numbers.

Table 20.4

Quantity of demand	Probability
0	0.05
1	0.25
2	0.40
3	0.15
4	0.10
5	0.05
	1.00

Let us assume that on the basis of past demands the probability distribution of demand given in Table 20.4 has been agreed upon. Then we can use the rule of association between the random numbers and demand as given in Table 20.5. We note that the probability of getting a random number between 00 and 04, for example, is 0.05 and the probability of 0 demand is also 0.05. Thus we can let the demand be 0 whatever the random number is between 00 and 04. Similarly, we can let the demand be 1 unit whenever the random number is between 05 and 29, since the probability of getting a random number between 05 and 29 is 0.25, the same as the probability that the demand will be 1 unit. The rest of Table 20.5 can also be understood in this way.

Simulated demands for a 10-day period are listed in Table 20.6.

Table 20.5

Random number	Associated demand
00–04	0
05–29	1
30–69	2
70–84	3
84–94	4
95–99	5

Cumulative Probabilities

The rule of association between random numbers and demands is related to the cumulative probability distribution of demand. The rule by which we assigned demands to random numbers is indicated by the two left-hand columns in Table 20.7. The cumulative probability distribution of demand is indicated by the two right-hand columns. The relation between the assignment rule and the cumulative probability of demand can also be illustrated by a graph, as shown in Figure 20.3.

Table 20.6

Day	Random number	Demand
1	84	4
2	61	2
3	59	2
4	63	2
5	92	5
6	50	2
7	42	2
8	15	1
9	73	3
10	62	2

Table 20.7

| Assignment rule | | Cumulative probability | |
Random number	Demand	Demand	Cumulative probability
00–04	0	0	0.05
05–29	1	1	0.30
30–69	2	2	0.70
70–84	3	3	0.85
85–94	4	4	0.95
95–99	5	5	1.00

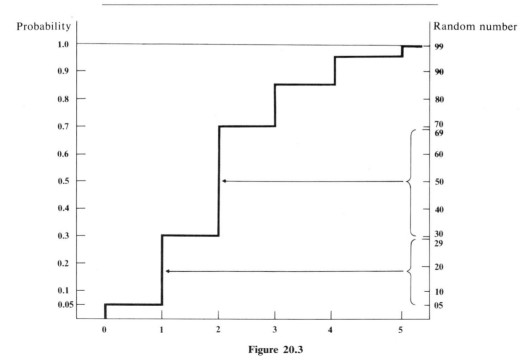

Figure 20.3

We observe that in Figure 20.3 the vertical line corresponding to a demand of 1 unit extends from 0.05 to 0.30 on the probability scale. The random numbers for the demand of 1 unit ranges from 05 to 29, the largest number being one less than 30. The vertical line corresponding to the demand of 2 units extends from 0.30 to 0.70 on the probability scale. The random numbers for the demand of 2 units ranges from 30 to 69, the largest number being again one less than 70. Similar relations hold for the other sizes of demand.

20.4   SIMULATION OF TELEPHONE NETWORK

A telephone call from one point in the circuit can reach another point by several different paths consisting of links which connect the intermediate points. If any path is open, the call can go through. The probability that a call will go through at any random instant is an important consideration in evaluating whether some additional paths should be provided between the two points. Even though such a probability can be calculated analytically, the calculations are extremely difficult in practice, the more so since there are many intermediate links. We can, however, estimate the probability by means of Monte Carlo simulation.

We assume that the diagram in Figure 20.4 depicts a simple telephone network. The nodes refer to different points in the network. The connecting links are the arcs between the nodes.

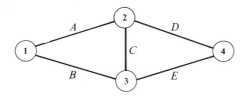

Figure 20.4

A call originating at node 1 can reach node 4 by one of four different paths. If a path is identified by the links that it contains, then the four different paths are:

$$\{A, D\}, \quad \{A, C, E\}, \quad \{B, C, D\}, \quad \{B, E\}.$$

Assuming that on the basis of past experience we have the following probabilities of the links being busy:

Link	Probability
A	0.5
B	0.6
C	0.8
D	0.6
E	0.5

then Table 20.8 gives the rule that may be used to decide whether a link is busy or not during the simulations. Suppose a five-digit random number happens to be

$$6 \quad 4 \quad 8 \quad 1 \quad 5.$$

Table 20.8

Link	Busy if random number is	Not busy if random number is
A	0, 1, 2, 3, or 4	5, 6, 7, 8, or 9
B	0, 1, 2, 3, 4, or 5	6, 7, 8, or 9
C	0, 1, 2, 3, 4, 5, 6, or 7	8, or 9
D	0, 1, 2, 3, 4, or 5	6, 7, 8, or 9
E	0, 1, 2, 3, or 4	5, 6, 7, 8, or 9

Then we can let these five digits correspond to:

A: not busy

B: busy

C: not busy

D: busy

E: not busy

We note that A, C, and E are not busy and together they constitute a path between node 1 and node 4. Therefore, the call will go through. This is one simulation run for the telephone network, where a *run* consists of taking one sample of random numbers and examining what the sample indicates about the telephone network.

By so repeating the simulation runs a large number of times we can obtain the percentage of times that the call will go through and use this percentage as the estimated value of the probability that the call will go through at any randomly selected instant.

For example, the results of ten simulation runs are as shown in Table 20.9. The right-hand column of the table shows that out of ten simulation runs the calls went through four times. Thus we may estimate the probability of the call going through at any randomly selected instant to be 0.4.

20.5 INVENTORY POLICY SIMULATION

In the chapter on inventory management we worked out the optimal inventory control policies by assuming the lead time to be constant. We pointed out that variable lead time is difficult to handle analytically. In this section we shall illustrate how variable lead time may be dealt with by means of Monte Carlo simulation.

Table 20.9

Runs	Random number					Status of the link*					Status† of the call
	A	B	C	D	E	A	B	C	D	E	
1	6	6	4	9	0	×	×		×		Yes
2	3	9	7	8	9		×		×	×	Yes
3	7	6	3	0	4	×	×				No
4	9	7	6	8	8	×	×		×	×	Yes
5	6	4	1	0	6	×				×	No
6	0	6	9	0	3		×	×			No
7	0	9	0	9	9		×		×	×	Yes
8	2	0	5	1	4						No
9	9	0	1	2	4	×					No
10	9	0	5	5	6	×				×	No

* × means that the link is not busy and blank space means that the link is busy.

† Yes means that the call will go through, and no means that the call will not go through.

Let us assume that daily demand has the probability distribution shown in the first two columns of Table 20.10. The cumulative probability distribution and random numbers corresponding to the demands are shown in the two right-hand columns. Thus the random number 4, for example, corresponds to a demand on that day of 30 units.

Table 20.10

Demand	Probability	Cumulative probability	Random numbers
10	0.1	0.1	0
20	0.2	0.3	1, 2
30	0.4	0.7	3, 4, 5, 6
40	0.2	0.9	7, 8
50	0.1	1.0	9
	1.0		

Next we assume that the lead time has the probability distribution indicated in the first two columns of Table 20.11. The cumulative probability distribution and the random numbers corresponding to the lead times are indicated in the two right-hand columns. Thus if the random number selected is 7, for example, then we will assume that the lead time is 4 days.

Now let us assume that the inventory policy under consideration is: monitor the inventory level at the beginning of every day and place an order for 150 units whenever the inventory level plus the quantity of unarrived previous orders is 100 units or less. Before actually adopting such a policy we would obviously want to find out its likely effect on the operations of the company.

Table 20.11

Lead time (days)	Probability	Cumulative probability	Random number
2	0.1	0.1	0
3	0.6	0.7	1, 2, 3, 4, 5, 6
4	0.3	1.0	7, 8, 9
	1.0		

The Monte Carlo method may then be used to determine the various operating characteristics of the given inventory policy, such as:

1. how often must orders be placed;
2. how frequently will the stock run out;
3. what the average level of inventory holding will be.

To start the simulation, we shall make the following three assumptions:

1. the beginning inventory is 120 units;
2. orders always arrive at the end of a day, so that they cannot be used to satisfy the demand on that day;
3. any demand that cannot be immediately satisfied will be satisfied after the arrival of the next order.

Since the beginning inventory is 120 units, an order will not be placed at the beginning of this day. Thus we write 0 under the heading "order placed" in Table 20.12. Since an order is not placed on this day, the lead time is irrelevant. Thus we leave a blank space under the heading "lead time." We next decide on the demand for the day by selecting a random number. The random number being 5, the demand is assumed to be 30 units as indicated under demand. If the demand is 30 units, then the end inventory will be 90 units, as indicated in the next column.

Next we simulate the second day. The beginning inventory is 90 units and there is no previously placed order. Therefore, we place an order for 150 units and recorded it under the heading "order placed." We then determine the lead time for this particular order by selecting a random number. The random number selected is 5. Therefore, we assume that the lead time will be 3 days, as indicated under the heading "lead time." We next determine the demand for this day by selecting a random number. The random number being 6, the demand is assumed to be 30 units. The end inventory is then 60 units.

Simulating the third day, we find that the beginning inventory is 60 units, with 150 additional units on order. Therefore, a new order is not placed at this time. We therefore proceed to determine the demand for the day by selecting a random number. The random number being 2, the demand is assumed to be 20 units.

On the fourth day the beginning inventory is 40 units and the previously placed order of 150 units has not arrived yet. No new order is placed. The demand for the day turns out to be 50 units. Thus the end inventory is zero and we record a shortage of 10 units. At the end of the day the order of 150 units arrives. We assume that 10 units of this order will have to be used to fill the unsatisfied demand for the day. The beginning inventory for the fifth day, therefore, will be 140 units, as indicated.

The remaining 15 days of our 20-day period are simulated in a similar manner. The simulation results are summarized in Table 20.12. Before proceeding further, the reader should examine carefully how these results have been obtained.

Table 20.12

Day	Beginning inventory	Order previously placed	Order placed	Lead time Random number	Lead time Days	Demand Random number	Demand Quantity	End inventory	Shortage	Order arrival
1	120	0	0			5	30	90		
2	90	0	150	5	3	6	30	60		
3	60	150	0			2	20	40		
4	40	150	0			9	50	0	10	150
5	140	0	0			0	10	130		
6	130	0	0			7	40	90		
7	90	0	150	9	4	5	30	60		
8	60	150	0			6	30	30		
9	30	150	0			2	20	10		
10	10	150	0			3	30	0	20	150
11	130	0	0			8	40	90		
12	90	0	150	2	3	7	40	50		
13	50	150	0			6	30	20		150
14	170	0	0			2	20	150		
15	150	0	0			4	30	120		
16	120	0	0			9	50	70		
17	70	0	150	6	3	2	20	50		
18	50	150	0			1	20	30		
19	30	150	0			8	40	0	10	150
20	140	0	0			5	30	110		

1,770

The results of our simulation lead us to the following conclusions: First, we ordered four times during the twenty-day period. Thus the average period between two successive orders is five days. Second, there were three occasions of stock-out during the period, or an average of once every seven days. Third, the sum of the beginning inventories for twenty days is 1770. Therefore, the average daily beginning inventory is 88.5 units.

20.6 PERT NETWORK SIMULATION

In our discussion of PERT network analysis we pointed out the difficulty of making probabilistic calculations for the completion time of entire projects. In this section we shall illustrate how such calculations may nevertheless be simulated.

Let us consider the network in Figure 20.5. Even though we usually assume

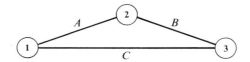

Figure 20.5

that the completion times of the activities in such a network have beta distributions, for the sake of simplicity we shall assume that the probability distributions of the activities are as shown in Table 20.13. We note for example, that there is a 50% chance that activity A will be completed during the 20th week, and a 50% chance that activity A will be completed during the 30th week.

Table 20.13

Activity A		Activity B		Activity C	
Completion time	Probability	Completion time	Probability	Completion time	Probability
20	0.5	15	0.6	40	0.5
30	0.5	25	0.4	50	0.5
	1.0		1.0		1.0

The critical path will consist of activities A and B, if for example, A and B take 20 and 25 weeks, respectively, and C takes 40 weeks. But if A and B take 20 and 25 weeks, respectively, and C takes 50 weeks, then the critical path will consist of C.

There are several things we want to know about the network in question, for example:

1. What is the probability of activity A being a part of a critical path?
2. What is the shape of the probability distribution for the project completion time?

To answer these questions, we will simulate the network with the following rule of association between random numbers and the activity completion times. For activity A:

Random number	Completion time
0, 1, 2, 3, or 4	20 weeks
5, 6, 7, 8, or 9	30 weeks

For activity B:

Random number	Completion time
0, 1, 2, 3, 4, or 5	15 weeks
6, 7, 8, or 9	25 weeks

And for activity C:

Random number	Completion time
0, 1, 2, 3, or 4	40 weeks
5, 6, 7, 8, or 9	50 weeks

Table 20.14 contains the result of twenty simulation runs.

Table 20.14

Simulation run	Random number	Completion time A	B	C	Critical path	Completion time for project (weeks)
1	554	⟨30⟩	⟨15⟩	40	C	⟨45⟩
2	135	20	15	⟨50⟩	C	50
3	575	⟨30⟩	⟨25⟩	50	A, B	55
4	697	⟨30⟩	⟨25⟩	50	A, B	55
5	563	⟨30⟩	⟨25⟩	40	A, B	55
6	729	30	15	⟨50⟩	C	50
7	848	30	15	⟨50⟩	C	50
8	431	20	15	⟨40⟩	C	40
9	767	⟨30⟩	⟨25⟩	50	A, B	55
10	416	20	15	⟨50⟩	C	50
11	025	20	15	⟨50⟩	C	50
12	896	⟨30⟩	⟨25⟩	50	A, B	55
13	462	⟨20⟩	⟨25⟩	40	A, B	45
14	700	⟨30⟩	⟨15⟩	40	C	45
15	077	20	25	⟨50⟩	C	50
16	007	20	15	⟨50⟩	C	50
17	000	20	15	⟨40⟩	C	40
18	585	⟨30⟩	⟨25⟩	50	A, B	55
19	543	⟨30⟩	⟨15⟩	40	C	45
20	553	⟨30⟩	⟨15⟩	40	A, B	45

The table shows that activity A was a part of a critical path 11 times out of 20 simulation runs. Thus we can estimate the probability of A being a part of a critical path to be 0.55. Similarly, we can estimate the probability of B being a part of a critical path to be 0.55 and that of C being a part of a critical path to be 0.45.

Knowing these probabilities will certainly help us in planning and coordinating the activities in the network. Suppose a probability is very high. Then we should be very careful in monitoring the activity in question, more so than in monitoring another activity with a lower probability of being a part of any critical path.

Table 20.15

Project completion time	Simulation result	Estimated probability
40 weeks	2 times	0.10
45 weeks	5 times	0.25
50 weeks	7 times	0.35
55 weeks	6 times	0.30
	20 times	1.00

We can next ascertain the estimated probability distribution of the project completion time on the basis of the information contained in the right-hand column of Table 20.14. We observe, for example, that 2 times out of 20 simulation runs, the project completion time was 40 weeks. Therefore, we can estimate the probability that the entire project will be completed during the 40th week to be 0.10. Similarly, the estimated probability for the project being completed during the 45th week is 0.25. The complete probability distribution of the completion time is shown in Table 20.15.

This kind of probability distribution is very useful. For example, the project manager is offered the contract to complete the entire project within 50 weeks. Before taking up the contract he would certainly want to know the likelihood that he may not be able to complete the project in 50 weeks. The above probability distribution shows that the estimated probability of the project not being completed within 50 weeks is 0.3.

20.7 SIMULATION OF WAITING LINES

In our discussion of waiting lines we were able to evaluate the operating characteristics of different waiting-line systems analytically by assuming that the arrival patterns and service times had some well-behaved theoretical probability distributions. If the probability distributions of the arrival patterns and service times are not so well behaved, the operating characteristics of waiting-line systems become very difficult to evaluate analytically. Nevertheless they can be evaluated by means of Monte Carlo simulation. We shall illustrate how this can be done for a single-channel waiting-line system.

Let us assume that at a tool crib of an aircraft manufacturer the probability distribution of elapse time between the arrivals of mechanics is:

Elapse time (minutes)	Probability
1	0.10
2	0.20
3	0.40
4	0.20
5	0.10
	1.00

Thus if one mechanic has just arrived, the probability is 0.4 that another mechanic will arrive 3 minutes later.

The probability distribution of the service time is:

Service time (minutes)	Probability
1	0.10
2	0.30
3	0.40
4	0.20
	1.00

Among the different operating characteristics we want to evaluate let us assume that we are particularly interested in the following two:

1. the average length of time that a mechanic will spend waiting in line;
2. the average length of time that a mechanic will spend in the system to check out a tool.

The assignment of random numbers for the elapse time between arrivals is shown in Table 20.16. The assignment of random numbers for the service time is shown in Table 20.17.

Table 20.16

Elapse time (minutes)	Cumulative probability	Random number
1	0.10	00–09
2	0.30	10–29
3	0.70	30–69
4	0.90	70–89
5	1.00	90–99

The simulation of the waiting line may proceed as follows. Assume that the tool crib opens at 8:00 A.M. First, we simulate mechanic arrivals by selecting random numbers. Assume that the first random number is 27, indicating that the first mechanic arrives two minutes after the tool crib opens, or at 8:02. Let

Table 20.17

Service time (minutes)	Cumulative probability	Random number
1	0.10	00–09
2	0.40	10–39
3	0.90	40–89
4	1.00	90–99

the next random number be 54: the second mechanic arrives three minutes after the first mechanic, or at 8:05. That is,

Random number	Elapsed time	Arrival time
27	2 minutes	8:02
54	3 minutes	8:05

which can also be illustrated as in Figure 20.6.

The successive simulated arrivals between 8:00 A.M. and 9:00 A.M. are listed in Table 20.18.

Table 20.18

Random number	Elapse time	Arrival time
27	2	8:02
54	3	8:05
69	3	8:08
49	3	8:11
03	1	8:12
65	3	8:15
91	5	8:20
28	2	8:22
69	3	8:25
91	5	8:30
01	1	8:31
88	4	8:35
57	3	8:38
21	2	8:40
70	4	8:44
69	3	8:47
70	4	8:51
66	3	8:54
31	3	8:57
61	3	9:00

The service for the first mechanic will then start at 8:02. To determine the time required to service this mechanic, we choose a random number again. Suppose the random number is 97: the simulated service time is four minutes,

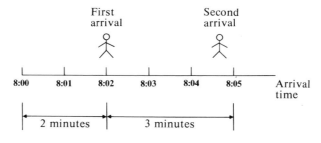

Figure 20.6

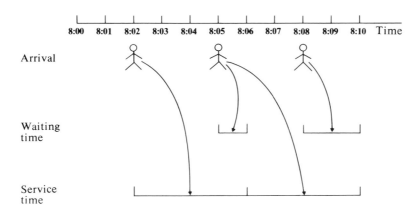

Figure 20.7

meaning that the service for this mechanic will be over at 8:06. However, the second mechanic has already arrived at 8:05. Since the service for him will start at 8:06, he will have to wait one minute before receiving the service. Suppose the random number is 95. Then it will again take four minutes to service the second mechanic. The service for this mechanic will be over at 8:10. But the third mechanic has arrived at 8:08. Thus he must wait two minutes before receiving his service.

The simulation results for the first 10 minutes may be illustrated as in Figure 20.7. The information contained in this diagram may be summarized in a table, as in Table 20.19. The simulation results for the entire one-hour period between 8:00 A.M. and 9:00 A. M. are shown in Table 20.20.

Now we can determine some of the operating characteristics of the tool crib waiting-line system. We note that the total waiting time of the twenty mechanics was 19 minutes. The average waiting time per mechanic is then 0.95 minute, or approximately one minute. We also note that it took 73 minutes altogether to service these twenty mechanics. Thus the average length of time that a mechanic spends in the system is 3.65 minutes.

20.8 EVALUATING ALTERNATIVE POLICIES AND CHANGING ENVIRONMENT

If, as our illustrations suggest, the Monte Carlo method can be used to study characteristics of a given policy in a given decision environment, then it should

Table 20.19

| Arrival | | | | Service time | | | | |
Random number	Elapsed time	Arrival time	Service begins	Random number	Time	Service ends	Waiting time	Total time
27	2	8:02	8:02	97	4	8:06	0	4
54	3	8:05	8:06	95	4	8:10	1	5
69	3	8:08	8:10				2	

Table 20.20

| Arrival | | | | Service time | | | | |
Random number	Elapsed time	Arrival time	Service begins	Random number	Time	Service ends	Waiting time	Total time
27	2	8:02	8:02	97	4	8:06	0	4
54	3	8:05	8:06	95	4	8:10	1	5
69	3	8:08	8:10	07	1	8:11	2	3
49	3	8:11	8:11	90	4	8:15	0	4
03	1	8:12	8:15	56	3	8:18	3	6
65	3	8:15	8:18	10	2	8:20	3	5
91	5	8:20	8:20	64	3	8:23	0	3
28	2	8:22	8:23	33	2	8:25	1	3
69	3	8:25	8:25	41	3	8:28	0	3
91	5	8:30	8:30	94	4	8:34	0	4
01	1	8:31	8:34	20	2	8:36	3	5
88	4	8:35	8:36	74	3	8:39	1	4
57	3	8:38	8:39	13	2	8:41	1	3
21	2	8:40	8:41	99	4	8:45	1	5
70	4	8:44	8:45	31	2	8:47	1	3
69	3	8:47	8:47	07	1	8:48	0	1
70	4	8:51	8:51	93	4	8:55	0	4
66	3	8:54	8:55	40	3	8:58	1	4
31	3	8:57	8:58	34	2	9:00	1	3
61	3	9:00	9:00	06	1	9:01	0	1
							19	73

also be usable in evaluating the characteristics of alternative policies in the same environment or the characteristics of the same policy in different environments.

Evaluating Alternative Policies

Consider our Monte Carlo simulation of the tool crib. We found the operating characteristics of the tool crib with just one clerk. Similarly, we can find the operating characteristics of having

1. 2 clerks,
2. 3 clerks,
3. 4 clerks, etc.

in the tool crib. These may be regarded as alternative policies. It would be common sense to assume that for the waiting-line system in question, placing 100 clerks in the tool crib is out of the question. That is, the number of alternative policies which we should evaluate is relatively small. By comparing the operating characteristics of the various policies we can determine the relative desirability of each policy in relation to the others. And indeed, we should be able to come up with an optimum policy, that is an optimal number of clerks to be placed in the tool crib, by means of Monte Carlo simulation without too much calculation.

Nevertheless, finding an optimal policy by means of Monte Carlo simulation is not usually so easy. To see this, consider our Monte Carlo simulation of an inventory control policy. The specific policy that we took up was placing an order for 150 units whenever the inventory on hand, plus what is on order, is 100 units or less. That is, in the simulation we used the order quantity of 150 units and the reorder level of 100 units. And an alternative policy was formulated by simply changing one or both of these quantities. But these particular quantities were selected arbitrarily. Therefore, to evaluate all the alternative policies would be an enormous task, indeed, too large to be contemplated. Thus we cannot rely on the Monte Carlo simulation to find the optimal policy.

We can, however, formulate the policies for simulation in such a way that we will eventually find a policy which is reasonably good, even if not truly optimal. Also during simulation there are ways to formulate the new policy to be simulated so that it is very likely to be superior to the previously simulated policies. These are methods of "simulation optimization."

Evaluating Alternative Environments

Let us again consider the tool crib simulation. To simulate the operation of the tool crib, we made specific and arbitrary assumptions about the arrival patterns of the mechanics and the service time distribution. We might well have simulated the tool crib operation with a different set of assumptions; that is, the policy of having one clerk in the tool crib might have been evaluated with different environmental conditions.

The fact that the Monte Carlo method can evaluate a given policy under different environmental settings makes it a very valuable planning tool. Business usually operates under constantly changing environments. A policy which is good under one set of conditions may turn out to be quite bad under new environmental conditions. Whenever we foresee a change in the environmental conditions, we can use Monte Carlo simulation to evaluate how well the given policy will fare under the new conditions.

20.9 SOME TECHNICAL ISSUES

Since the purpose of this chapter is to acquaint the reader with the application of the Monte Carlo simulation technique to different types of decision problems, we have used very simple illustrative examples. Actual decision problems are likely to be much more complex than those described in the preceding sections.

A number of technical issues often arise in the design and execution of complex simulation experiments. Detailed considerations of these issues are beyond the scope of this chapter. We shall simply describe what some of the issues are without getting into any details.

Computer Languages

Since most simulation experiments are done on computers, the question of which computer language to use in writing the program is a legitimate issue.

We can use FORTRAN, ALGOL, PL/1, and other general-purpose languages. An advantage of using these languages is that an experienced programmer is usually already familiar with one or more of them. However, there are also several drawbacks in using these languages for the purpose of writing a simulation program. In all simulation experiments there is a need to perform routine operations which are peculiar to these experiments, for example (1) generating random phenomena, (2) gathering statistics on the simulation results, and (3) arranging the outputs in proper formats. The programmer using one of the general-purpose languages will have to write the subroutines for each of these standard simulation routines.

There are several computer languages specifically developed for simulation that have built-in routines to generate random phenomena, tabulate statistics, and prepare the output in some prescribed formats. Two of the better known of these languages are SIMSCRIPT and GPSS (General Purpose Systems Simulator).

Variance-Reducing Technique

One problem that arises in statistical sampling is to find an estimator that is more efficient than other estimators. An estimator is said to be more efficient than other estimators if it has a smaller variance than the others.

A similar problem arises in Monte Carlo simulation. As we pointed out earlier, this simulation in a sense amounts to taking a sample from a probability distribution. Therefore, the statistics we gather in a Monte Carlo simulation are likely to have the variances associated with them. Since a simulation run is equivalent to one sample observation, the variances associated with these statistics will become smaller and smaller as we increase the number of simulation runs.

However, increasing the number of simulation runs will require additional calculations and therefore more computer time. Therefore, if possible, we usually want the simulation experiments to be so designed that the variances for the statistics will be relatively small for a given number of simulation runs. There are ways of designing simulation experiments so that the variances of the statistics are smaller than those associated with the crude simulation techniques which we have used as illustrations. These techniques are known as the *variance-reducing techniques*.

EXERCISES

1. The system depicted in Figure 20.8 will work if both the subsystems 1 and 2 work. Each of the subsystems will work if either of its two components work. The probability of each component working is indicated in the figure. The components work independently of each other.

> **a.** Calculate the reliability coefficient for the system by applying the laws of probability.
> **b.** Estimate the reliability coefficient for the system by twenty Monte Carlo simulation runs.

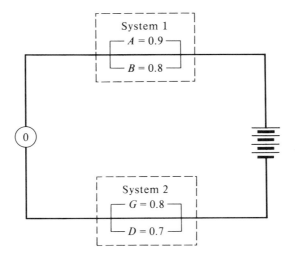

Figure 20.8

2. The automatic guidance system of a space vehicle has a 0.95 probability of working during the entire flight. A monitoring system is installed in the vehicle to signal to ground control whenever the guidance system is not working. The probability of the monitoring system successfully sending the message when the guidance system is out of order is 0.9. If the ground control receives such a message, it will try to guide the vehicle from the ground during the remaining flight. The probability that ground control can successfully guide the vehicle in the event of failure of the automatic guidance system, is 0.8.

    a. Calculate analytically the probability that the space vehicle will be under proper guidance during the entire flight.
    b. Estimate the same probability by conducting simulation runs.

3. The following table summarizes Eastgate Department Store's daily sales records of a certain model of television set for the past 100 days:

Number of sets sold	Number of days
0	10
1	15
2	25
3	30
4	15
5	05

100

Simulate the daily sales for the next twenty days on the basis of these statistics.

4. The diagram in Figure 20.9 depicts a simple telephone network. The nodes represent different points in the network, and the arcs are the connecting links. A call can go through a link in either direction if the latter is not busy. The probability of a

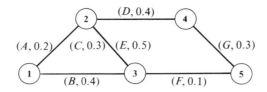

Figure 20.9

link being busy is indicated by the number in the parentheses. We want to find out the probability that a call originating at node 1 will reach node 5. Estimate this probability by means of a Monte Carlo simulation.

Table 20.21

Demanded	Probability
0	0.05
1	0.10
2	0.10
3	0.15
4	0.20
5	0.20
6	0.15
7	0.05

5. Table 20.21 shows the probability distribution of weekly demand for a certain model of refrigerator at Westgate Department Store. The probability distribution for the lead time is:

Lead time (in weeks)	Probability
2	0.3
3	0.5
4	0.2
	1.0

The inventory policy under consideration is: monitor the inventory level at the beginning of each week and place an order for 25 refrigerators whenever the inventory level, plus the quantity on order but not yet arrived, is 15 units or less. The store has 15 units at the beginning of this week. Any order arriving in a given week always arrives so that it cannot be used to fill the demand in that week. Any demand which is not met during the week is lost.

By conducting a Monte Carlo simulation of 30 weeks, determine the following characteristics of the policy under consideration.

    a. How often will the store have to place orders for refrigerators?
    b. What will be the average level of weekly beginning inventory?
    c. How often will the stock run out?
    d. What will be the average weekly sales loss due to inventory stock-out?

6. In Exercise 5 assume that there is an order cost of $100 per order. The inventory holding cost is $40 per unit for 30 weeks. The unit profit margin on the refrigerators is $90. Then on the basis of your simulation results, what is the total 30-week cost of the inventory management policy under consideration?

7. For Exercise 5 formulate an inventory management policy that you believe to be reasonably good. Compare the total 30-week cost of your policy with that given in Exercise 5 by carrying out a Monte Carlo simulation.

8. Figure 20.10 shows a PERT network. The probability distribution of the completion time of each activity is given in Table 20.22. Use a Monte Carlo simulation of 20 runs to answer the following questions.

    a. What is the probability that each activity will be a part of a critical path?
    b. What is the probability distribution of the completion time for the entire project?
    c. What is the probability that the entire project will be completed within 20 weeks?

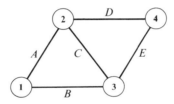

Figure 20.10

Table 20.22

Completion	Probabilities				
time (weeks)	A	B	C	D	E
4					0.20
5			0.10		0.30
6	0.10		0.20		0.30
7	0.20	0.15	0.40	0.10	0.20
8	0.40	0.25	0.20	0.20	
9	0.20	0.30	0.10	0.40	
10	0.10	0.20		0.20	
11		0.10		0.10	
	1.00	1.00	1.00	1.00	1.00

9. At the repair shop of Browncab Taxi Company the cars to be repaired are brought into the shop at the beginning of each day. The probability distribution of the number of cars that come into the shop on any given day is:

Number of cars	Probability
4	0.05
5	0.10
6	0.20
7	0.30
8	0.25
9	0.10
	1.00

The shop has the capacity to repair all the cars on the same day that they come in. However, the union is proposing that the shop repair no more than seven cars a day. Use a Monte Carlo simulation of 30 days to answer the following questions.

a. What is the average number of cars waiting to be repaired on any given day?
b. The cost in lost revenue of a car in the repair shop is $30 per day. What is the average daily cost attributable to cars being in the repair shop?

10. World Wide Shipping Company has one unloading berth at a West Coast port. The probability distribution of the elapsed time between the arrivals of cargo ships at the port is:

Elapse time (in days)	Probability
0	0.1
1	0.2
2	0.4
3	0.3
	1.0

The probability distribution of time required to unload the ships is:

Unloading time (in days)	Probability
1	0.7
2	0.2
3	0.1
	1.0

Assume that ships arrive at the beginning of the day so that unless the berth is busy the unloading operation can commence on the day of their arrival. Use a Monte Carlo simulation of 50 days to answer the following questions.

a. What is the probability that an arriving ship will have to wait before docking?
b. What is the average number of ships waiting to dock at any time?
c. On the average how long does a ship have to wait before docking?

d. What is the average time that a ship has to be in port to be unloaded, including the waiting time?

e. Suppose the revenue lost by a ship while waiting or unloading is $5000 per day. What is the average revenue loss per day due to waiting and unloading?

11. In Exercise 10 the daily cost of operating another berth is $1500. Will it be beneficial to World Wide Shipping to add another berth? Answer the question by conducting a Monte Carlo simulation.

APPENDIXES

APPENDIX 1: AREAS FOR THE STANDARD NORMAL PROBABILITY DISTRIBUTION

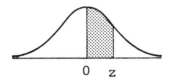

Example: The table shows that $p(0 \leq z \leq 1) = 0.3413$.

z	.00	.01	.02	.03	.04	.05	.06	.07	.08	.09
0.0	.0000	.0040	.0080	.0120	.0160	.0199	.0239	.0279	.0319	.0359
0.1	.0398	.0438	.0478	.0517	.0557	.0596	.0636	.0675	.0714	.0753
0.2	.0793	.0832	.0871	.0910	.0948	.0987	.1026	.1064	.1103	.1141
0.3	.1179	.1217	.1255	.1293	.1331	.1368	.1406	.1443	.1480	.1517
0.4	.1554	.1591	.1628	.1664	.1700	.1736	.1772	.1808	.1844	.1879
0.5	.1915	.1950	.1985	.2019	.2054	.2088	.2123	.2157	.2190	.2224
0.6	.2257	.2291	.2324	.2357	.2389	.2422	.2454	.2486	.2518	.2549
0.7	.2580	.2612	.2642	.2673	.2704	.2734	.2764	.2794	.2823	.2852
0.8	.2881	.2910	.2939	.2967	.2995	.3023	.3051	.3078	.3106	.3133
0.9	.3159	.3186	.3212	.3238	.3264	.3289	.3315	.3340	.3365	.3389
1.0	.3413	.3438	.3461	.3485	.3508	.3531	.3554	.3577	.3599	.3621
1.1	.3643	.3665	.3686	.3708	.3729	.3749	.3770	.3790	.3810	.3830
1.2	.3849	.3869	.3888	.3907	.3925	.3944	.3962	.3980	.3997	.4015
1.3	.4032	.4049	.4066	.4082	.4099	.4115	.4131	.4147	.4162	.4177
1.4	.4192	.4207	.4222	.4236	.4251	.4265	.4279	.4292	.4306	.4319
1.5	.4332	.4345	.4357	.4370	.4382	.4394	.4406	.4418	.4429	.4441
1.6	.4452	.4463	.4474	.4484	.4495	.4505	.4515	.4525	.4535	.4545
1.7	.4554	.4564	.4573	.4582	.4591	.4599	.4608	.4616	.4625	.4633
1.8	.4641	.4649	.4656	.4664	.4671	.4678	.4686	.4693	.4699	.4706
1.9	.4713	.4719	.4726	.4732	.4738	.4744	.4750	.4756	.4761	.4767
2.0	.4772	.4778	.4783	.4788	.4793	.4798	.4803	.4808	.4812	.4817
2.1	.4821	.4826	.4830	.4834	.4838	.4842	.4846	.4850	.4854	.4857
2.2	.4861	.4864	.4868	.4871	.4875	.4878	.4881	.4884	.4887	.4890
2.3	.4893	.4896	.4898	.4901	.4904	.4906	.4909	.4911	.4913	.4916
2.4	.4918	.4920	.4922	.4925	.4927	.4929	.4931	.4932	.4934	.4936
2.5	.4938	.4940	.4941	.4943	.4945	.4946	.4948	.4949	.4951	.4952
2.6	.4953	.4955	.4956	.4957	.4959	.4960	.4961	.4962	.4963	.4964
2.7	.4965	.4966	.4967	.4968	.4969	.4970	.4971	.4972	.4973	.4974
2.8	.4974	.4975	.4976	.4977	.4977	.4978	.4979	.4979	.4980	.4981
2.9	.4981	.4982	.4982	.4983	.4984	.4984	.4985	.4985	.4986	.4986
3.0	.49865	.4987	.4987	.4988	.4988	.4989	.4989	.4989	.4990	.4990
4.0	.49997									

APPENDIX 2: POISSON PROBABILITIES*

λ

k	0.1	0.2	0.3	0.4	0.5	0.6	0.7	0.8	0.9	1.0
0	.9048	.8187	.7408	.6703	.6065	.5488	.4966	.4493	.4066	.3679
1	.0905	.1637	.2222	.2681	.3033	.3293	.3476	.3595	.3659	.3679
2	.0045	.0164	.0333	.0536	.0758	.0988	.1217	.1438	.1647	.1839
3	.0002	.0011	.0033	.0072	.0126	.0198	.0284	.0383	.0494	.0613
4	.0000	.0001	.0002	.0007	.0016	.0030	.0050	.0077	.0111	.0153
5	.0000	.0000	.0000	.0001	.0002	.0004	.0007	.0012	.0020	.0031
6	.0000	.0000	.0000	.0000	.0000	.0000	.0001	.0002	.0003	.0005
7	.0000	.0000	.0000	.0000	.0000	.0000	.0000	.0000	.0000	.0001

λ

k	1.1	1.2	1.3	1.4	1.5	1.6	1.7	1.8	1.9	2.0
0	.3329	.3012	.2725	.2466	.2231	.2019	.1827	.1653	.1496	.1353
1	.3662	.3614	.3543	.3452	.3347	.3230	.3106	.2975	.2842	.2707
2	.2014	.2169	.2303	.2417	.2510	.2584	.2640	.2678	.2700	.2707
3	.0738	.0867	.0998	.1128	.1255	.1378	.1496	.1607	.1710	.1804
4	.0203	.0260	.0324	.0395	.0471	.0551	.0636	.0723	.0812	.0902
5	.0045	.0062	.0084	.0111	.0141	.0176	.0216	.0260	.0309	.0361
6	.0008	.0012	.0018	.0026	.0035	.0047	.0061	.0078	.0098	.0120
7	.0001	.0002	.0003	.0005	.0008	.0011	.0015	.0020	.0027	.0034
8	.0000	.0000	.0001	.0001	.0001	.0002	.0003	.0005	.0006	.0009
9	.0000	.0000	.0000	.0000	.0000	.0000	.0001	.0001	.0001	.0002

λ

k	2.1	2.2	2.3	2.4	2.5	2.6	2.7	2.8	2.9	3.0
0	.1225	.1108	.1003	.0907	.0821	.0743	.0672	.0608	.0550	.0498
1	.2572	.2438	.2306	.2177	.2052	.1931	.1815	.1703	.1596	.1494
2	.2700	.2681	.2652	.2613	.2565	.2510	.2450	.2384	.2314	.2240
3	.1890	.1966	.2033	.2090	.2138	.2176	.2205	.2225	.2237	.2240
4	.0992	.1082	.1169	.1254	.1336	.1414	.1488	.1557	.1622	.1680
5	.0417	.0476	.0538	.0602	.0668	.0735	.0804	.0872	.0940	.1008
6	.0146	.0174	.0206	.0241	.0278	.0319	.0362	.0407	.0455	.0504
7	.0044	.0055	.0068	.0083	.0099	.0118	.0139	.0163	.0188	.0216
8	.0011	.0015	.0019	.0025	.0031	.0038	.0047	.0057	.0068	.0081
9	.0003	.0004	.0005	.0007	.0009	.0011	.0014	.0018	.0022	.0027
10	.0001	.0001	.0001	.0002	.0002	.0003	.0004	.0005	.0006	.0008
11	.0000	.0000	.0000	.0000	.0000	.0001	.0001	.0001	.0002	.0002
12	.0000	.0000	.0000	.0000	.0000	.0000	.0000	.0000	.0000	.0001

λ

k	3.1	3.2	3.3	3.4	3.5	3.6	3.7	3.8	3.9	4.0
0	.0450	.0408	.0369	.0334	.0302	.0273	.0247	.0224	.0202	.0183
1	.1397	.1304	.1217	.1135	.1057	.0984	.0915	.0850	.0789	.0733
2	.2165	.2087	.2008	.1929	.1850	.1771	.1692	.1615	.1539	.1465
3	.2237	.2226	.2209	.2186	.2158	.2125	.2087	.2046	.2001	.1954
4	.1734	.1781	.1823	.1858	.1888	.1912	.1931	.1944	.1951	.1954
5	.1075	.1140	.1203	.1264	.1322	.1377	.1429	.1477	.1522	.1563
6	.0555	.0608	.0662	.0716	.0771	.0826	.0881	.0936	.0989	.1042
7	.0246	.0278	.0312	.0348	.0385	.0425	.0466	.0508	.0551	.0595
8	.0095	.0111	.0129	.0148	.0169	.0191	.0215	.0241	.0269	.0298
9	.0033	.0040	.0047	.0056	.0066	.0076	.0089	.0102	.0116	.0132

*Reproduced by permission of the publisher from *CRC Handbook of Tables for Mathematics,* Revised 4th ed., 1975, Samuel Selby (ed.). Cleveland: CRC Press, Inc.

k	3.1	3.2	3.3	3.4	3.5	3.6	3.7	3.8	3.9	4.0
10	.0010	.0013	.0016	.0019	.0023	.0028	.0033	.0039	.0045	.0053
11	.0003	.0004	.0005	.0006	.0007	.0009	.0011	.0013	.0016	.0019
12	.0001	.0001	.0001	.0002	.0002	.0003	.0003	.0004	.0005	.0006
13	.0000	.0000	.0000	.0000	.0001	.0001	.0001	.0001	.0002	.0002
14	.0000	.0000	.0000	.0000	.0000	.0000	.0000	.0000	.0000	.0001

k	4.1	4.2	4.3	4.4	4.5	4.6	4.7	4.8	4.9	5.0
0	.0166	.0150	.0136	.0123	.0111	.0101	.0091	.0082	.0074	.0067
1	.0679	.0630	.0583	.0540	.0500	.0462	.0427	.0395	.0365	.0337
2	.1393	.1323	.1254	.1188	.1125	.1063	.1005	.0948	.0894	.0842
3	.1904	.1852	.1798	.1743	.1687	.1631	.1574	.1517	.1460	.1404
4	.1951	.1944	.1933	.1917	.1898	.1875	.1849	.1820	.1789	.1755
5	.1600	.1633	.1662	.1687	.1708	.1725	.1738	.1747	.1753	.1755
6	.1093	.1143	.1191	.1237	.1281	.1323	.1362	.1398	.1432	.1462
7	.0640	.0686	.0732	.0778	.0824	.0869	.0914	.0959	.1002	.1044
8	.0328	.0360	.0393	.0428	.0463	.0500	.0537	.0575	.0614	.0653
9	.0150	.0168	.0188	.0209	.0232	.0255	.0280	.0307	.0334	.0363
10	.0061	.0071	.0081	.0092	.0104	.0118	.0132	.0147	.0164	.0181
11	.0023	.0027	.0032	.0037	.0043	.0049	.0056	.0064	.0073	.0082
12	.0008	.0009	.0011	.0014	.0016	.0019	.0022	.0026	.0030	.0034
13	.0002	.0003	.0004	.0005	.0006	.0007	.0008	.0009	.0011	.0013
14	.0001	.0001	.0001	.0001	.0002	.0002	.0003	.0003	.0004	.0005
15	.0000	.0000	.0000	.0000	.0001	.0001	.0001	.0001	.0001	.0002

k	5.1	5.2	5.3	5.4	5.5	5.6	5.7	5.8	5.9	6.0
0	.0061	.0055	.0050	.0045	.0041	.0037	.0033	.0030	.0027	.0025
1	.0311	.0287	.0265	.0244	.0225	.0207	.0191	.0176	.0162	.0149
2	.0793	.0746	.0701	.0659	.0618	.0580	.0544	.0509	.0477	.0446
3	.1348	.1293	.1239	.1185	.1133	.1082	.1033	.0985	.0938	.0892
4	.1719	.1681	.1641	.1600	.1558	.1515	.1472	.1428	.1383	.1339
5	.1753	.1748	.1740	.1728	.1714	.1697	.1678	.1656	.1632	.1606
6	.1490	.1515	.1537	.1555	.1571	.1584	.1594	.1601	.1605	.1606
7	.1086	.1125	.1163	.1200	.1234	.1267	.1298	.1326	.1353	.1377
8	.0692	.0731	.0771	.0810	.0849	.0887	.0925	.0962	.0998	.1033
9	.0392	.0423	.0454	.0486	.0519	.0552	.0586	.0620	.0654	.0688
10	.0200	.0220	.0241	.0262	.0285	.0309	.0334	.0359	.0386	.0413
11	.0093	.0104	.0116	.0129	.0143	.0157	.0173	.0190	.0207	.0225
12	.0039	.0045	.0051	.0058	.0065	.0073	.0082	.0092	.0102	.0113
13	.0015	.0018	.0021	.0024	.0028	.0032	.0036	.0041	.0046	.0052
14	.0006	.0007	.0008	.0009	.0011	.0013	.0015	.0017	.0019	.0022
15	.0002	.0002	.0003	.0003	.0004	.0005	.0006	.0007	.0008	.0009
16	.0001	.0001	.0001	.0001	.0001	.0002	.0002	.0002	.0003	.0003
17	.0000	.0000	.0000	.0000	.0000	.0000	.0001	.0001	.0001	.0001

	λ									
k	6.1	6.2	6.3	6.4	6.5	6.6	6.7	6.8	6.9	7.0
0	.0022	.0020	.0018	.0017	.0015	.0014	.0012	.0011	.0010	.0009
1	.0137	.0126	.0116	.0106	.0098	.0090	.0082	.0076	.0070	.0064
2	.0417	.0390	.0364	.0340	.0318	.0296	.0276	.0258	.0240	.0223
3	.0848	.0806	.0765	.0726	.0688	.0652	.0617	.0584	.0552	.0521
4	.1294	.1249	.1205	.1162	.1118	.1076	.1034	.0992	.0952	.0912
5	.1579	.1549	.1519	.1487	.1454	.1420	.1385	.1349	.1314	.1277
6	.1605	.1601	.1595	.1586	.1575	.1562	.1546	.1529	.1511	.1490
7	.1399	.1418	.1435	.1450	.1462	.1472	.1480	.1486	.1489	.1490
8	.1066	.1099	.1130	.1160	.1188	.1215	.1240	.1263	.1284	.1304
9	.0723	.0757	.0791	.0825	.0858	.0891	.0923	.0954	.0985	.1014
10	.0441	.0469	.0498	.0528	.0558	.0588	.0618	.0649	.0679	.0710
11	.0245	.0265	.0285	.0307	.0330	.0353	.0377	.0401	.0426	.0452
12	.0124	.0137	.0150	.0164	.0179	.0194	.0210	.0227	.0245	.0264
13	.0058	.0065	.0073	.0081	.0089	.0098	.0108	.0119	.0130	.0142
14	.0025	.0029	.0033	.0037	.0041	.0046	.0052	.0058	.0064	.0071
15	.0010	.0012	.0014	.0016	.0018	.0020	.0023	.0026	.0029	.0033
16	.0004	.0005	.0005	.0006	.0007	.0008	.0010	.0011	.0013	.0014
17	.0001	.0002	.0002	.0002	.0003	.0003	.0004	.0004	.0005	.0006
18	.0000	.0001	.0001	.0001	.0001	.0001	.0001	.0002	.0002	.0002
19	.0000	.0000	.0000	.0000	.0000	.0000	.0000	.0001	.0001	.0001

	λ									
k	7.1	7.2	7.3	7.4	7.5	7.6	7.7	7.8	7.9	8.0
0	.0008	.0007	.0007	.0006	.0006	.0005	.0005	.0004	.0004	.0003
1	.0059	.0054	.0049	.0045	.0041	.0038	.0035	.0032	.0029	.0027
2	.0208	.0194	.0180	.0167	.0156	.0145	.0134	.0125	.0116	.0107
3	.0492	.0464	.0438	.0413	.0389	.0366	.0345	.0324	.0305	.0286
4	.0874	.0836	.0799	.0764	.0729	.0696	.0663	.0632	.0602	.0573
5	.1241	.1204	.1167	.1130	.1094	.1057	.1021	.0986	.0951	.0916
6	.1468	.1445	.1420	.1394	.1367	.1339	.1311	.1282	.1252	.1221
7	.1489	.1486	.1481	.1474	.1465	.1454	.1442	.1428	.1413	.1396
8	.1321	.1337	.1351	.1363	.1373	.1382	.1388	.1392	.1395	.1396
9	.1042	.1070	.1096	.1121	.1144	.1167	.1187	.1207	.1224	.1241
10	.0740	.0770	.0800	.0829	.0858	.0887	.0914	.0941	.0967	.0993
11	.0478	.0504	.0531	.0558	.0585	.0613	.0640	.0667	.0695	.0722
12	.0283	.0303	.0323	.0344	.0366	.0388	.0411	.0434	.0457	.0481
13	.0154	.0168	.0181	.0196	.0211	.0227	.0243	.0260	.0278	.0296
14	.0078	.0086	.0095	.0104	.0113	.0123	.0134	.0145	.0157	.0169
15	.0037	.0041	.0046	.0051	.0057	.0062	.0069	.0075	.0083	.0090
16	.0016	.0019	.0021	.0024	.0026	.0030	.0033	.0037	.0041	.0045
17	.0007	.0008	.0009	.0010	.0012	.0013	.0015	.0017	.0019	.0021
18	.0003	.0003	.0004	.0004	.0005	.0006	.0006	.0007	.0008	.0009
19	.0001	.0001	.0001	.0002	.0002	.0002	.0003	.0003	.0003	.0004
20	.0000	.0000	.0001	.0001	.0001	.0001	.0001	.0001	.0001	.0002
21	.0000	.0000	.0000	.0000	.0000	.0000	.0000	.0000	.0001	.0001

λ

k	8.1	8.2	8.3	8.4	8.5	8.6	8.7	8.8	8.9	9.0
0	.0003	.0003	.0002	.0002	.0002	.0002	.0002	.0002	.0001	.0001
1	.0025	.0023	.0021	.0019	.0017	.0016	.0014	.0013	.0012	.0011
2	.0100	.0092	.0086	.0079	.0074	.0068	.0063	.0058	.0054	.0050
3	.0269	.0252	.0237	.0222	.0208	.0195	.0183	.0171	.0160	.0150
4	.0544	.0517	.0491	.0466	.0443	.0420	.0398	.0377	.0357	.0337
5	.0882	.0849	.0816	.0784	.0752	.0722	.0692	.0663	.0635	.0607
6	.1191	.1160	.1128	.1097	.1066	.1034	.1003	.0972	.0941	.0911
7	.1378	.1358	.1338	.1317	.1294	.1271	.1247	.1222	.1197	.1171
8	.1395	.1392	.1388	.1382	.1375	.1366	.1356	.1344	.1332	.1318
9	.1256	.1269	.1280	.1290	.1299	.1306	.1311	.1315	.1317	.1318
10	.1017	.1040	.1063	.1084	.1104	.1123	.1140	.1157	.1172	.1186
11	.0749	.0776	.0802	.0828	.0853	.0878	.0902	.0925	.0948	.0970
12	.0505	.0530	.0555	.0579	.0604	.0629	.0654	.0679	.0703	.0728
13	.0315	.0334	.0354	.0374	.0395	.0416	.0438	.0459	.0481	.0504
14	.0182	.0196	.0210	.0225	.0240	.0256	.0272	.0289	.0306	.0324
15	.0098	.0107	.0116	.0126	.0136	.0147	.0158	.0169	.0182	.0194
16	.0050	.0055	.0060	.0066	.0072	.0079	.0086	.0093	.0101	.0109
17	.0024	.0026	.0029	.0033	.0036	.0040	.0044	.0048	.0053	.0058
18	.0011	.0012	.0014	.0015	.0017	.0019	.0021	.0024	.0026	.0029
19	.0005	.0005	.0006	.0007	.0008	.0009	.0010	.0011	.0012	.0014
20	.0002	.0002	.0002	.0003	.0003	.0004	.0004	.0005	.0005	.0006
21	.0001	.0001	.0001	.0001	.0001	.0002	.0002	.0002	.0002	.0003
22	.0000	.0000	.0000	.0000	.0001	.0001	.0001	.0001	.0001	.0001

λ

k	9.1	9.2	9.3	9.4	9.5	9.6	9.7	9.8	9.9	10
0	.0001	.0001	.0001	.0001	.0001	.0001	.0001	.0001	.0001	.0000
1	.0010	.0009	.0009	.0008	.0007	.0007	.0006	.0005	.0005	.0005
2	.0046	.0043	.0040	.0037	.0034	.0031	.0029	.0027	.0025	.0023
3	.0140	.0131	.0123	.0115	.0107	.0100	.0093	.0087	.0081	.0076
4	.0319	.0302	.0285	.0269	.0254	.0240	.0226	.0213	.0201	.0189
5	.0581	.0555	.0530	.0506	.0483	.0460	.0439	.0418	.0398	.0378
6	.0881	.0851	.0822	.0793	.0764	.0736	.0709	.0682	.0656	.0631
7	.1145	.1118	.1091	.1064	.1037	.1010	.0982	.0955	.0928	.0901
8	.1302	.1286	.1269	.1251	.1232	.1212	.1191	.1170	.1148	.1126
9	.1317	.1315	.1311	.1306	.1300	.1293	.1284	.1274	.1263	.1251
10	.1198	.1210	.1219	.1228	.1235	.1241	.1245	.1249	.1250	.1251
11	.0991	.1012	.1031	.1049	.1067	.1083	.1098	.1112	.1125	.1137
12	.0752	.0776	.0799	.0822	.0844	.0866	.0888	.0908	.0928	.0948
13	.0526	.0549	.0572	.0594	.0617	.0640	.0662	.0685	.0707	.0729
14	.0342	.0361	.0380	.0399	.0419	.0439	.0459	.0479	.0500	.0521
15	.0208	.0221	.0235	.0250	.0265	.0281	.0297	.0313	.0330	.0347
16	.0118	.0127	.0137	.0147	.0157	.0168	.0180	.0192	.0204	.0217
17	.0063	.0069	.0075	.0081	.0088	.0095	.0103	.0111	.0119	.0128
18	.0032	.0035	.0039	.0042	.0046	.0051	.0055	.0060	.0065	.0071
19	.0015	.0017	.0019	.0021	.0023	.0026	.0028	.0031	.0034	.0037

					λ					
k	9.1	9.2	9.3	9.4	9.5	9.6	9.7	9.8	9.9	10
20	.0007	.0008	.0009	.0010	.0011	.0012	.0014	.0015	.0017	.0019
21	.0003	.0003	.0004	.0004	.0005	.0006	.0006	.0007	.0008	.0009
22	.0001	.0001	.0002	.0002	.0002	.0002	.0003	.0003	.0004	.0004
23	.0000	.0001	.0001	.0001	.0001	.0001	.0001	.0001	.0002	.0002
24	.0000	.0000	.0000	.0000	.0000	.0000	.0000	.0001	.0001	.0001

					λ					
k	11	12	13	14	15	16	17	18	19	20
0	.0000	.0000	.0000	.0000	.0000	.0000	.0000	.0000	.0000	.0000
1	.0002	.0001	.0000	.0000	.0000	.0000	.0000	.0000	.0000	.0000
2	.0010	.0004	.0002	.0001	.0000	.0000	.0000	.0000	.0000	.0000
3	.0037	.0018	.0008	.0004	.0002	.0001	.0000	.0000	.0000	.0000
4	.0102	.0053	.0027	.0013	.0006	.0003	.0001	.0001	.0000	.0000
5	.0224	.0127	.0070	.0037	.0019	.0010	.0005	.0002	.0001	.0001
6	.0411	.0255	.0152	.0087	.0048	.0026	.0014	.0007	.0004	.0002
7	.0646	.0437	.0281	.0174	.0104	.0060	.0034	.0018	.0010	.0005
8	.0888	.0655	.0457	.0304	.0194	.0120	.0072	.0042	.0024	.0013
9	.1085	.0874	.0661	.0473	.0324	.0213	.0135	.0083	.0050	.0029
10	.1194	.1048	.0859	.0663	.0486	.0341	.0230	.0150	.0095	.0058
11	.1194	.1144	.1015	.0844	.0663	.0496	.0355	.0245	.0164	.0106
12	.1094	.1144	.1099	.0984	.0829	.0661	.0504	.0368	.0259	.0176
13	.0926	.1056	.1099	.1060	.0956	.0814	.0658	.0509	.0378	.0271
14	.0728	.0905	.1021	.1060	.1024	.0930	.0800	.0655	.0514	.0387
15	.0534	.0724	.0885	.0989	.1024	.0992	.0906	.0786	.0650	.0516
16	.0367	.0543	.0719	.0866	.0960	.0992	.0963	.0884	.0772	.0646
17	.0237	.0383	.0550	.0713	.0847	.0934	.0963	.0936	.0863	.0760
18	.0145	.0256	.0397	.0554	.0706	.0830	.0909	.0936	.0911	.0844
19	.0084	.0161	.0272	.0409	.0557	.0699	.0814	.0887	.0911	.0888
20	.0046	.0097	.0177	.0286	.0418	.0559	.0692	.0798	.0866	.0888
21	.0024	.0055	.0109	.0191	.0299	.0426	.0560	.0684	.0783	.0846
22	.0012	.0030	.0065	.0121	.0204	.0310	.0433	.0560	.0676	.0769
23	.0006	.0016	.0037	.0074	.0133	.0216	.0320	.0438	.0559	.0669
24	.0003	.0008	.0020	.0043	.0083	.0144	.0226	.0328	.0442	.0557
25	.0001	.0004	.0010	.0024	.0050	.0092	.0154	.0237	.0336	.0446
26	.0000	.0002	.0005	.0013	.0029	.0057	.0101	.0164	.0246	.0343
27	.0000	.0001	.0002	.0007	.0016	.0034	.0063	.0109	.0173	.0254
28	.0000	.0000	.0001	.0003	.0009	.0019	.0038	.0070	.0117	.0181
29	.0000	.0000	.0001	.0002	.0004	.0011	.0023	.0044	.0077	.0125
30	.0000	.0000	.0000	.0001	.0002	.0006	.0013	.0026	.0049	.0083
31	.0000	.0000	.0000	.0000	.0001	.0003	.0007	.0015	.0030	.0054
32	.0000	.0000	.0000	.0000	.0001	.0001	.0004	.0009	.0018	.0034
33	.0000	.0000	.0000	.0000	.0000	.0001	.0002	.0005	.0010	.0020
34	.0000	.0000	.0000	.0000	.0000	.0000	.0001	.0002	.0006	.0012
35	.0000	.0000	.0000	.0000	.0000	.0000	.0000	.0001	.0003	.0007
36	.0000	.0000	.0000	.0000	.0000	.0000	.0000	.0001	.0002	.0004
37	.0000	.0000	.0000	.0000	.0000	.0000	.0000	.0000	.0001	.0002
38	.0000	.0000	.0000	.0000	.0000	.0000	.0000	.0000	.0000	.0001
39	.0000	.0000	.0000	.0000	.0000	.0000	.0000	.0000	.0000	.0001

APPENDIX 3: BUSY-PERIOD PROBABILITIES FOR WAITING-LINE SYSTEMS WITH POISSON ARRIVALS AND EXPONENTIAL SERVICE TIMES

✧ M ✧

RHO	1.00	2.00	3.00	4.00	5.00	6.00	7.00	8.00	9.00
0.10	0.1000	0.0048	0.0002						
0.20	0.2000	0.0182	0.0012						
0.30	0.3000	0.0391	0.0037	0.0003					
0.40	0.4000	0.0667	0.0082	0.0008					
0.50	0.5000	0.1000	0.0152	0.0018	0.0002				
0.60	0.6000	0.1385	0.0247	0.0035	0.0004				
0.70	0.7000	0.1815	0.0369	0.0060	0.0008				
0.80	0.8000	0.2286	0.0520	0.0096	0.0015	0.0002			
0.90	0.9000	0.2793	0.0700	0.0143	0.0024	0.0004			
1.00	1.0000	0.3333	0.0909	0.0204	0.0038	0.0006			
1.10		0.3903	0.1146	0.0279	0.0057	0.0010	0.0002		
1.20		0.4500	0.1412	0.0370	0.0082	0.0016	0.0003		
1.30		0.5121	0.1704	0.0478	0.0114	0.0023	0.0004		
1.40		0.5765	0.2024	0.0603	0.0153	0.0034	0.0006	0.0001	
1.50		0.6429	0.2368	0.0746	0.0201	0.0047	0.0010	0.0002	
1.60		0.7111	0.2738	0.0907	0.0259	0.0064	0.0014	0.0003	
1.70		0.7811	0.3131	0.1087	0.0326	0.0085	0.0020	0.0004	
1.80		0.8526	0.3547	0.1285	0.0405	0.0111	0.0027	0.0006	0.0001
1.90		0.9256	0.3985	0.1503	0.0495	0.0143	0.0036	0.0008	0.0002
2.00		1.0000	0.4444	0.1739	0.0597	0.0180	0.0048	0.0011	0.0002

RHO denotes the traffic intensity ratio; M denotes the number of service channels.

* M *

RHO	3.00	4.00	5.00	6.00	7.00	8.00	9.00	10.00	11.00	12.00
2.10	0.4923	0.1994	0.0712	0.0224	0.0062	0.0016	0.0003			
2.20	0.5422	0.2268	0.0839	0.0275	0.0080	0.0021	0.0005	0.0001		
2.30	0.5938	0.2560	0.0980	0.0333	0.0101	0.0027	0.0007	0.0001		
2.40	0.6472	0.2870	0.1135	0.0400	0.0126	0.0035	0.0009	0.0002		
2.50	0.7022	0.3199	0.1304	0.0474	0.0154	0.0045	0.0012	0.0003		
2.60	0.7589	0.3544	0.1487	0.0558	0.0188	0.0057	0.0016	0.0004		
2.70	0.8171	0.3907	0.1684	0.0652	0.0227	0.0071	0.0020	0.0005	0.0001	
2.80	0.8767	0.4287	0.1895	0.0755	0.0271	0.0088	0.0026	0.0007	0.0002	
2.90	0.9377	0.4682	0.2121	0.0868	0.0320	0.0107	0.0032	0.0009	0.0002	
3.00	1.0000	0.5094	0.2362	0.0991	0.0376	0.0129	0.0040	0.0012	0.0003	
3.10		0.5522	0.2616	0.1126	0.0439	0.0155	0.0050	0.0015	0.0004	
3.20		0.5964	0.2886	0.1271	0.0509	0.0185	0.0061	0.0019	0.0005	0.0001
3.30		0.6422	0.3169	0.1427	0.0585	0.0219	0.0074	0.0023	0.0007	0.0002
3.40		0.6893	0.3467	0.1595	0.0670	0.0256	0.0090	0.0029	0.0008	0.0002
3.50		0.7379	0.3778	0.1775	0.0762	0.0299	0.0107	0.0035	0.0011	0.0003
3.60		0.7878	0.4104	0.1966	0.0862	0.0346	0.0127	0.0043	0.0013	0.0004
3.70		0.8390	0.4443	0.2168	0.0971	0.0399	0.0150	0.0052	0.0017	0.0005
3.80		0.8914	0.4796	0.2383	0.1089	0.0457	0.0176	0.0062	0.0020	0.0006
3.90		0.9451	0.5162	0.2609	0.1215	0.0521	0.0205	0.0074	0.0025	0.0008
4.00		1.0000	0.5541	0.2848	0.1351	0.0590	0.0238	0.0088	0.0030	0.0010

* M *

RHO	5.00	6.00	7.00	8.00	9.00	10.00	11.00	12.00	13.00	14.00
4.10	0.5933	0.3098	0.1496	0.0667	0.0274	0.0104	0.0036	0.0012	0.0004	0.0001
4.20	0.6338	0.3360	0.1651	0.0749	0.0314	0.0122	0.0044	0.0015	0.0005	0.0001
4.30	0.6755	0.3634	0.1815	0.0839	0.0358	0.0142	0.0052	0.0018	0.0006	0.0002
4.40	0.7184	0.3919	0.1988	0.0935	0.0407	0.0164	0.0061	0.0021	0.0007	0.0002
4.50	0.7625	0.4217	0.2172	0.1039	0.0460	0.0189	0.0072	0.0026	0.0008	0.0003
4.60	0.8078	0.4525	0.2366	0.1150	0.0519	0.0217	0.0084	0.0031	0.0010	0.0003
4.70	0.8542	0.4846	0.2570	0.1269	0.0582	0.0248	0.0098	0.0036	0.0012	0.0004
4.80	0.9017	0.5178	0.2783	0.1395	0.0651	0.0282	0.0114	0.0043	0.0015	0.0005
4.90	0.9503	0.5521	0.3007	0.1530	0.0725	0.0320	0.0131	0.0050	0.0018	0.0006
5.00	1.0000	0.5875	0.3241	0.1673	0.0805	0.0361	0.0151	0.0059	0.0021	0.0007
5.10		0.6240	0.3486	0.1824	0.0891	0.0406	0.0173	0.0069	0.0025	0.0009
5.20		0.6617	0.3740	0.1983	0.0983	0.0455	0.0197	0.0079	0.0030	0.0011
5.30		0.7004	0.4005	0.2151	0.1081	0.0508	0.0223	0.0092	0.0035	0.0013
5.40		0.7401	0.4280	0.2327	0.1186	0.0566	0.0252	0.0105	0.0041	0.0015
5.50		0.7809	0.4564	0.2512	0.1298	0.0628	0.0284	0.0121	0.0048	0.0018
5.60		0.8227	0.4859	0.2706	0.1416	0.0695	0.0319	0.0138	0.0056	0.0021
5.70		0.8656	0.5164	0.2909	0.1541	0.0766	0.0357	0.0156	0.0064	0.0025
5.80		0.9094	0.5479	0.3120	0.1673	0.0843	0.0399	0.0177	0.0074	0.0029
5.90		0.9542	0.5804	0.3340	0.1813	0.0925	0.0444	0.0200	0.0084	0.0034
6.00		1.0000	0.6138	0.3570	0.1960	0.1013	0.0492	0.0225	0.0096	0.0039

* M *

RHO	7.00	8.00	9.00	10.00	11.00	12.00	13.00	14.00	15.00	16.00
6.10	0.6482	0.3808	0.2114	0.1106	0.0545	0.0252	0.0110	0.0045	0.0017	0.0006
6.20	0.6836	0.4055	0.2276	0.1205	0.0601	0.0282	0.0124	0.0052	0.0020	0.0008
6.30	0.7200	0.4311	0.2445	0.1310	0.0661	0.0314	0.0141	0.0059	0.0024	0.0009
6.40	0.7572	0.4576	0.2622	0.1420	0.0726	0.0349	0.0159	0.0068	0.0027	0.0010
6.50	0.7954	0.4850	0.2807	0.1537	0.0795	0.0388	0.0178	0.0077	0.0032	0.0012
6.60	0.8345	0.5133	0.3000	0.1660	0.0868	0.0429	0.0200	0.0088	0.0036	0.0014
6.70	0.8746	0.5425	0.3200	0.1790	0.0947	0.0473	0.0223	0.0099	0.0042	0.0017
6.80	0.9155	0.5726	0.3409	0.1926	0.1030	0.0521	0.0249	0.0112	0.0048	0.0019
6.90	0.9573	0.6035	0.3625	0.2068	0.1118	0.0572	0.0276	0.0126	0.0055	0.0022
7.00	1.0000	0.6353	0.3849	0.2217	0.1211	0.0626	0.0306	0.0142	0.0062	0.0026
7.10		0.6680	0.4082	0.2373	0.1310	0.0685	0.0339	0.0159	0.0070	0.0030
7.20		0.7015	0.4322	0.2536	0.1413	0.0747	0.0374	0.0177	0.0079	0.0034
7.30		0.7359	0.4571	0.2706	0.1523	0.0813	0.0411	0.0197	0.0090	0.0039
7.40		0.7712	0.4827	0.2882	0.1637	0.0883	0.0452	0.0219	0.0101	0.0044
7.50		0.8072	0.5091	0.3066	0.1758	0.0958	0.0495	0.0243	0.0113	0.0050
7.60		0.8442	0.5364	0.3257	0.1884	0.1037	0.0542	0.0268	0.0126	0.0056
7.70		0.8819	0.5644	0.3455	0.2017	0.1120	0.0591	0.0296	0.0141	0.0064
7.80		0.9205	0.5933	0.3660	0.2155	0.1208	0.0644	0.0326	0.0157	0.0072
7.90		0.9598	0.6229	0.3872	0.2299	0.1301	0.0700	0.0358	0.0174	0.0081
8.00		1.0000	0.6533	0.4092	0.2450	0.1398	0.0760	0.0393	0.0193	0.0090

* M *

RHO	9.00	10.00	11.00	12.00	13.00	14.00	15.00	16.00	17.00	18.00
8.10	0.6845	0.4319	0.2606	0.1501	0.0823	0.0430	0.0213	0.0101	0.0045	0.0019
8.20	0.7165	0.4553	0.2769	0.1608	0.0890	0.0469	0.0235	0.0112	0.0051	0.0022
8.30	0.7493	0.4794	0.2938	0.1721	0.0961	0.0512	0.0259	0.0125	0.0057	0.0025
8.40	0.7828	0.5043	0.3114	0.1839	0.1036	0.0557	0.0285	0.0139	0.0064	0.0029
8.50	0.8171	0.5299	0.3296	0.1962	0.1115	0.0605	0.0312	0.0154	0.0072	0.0032
8.60	0.8522	0.5562	0.3485	0.2091	0.1199	0.0656	0.0342	0.0170	0.0081	0.0036
8.70	0.8880	0.5832	0.3680	0.2225	0.1286	0.0710	0.0374	0.0188	0.0090	0.0041
8.80	0.9246	0.6110	0.3881	0.2364	0.1378	0.0767	0.0408	0.0207	0.0100	0.0046
8.90	0.9619	0.6395	0.4090	0.2509	0.1474	0.0828	0.0444	0.0227	0.0111	0.0052
9.00	1.0000	0.6687	0.4305	0.2660	0.1575	0.0892	0.0482	0.0249	0.0123	0.0058
9.10		0.6987	0.4526	0.2817	0.1681	0.0959	0.0523	0.0273	0.0136	0.0065
9.20		0.7293	0.4754	0.2979	0.1791	0.1030	0.0567	0.0298	0.0150	0.0072
9.30		0.7607	0.4989	0.3148	0.1906	0.1105	0.0613	0.0325	0.0165	0.0080
9.40		0.7928	0.5231	0.3322	0.2026	0.1184	0.0662	0.0354	0.0181	0.0089
9.50		0.8256	0.5479	0.3502	0.2151	0.1267	0.0714	0.0386	0.0199	0.0098
9.60		0.8591	0.5734	0.3688	0.2281	0.1353	0.0769	0.0419	0.0218	0.0109
9.70		0.8933	0.5996	0.3881	0.2416	0.1444	0.0827	0.0454	0.0238	0.0120
9.80		0.9282	0.6264	0.4079	0.2556	0.1539	0.0888	0.0491	0.0260	0.0132
9.90		0.9637	0.6539	0.4283	0.2702	0.1638	0.0953	0.0531	0.0284	0.0145
10.00		1.0000	0.6821	0.4494	0.2853	0.1741	0.1020	0.0573	0.0309	0.0159

APPENDIX 4: EXPONENTIAL FUNCTIONS*

x	e^x	$\mathrm{Log}_{10}\left(e^x\right)$	e^{-x}	x	e^x	$\mathrm{Log}_{10}\left(e^x\right)$	e^{-x}
0.00	1.0000	0.00000	1.000000	**0.50**	1.6487	0.21715	0.606531
0.01	1.0101	.00434	0.990050	0.51	1.6653	.22149	.600496
0.02	1.0202	.00869	.980199	0.52	1.6820	.22583	.594521
0.03	1.0305	.01303	.970446	0.53	1.6989	.23018	.588605
0.04	1.0408	.01737	.960789	0.54	1.7160	.23452	.582748
0.05	1.0513	0.02171	0.951229	**0.55**	1.7333	0.23886	0.576950
0.06	1.0618	.02606	.941765	0.56	1.7507	.24320	.571209
0.07	1.0725	.03040	.932394	0.57	1.7683	.24755	.565525
0.08	1.0833	.03474	.923116	0.58	1.7860	.25189	.559898
0.09	1.0942	.03909	.913931	0.59	1.8040	.25623	.554327
0.10	1.1052	0.04343	0.904837	**0.60**	1.8221	0.26058	0.548812
0.11	1.1163	.04777	.895834	0.61	1.8404	.26492	.543351
0.12	1.1275	.05212	.886920	0.62	1.8589	.26926	.537944
0.13	1.1388	.05646	.878095	0.63	1.8776	.27361	.532592
0.14	1.1503	.06080	.869358	0.64	1.8965	.27795	.527292
0.15	1.1618	0.06514	0.860708	**0.65**	1.9155	0.28229	0.522046
0.16	1.1735	.06949	.852144	0.66	1.9348	.28663	.516851
0.17	1.1853	.07383	.843665	0.67	1.9542	.29098	.511709
0.18	1.1972	.07817	.835270	0.68	1.9739	.29532	.506617
0.19	1.2092	.08252	.826959	0.69	1.9937	.29966	.501576
0.20	1.2214	0.08686	0.818731	**0.70**	2.0138	0.30401	0.496585
0.21	1.2337	.09120	.810584	0.71	2.0340	.30835	.491644
0.22	1.2461	.09554	.802519	0.72	2.0544	.31269	.486752
0.23	1.2586	.09989	.794534	0.73	2.0751	.31703	.481909
0.24	1.2712	.10423	.786628	0.74	2.0959	.32138	.477114
0.25	1.2840	0.10857	0.778801	**0.75**	2.1170	0.32572	0.472367
0.26	1.2969	.11292	.771052	0.76	2.1383	.33006	.467666
0.27	1.3100	.11726	.763379	0.77	2.1598	.33441	.463013
0.28	1.3231	.12160	.755784	0.78	2.1815	.33875	.458406
0.29	1.3364	.12595	.748264	0.79	2.2034	.34309	.453845
0.30	1.3499	0.13029	0.740818	**0.80**	2.2255	0.34744	0.449329
0.31	1.3634	.13463	.733447	0.81	2.2479	.35178	.444858
0.32	1.3771	.13897	.726149	0.82	2.2705	.35612	.440432
0.33	1.3910	.14332	.718924	0.83	2.2933	.36046	.436049
0.34	1.4049	.14766	.711770	0.84	2.3164	.36481	.431711
0.35	1.4191	0.15200	0.704688	**0.85**	2.3396	0.36915	0.427415
0.36	1.4333	.15635	.697676	0.86	2.3632	.37349	.423162
0.37	1.4477	.16069	.690734	0.87	2.3869	.37784	.418952
0.38	1.4623	.16503	.683861	0.88	2.4109	.38218	.414783
0.39	1.4770	.16937	.677057	0.89	2.4351	.38652	.410656
0.40	1.4918	0.17372	0.670320	**0.90**	2.4596	0.39087	0.406570
0.41	1.5068	.17806	.663650	0.91	2.4843	.39521	.402524
0.42	1.5220	.18240	.657047	0.92	2.5093	.39955	.398519
0.43	1.5373	.18675	.650509	0.93	2.5345	.40389	.394554
0.44	1.5527	.19109	.644036	0.94	2.5600	.40824	.390628
0.45	1.5683	0.19543	0.637628	**0.95**	2.5857	0.41258	0.386741
0.46	1.5841	.19978	.631284	0.96	2.6117	.41692	.382893
0.47	1.6000	.20412	.625002	0.97	2.6379	.42127	.379083
0.48	1.6161	.20846	.618783	0.98	2.6645	.42561	.375311
0.49	1.6323	.21280	.612626	0.99	2.6912	.42995	.371577
0.50	1.6487	0.21715	0.606531	**1.00**	2.7183	0.43429	0.367879

*Reproduced by permission of the publisher from *CRC Standard Mathematical Tables*, 23rd ed., 1975, Samuel Selby (ed.). Cleveland: CRC Press, Inc.

x	e^x	$\text{Log}_{10}\left(e^x\right)$	e^{-x}	x	e^x	$\text{Log}_{10}\left(e^x\right)$	e^{-x}
1.00	2.7183	0.43429	0.367879	1.50	4.4817	0.65144	0.223130
1.01	2.7456	.43864	.364219	1.51	4.5267	.65578	.220910
1.02	2.7732	.44298	.360595	1.52	4.5722	.66013	.218712
1.03	2.8011	.44732	.357007	1.53	4.6182	.66447	.216536
1.04	2.8292	.45167	.353455	1.54	4.6646	.66881	.214381
1.05	2.8577	0.45601	0.349938	1.55	4.7115	0.67316	0.212248
1.06	2.8864	.46035	.346456	1.56	4.7588	.67750	.210136
1.07	2.9154	.46470	.343009	1.57	4.8066	.68184	.208045
1.08	2.9447	.46904	.339596	1.58	4.8550	.68619	.205975
1.09	2.9743	.47338	.336216	1.59	4.9037	.69053	.203926
1.10	3.0042	0.47772	0.332871	1.60	4.9530	0.69487	0.201897
1.11	3.0344	.48207	.329559	1.61	5.0028	.69921	.199888
1.12	3.0649	.48641	.326280	1.62	5.0531	.70356	.197899
1.13	3.0957	.49075	323033	1.63	5.1039	.70790	.195930
1.14	3.1268	.49510	.319819	1.64	5.1552	.71224	.193980
1.15	3.1582	0.49944	0.316637	1.65	5.2070	0.71659	0.192050
1.16	3.1899	.50378	.313486	1.66	5.2593	.72093	.190139
1.17	3.2220	.50812	310367	1.67	5.3122	.72527	.188247
1.18	3.2544	.51247	307279	1.68	5.3656	.72961	.186374
1.19	3.2871	.51681	.304221	1.69	5.4195	.73396	.184520
1.20	3.3201	0.52115	0.301194	1.70	5.4739	0.73830	0.182684
1.21	3.3535	.52550	.298197	1.71	5.5290	.74264	.180866
1.22	3.3872	.52984	.295230	1.72	5.5845	.74699	.179066
1.23	3.4212	.53418	.292293	1.73	5.6407	.75133	.177284
1.24	3.4556	.53853	.289384	1.74	5.6973	75567	175520
1.25	3.4903	0.54287	0.286505	1.75	5.7546	0.76002	0.173774
1.26	3.5254	.54721	.283654	1.76	5.8124	.76436	.172045
1.27	3.5609	.55155	.280832	1.77	5.8709	.76870	170333
1.28	3.5966	.55590	.278037	1.78	5.9299	.77304	168638
1.29	3.6328	.55024	.275271	1.79	5.9895	.77739	.166960
1.30	3.6693	0.56458	0.272532	1.80	6.0496	0.78173	0.165299
1.31	3.7062	.56893	.269820	1.81	6.1104	.78607	.163654
1.32	3.7434	.57327	.267135	1.82	6.1719	.79042	.162026
1.33	3.7810	.57761	.264477	1.83	6.2339	.79476	.160414
1.34	3.8190	.58195	.261846	1.84	6.2965	79910	.158817
1.35	3.8574	0.58630	0.259240	1.85	6.3598	0.80344	0.157237
1.36	3.8962	.59064	.256661	1.86	6.4237	.80779	.155673
1.37	3.9354	.59498	.254107	1.87	6.4383	.81213	.154124
1.38	3.9749	.59933	.251579	1.88	6.5535	.81647	.152590
1.39	4.0149	.60367	.249075	1.89	6.6194	.82082	.151072
1.40	4.0552	0.60801	0.246597	1.90	6.6859	0.82516	0.149569
1.41	4.0960	.61236	.244143	1.91	6.7531	.82950	.148080
1.42	4.1371	.61670	.241714	1.92	6.8210	.83385	.146607
1.43	4.1787	.62104	.239309	1.93	6.8895	.83819	.145148
1.44	4.2207	.62538	.236928	1.94	6.9588	.84253	.143704
1.45	4.2631	0.62973	0.234570	1.95	7.0287	0.84687	0.142274
1.46	4.3060	.63407	.232236	1.96	7.0993	.85122	.140858
1.47	4.3492	.63841	.229925	1.97	7.1707	.85556	.139457
1.48	4.3929	.64276	.227638	1.98	7.2427	.85990	.138069
1.49	4.4371	.64710	.225373	1.99	7.3155	.86425	.136695
1.50	4.4817	0.65144	0.223130	2.00	7.3891	0.86859	0.135335

x	e^x	$Log_{10}\left(e^x\right)$	e^{-x}	x	e^x	$Log_{10}\left(e^x\right)$	e^{-x}
2.00	7.3891	0.86859	0.135335	**2.50**	12.182	1.08574	0.082085
2.01	7.4633	.87293	.133989	2.51	12.305	1.09008	.081268
2.02	7.5383	.87727	.132655	2.52	12.429	1.09442	.080460
2.03	7.6141	.88162	.131336	2.53	12.554	1.09877	.079659
2.04	7.6906	.88596	.130029	2.54	12.680	1.10311	.078866
2.05	7.7679	0.89030	0.128735	**2.55**	12.807	1.10745	0.078082
2.06	7.8460	.89465	.127454	2.56	12.936	1.11179	.077305
2.07	7.9248	.89899	.126186	2.57	13.066	1.11614	.076536
2.08	8.0045	.90333	.124930	2.58	13.197	1.12048	.075774
2.09	8.0849	.90768	.123687	2.59	13.330	1.12482	.075020
2.10	8.1662	0.91202	0.122456	**2.60**	13.464	1.12917	0.074274
2.11	8.2482	.91636	.121238	2.61	13.599	1.13351	.073535
2.12	8.3311	.92070	.120032	2.62	13.736	1.13785	.072803
2.13	8.4149	.92505	.118837	2.63	13.874	1.14219	.072078
2.14	8.4994	.92939	.117655	2.64	14.013	1.14654	.071361
2.15	8.5849	0.93373	0.116484	**2.65**	14.154	1.15088	0.070651
2.16	8.6711	.93808	.115325	2.66	14.296	1.15522	.069948
2.17	8.7583	.94242	.114178	2.67	14.440	1.15957	.069252
2.18	8.8463	.94676	.113042	2.68	14.585	1.16391	.068563
2.19	8.9352	.95110	.111917	2.69	14.732	1.16825	.067881
2.20	9.0250	0.95545	0.110803	**2.70**	14.880	1.17260	0.067206
2.21	9.1157	.95979	.109701	2.71	15.029	1.17694	.066537
2.22	9.2073	.96413	.108609	2.72	15.180	1.18128	.065875
2.23	9.2999	.96848	.107528	2.73	15.333	1.18562	.065219
2.24	9.3933	.97282	.106459	2.74	15.487	1.18997	.064570
2.25	9.4877	0.97716	0.105399	**2.75**	15.643	1.19431	0.063928
2.26	9.5831	.98151	.104350	2.76	15.800	1.19865	.063292
2.27	9.6794	.98585	.103312	2.77	15.959	1.20300	.062662
2.28	9.7767	.99019	.102284	2.78	16.119	1.20734	.062039
2.29	9.8749	.99453	.101266	2.79	16.281	1.21168	.061421
2.30	9.9742	0.99888	0.100259	**2.80**	16.445	1.21602	0.060810
2.31	10.074	1.00322	.099261	2.81	16.610	1.22037	.060205
2.32	10.176	1.00756	.098274	2.82	16.777	1.22471	.059606
2.33	10.278	1.01191	.097296	2.83	16.945	1.22905	.059013
2.34	10.381	1.01625	.096328	2.84	17.116	1.23340	.058426
2.35	10.486	1.02059	0.095369	**2.85**	17.288	1.23774	0.057844
2.36	10.591	1.02493	.094420	2.86	17.462	1.24208	.057269
2.37	10.697	1.02928	.093481	2.87	17.637	1.24643	.056699
2.38	10.805	1.03362	.092551	2.88	17.814	1.25077	.056135
2.39	10.913	1.03796	.091630	2.89	17.993	1.25511	.055576
2.40	11.023	1.04231	0.090718	**2.90**	18.174	1.25945	0.055023
2.41	11.134	1.04665	.089815	2.91	18.357	1.26380	.054476
2.42	11.246	1.05099	.088922	2.92	18.541	1.26814	.053934
2.43	11.359	1.05534	.088037	2.93	18.728	1.27248	.053397
2.44	11.473	1.05968	.087161	2.94	18.916	1.27683	.052866
2.45	11.588	1.06402	0.086294	**2.95**	19.106	1.28117	0.052340
2.46	11.705	1.06836	.085435	2.96	19.298	1.28551	.051819
2.47	11.822	1.07271	.084585	2.97	19.492	1.28985	.051303
2.48	11.941	1.07705	.083743	2.98	19.688	1.29420	.050793
2.49	12.061	1.08139	.082910	2.99	19.886	1.29854	.050287
2.50	12.182	1.08574	0.082085	**3.00**	20.086	1.30288	0.049787

x	e^x	$\text{Log}_{10}\left(e^x\right)$	e^{-x}	x	e^x	$\text{Log}_{10}\left(e^x\right)$	e^{-x}
3.00	20.086	1.30288	0.049787	**3.50**	33.115	1.52003	0.030197
3.01	20.287	1.30723	.049292	3.51	33.448	1.52437	.029897
3.02	20.491	1.31157	.048801	3.52	33.784	1.52872	.029599
3.03	20.697	1.31591	.048316	3.53	34.124	1.53306	.029305
3.04	20.905	1.32026	.047835	3.54	34.467	1.53740	.029013
3.05	21.115	1.32460	0.047359	**3.55**	34.813	1.54175	0.028725
3.06	21.328	1.32894	.046888	3.56	35.163	1.54609	.028439
3.07	21.542	1.33328	.046421	3.57	35.517	1.55043	.028156
3.08	21.758	1.33763	.045959	3.58	35.874	1.55477	.027876
3.09	21.977	1.34197	.045502	3.59	36.234	1.55912	.027598
3.10	22.198	1.34631	0.045049	**3.60**	36.598	1.56346	0.027324
3.11	22.421	1.35066	.044601	3.61	36.966	1.56780	.027052
3.12	22.646	1.35500	.044157	3.62	37.338	1.57215	.026783
3.13	22.874	1.35934	.043718	3.63	37.713	1.57649	.026516
3.14	23.104	1.36368	.043283	3.64	38.092	1.58083	.026252
3.15	23.336	1.36803	0.042852	**3.65**	38.475	1.58517	0.025991
3.16	23.571	1.37237	.042426	3.66	38.861	1.58952	.025733
3.17	23.807	1.37671	.042004	3.67	39.252	1.59386	.025476
3.18	24.047	1.38106	.041586	3.68	39.646	1.59820	.025223
3.19	24.288	1.38540	.041172	3.69	40.045	1.60255	.024972
3.20	24.533	1.38974	0.040762	**3.70**	40.447	1.60689	0.024724
3.21	24.779	1.39409	.040357	3.71	40.854	1.61123	.024478
3.22	25.028	1.39843	.039955	3.72	41.264	1.61558	.024234
3.23	25.280	1.40277	.039557	3.73	41.679	1.61992	.023993
3.24	25.534	1.40711	.039164	3.74	42.098	1.62426	.023754
3.25	25.790	1.41146	0.038774	**3.75**	42.521	1.62860	0.023518
3.26	26.050	1.41580	.038388	3.76	42.948	1.63295	.023284
3.27	26.311	1.42014	.038006	3.77	43.380	1.63729	.023052
3.28	26.576	1.42449	.037628	3.78	43.816	1.64163	.022823
3.29	26.843	1.42883	.037254	3.79	44.256	1.64598	.022596
3.30	27.113	1.43317	0.036883	**3.80**	44.701	1.65032	0.022371
3.31	27.385	1.43751	.036516	3.81	45.150	1.65466	.022148
3.32	27.660	1.44186	.036153	3.82	45.604	1.65900	.021928
3.33	27.938	1.44620	.035793	3.83	46.063	1.66335	.021710
3.34	28.219	1.45054	.035437	3.84	46.525	1.66769	.021494
3.35	28.503	1.45489	0.035084	**3.85**	46.993	1.67203	0.021280
3.36	28.789	1.45923	.034735	3.86	47.465	1.67638	.021068
3.37	29.079	1.46357	.034390	3.87	47.942	1.68072	.020858
3.38	29.371	1.46792	.034047	3.88	48.424	1.68506	.020651
3.39	29.666	1.47226	.033709	3.89	48.911	1.68941	.020445
3.40	29.964	1.47660	0.033373	**3.90**	49.402	1.69375	0.020242
3.41	30.265	1.48094	.033041	3.91	49.899	1.69809	.020041
3.42	30.569	1.48529	.032712	3.92	50.400	1.70243	.019841
3.43	30.877	1.48963	.032387	3.93	50.907	1.70678	.019644
3.44	31.187	1.49397	.032065	3.94	51.419	1.71112	.019448
3.45	31.500	1.49832	0.031746	**3.95**	51.935	1.71546	0.019255
3.46	31.817	1.50266	.031430	3.96	52.457	1.71981	.019063
3.47	32.137	1.50700	.031117	3.97	52.985	1.72415	.018873
3.48	32.460	1.51134	.030807	3.98	53.517	1.72849	.018686
3.49	32.786	1.51569	.030501	3.99	54.055	1.73283	.018500
3.50	33.115	1.52003	0.030197	**4.00**	54.598	1.73718	0.018316

x	e^x	$\mathrm{Log}_{10}\left(e^x\right)$	e^{-x}	x	e^x	$\mathrm{Log}_{10}\left(e^x\right)$	e^{-x}
4.00	54.598	1.73718	0.018316	**4.50**	90.017	1.95433	0.011109
4.01	55.147	1.74152	.018133	4.51	90.922	1.95867	.010998
4.02	55.701	1.74586	.017953	4.52	91.836	1.96301	.010889
4.03	56.261	1.75021	.017774	4.53	92.759	1.96735	.010781
4.04	56.826	1.75455	.017597	4.54	93.691	1.97170	.010673
4.05	57.397	1.75889	0.017422	**4.55**	94.632	1.97604	0.010567
4.06	57.974	1.76324	.017249	4.56	95.583	1.98038	.010462
4.07	58.557	1.76758	.017077	4.57	96.544	1.98473	.010358
4.08	59.145	1.77192	.016907	4.58	97.514	1.98907	.010255
4.09	59.740	1.77626	.016739	4.59	98.494	1.99341	.010153
4.10	60.340	1.78061	0.016573	**4.60**	99.484	1.99775	0.010052
4.11	60.947	1.78495	.016408	4.61	100.48	2.00210	.009952
4.12	61.559	1.78929	.016245	4.62	101.49	2.00644	.009853
4.13	62.178	1.79364	.016083	4.63	102.51	2.01078	.009755
4.14	62.803	1.79798	.015923	4.64	103.54	2.01513	.009658
4.15	63.434	1.80232	0.015764	**4.65**	104.58	2.01947	0.009562
4.16	64.072	1.80667	.015608	4.66	105.64	2.02381	.009466
4.17	64.715	1.81101	.015452	4.67	106.70	2.02816	.009372
4.18	65.366	1.81535	.015299	4.68	107.77	2.03250	.009279
4.19	66.023	1.81969	.015146	4.69	108.85	2.03684	.009187
4.20	66.686	1.82404	0.014996	**4.70**	109.95	2.04118	0.009095
4.21	67.357	1.82838	.014846	4.71	111.05	2.04553	.009005
4.22	68.033	1.83272	.014699	4.72	112.17	2.04987	.008915
4.23	68.717	1.83707	.014552	4.73	113.30	2.05421	.008826
4.24	69.408	1.84141	.014408	4.74	114.43	2.05856	.008739
4.25	70.105	1.84575	0.014264	**4.75**	115.58	2.06290	0.008652
4.26	70.810	1.85009	.014122	4.76	116.75	2.06724	.008566
4.27	71.522	1.85444	.013982	4.77	117.92	2.07158	.008480
4.28	72.240	1.85878	.013843	4.78	119.10	2.07593	.008396
4.29	72.966	1.86312	.013705	4.79	120.30	2.08027	.008312
4.30	73.700	1.86747	0.013569	**4.80**	121.51	2.08461	0.008230
4.31	74.440	1.87181	.013434	4.81	122.73	2.08896	.008148
4.32	75.189	1.87615	.013300	4.82	123.97	2.09330	.008067
4.33	75.944	1.88050	.013168	4.83	125.21	2.09764	.007987
4.34	76.708	1.88484	.013037	4.84	126.47	2.10199	.007907
4.35	77.478	1.88918	0.012907	**4.85**	127.74	2.10633	0.007828
4.36	78.257	1.89352	.012778	4.86	129.02	2.11067	.007750
4.37	79.044	1.89787	.012651	4.87	130.32	2.11501	.007673
4.38	79.838	1.90221	.012525	4.88	131.63	2.11936	.007597
4.39	80.640	1.90655	.012401	4.89	132.95	2.12370	.007521
4.40	81.451	1.91090	0.012277	**4.90**	134.29	2.12804	0.007447
4.41	82.269	1.91524	.012155	4.91	135.64	2.13239	.007372
4.42	83.096	1.91958	.012034	4.92	137.00	2.13673	.007299
4.43	83.931	1.92392	.011914	4.93	138.38	2.14107	.007227
4.44	84.775	1.92827	.011796	4.94	139.77	2.14541	.007155
4.45	85.627	1.93261	0.011679	**4.95**	141.17	2.14976	0.007083
4.46	86.488	1.93695	.011562	4.96	142.59	2.15410	.007013
4.47	87.357	1.94130	.011447	4.97	144.03	2.15844	.006943
4.48	88.235	1.94564	.011333	4.98	145.47	2.16279	.006874
4.49	89.121	1.94998	.011221	4.99	146.94	2.16713	.006806
4.50	90.017	1.95433	0.011109	**5.00**	148.41	2.17147	0.006738

x	e^x	$Log_{10}\left(e^x\right)$	e^{-x}	x	e^x	$Log_{10}\left(e^x\right)$	e^{-x}
5.00	148.41	2.17147	0.006738	**5.50**	244.69	2.38862	0.0040868
5.01	149.90	2.17582	.006671	5.55	257.24	2.41033	.0038875
5.02	151.41	2.18016	.006605	5.60	270.43	2.43205	.0036979
5.03	152.93	2.18450	.006539	5.65	284.29	2.45376	.0035175
5.04	154.47	2.18884	.006474	5.70	298.87	2.47548	.0033460
5.05	156.02	2.19319	0.006409	**5.75**	314.19	2.49719	0.0031828
5.06	157.59	2.19753	.006346	5.80	330.30	2.51891	.0030276
5.07	159.17	2.20187	.006282	5.85	347.23	2.54062	.0028799
5.08	160.77	2.20622	.006220	5.90	365.04	2.56234	.0027394
5.09	162.39	2.21056	.006158	5.95	383.75	2.58405	.0026058
5.10	164.02	2.21490	0.006097	**6.00**	403.43	2.60577	0.0024788
5.11	165.67	2.21924	.006036	6.05	424.11	2.62748	.0023579
5.12	167.34	2.22359	.005976	6.10	445.86	2.64920	.0022429
5.13	169.02	2.22793	.005917	6.15	468.72	2.67091	.0021335
5.14	170.72	2.23227	.005858	6.20	492.75	2.69263	.0020294
5.15	172.43	2.23662	0.005799	**6.25**	518.01	2.71434	0.0019305
5.16	174.16	2.24096	.005742	6.30	544.57	2.73606	.0018363
5.17	175.91	2.24530	.005685	6.35	572.49	2.75777	.0017467
5.18	177.68	2.24965	.005628	6.40	601.85	2.77948	.0016616
5.19	179.47	2.25399	.005572	6.45	632.70	2.80120	.0015805
5.20	181.27	2.25833	0.005517	**6.50**	665.14	2.82291	0.0015034
5.21	183.09	2.26267	.005462	6.55	699.24	2.84463	.0014301
5.22	184.93	2.26702	.005407	6.60	735.10	2.86634	.0013604
5.23	186.79	2.27136	.005354	6.65	772.78	2.88806	.0012940
5.24	188.67	2.27570	.005300	6.70	812.41	2.90977	.0012309
5.25	190.57	2.28005	0.005248	**6.75**	854.06	2.93149	0.0011709
5.26	192.48	2.28439	.005195	6.80	897.85	2.95320	.0011138
5.27	194.42	2.28873	.005144	6.85	943.88	2.97492	.0010595
5.28	196.37	2.29307	.005092	6.90	992.27	2.99663	.0010078
5.29	198.34	2.29742	.005042	6.95	1043.1	3.01835	.0009586
5.30	200.34	2.30176	0.004992	**7.00**	1096.6	3.04006	0.0009119
5.31	202.35	2.30610	.004942	7.05	1152.9	3.06178	.0008674
5.32	204.38	2.31045	.004893	7.10	1212.0	3.08349	.0008251
5.33	206.44	2.31479	.004844	7.15	1274.1	3.10521	.0007849
5.34	208.51	2.31913	.004796	7.20	1339.4	3.12692	.0007466
5.35	210.61	2.32348	0.004748	**7.25**	1408.1	3.14863	0.0007102
5.36	212.72	2.32782	.004701	7.30	1480.3	3.17035	.0006755
5.37	214.86	2.33216	.004654	7.35	1556.2	3.19206	.0006426
5.38	217.02	2.33650	.004608	7.40	1636.0	3.21378	.0006113
5.39	219.20	2.34085	.004562	7.45	1719.9	3.23549	.0005814
5.40	221.41	2.34519	0.004517	**7.50**	1808.0	3.25721	0.0005531
5.41	223.63	2.34953	.004472	7.55	1900.7	3.27892	.0005261
5.42	225.88	2.35388	.004427	7.60	1998.2	3.30064	.0005005
5.43	228.15	2.35822	.004383	7.65	2100.6	3.32235	.0004760
5.44	230.44	2.36256	.004339	7.70	2208.3	3.34407	.0004528
5.45	232.76	2.36690	0.004296	**7.75**	2321.6	3.36578	0.0004307
5.46	235.10	2.37125	.004254	7.80	2440.6	3.38750	.0004097
5.47	237.46	2.37559	.004211	7.85	2565.7	3.40921	.0003898
5.48	239.85	2.37993	.004169	7.90	2697.3	3.43093	.0003707
5.49	242.26	2.38428	.004128	7.95	2835.6	3.45264	.0003527
5.50	244.69	2.38862	0.004087	**8.00**	2981.0	3.47436	0.0003355

x	e^x	$Log_{10}\left(e^x\right)$	e^{-x}	x	e^x	$Log_{10}\left(e^x\right)$	e^{-x}
8.00	2981.0	3.47436	0.0003355	**9.00**	8103.1	3.90865	0.0001234
8.05	3133.8	3.49607	.0003191	9.05	8518.5	3.93037	.0001174
8.10	3294.5	3.51779	.0003035	9.10	8955.3	3.95208	.0001117
8.15	3463.4	3.53950	.0002887	9.15	9414.4	3.97379	.0001062
8.20	3641.0	3.56121	.0002747	9.20	9897.1	3.99551	.0001010
8.25	3827.6	3.58293	0.0002613	**9.25**	10405	4.01722	0.0000961
8.30	4023.9	3.60464	.0002485	9.30	10938	4.03894	.0000914
8.35	4230.2	3.62636	.0002364	9.35	11499	4.06065	.0000870
8.40	4447.1	3.64807	.0002249	9.40	12088	4.08237	.0000827
8.45	4675.1	3.66979	.0002139	9.45	12708	4.10408	.0000787
8.50	4914.8	3.69150	0.0002035	**9.50**	13360	4.12580	0.0000749
8.55	5166.8	3.71322	.0001935	9.55	14045	4.14751	.0000712
8.60	5431.7	3.73493	.0001841	9.60	14765	4.16923	.0000677
8.65	5710.1	3.75665	.0001751	9.65	15522	4.19094	.0000644
8.70	6002.9	3.77836	.0001666	9.70	16318	4.21266	.0000613
8.75	6310.7	3.80008	0.0001585	**9.75**	17154	4.23437	0.0000583
8.80	6634.2	3.82179	.0001507	9.80	18034	4.25609	.0000555
8.85	6974.4	3.84351	.0001434	9.85	18958	4.27780	.0000527
8.90	7332.0	3.86522	.0001364	9.90	19930	4.29952	.0000502
8.95	7707.9	3.88694	.0001297	9.95	20952	4.32123	0.0000477
9.00	8103.1	3.90865	0.0001234	10.00	22026	4.34294	0.0000454

APPENDIX 5: RANDOM NUMBERS*

```
09 18 82 00 97    32 82 53 95 27    04 22 08 63 04    83 38 98 73 74    64 27 85 80 44
90 04 58 54 97    51 98 15 06 54    94 93 88 19 97    91 87 07 61 50    68 47 66 46 59
73 18 95 02 07    47 67 72 62 69    62 29 06 44 64    27 12 46 70 18    41 36 18 27 60
75 76 87 64 90    20 97 18 17 49    90 42 91 22 72    95 37 50 58 71    93 82 34 31 78
54 01 64 40 56    66 28 13 10 03    00 68 22 73 98    20 71 45 32 95    07 70 61 78 13

08 35 86 99 10    78 54 24 27 85    13 66 15 88 73    04 61 89 75 53    31 22 30 84 20
28 30 60 32 64    81 33 31 05 91    40 51 00 78 93    32 60 46 04 75    94 11 90 18 40
53 84 08 62 33    81 59 41 36 28    51 21 59 02 90    28 46 66 87 95    77 76 22 07 91
91 75 75 37 41    61 61 36 22 69    50 26 39 02 12    55 78 17 65 14    83 48 34 70 55
89 41 59 26 94    00 39 75 83 91    12 60 71 76 46    48 94 97 23 06    94 54 13 74 08

77 51 30 38 20    86 83 42 99 01    68 41 48 27 74    51 90 81 39 80    72 89 35 55 07
19 50 23 71 74    69 97 92 02 88    55 21 02 97 73    74 28 77 52 51    65 34 46 74 15
21 81 85 93 13    93 27 88 17 57    05 68 67 31 56    07 08 28 50 46    31 85 33 84 52
51 47 46 64 99    68 10 72 36 21    94 04 99 13 45    42 83 60 91 91    08 00 74 54 49
99 55 96 83 31    62 53 52 41 70    69 77 71 28 30    74 81 97 81 42    43 86 07 28 34

33 71 34 80 07    93 58 47 28 69    51 92 66 47 21    58 30 32 98 22    93 17 49 39 72
85 27 48 68 93    11 30 32 92 70    28 83 43 41 37    73 51 59 04 00    71 14 84 36 43
84 13 38 96 40    44 03 55 21 66    73 85 27 00 91    61 22 26 05 61    62 32 71 84 23
56 73 21 62 34    17 39 59 61 31    10 12 39 16 22    85 49 65 75 60    81 60 41 88 80
65 13 85 68 06    87 64 88 52 61    34 31 36 58 61    45 87 52 10 69    85 64 44 72 77

38 00 10 21 76    81 71 91 17 11    71 60 29 29 37    74 21 96 40 49    65 58 44 96 98
37 40 29 63 97    01 30 47 75 86    56 27 11 00 86    47 32 46 26 05    40 03 03 74 38
97 12 54 03 48    87 08 33 14 17    21 81 53 92 50    75 23 76 20 47    15 50 12 95 78
21 82 64 11 34    47 14 33 40 72    64 63 88 59 02    49 13 90 64 41    03 85 65 45 52
73 13 54 27 42    95 71 90 90 35    85 79 47 42 96    08 78 98 81 56    64 69 11 92 02

07 63 87 79 29    03 06 11 80 72    96 20 74 41 56    23 82 19 95 38    04 71 36 69 94
60 52 88 34 41    07 95 41 98 14    59 17 52 06 95    05 53 35 21 39    61 21 20 64 55
83 59 63 56 55    06 95 89 29 83    05 12 80 97 19    77 43 35 37 83    92 30 15 04 98
10 85 06 27 46    99 59 91 05 07    13 49 90 63 19    53 07 57 18 39    06 41 01 93 62
39 82 09 89 52    43 62 26 31 47    64 42 18 08 14    43 80 00 93 51    31 02 47 31 67

59 58 00 64 78    75 56 97 88 00    88 83 55 44 86    23 76 80 61 56    04 11 10 84 08
38 50 80 73 41    23 79 34 87 63    90 82 29 70 22    17 71 90 42 07    95 95 44 99 53
30 69 27 06 68    94 68 81 61 27    56 19 68 00 91    82 06 76 34 00    05 46 26 92 00
65 44 39 56 59    18 28 82 74 37    49 63 22 40 41    08 33 76 56 76    96 29 99 08 36
27 26 75 02 64    13 19 27 22 94    07 47 74 46 06    17 98 54 89 11    97 34 13 03 58

91 30 70 69 91    19 07 22 42 10    36 69 95 37 28    28 82 53 57 93    28 97 66 62 52
68 43 49 46 88    84 47 31 36 22    62 12 69 84 08    12 84 38 25 90    09 81 59 31 46
48 90 81 58 77    54 74 52 45 91    35 70 00 47 54    83 82 45 26 92    54 13 05 51 60
06 91 34 51 97    42 67 27 86 01    11 88 30 95 28    63 01 19 89 01    14 97 44 03 44
10 45 51 60 19    14 21 03 37 12    91 34 23 78 21    88 32 58 08 51    43 66 77 08 83

12 88 39 73 43    65 02 76 11 84    04 28 50 13 92    17 97 41 50 77    90 71 22 67 69
21 77 83 09 76    38 80 73 69 61    31 64 94 20 96    63 28 10 20 23    08 81 64 74 49
19 52 35 95 15    65 12 25 96 59    86 28 36 82 58    69 57 21 37 98    16 43 59 15 29
67 24 55 26 70    35 58 31 65 63    79 24 68 66 86    76 46 33 42 22    26 65 59 08 02
60 58 44 73 77    07 50 03 79 92    45 13 42 65 29    26 76 08 36 37    41 32 64 43 44

53 85 34 13 77    36 06 69 48 50    58 83 87 38 59    49 36 47 33 31    96 24 04 36 42
24 63 73 87 36    74 38 48 93 42    52 62 30 79 92    12 36 91 86 01    03 74 28 38 73
83 08 01 24 51    38 99 22 28 15    07 75 95 17 77    97 37 72 75 85    51 97 23 78 67
16 44 42 43 34    36 15 19 90 73    27 49 37 09 39    85 13 03 25 52    54 84 65 47 59
60 79 01 81 57    57 17 86 57 62    11 16 17 85 76    45 81 95 29 79    65 13 00 48 60
```

```
10 09 73 25 33    76 52 01 35 86    34 67 35 48 76    80 95 90 91 17    39 29 27 49 45
37 54 20 48 05    64 89 47 42 96    24 80 52 40 37    20 63 61 04 02    00 82 29 16 65
08 42 26 89 53    19 64 50 93 03    23 20 90 25 60    15 95 33 47 64    35 08 03 36 06
99 01 90 25 29    09 37 67 07 15    38 31 13 11 65    88 67 67 43 97    04 43 62 76 59
12 80 79 99 70    80 15 73 61 47    64 03 23 66 53    98 95 11 68 77    12 17 17 68 33

66 06 57 47 17    34 07 27 68 50    36 69 73 61 70    65 81 33 98 85    11 19 92 91 70
31 06 01 08 05    45 57 18 24 06    35 30 34 26 14    86 79 90 74 39    23 40 30 97 32
85 26 97 76 02    02 05 16 56 92    68 66 57 48 18    73 05 38 52 47    18 62 38 85 79
63 57 33 21 35    05 32 54 70 48    90 55 35 75 48    28 46 82 87 09    83 49 12 56 24
73 79 64 57 53    03 52 96 47 78    35 80 83 42 82    60 93 52 03 44    35 27 38 84 35

98 52 01 77 67    14 90 56 86 07    22 10 94 05 58    60 97 09 34 33    50 50 07 39 98
11 80 50 54 31    39 80 82 77 32    50 72 56 82 48    29 40 52 42 01    52 77 56 78 51
83 45 29 96 34    06 28 89 80 83    13 74 67 00 78    18 47 54 06 10    68 71 17 78 17
88 68 54 02 00    86 50 75 84 01    36 76 66 79 51    90 36 47 64 93    29 60 91 10 62
99 59 46 73 48    87 51 76 49 69    91 82 60 89 28    93 78 56 13 68    23 47 83 41 13

65 48 11 76 74    17 46 85 09 50    58 04 77 69 74    73 03 95 71 86    40 21 81 65 44
80 12 43 56 35    17 72 70 80 15    45 31 82 23 74    21 11 57 82 53    14 38 55 37 63
74 35 09 98 17    77 40 27 72 14    43 23 60 02 10    45 52 16 42 37    96 28 60 26 55
69 91 62 68 03    66 25 22 91 48    36 93 68 72 03    76 62 11 39 90    94 40 05 64 18
09 89 32 05 05    14 22 56 85 14    46 42 75 67 88    96 29 77 88 22    54 38 21 45 98

91 49 91 45 23    68 47 92 76 86    46 16 28 35 54    94 75 08 99 23    37 08 92 00 48
80 33 69 45 98    26 94 03 68 58    70 29 73 41 35    53 14 03 33 40    42 05 08 23 41
44 10 48 19 49    85 15 74 79 54    32 97 92 65 75    57 60 04 08 81    22 22 20 64 13
12 55 07 37 42    11 10 00 20 40    12 86 07 46 97    96 64 48 94 39    28 70 72 58 15
63 60 64 93 29    16 50 53 44 84    40 21 95 25 63    43 65 17 70 82    07 20 73 17 90

61 19 69 04 46    26 45 74 77 74    51 92 43 37 29    65 39 45 95 93    42 58 26 05 27
15 47 44 52 66    95 27 07 99 53    59 36 78 38 48    82 39 61 01 18    33 21 15 94 66
94 55 72 85 73    67 89 75 43 87    54 62 24 44 31    91 19 04 25 92    92 92 74 59 73
42 48 11 62 13    97 34 40 87 21    16 86 84 87 67    03 07 11 20 59    25 70 14 66 70
23 52 37 83 17    73 20 88 98 37    68 93 59 14 16    26 25 22 96 63    05 52 28 25 62

04 49 35 24 94    75 24 63 38 24    45 86 25 10 25    61 96 27 93 35    65 33 71 24 72
00 54 99 76 54    64 05 18 81 59    96 11 96 38 96    54 69 28 23 91    23 28 72 95 29
35 96 31 53 07    26 89 80 93 54    33 35 13 54 62    77 97 45 00 24    90 10 33 93 33
59 80 80 83 91    45 42 72 68 42    83 60 94 97 00    13 02 12 48 92    78 56 52 01 06
46 05 88 52 36    01 39 09 22 86    77 28 14 40 77    93 91 08 36 47    70 61 74 29 41

32 17 90 05 97    87 37 92 52 41    05 56 70 70 07    86 74 31 71 57    85 39 41 18 38
69 23 46 14 06    20 11 74 52 04    15 95 66 00 00    18 74 39 24 23    97 11 89 63 38
19 56 54 14 30    01 75 87 53 79    40 41 92 15 85    66 67 43 68 06    84 96 28 52 07
45 15 51 49 38    19 47 60 72 46    43 66 79 45 43    59 04 79 00 33    20 82 66 95 41
94 86 43 19 94    36 16 81 08 51    34 88 88 15 53    01 54 03 54 56    05 01 45 11 76

98 08 62 48 26    45 24 02 84 04    44 99 90 88 96    39 09 47 34 07    35 44 13 18 80
33 18 51 62 32    41 94 15 09 49    89 43 54 85 81    88 69 54 19 94    37 54 87 30 43
80 95 10 04 06    96 38 27 07 74    20 15 12 33 87    25 01 62 52 98    94 62 46 11 71
79 75 24 91 40    71 96 12 82 96    69 86 10 25 91    74 85 22 05 39    00 38 75 95 79
18 63 33 25 37    98 14 50 65 71    31 01 02 46 74    05 45 56 14 27    77 93 89 19 36

74 02 94 39 02    77 55 73 22 70    97 79 01 71 19    52 52 75 80 21    80 81 45 17 48
54 17 84 56 11    80 99 33 71 43    05 33 51 29 69    56 12 71 92 55    36 04 09 03 24
11 66 44 98 83    52 07 98 48 27    59 38 17 15 39    09 97 33 34 40    88 46 12 33 56
48 32 47 79 28    31 24 96 47 10    02 29 53 68 70    32 30 75 75 46    15 02 00 99 94
69 07 49 41 38    87 63 79 19 76    35 58 40 44 01    10 51 82 16 15    01 84 87 69 38
```

BIBLIOGRAPHY

Chapter 1

Ackoff, R. L., and P. Rivett, *A Manager's Guide to Operations Research*. New York: Wiley, 1963.

Ackoff, R. L., and M. W. Sasieni, *Fundamentals of Operations Research*. New York: Wiley, 1968.

Baumol, W. J., *Economic Theory and Operations Analysis*. Englewood Cliffs, N.J.: Prentice-Hall, 1972.

Bierman, H., C. P. Bonini, Jr., and W. J. Hausemann, *Quantitative Analysis for Business Decisions*. Homewood, Ill.: Richard D. Irwin, 1975.

Carlson, P. G., *Quantitative Methods for Managers*. New York: Harper & Row, 1967.

Carr, C. R., and C. H. Howe, *Quantitative Decision Procedures in Management and Economics*. New York: McGraw-Hill, 1964.

Hertz, D. B., and R. T. Eddison. *Progress in Operations Research*, Vol. II. New York: Wiley, 1964.

Hillier, F. S., and G. T. Lieberman, *Introduction to Operations Research*. San Francisco: Holden-Day, 1975.

Horowitz, I., *An Introduction to Quantitative Business Analysis*. New York: McGraw-Hill, 1972.

Levin, R., and C. Kirkpatrick, *Quantitative Approaches to Management*. New York: McGraw-Hill, 1975.

Miller, D. W., and M. K. Starr, *Executive Decisions and Operations Research*. Englewood Cliffs, N.J.: Prentice-Hall, 1969.

Richmond, S. B., *Operations Research for Management Decisions*. New York: Ronald Press, 1968.

Thierauf, R. J., *Decision Making through Operations Research*. New York: Wiley, 1970.

Wagner, H. M., *Principles of Operations Research*. Englewood Cliffs, N.J.: Prentice-Hall, 1975.

Chapter 2

Ackoff, R. J., and M. W. Sasieni, *Fundamentals of Operations Research*. New York: Wiley, 1968.

Bowman, E. H., and R. B. Fetter, *Analysis of Production and Operations Management*. Homewood, Ill.: Richard D. Erwin, 1967.

Buffa, E. S., *Modern Production Management: Problems and Models*. New York: Wiley, 1968.

Churchman, C. W., H. L. Ackoff, and E. L. Arnoff, *Introduction to Operations Research*. New York: Wiley, 1957.

Day, R. L., *Marketing Models, Quantitative and Behavioral*. Scranton, Pa.: International Textbook, 1964.

Gershefski, G. Q., "Corporate models—the state of the art." *Management Science*, **16**(6), February 1970.

Kaufmann, A., *Methods and Models for Operations Research*. Englewood Cliffs, N.J.: Prentice-Hall, 1963.

Teichroew, D., *An Introduction to Management Science Deterministic Models*. New York: Wiley, 1964.

Chapter 3

Goldberg, S., *Probability: An Introduction*. Englewood Cliffs, N.J.: Prentice-Hall, 1960.

Hodges, J., and E. Lehman, *Basic Concepts of Probability and Statistics*. San Francisco: Holden-Day, 1964.

Kim, C., *Statistical Analysis for Inference and Decision*. Hinsdale, Ill.: Dryden Press, 1973.

Mosteller, F., R. Rourke, and G. Thomas, Jr., *Probability and Statistics*. Reading, Mass.: Addison-Wesley, 1961.

Parzen, E., *Modern Probability Theory and Its Application*. New York: Wiley, 1960.

Wolf, F. L., *Elements of Probability and Statistics*. New York: McGraw-Hill, 1962.

Chapter 4

Bross, I. D. J., *Design for Decision*. New York: Macmillan, 1953.

Chernoff, H., and L. E. Moses, *Elementary Decision Theory*. New York: Wiley, 1959.

Dyckman, T. R., S. Smidt, and A. K. McAdams, *Management Decision Making Under Uncertainty*. New York: Macmillan, 1969.

Forester, J., *Statistical Selection of Business Strategies*. Homewood, Ill.: Richard D. Irwin, 1968.

Hadley, G., *Introduction to Probability and Statistical Decision Theory*. San Francisco: Holden-Day, 1967.

Kim, C., *Statistical Analysis for Inference and Decision*. Hinsdale, Ill.: Dryden Press, 1973.

Peters, W. S., and G. W. Summers, *Statistical Analysis for Business Decisions*. Englewood Cliffs, N.J.: Prentice-Hall, 1968.

Pratt, J. W., H. Raiffa, and R. O. Schlaifer, *Introduction to Statistical Decision Theory*. New York: McGraw-Hill, 1965.

Raiffa, H., *Decision Analysis*. Reading, Mass.: Addison-Wesley, 1968.

Savage, L. J., *The Foundations of Statistics*. New York, Wiley, 1954.

Schlaifer, R., *Analysis of Decisions Under Uncertainty*. New York: McGraw-Hill, 1969.

Chapters 5 and 6

Horngren, C. T., *Accounting for Management Control: An Introduction*. Englewood Cliffs, N.J.: Prentice-Hall, 1970.

Keller, I. W., and W. L. Ferrara, *Management Accounting for Profit Control*. New York: McGraw-Hill, 1966.

Kim, C., "A stochastic cost volume profit analysis," *Decision Sciences*, **4**(3), July 1973.

Rappaport, A. (ed.), *Information for Decision Making*. Englewood Cliffs, N.J.: Prentice-Hall, 1975.

Tucker, S. P., *The Breakeven System: A Tool for Profit Planning*. Englewood Cliffs, N.J.: Prentice-Hall, 1963.

Willis, P. J., *Price, Cost and Output*. Oxford: Blackwell & Mott, 1961.

Chapters 7 and 8

Buchan, J., and E. Koenigsberg, *Scientific Inventory Management*. Englewood Cliffs, N.J.: Prentice-Hall, 1963.

Buffa, E. S., and W. H. Taubert, *Production-Inventory Systems: Planning and Control*. Homewood, Ill.: Richard D. Irwin, 1972.

Hadley, G., and T. M. Whitin, *Analysis of Inventory Systems*. Englewood Cliffs, N.J.: Prentice-Hall, 1963.

Magee, J. F., and D. M. Boodman, *Production Planning and Inventory Control*. New York: McGraw-Hill, 1967.

Naddor, E., *Inventory Systems*. New York: Wiley, 1966.

Niland, P., *Production Planning, Scheduling and Inventory Control: A Text and Cases*. New York: Macmillan, 1972.

Starr, M., and D. Miller, *Inventory Control: Theory and Practice*. Englewood Cliffs, N.J.: Prentice-Hall, 1962.

Chapters 9, 10, 11

Beale, E. M. L., *Mathematical Programming in Practice*. New York: Wiley, 1968.

Charnes, A., and W. W. Cooper, *Management Models and Industrial Applications of Linear Programming* (2 vols.). New York: Wiley, 1963.

Daellenbach, H. G., and E. J. Bell, *User's Guide to Linear Programming*. Englewood Cliffs, N.J.: Prentice-Hall, 1970.

Dantzig, G. B., *Linear Programming and Extensions*. Princeton, N.J.: Princeton University Press, 1963.

Driebeck, N. J., *Applied Linear Programming*. Reading, Mass.: Addison-Wesley, 1969.

Hadley, G., *Linear Programming*. Reading, Mass.: Addison-Wesley, 1962.

Kim, C., *Introduction to Linear Programming*. New York: Holt, Rinehart & Winston, 1972.

Levin, R. I., and R. P. Lamone, *Linear Programming for Management Decisions*. Homewood, Ill.: Richard D. Irwin, 1969.

Stockton, R. S., *Introduction to Linear Programming*. Boston: Allyn and Bacon, 1960.

Strum, J. E., *Introduction to Linear Programming*. San Francisco: Holden-Day, 1972.

Chapter 12

Berge, C., and A. Ghouila-Houri, *Programming, Games and Transportation Networks* (translated from French by Maxine Merrington and C. Ramanujacharyulu). New York: Wiley, 1965.

Busacker, R. G., and T. L. Saaty, *Finite Graphs and Networks: An Introduction with Applications*. New York: McGraw-Hill, 1965.

Elmaghraby, S. E., *Some Network Models in Management Science*. Berlin: Springer-Verlag, 1970.

Ford, L. R., Jr., and D. R. Fulkerson, *Flows in Networks*. Princeton, N.J.: Princeton University Press, 1962.

Frank, H., and I. T. Frisch, *Communication, Transmission and Transportation Networks*. Reading, Mass.: Addison-Wesley, 1971.

Price, W. L., *Graphs and Networks*. London: Butterworths, 1971.

Chapter 13

Archibald, R. D., and R. L. Villoria, *Network-Based Management Systems (PERT/CPM)*. New York: Wiley, 1966.

Baker, B. N., *An Introduction to PERT-CPM*. Homewood, Ill.: Richard D. Irwin, 1964.

Battersby, A., *Network Analysis for Planning and Scheduling*. New York: Wiley, 1970.

Evarts, H. F., *Introduction to PERT*. Boston: Allyn and Bacon, 1964.

Levin, R., and C. A. Kirkpatrick, *Planning and Control with PERT/CPM*. New York: McGraw-Hill, 1966.

McLaren, K. G., and E. L. Buesnel, *Network Analysis in Project Management*. London: Cassell, 1969.

Moder, J. J., and C. R. Phillips. *Project Management with CPM and PERT*. New York: Van Nostrand, 1970.

Shaffer, L. R., J. B. Ritter, and W. L. Meyer, *Critical Path Method*. New York: McGraw-Hill, 1965.

Stillian, G. N., *et al. PERT: A New Management Planning and Control Technique*. New York: American Management Association, 1963.

Wiest, J. D., and F. Levy, *A Management Guide to PERT/CPM*. Englewood Cliffs, N.J.: Prentice-Hall, 1969.

Chapters 14 and 15

Abadie, J. (ed.), *Integer and Nonlinear Programming*. New York: American Elsevier, 1970.

Garfinkel, R. S., and G. L. Nemhauser, *Integer Programming*. New York: Wiley, 1972.

Geoffrion, A. M., and R. E. Marsten, "Integer programming algorithms: A framework and state-of-the-art survey," *Management Science*, **18**(9), 465–491 (May 1972).

Greenburg, H., *Integer Programming*. New York: Academic Press, 1971.

Hu, T. C., *Integer Programming and Network Flows*. Reading, Mass.: Addison-Wesley, 1969.

Lawler, E. L., and D. E. Wood, "Branch-and-Bound Methods: A Survey." *Operations Research*, **14**(4), 669–719 (1966).

Plane, D. R., and C. McMillan, Jr., *Discrete Optimization*. Englewood Cliffs, N.J.: Prentice-Hall, 1971.

Zionts, S., *Linear and Integer Programming*. Englewood Cliffs, N.J.: Prentice-Hall, 1971.

Chapter 16

Beckman, M. J., *Dynamic Programming of Economic Decisions*. Berlin: Springer-Verlag, 1968.

Bellman, R. E., *Dynamic Programming*. Princeton, N.J.: Princeton University Press, 1957.

Bellman, R., and S. Dreyfus, *Applied Dynamic Programming*. Princeton, N.J.: Princeton University Press, 1962.

Kaufmann, A., and R. Cruon, *Dynamic Programming: Sequential Scientific Management* (translated from French by Henry C. Sneyd). New York: Academic Press, 1967.

Nemhauser, G. L., *Introduction to Dynamic Programming*. New York: Wiley, 1966.

White, D. J., *Dynamic Programming*. Edinburgh: Oliver & Boyd; San Francisco: Holden-Day, 1969.

Chapter 17

Derman, C., *Finite State Markov Decision Processes*. New York: Academic Press, 1970.

Freedman, D., *Markov Chains*. San Francisco: Holden-Day, 1971.

Howard, R. A., *Dynamic Programming and Markov Processes*. Cambridge, Mass.: M.I.T. Press, 1960.

Howard, R. A., *Dynamic Probabilistic Systems* (2 vols.). New York: Wiley, 1971.

Kemeny, J. G., J. L. Snell, and G. L. Thompson, *Finite Markov Chains*. Englewood Cliffs, N.J.: Prentice-Hall, 1959.

Martin, J. J., *Bayesian Decision Problems and Markov Chains*. New York: Wiley, 1967.

Chapter 18

Benes, V. E., *General Stochastic Process in the Theory of Queues*. Reading, Mass.: Addison-Wesley, 1963.

Cohen, J. W., *The Single-Server Queue*. Amsterdam: North-Holland, 1969.

Cox, D. R., and W. L. Smith, *Queues*. New York: Wiley, 1961.

Cooper, R. B., *Introduction to Queuing Theory*. New York: Macmillan, 1972.

Lee, A. M., *Applied Queueing Theory*. New York: St. Martin's Press, 1966.

Morse, P. M., *Queues, Inventories and Maintenance*. New York: Wiley, 1958.

Prabhu, N. U., *Queues and Inventories*. New York: Wiley, 1965.

Riordan, J., *Stochastic Service Systems*. New York: Wiley, 1962.

Saaty, T. L., *Elements of Queueing Theory with Applications*. New York: McGraw-Hill, 1961.

Takács, L., *Introduction to the Theory of Queues*. Oxford: Oxford University Press, 1962.

Chapter 19

Davis, M. D., *Game Theory, a Nontechnical Introduction*. New York: Basic Books, 1970.

Dresher, M., *Games of Strategy, Theory and Applications*. Englewood Cliffs, N.J.: Prentice-Hall, 1961.

Glicksman, A. M., *An Introduction to Linear Programming and the Theory of Games*. New York: Wiley, 1963.

Levin. R. I., and R. B. Desjardins, *Theory of Games and Strategies*. Scranton, Pa.: International Textbook, 1970.

Luce, R. D., and H. Raiffa, *Games and Decisions*. New York: Wiley, 1957.

McKinsey, J. C. C., *Introduction to the Theory of Games*. New York: McGraw-Hill, 1952.

Rapoport, A., *Two Person Game Theory*. Ann Arbor, Mich.: University of Michigan Press, 1966.

Von Neumann, J., and O. Morgenstern, *Theory of Games and Economic Behavior*. Princeton, N.J.: Princeton University Press, 1944.

Williams, J. D., *The Compleat Strategyst*. New York: McGraw-Hill, 1966.

Chapter 20

Balderston, F. E., and A. C. Haggatt, *Simulation of Marketing Processes*. Berkeley, Calif.: Institute of Business and Economic Research, University of California, 1962.

Basil, D. C., P. R. Cone, and J. A. Fleming, *Executive Decision Making Through Simulation*. Columbus, O.: Charles E. Merrill, 1965.

Bonini, C. P., *Simulation of Information and Decision Systems in the Firm*. Englewood Cliffs, N.J.: Prentice-Hall, 1963.

Charafas, D. N., *Systems and Simulation*. New York: Academic Press, 1965.

Emshoff, J. R., and R. L. Sisson, *Design and Use of Computer Simulation Models*. New York: Macmillan, 1970.

Evans, G. W., G. F. Wallace, and G. L. Sutherland, *Simulation Using Digital Computers*. Englewood Cliffs, N.J.: Prentice-Hall, 1967.

Hammersley, J. M., and D. C. Handscomb, *Monte Carlo Methods*. New York: Wiley, 1964.

Mihram, G., *Simulation: Statistical Foundations and Methodology*. New York: Academic Press, 1972.

McMillan, C., and R. F. Gonzales, *Systems Analysis, A Computer Approach to Decision Models*. Homewood, Ill.: Richard D. Irwin, 1968.

Meier, R., W. T. Newell, and H. L. Pazer, *Simulation in Business and Economics*. Englewood Cliffs, N.J.: Prentice-Hall, 1969.

Naylor, T. H., J. L. Balintfy, D. S. Burdick, and D. Chu, *Computer Simulation Techniques*. New York: Wiley, 1966.

Schmidt, J. W., and R. E. Taylor, *Simulation and Analysis of Industrial Systems*. Homewood, Ill.: Richard D. Irwin, 1970.

Tocher, K. D., *The Art of Simulation*. London: English Universities Press, 1963.

INDEX